Philosophies of Work in the Platonic Tradition

Also available from Bloomsbury:

Creation and the Function of Art, by Jason Tuckwell
Michel Henry's Practical Philosophy, edited by Jeffrey Hanson,
Brian Harding, and Michael R. Kelly
Resistance, Revolution and Fascism, by Anthony Faramelli
*Rewriting Contemporary Political Philosophy with Plato and
Aristotle*, by Paul Schollmeier

Philosophies of Work in the Platonic Tradition

A History of Labor and Human Flourishing

Jeffrey Hanson

BLOOMSBURY ACADEMIC
LONDON • NEW YORK • OXFORD • NEW DELHI • SYDNEY

BLOOMSBURY ACADEMIC
Bloomsbury Publishing Plc
50 Bedford Square, London, WC1B 3DP, UK
1385 Broadway, New York, NY 10018, USA
29 Earlsfort Terrace, Dublin 2, Ireland

BLOOMSBURY, BLOOMSBURY ACADEMIC and the Diana logo are
trademarks of Bloomsbury Publishing Plc

First published in Great Britain 2022
This paperback edition published 2023

Copyright © Jeffrey Hanson, 2022

Jeffrey Hanson has asserted his right under the Copyright, Designs and
Patents Act, 1988, to be identified as Author of this work.

Cover image: Sergio Barrios / EyeEm / Getty Images

All rights reserved. No part of this publication may be reproduced or transmitted in
any form or by any means, electronic or mechanical, including photocopying,
recording, or any information storage or retrieval system, without prior
permission in writing from the publishers.

Bloomsbury Publishing Plc does not have any control over, or responsibility for, any
third-party websites referred to or in this book. All internet addresses given in this
book were correct at the time of going to press. The author and publisher regret any
inconvenience caused if addresses have changed or sites have ceased to exist, but
can accept no responsibility for any such changes.

A catalogue record for this book is available from the British Library.

A catalog record for this book is available from the Library of Congress.

ISBN: HB: 978-1-3501-5093-5
PB: 978-1-3502-9946-7
ePDF: 978-1-3501-5095-9
eBook: 978-1-3501-5096-6

Typeset by Newgen KnowledgeWorks Pvt. Ltd., Chennai, India

To find out more about our authors and books visit www.bloomsbury.com
and sign up for our newsletters.

To my best friend, "Death, the Hooded Man"
"Of making many books there is no end."
—Ecclesiastes 12:12

Contents

Introduction	1
Part One Ancient Greece	
1 Work among the Ancient Greeks	11
2 Plato on Work	21
Part Two The Middle Ages	
3 The Early Medieval Period	67
4 The Late Medieval Period	105
Part Three The Modern Era	
5 Petrarch	123
6 Martin Luther	133
7 John Ruskin	157
8 Simone Weil	177
Conclusion	197
Notes	203
Bibliography	263
Index of Biblical Citations	275
General Index	277

Introduction

US presidential candidate Republican senator Marco Rubio made headlines in a 2015 debate when he exclaimed, "I don't know why we have stigmatized vocational education. Welders make more money than philosophers. We need more welders and less philosophers."[1] Responses to his apparently impromptu remark took two predictable forms. First, many critics hastened to point out that according to the Bureau of Labor Statistics, university professors of philosophy and religion had a higher median income than welders, though presumably this was not meant as an insult to welders.[2] The second reaction, not actually opposed to the first, was to defend the integrity of philosophy on the basis of its career relevance and income potential. Then executive director of the American Philosophical Association Amy E. Ferrer argued,

> Rubio's refrain about the value of philosophy is unfortunate—and misinformed. Philosophy teaches many of the skills most valued in today's economy: critical thinking, analysis, effective written and verbal communication, problem solving, and more. And philosophy majors' success is borne out in both data—which show that philosophy majors consistently outperform nearly all other majors on graduate entrance exams such as the GRE and LSAT, and that philosophy ties with mathematics for the highest percentage increase from starting to midcareer salary.[3]

This anecdote points up a quandary about work and the way to value it. The president of the nation's largest and most important professional organization representing the views and interests of professors of philosophy leapt to the defense of a perceived attack on the profession she officially represented by citing data proving that her discipline is as lucrative as any other field of academic study and as helpful to employment prospects. Given that it was the reputation of professional philosophy that was in question, is it not surprising that the field was defended not in philosophical terms but in terms of its effectiveness in meeting market demands?

Despite occasional outbursts like Senator Rubio's and the runaway success of best sellers like Matthew Crawford's enlightening *Shop Class as Soulcraft* (as unpredicted a popular hit as its generational forebear, Robert Pirsig's *Zen and the Art of Motorcycle Maintenance*), most Americans and perhaps most Westerners generally hold difficult or physical labor in low esteem and normally think of the reward of most if not all work as being strictly instrumental if not altogether mercenary.

This book is written to offer conceptual resources in support of a loftier view of work, with an aim to vindicating its value in philosophical terms that do not appeal to salary or prestige. If we are to resolve the current quandary about how to value work, we will have to do so in terms that are philosophically robust and do not reduce to the perceived value of incentives to work. I have discovered that Western civilization's most promising available ways of thinking about the value of work are in the tradition of thinking beginning with Plato and running through his long line of inheritors, up to Simone Weil.

The core Platonic doctrine that undergirds the argument of this book comes from Book II of the *Republic*. There Socrates and his friends are proposing to defend justice as desirable in itself, apart from any cultural or circumstantial incentive to be just. As a preliminary to his argument, which will last for several books, Socrates outlines three different kinds of good. First, he argues, "there is a kind of good we welcome, not because we desire what comes from it, but because we welcome it for its own sake—joy, for example, and all the harmless pleasures that have no results beyond the joy of having them." Second, "there is a kind of good we like for its own sake and also for the sake of what comes from it—knowing, for example, and seeing and being healthy." Third, and finally, there is a "kind of good, such as physical training, medical treatment when sick, medicine itself, and the other ways of making money," which "we'd say that these are onerous but beneficial to us, and we wouldn't choose them for their own sakes, but for the sake of the rewards and other things that come from them."[4] The point of this taxonomy is that Socrates names the second class of goods the best, those that are desirable in themselves and for their benefits.

This dichotomy is what would seem to underpin at least implicitly the debate about work today, exemplified in the Rubio/Ferrer exchange. It would appear from the state of dialogue today about work that the majority of interlocutors imagine these are the only two options: either work or certain forms of work are good in themselves and worth defending in their own right or they are instrumentally good and worth defending only in view of the benefits they bring.[5] In this book I exposit the Platonic tradition of reflection on work because I think for this tradition a third option is available: work is both good in itself, as making a distinct contribution to human life lived fully, and good for the benefits it brings about. The latter, I take it, are obvious.

The essential point is that such rationalizations in favor of work's value are not, according to the Platonic conceptuality, necessarily in competition with work's instrumental benefits. This book is an effort at tracing out the Platonic lineage and explaining its value for appraising work as an element of a happy and flourishing human life, desirable quite apart from its financial rewards.

Contrary to the stereotypical view of the first great Western philosopher, according to which he is in flight from the concrete reality of the terrestrial realm and focuses entirely on the airy heights wherein are found the "Forms," I take Plato to be more congenial to the topic of work than Aristotle, who is allegedly more invested in the ordinary world of sensory experience. Aristotle will insist on a sharp distinction between theory and production (for the Platonic tradition these two will always travel together), and he denies that the divine does anything productive (while Plato attributes the ordering of the cosmos to a demiurge or worker). For Plato both the divine worker and the philosopher begin in contemplation, but their contemplation always issues in practical production.

For the Platonic tradition, theory is always higher than practice. That priority will be upheld in the pages to come. However, work is seen as responsive to reality. In the words of Michael Hanby, "human making ... must first let the world *be*, treating it as having its own inner integrity and as something good and beautiful in its own right, and not as something first to be commanded or controlled."[6] This is certainly true of the thinkers studied in this book. Plato will frame the skills and crafts practiced by the ordinary Athenians of his day as opportunities to glimpse in a limited way the highest realities that the philosopher contemplates in full. What most people did as what we would call a job is for Plato a kind of knowing. It is not the whole of knowledge and cannot be, but it is a mastery of some part of reality and a constructive response to it that repairs a genuine need and secures a worthwhile good. The carpenter, for example, knows wood, what it can bear, how it can be shaped and cut and joined in order to produce a worthwhile object that in its small but inimitable way partakes of the eternal verities of form and beauty.

In this way work in an ordinary sense, and this again will be true for all the thinkers examined in this book, is never merely an external phenomenon but also an inner dynamic. One effort on the part of an organizational psychologist to take a more philosophical approach to work has resulted in this definition: "an agentic activity done with the purpose of changing the environment."[7] While defensible as a definition of contemporary work, this definition misses out an entire dimension upheld by the Platonic tradition, which instead sees work as needed for any good at all and therefore not primarily about altering the environment. Speaking about Saint Paul and Augustine (about whom much will be said in this book), the historian Rémi Brague aptly observes that for early Christian thinking "work, however, is not valorized as a transformation of nature, but rather as a labor on oneself."[8] For the worker in the Platonic tradition, while work is done in relation to reality, it is also always done on oneself. We will see that the early monks understood this and did work that precisely was not intended to make a profound change in the world but to change the self. They knew that what we do repeatedly, day in and day out, makes us who we are.

Finally, in this tradition work and morality are linked. All making is moral, and this is true in the first instance because work shapes the worker and because the limited but intrinsic goods of work are also set in a social order, the justice of which is partly measured by the work done in it. This connection again will be forged by Plato and extend all the way to Simone Weil. Plato sees an isomorphism between the individual soul and the polis, and the latter exists according to him ultimately to allow for a just social order within which each individual can pursue her appointed task. The celebrated definition of justice in the *Republic* as each person doing his own job at first seems like a practical postulate but in the end rises to the level of a philosophical principle. This is because work is a way of participating in the justice that arises in a community wherein each person is not looking merely to his outward task but is also looking after the quality of his own soul, a parallelism that is explicit in Plato and at least implicit in his many followers.

In what follows then I trace out these major themes from their origins in ancient Greek thought to the twentieth century. In each case these fundamental points will find various expressions and emphases. I hope thereby to unearth some traditional wisdom for thinking about work today that is nonreductive. There is of course much more that could be said about issues related to work, but where these require expertise in economics or public policy, I am not competent to speak.[9] I write as someone interested in philosophy for people interested in philosophy, and my desire is to see philosophers speak about work with more depth and appreciation for its inherent goods.

The nature of these goods has been given a prolonged and detailed analysis by Alasdair MacIntyre, who over the course of many years' speculation and refinement with critical interlocutors has developed an account of human practices that distinguishes between goods internal to such practices and goods external to them, or proper ends chosen for themselves and those goods chosen for the sake of something else.[10] The former he has more lately taken to calling "goods of excellence" and the latter "goods of effectiveness."[11] This book finds this distinction potentially useful, and when herein I speak about goods internal to work it is this sort of conceptuality I have in mind, which may be familiar to contemporary philosophical readers who also have engaged in some study of work.[12] According to what is now a familiar discussion and an oft-cited example, MacIntyre argues that taking on board a practice is a matter of being introduced to the internal good that can only be obtained by that practice and tutoring a desire for that good. External goods may play a role in motivating the practice for noninitiates and beginners, but truly to be masterful in a practice is to pursue it not for the sake of any available external good but for the sake of the irreplaceable good internal to the practice itself. So a child may be offered candy in exchange for playing chess and may be promised further candy to come should the child win a game, but the child is not a chess player in the full sense until she or he has learned to appreciate chess for its own sake and practice it in full appreciation of and tutored desire for its characteristic internal good, which MacIntyre himself calls "a certain highly particular kind of analytical skill, strategic imagination, and competitive intensity."[13]

It is this good that is essential to making chess what it is, and no other practice can instill quite the same sort of analytical skill, strategic imagination, or competitive intensity, though similar such goods are available in comparable practices. Still, to master chess is to pursue this highly specific good, only available in chess. External goods are widely available and travel together with many practices: It is possible to make money in a variety of ways, and money may flow into the earner's pockets regardless of the practice that the earner pursues or how excellent she or he is at that practice. Mastery of a practice may be compatible with external goods—fame, publicity, wealth—but where external goods threaten the integrity of a practice the true practitioner must eschew them in favor of single-hearted devotion to the internal good of their practice. External incentives may be expedient for the immature and inexperienced, but the true practitioner will not require such blandishments, and even spurn them if they threaten the practice's internal good.

Formation in practices is thus also formation of character. By being introduced to a practice, a child is also being inculcated in virtues, which are needed to discern and pursue the goods peculiar to them. Cheating at chess may bring candy, but as Kelvin

Knight puts it, "one will only learn how to become a better chess player by cultivating personal excellence in the emulation of standards established by others."[14] Practices then are what Knight calls the school of the virtues, in which goods distinctive of practices are acquired along with the more traditional virtues like self-control, friendship with fellow practitioners, justice in acknowledging others' achievements and their earned deserts, truthfulness with oneself and others, and "courage in defending achievements against institutional corruption or repression."[15] Persons of character may accept external goods, but they will not accept any substitute for the internal good to which their practice is devoted. It is worth remembering that both internal and external goods are genuine, and they need not always be in competition. As MacIntyre himself allows,

> It would be a large misconception to suppose that allegiance to goods of the one kind necessarily excluded allegiance to goods of the other. ... Thus the goods of excellence cannot be systematically cultivated unless at least some of the goods of effectiveness are also pursued. On the other hand it is difficult in most social contexts to pursue the goods of effectiveness without cultivating at least to some degree the goods of excellence.[16]

Here MacIntyre's distinction maps well onto the categories from Plato we have already examined: the best category of good comprises both goods of excellence and goods of effectiveness together; they are chosen for themselves and for the sake of something else.

The threat of the two pulling apart, however, is ever-present, because institutions are not the natural school of virtues but rather the peddlers of external goods. "Institutional corruption or repression" is ineradicable, and courage against this danger will always be needed by the practitioner. Wherever the external goods overpower internal goods, virtue is eroded. Because the pernicious influence of institutions is especially strong in the contemporary era, an objection against using MacIntyre's conceptuality in application to work may arise. I am (all too briefly) introducing his distinction between internal and external goods because it is a useful one for the analysis, and I will claim that what is interesting about the authors examined in this volume is that they offer various accounts of, insights into, and strategies to promote the goods internal to different kinds of labor. MacIntyre himself however is a critic of contemporary work and sometimes writes as if internal goods are not available to work as it is practiced today and within modern capitalist economies. Such economies elevate the vice of *pleonexia* into a pseudo-virtue and chase after external goods in preference to internal goods, with the result that it becomes at least difficult if not impossible to secure the internal goods of work when that work is under heavy institutional pressure.[17]

This objection however is not fatal, because the authors surveyed herein are already very much aware of this problem. Indeed, I will show that Plato has already anticipated it. That work may be compromised in any given setting is a danger to which the writers herein are already attuned. That work in the modern era may be more susceptible to enticement away from its internal goods in favor of external goods is certainly arguable, and some authors studied herein will put forth their own versions of just such an argument. Such a judgment however is an empirical one not a philosophical one. MacIntyre himself seems to concede this at various points. While certainly standing by his assessment that "exploitative structures of both free market and state capitalism make it often difficult and at times impossible to achieve the goods of the workplace through excellent work," he nevertheless gives examples of exceptional labor situations in which work devoted to the internal goods of the practices enshrined and defended in those situations is done well and for its own sake.[18]

Citing the very different but nevertheless convergent examples of W. Edwards Deming, who revolutionized automobile manufacturing in Japan, and Wendell Berry, the agrarian, MacIntyre points out that neither man "ignores the need to be productive, the fact that it is the production of worthwhile goods that gives productive work its point and purpose, but both take it that such work serves a common good to which each worker contributes."[19] MacIntyre's estimation of Tom Burns's studies of the British Broadcasting Corporation's early work ethos (and its unfavorable contrast to a later, managerial ethos)[20] and the Cummins engine company leads him to the same conclusion: that there is a difference between work done for external goods and work done for internal goods and that the latter are still available even when under considerable threat.[21] The fishing community of Thorupstrand, Denmark, and the collective organization of the Monte Azul favela in São Paulo, Brazil, are also instructive examples of what is yet possible in contemporary workplaces.[22] When work is organized around internal goods, "workers are able to pursue ends that they themselves have identified as worthwhile, in the pursuit of which they hold themselves to standards of excellence that they have made their own," while with those workers rests "primary responsibility for the quality of the end products of the work ... who in this respect are treated as agents with rational and aesthetic powers, even though their labor is still exploited."[23] Even in labor situations that MacIntyre deems exploitative, then, it is still possible that at work

> desires are educated and transformed. Distinctions are made between real and apparent goods, between objects of desire that agents have good reason to pursue and objects of desire that need to be set aside if excellence is to be achieved. Feelings are transformed as what agents care about changes. What agents want for and from themselves and for and from others is no longer what it was. More experienced workers become teachers. Managers become enablers.[24]

Much of what this book is concerned with is how philosophers in the Platonic tradition have sought to address the obstacles to work that is good in these ways and overcome those obstacles.[25]

A final word should be said too about the tradition that concerns this book. All traditions are retrospectively, not prospectively, formed. The thinkers herein have affiliations that I believe are broadly in line with Platonism, but readers will have to assess for themselves whether the story I tell is fully convincing. A self-identifying Platonist like Simone Weil, writing centuries after Plato himself, will not of course reproduce exactly his metaphysics or any other aspect of his thought. However, I have already identified themes that I think are characteristic of the Platonic tradition when it comes to the question of labor, and those themes will recur over the centuries from Plato on. No one studied in this book is included because they tick all the boxes on a putative checklist of features that would "count" as making one a Platonist; they are included because they sustain and develop some characteristic ideas that are first given shape in Plato's writings. Plato's inheritors explore further these ideas; they are not governed by them. I am not a Plato scholar or even a classicist, so my aim here is simply to establish—with considerable help from actual Plato scholars—that there is in his writings a coherent and potentially fruitful resource for thinking about the internal goods of work, an awareness of the dangers to those goods, and a set of defensible strategies for mitigating those dangers. The remaining chapters will tell the story of how this inspirational material will be reinvented by Plato's creative followers.

Part One

Ancient Greece

Our study begins with the origins of Western philosophy itself, in the cultural milieu of fourth-century BC Athens. In the first section of this chapter, general attitudes about different kinds of work will be examined, with particular attention to the pre-Socratic world of Hesiod and Homer, the two poets rightly called the educators of ancient Greece.

The second section traces Plato's complex response to different sorts of work and his effort to define the life of philosophical contemplation as a sort of work worthy of its own, indeed paramount, respect. It will be shown that this project was carried forward by Plato at the price of denigrating other forms of work that the Greeks called "banausic," denoting labor requiring the application of fire by forging or furnace work. The prejudice against banausic labor runs deep in Greek culture, mythically associated as it was with the god Hephaestus, the only member of the divine pantheon who undertook productive labor and with it was cursed by ugliness and deformity (again uniquely among the Olympian divinities). At the same time, we will discover that Plato had a lively interest in crafts though he consistently marked out their limits.

A comprehensive survey of the ancient Greeks' attitudes to work obviously cannot be provided here. A number of social and historical studies are already available.[1] My aim here is simply to furnish the requisite background for appreciating the philosophical world's response to the question of work and point up those features of Greek society's deployment of and writing about work that are necessary to understand what Plato says about work in the context of his culture's general attitudes and foundational writings. This section is organized around major types of work as the Greeks understood them and will provide the basis upon which later sections will engage with the expressly philosophical writings of Plato as he touches upon questions of work.

1

Work among the Ancient Greeks

As Jean-Pierre Vernant pointed out, "In Greek there is no term that corresponds to 'work.'"[1] Instead there is a complex of terms that orbit around what we would call work in a contemporary vernacular. The term *ponos* could be applied to any activity involving effort or labor; it applies equally to pedestrian effort as to the choice Hercules makes to embrace a life of effort rather than ease,[2] though the storied labors of Hercules are obviously mythic in scope and grandeur and thus not the sort of exploit we would ordinarily call "work." Similarly *ergon* can refer to farming or commercial activity (though it is etymologically related to the former) and even more broadly to any thing's characteristic activity. For the Greeks everything has its own *telos*, and this *telos* is achieved by *ergon*, and whenever that *ergon* is done well, *arête*—virtue or excellence—is the result. Apart from these categories there is the class of activities belonging to *technai*, which require specialized knowledge and aim at the production of a thing separate from the practice of the techne itself, and *prattein*, which produce nothing apart from their own activity.[3] Yet another distinction must be drawn between the *demiourgoi*, who work for the benefit of the community as a whole, and those whose work is undertaken within the *oichos*, the extended household that formed the bedrock of ancient Greek societies, and for its direct benefit only.[4]

This distinction is also commented upon by Moses Finley, who concentrates his explanation on the Homeric era. Only twice do the Homeric poems use this term, once by Eumaeus, who calls *demiourgoi* those elites among specialist workers who "supplied essential needs in a way that neither the lords nor the non-specialists among their followers" were able. Finley asserts that this class "floated in mid-air in the social hierarchy."[5] Not necessarily on retainer but possibly paid piecemeal, the demiourgoi had the name and status they did, not on the basis of payment but because of their availability to the whole *demos* or general population.[6] More secure in their roles are those workers attached to the *oichos*. Finley reminds his reader,

> The authoritarian household, the *oikos*, was the centre around which life was organized, from which flowed not only the satisfaction of material needs, including security, but ethical norms and values, duties, obligations and responsibilities, social relationships, and relations with the gods. The *oikos* was not merely the family, it was all the people of the household together with its land and its goods,

hence the term "economics," which denotes the management of the estate.⁷ The oichos was supported by workers who were attached to the household and traded mobility for an acknowledged place of security and belonging, which the demiourgoi did not have, though the range of their itineracy is unknown.⁸ Worst of all was to be a *thes*, a hireling who had no permanent position in any oichos and could be contracted and dismissed at will.⁹

These variations do not necessarily suggest that the Greeks had no concept of work at all but that they acknowledged a wide variety of practical efforts that had distinct characteristics.¹⁰ While all cultures, it would seem, share the intuition that work at least can be a burden, we will see in what follows that the blanket assertion that "to the Greeks work was a curse and nothing else" cannot be sustained.¹¹

Farming

Agriculture was the fundamental and most widespread form of work practiced in ancient Greece. Our catalog of different sorts of occupation begins here because farming was widely regarded in ancient Greece as not only the most prevalent and essential form of work but also the one requiring the least amount of technical (in the etymological sense of the word) expertise. Noting the etymological connection between ergon, the already mentioned word we can translate as "work," and the word for "field," Vernant expands upon the primordial nature of cultivation of grain according to Hesiod. By contrast to the maintenance of fruit trees, which yield their bounty as part of the rhythm of seasons marked by festivals and feast days that mark the human relationship to the gods,¹² cultivation of grains requires effort overseen by the goddess Demeter, who does not so much distribute her gifts with the profligacy of a fruit tree as regulate equitably the reward of the harvest in proportion to the work invested.¹³ The farmer, correspondingly, "does not feel that he is applying a cultivation technique to the soil or that he is practising a trade."¹⁴ Again by contrast to the growth of fruit trees, grains are cultivated not under the seasonal calendar of festival exuberance but the steady application of daily tasks.

The most ancient record of how these tasks are to be pursued rightly is that of Hesiod, who in his *Works and Days* advocates for the value of effort to his benighted brother, Perses. Vernant sees in the agricultural sphere a strong connection to the cultural in general and to the cult in specific. In his interpretation, what ties the theological and the moral to the agricultural is "punctilious ritualism."¹⁵ It is this attentiveness to duty that makes Hesiod's farming life one of both work and devotion, where both elements are required for success with men and gods. For this reason, to the Greek mind farming is not a matter of producing any useful or valued commodity but an activity closer to religious behavior.¹⁶

Finley too sees that farming was one area of work that required no special skill, though he does not stress, like Vernant, an overly strong connection to religiosity. "For the basic work of pasturage and tillage in the fields, of stewardship and service in the house, there was no need of specialists: every man in Ithaca could herd and plough, saw and carve, and those commoners who had their own holdings worked them themselves."[17] The wide-ranging ability to work the fields means in Finley's account that the contribution of the demiourgoi to the regular running of the oichos was relatively small.[18] The goal of the oichos was no more ambitious than self-sufficiency. David Tandy and Walter Neale notice that Hesiod seems primarily invested in the goal of keeping hunger (which he mentions seven times in *Works and Days*) and debt at bay, devoting little discussion to the possibility of exporting excess production and whatever profit might be made from it.[19]

Farming, as both Xenophon and Hesiod maintain, requires only attentiveness to what nature and the gods that oversee nature teach to the mindful and diligent observer. Xenophon's Socrates asserts to Critobulus, "because the earth is divine, she teaches justice to those who have the ability to learn from her. She gives the greatest benefits in return to those who cultivate her best."[20] There is in the ancient Greek world a widespread conviction that the act of farming has its own fundamental justice, where effort correlates neatly to benefit. Nature has no secrets when it comes to cultivation but is open to anyone ready to learn her lessons. As Hesiod counsels his brother Perses,

> work the works that the gods have assigned to people, lest at some time with your children and wife and with an ache in your spirit you may seek sustenance among your neighbors, and they do not care. For twice, perhaps three times, you will get results. But if you vex them further, you will not achieve a thing; you will make many vain arguments, and your repertoire of words will be of no use. I command you to consider discharge of *chrea* [debt] and avoidance of hunger.[21]

A number of key points are touched on in this passage. First, Hesiod encourages above all the avoidance of want and debt, which Tandy and Neale explain at length in their introduction.[22] They conclude that while a compelling case can be made that the most deleterious consequence of debt in Hesiod's day was not so much loss of land itself (which was not an alienable property in the economy of the time)[23] but loss of control of the land's production, it nevertheless seems that Perses has lost control of his lot of land (*kleros*) altogether. Second, Hesiod regards neighbors, who all struggled for at best relative autarchy and were unable to depend on a centralized authority or dispenser of emergency resources,[24] as an insufficient bulwark against hunger and debt. Third and finally, Hesiod does indicate here that the tasks assigned to the would-be farmer and requiring his attention are assigned by the gods. Because of this, farming can yield results in a way that neighbors cannot deliver.

Those results only come by exertion and fidelity to the tasks, but nature's demands are clear and not a matter of esoteric knowledge. For instance, Hesiod counsels Perses to cut wood when it is "least worm-eaten when cut with the iron: it drops its leaves to the ground and ceases from sprouting. Precisely then, remember to cut wood, the work of that season."[25] So here the clue to the time to hew perhaps is that wood drops its leaves and stops sprouting. Hesiod's advice along these lines to Perses is sound but in a way not needful (unless you are a "fool," as Hesiod repeatedly calls his brother).[26] There is a kind of equity to farming, according to which effort is reliably rewarded. As Hesiod says, "Turn up [the soil] in the spring; in the summer a once-plowed [fallow] field will not deceive you."[27]

Xenophon too argues that nature teaches its ways without special instruction. In Vernant's words,

> Xenophon's descriptions of the sowing, weeding, harvesting, threshing, winnowing, and of the cultivation of fruit trees, are all aimed at showing us not human skills, but "nature" at work in these operations. For instance, where do we get viticulture from if not from the vine itself? By climbing up the trees, the vine itself teaches us to give it a support; by spreading its leafy shoots when the grapes are still young, it teaches us to shade the exposed parts; by shedding its leaves, it teaches us to pick them off so that the fruit can ripen when the sun has become temperate.[28]

As in Hesiod's instructions about when to cut wood, it is the natural process itself that provides the hint as to what the farmer should do at every season. Because special skills are not required, Xenophon's gentleman farmer Ischomachus (whose instruction Socrates recounts in the center of the dialogue) claims that cultivation provides an entirely equitable measure of a man's worth:

> For she [nature] doesn't make a display in order to deceive, but speaks the truth and reveals clearly what she can do and what she can't. By providing all that she has in a form that is easy to learn and understand, I think the earth constitutes the best test of evil and lazy men. For in other occupations, those who avoid working offer ignorance as an excuse, but that is not possible in the case of farming; because everyone knows that the earth responds well to good treatment.[29]

It is for this reason that Ischomachus, much earlier in his discussion with Socrates, asserts that farming "is most beneficial and pleasant to work at, and most lovely and most dear to gods and men, and, in addition, it is very easy to learn."[30] This is in fact Ischomachus's first substantive response to Socrates's request that he teach his questioner how to farm. The specifics of Ischomachus's advice are not of interest here, aside from the respect in which, already mentioned, they provide clues to the correlation inherent in farming between what nature provides and how attentive human effort is best able to increase its yield. Interestingly, it is on this basis that Ischomachus maintains that farming is easy to learn, even for someone like Socrates, who characteristically protests his own ignorance of the matter. Ischomachus maintains that even a novice like Socrates would not require special training, which makes farming different from medicine, which one cannot learn simply by beginning to examine patients (to use Socrates's own counterexample).[31] Observation is the essential first step according to the gentleman farmer. To find out what the soil will sustain, for instance, Ischomachus contends,

> You can learn simply by looking at the crops and the trees on another man's soil what it can produce and what it can't. When a man has learned this, there is no point in persisting in struggling against the decrees of the gods; he is not likely to obtain provisions by sowing and planting what he wants, rather than what the soil prefers to produce and nurture.[32]

For some pages thereafter, Ischomachus becomes the questioner and Socrates the answerer, reversing their normal Platonic roles. Xenophon's Socrates is led to acknowledge the wisest way of proceeding through the various elements of agricultural practice by observing what nature itself suggests and imitating accordingly. At some point Socrates evinces the sort of surprise usually reserved in Plato's writings for his interlocutors:

> "I didn't realize I knew all that," I said. "And this has made me wonder for some time now whether I also know without realizing it how to smelt gold, and to play the flute, and to paint. For no one taught me these subjects, nor did anyone teach me farming, and I watch men employed in these other occupations, just as I watch men farming." "Well," Ischomachus said, "didn't I tell you just now that farming is a most noble occupation, because it is easiest to learn?"[33]

Continuing in this vein, Ischomachus cements the point by demonstrating again that Socrates can infer a great deal about planting of trees (the other great concern of Greek agriculture remarked upon above by Vernant) as well, again by observation. At the same time, Ischomachus discounts as "not possible" that the same methods should yield success when attempting to learn flute-playing or painting (again to use Socrates's own contrasts).[34] The key distinction seems to be that nature itself is doing the teaching rather than another expert craftsman or perhaps even an expert farmer like Ischomachus himself. Ischomachus concludes his instruction by claiming that "farming is such a humane and gentle occupation that she makes those who see her and hear her immediately knowledgeable about her. And she herself ... also gives many lessons about how one might treat her best."[35] At this point though a perhaps unsurprising objection crops up: "How is it, Ischomachus," Socrates asks, "if it's so easy, as you say, to learn the principles relevant to farming, and everyone has an equal amount of knowledge about what should be done, not everyone does equally well, but some live in plenty and have a surplus, whereas others cannot provide themselves with the necessities, but even get into debt as well?"[36]

Here we touch upon the second key ingredient of successful farming according to Ischomachus; the difference between the prosperous and the impoverished is not attributable to knowledge or lack thereof but to concern (*epimeleia*) or the lack thereof. In Ischomachus's opinion no oichos is ruined because the farmer did not know the proper methods but because he was not diligent in applying them.[37] How to go about farming is plain, so the difference between success and failure comes down to hard work, which is why Ischomachus claims as we saw above that farming is a perfect test of character: "So too in working, there is a great difference in achievement between those who work at their assignments and those who do not work, but find excuses for not working and are allowed to work slowly."[38] Indeed, not only is there a great difference here, it is *the* difference, "for those who are capable of paying attention to it, and who farm energetically, it provides a most effective way of making money."[39]

One can imagine Hesiod agreeing with Ischomachus here, as he too counsels Perses with the need for energetic expenditure of effort coupled with straightforward attentiveness to what nature instructs. Ischomachus's commitment to work is so thoroughgoing that he has remained faithful to the advice of his father, whom he lauds as a successful and hardworking farmer himself, to avoid purchasing land that is already cultivated and thus expensive and not likely to sustain improvement in favor of land that has been neglected and is thus capable of significant improvement. Not only does this strategy yield profit, which both Ischomachus and his father pursued, but it also affords "pleasure," inasmuch as Ischomachus's father "regarded every possession or living creature that was constantly improving as particularly delightful."[40]

This part of Xenophon's *Oeconomicus* stands alongside *Works and Days* as one of the greatest paeans to hard work that the ancient Greek world produced. Work is here presented as affording its own particular pleasure, evinced by Ischomachus's father's practice of selling off land he had improved in order to "buy another uncultivated plot immediately to replace it." Intriguingly, Ischomachus claims this was not because of his father's love of financial gain but because "he loved working."[41]

Crafts

Interestingly, both Tandy and Neale and Finley seize upon Achilles's offer of five years' use of iron as a prize for the funeral games of Patroclus in the *Iliad* as illustrative of the rarity and value of metal and its usefulness to the daily operation of an oichos.[42] Metal, though prized, requires dedicated effort and special skills, skills that exceed what farming demands. As Vernant documents, Xenophon contrasts farming with crafts calling for techne, skill that knows and applies the appropriate means to secure a specific end.[43] By contrast with nature, who reveals all her secrets, the craftsman guards his secrets, requiring apprenticeship and initiation.[44] Recall too that Xenophon allowed the would-be craftsman to plead ignorance, since the essential knowledge required for any craft is not obvious to the dilettante, while the would-be farmer need only overcome sloth and apply effort to the task.

Vernant identifies two key attitudes about techne in Greek culture: first, that the practice of specialized activities in concert contributes to social stability, and second, that it lays out rules for success in the various areas of human endeavor.[45] These are valuable characteristics because people were thought to settle together out of respective needs that the practice of techne can address.[46] Technai thus fundamentally serve needs (chrea)[47] and are both defined and limited by them.[48] Every individual has a plurality of needs but limited capacity and resources to meet them, so the coming together of needs and capacities to meet them is a natural arrangement as much as a political one; furthermore, it is an arrangement that promotes the good of human activities in general.[49] Thus all technai are limited in both number and scope since they serve a limited set of human needs.[50]

An illustrative contrast can be made to the manner in which the mythological Cyclopes were understood to live. John Peter Oleson points out that according to this fantastical scenario,

> A tribe of one-eyed giants, the Cyclopes, lived on a fertile island with a beneficent climate that provided wheat, barley, and grapes (the basis for the ancient Greek

diet) spontaneously, without any need for plowing or sowing. As a result, Homer concludes, they had no need for assemblies or laws, shipwrights, or other technologies, each family living apart in caves and herding flocks of sheep in a modified hunting-gathering culture.[51]

Where there is no need, there is no need for work or techne. Aristotle declared that only people lived by nature in a polis, while only a beast or a god lives alone.[52] The Cyclopes seem to vindicate this intuition, being beasts who do not live in community, do not have immediate needs, and do not therefore require or make use of technai.

Technai then exist to address needs, and they aim at the use to which their products are intended to be put. This use is most satisfactorily achieved when the product of a given techne most completely corresponds to its *eidos* or form. Because artificial objects as well as natural ones have final causes or teloi, the eidos or form governs this telos, and the most successful craftsman is the one who achieves conformity to the eidos well.[53] Technai undertaken in pursuit of artificial objects that answer to no immediate need stimulate pleasures superfluous to need. As Vernant notices though, the entire realm of production of appearances can also be extended to include sophistry and banking or commerce. These latter produce not goods connected to *physis*, the realm of natural need, but *nomos*, the realm of conventional tokens.

This distinction is relevant to Plato's entire thought experiment in the *Republic*; having agreed with his interlocutors that insight into the political order at large and how justice is found in the city will be isomorphic with the order between the parts of the soul and how justice is found in the individual, at first Socrates sketches a society adapted strictly to need: "because people need many things, and because one person calls on a second out of one need and on a third out of a different need, many people gather in a single place to live together as partners and helpers. And such a settlement is called a city."[54] The primary needs of human beings being food, shelter, and clothing, the city will require farmers, builders, and weavers, that is, practitioners of basic technai.[55] With the further recognition that the products of each techne are best attained when each craftsman pursues the techne to which he is most naturally suited, Socrates and his interlocutors conclude that "carpenters, metal workers, and many other craftsmen of that sort will share our little city and make it bigger," because the farmers, builders, and weavers will not be makers of their own tools, which are nevertheless requisite for their respective technai.[56]

The proliferation of various kinds of craftsmen though is no hindrance to a downright idyllic social existence, Socrates's description of which is worth quoting in full:

> Let's see what sort of life our citizens will lead when they've been provided for in the way we have been describing. They'll produce bread, wine, clothes, and shoes, won't they? They'll build houses, work naked and barefoot in the summer, and wear adequate clothing and shoes in the winter. For food, they'll knead and cook the flour and meal they've made from wheat and barley. They'll put their honest cakes and loaves on reeds or clean leaves, and, reclining on beds strewn with yew and myrtle, they'll feast with their children, drink their wine, and, crowned with

wreaths, hymn the gods. They'll enjoy sex with one another but bear no more children than their resources allow, lest they fall into either poverty or war.[57]

Socrates's description of this romantic arrangement is "interrupted" by Glaucon, who protests at the austerity of this imagined citizenry.[58] Under pressure from the younger man, Socrates avers that the group is apparently then not looking for the origin of cities in general but the origin of a *"luxurious* city."[59] Intriguingly, Socrates here does something very rare for him: He asserts his own, apparently sincere, and unsolicited opinion:

> Yet the true city, in my opinion, is the one we've described, the healthy one, as it were. But let's study a city with a fever, if that's what you want. There's nothing to stop us. The things I mentioned earlier and the way of life I described won't satisfy some people, it seems, but couches, tables, and other furniture will have to be added, and, of course, all sorts of delicacies, perfumed oils, incense, prostitutes, and pastries. We mustn't provide them only with the necessities we mentioned at first, such as houses, clothes, and shoes, but painting and embroidery must be begun, and gold, ivory, and the like acquired. Isn't that so?[60]

Notice that a transition has been effectuated from a community based on need to one accommodating pleasures as well as addressing needs. In Socrates's estimation it would appear that the luxuries that he catalogues do not answer to any genuine human need but are superfluities. In a rare moment of candor, he asserts that the true community is the one he outlined at first, which he proceeds to contrast almost point-for-point with the feverish city and its new roster of pleasures corresponding to the simple satisfactions of the healthy city. Where the healthy city has wholesome food, the feverish city has delicacies and pastries; clothing in the healthy city is functional and relinquished altogether when not necessary, while the feverish city clothes its citizens in embroidery; the healthy city serves food on reeds, while the feverish city demands tables; where the healthy city's inhabitants recline on fronds, the feverish city's citizens lie on couches; sex in the healthy city is for enjoyment and manageable levels of procreation, while the feverish city offers prostitution;[61] finally, and perhaps most significantly, while the piety of the healthy city's citizens is evident in their hymns, there is no mention made of the gods in connection with the feverish city. In a disturbing extrapolation from this new premise, Socrates and his friends agree that such a city, with its demands for illusory goods and services that do not strictly answer to need, will inevitably fall into war with its neighbors as a result of excessive demand for resources that are in the control of the city's nearest competitors for the same scarce resources.[62] This is yet another point of contrast with the healthy city, wherein Socrates says the people maintain sustainable levels of population and demand for resources precisely to avoid the extremes of poverty and lust for conquest fueled by acquisitiveness. The decisive new addition to the city that Socrates and his interlocutors proceed to develop is its embrace of technai that do not correlate to the satisfaction of human needs but produce objects superfluous to those needs.

Significant perhaps, but not often noticed, is that the conversation was already on the very verge of ascertaining the character of justice, the point of the whole book. Having declared that the healthy city is complete, Socrates initially inquires, "where are justice and injustice to be found in it?" Adeimantus confesses, 'I have no idea, Socrates, unless it was somewhere in some need that these people have of one another."[63] This may have been the germ of the ultimate answer that justice is a matter of each person (and part of the soul) doing his or her own job. The embarkation on the extended discussion of the "sick" city is thus in one sense a sidetrack from what seemed in the first instance to be an imminent arrival at the point of resolving the basic question about justice. It could thus be argued that the production of objects superfluous to human need prolongs at least if not complicates altogether the question of justice. We will continue to develop this thought, but the point is that the technai are natural and necessary and their practice correlates strongly with just order in the soul and society.

Banausia

One special category of crafts deserves particular attention. The topic can be introduced most effectively by returning to a remark from Xenophon, in which Socrates voices an apparently commonplace sentiment. In response to Critobulus's question as to which branches of knowledge are honorable and worth pursuing, Socrates immediately sets aside "the so-called banausic occupations," which he claims without contradiction or qualification

> are both denounced and, quite rightly, held in very low esteem by states. For they utterly ruin the bodies of those who work at them and those of their supervisors, by forcing them to lead a sedentary life and to stay indoors, and some of them even to spend the whole day by the fire. When their bodies become effeminate, their souls too become much weaker. Furthermore, the so-called "banausic" occupations leave a man no spare time to be concerned about his friends and city. Consequently such men seem to treat their friends badly and to defend their countries badly too. In fact, in some cities, especially in those reputed to excel in war, none of the citizens is permitted to work at the banausic occupations.[64]

The word "banausic" derives from the Greek term for "furnace," and it refers to crafts that depend on the use of fire like smithing and pottery, in particular, but more broadly construed can connote vulgarity and tastelessness.[65] A disdain for this sort of work was apparently widespread in ancient Greece and, as we will see, serves an important rhetorical function in the discourses of Plato. Lest Xenophon's testimony of Socrates's condemnation of banausic crafts be taken as unrepresentative, Plato's Socrates also condemns those whose "souls are cramped and spoiled by the mechanical nature of their work, in just the way that their bodies are mutilated by their crafts and labors."[66] Oleson documents the extent to which the ancient world was in agreement on this point, citing both Greek and Roman authors,[67] but he rejects Finley's argument that this widespread aversion to banausic labor caused a lack of technological progress in the ancient world; indeed the mammoth volume he edited is intended to provide significant evidence that technology flourished in the cultures of Greece and Rome.[68]

Nevertheless, a palpable distaste for the banausic persisted from early to late in the ancient world. On the earliest end, it is possible that Hesiod's counsel to Perses that he "pass by the smith's seat and the warm talk-hall in wintertime, when the cold keeps men back from their works"[69] is not just, as Vernant speculates, a sign of Hesiod's disinterest in town life[70] but possibly also a slight against forging and smithing as activities alien and subordinate to the high calling of farming. Further evidence for this potential reading is gleaned from the context. Coupled with the smith's seat is the "talk-hall," (*lerche*) which was a warm resort for the homeless and thus a place of idleness or eating and drinking without the high-toned conversation of a typical symposium.[71] As Tandy and Neale observe, in the *Odyssey* Penelope dismisses her husband, disguised as an indigent seeking shelter, with the suggestion that he is either insane or drunk and ought to go sleep in a smithy or a "talk-hall" with the other gossips and chatterers. So the smith's place of work was associated with indigence and vulgarity. On the late end, we see Cicero echoing a centuries-long verdict against banausia when he writes in the *De officiis* that "all mechanics are engaged in vulgar trades; for no workshop can have anything liberal about it." The banausic crafts he thereby positions as less desirable than tax-gathering and usury, hired labor involving mere manual labor rather than any artistic skill, and price-gouging retailers who are middlemen between wholesalers and purchasers, whose meager profits depend on markup. Below the banausic arts are only "those trades which cater to sensual pleasures" and the fripperies of perfumers and performers.[72]

The cultural consensus that banausic crafts warped body and soul was also encoded in myth. As Finley put it, "much of the psychology of labour, with its ambivalence between admiration of skill and craft and its rejection of the labourer as essentially and irretrievably an inferior being, found its expression on Olympus." Homer humanized the gods and thus included work within their otherwise divine life, but this would seem to imply an equality between labor and the nobler pursuits of the gods. The dilemma is that "only a god could make swords for gods, yet somehow he must be a being apart from the other gods."[73] The solution was to conceive of the only ugly god: Hephaestus, who expertly and tirelessly worked at the forge but was deformed and repellent, a source of ridicule among the other denizens of Olympus. Limping from birth, Hephaestus was hulking and unattractive. His coupling with Aphrodite captures the sportive contradiction between his undeniable skill but detestable exterior. Even among the gods, then, banausia was to be mocked and scorned. Remembering though Hephaestus's revenge upon his wife's infidelity with Ares, by means of forged bonds that snared the adulterers in their bed, whereupon Hephaestus invites the rest of the gods to laugh at them for once, proves that the banausic arts are still undeniably skillful, even against the most beautiful and most warlike of the Olympians.[74]

2

Plato on Work

Plato on Techne

The first and most obvious point to make about Plato's thinking about work in its various forms is that it is staggering in scope and continuous across his entire corpus. By one count, the word "techne" in its various inflections occurs 675 times in the dialogues, and words derived from "techne" occur 187 times.[1] One tabulation produced by Robert Brumbaugh's "casual and partial sample of references to crafts" includes Plato referring to "Bath attending; Blacksmithing; Building (with masonry); Carpentry; Butchering; Carving; Cabinetmaking; Clothesmaking; Cobbling; the art of Commerce; Cooking; Barbering; Coppersmithing; Dyeing; Embroidery; Flutemaking; Thread spinning; Gold refining; Statue carving; Minting of coinage; Navigation," not to mention his particular favorites and more frequently cited references to "the General's (art of Warfare); Hunting; Medicine; Lawgiving; Measuring; or even Weaving."[2] Brumbaugh further argues that not only are these references not merely in passing or superficial, but Plato actually seems to have more than an outsider's familiarity with certain arts and crafts—hunting and warfare certainly and medicine besides, but also carpentry and particularly spinning and weaving, certain details of which Plato preserves and are found in no other ancient author.[3] At the very least, then, we can say that Plato is a constant admirer and interested observer of craftsmanship and that he deploys allusions to a wide variety of crafts and artisanal practices.

A natural question that arises is to what sort of purpose or purposes Plato devotes these allusions. The classic position has been that Plato seizes upon techne as a model for his own view of what philosophical knowledge must consist in. Early and straightforward deployments of this analogy can be found in the *Laches* and the *Apology* most obviously.[4] In the former dialogue, a debate between two generals over whether armor fighting is valuable for promoting excellence reaches an impasse, and Socrates is called upon to cast the deciding vote.[5] Shocked at his interlocutors' readiness to pursue a course of moral action on the basis of majority vote, Socrates proposes that the wiser tactic would be "to investigate first of all whether any one of us is an expert in the subject we are debating, or not. And if one of us is, then we should listen to him even if he is only one, and disregard the others. But if no one of us is an expert, then we must look for someone who is," and he argues further that the procedure they adopt has the most momentous consequences, inasmuch as what is at stake is the quality of their sons and the future fortunes of the oichos.[6]

Similarly in the *Apology*, Socrates recounts a discussion with Callias, father to two sons. Socrates himself draws an analogy between the expertise required to raise domestic animals and to rear children into a life of excellence.

> "Callias," I said, "if your sons were colts or calves, we could find and engage a supervisor for them who would make them excel in their proper qualities, some horse breeder or farmer. Now since they are men, whom do you have in mind to supervise them? Who is an expert in this kind of excellence, the human and social kind?"

Callias's ready answer is that the sophist Evenus of Paros is the one he has paid to provide this expertise.[7] Passages like these seem to suggest a straightforward analogy between technical expertise that concerns more mundane affairs like military science and animal husbandry and an alluded-to more comprehensive human or specifically ethical expertise. As Roochnik summarizes passages of this sort, "These passages are critical, for they seem to answer a fundamental question permeating Plato's early dialogues, and perhaps all of them: What is 'moral knowledge,' knowledge of the arête of the *psuche*, of how to live an excellent life? It seems to be analogous to a techne."[8]

Indeed, as Roochnik goes on to schematize a variety of basic positions in the scholarly literature on this question, there is widespread agreement on this point. He shapes what he calls a "standard account of techne," according to which "in the early dialogues Socrates' use of the techne analogy represents Plato's assertion of a serious theoretical model of moral knowledge as a guide and telos of his philosophizing. On this reading, Plato hopes for and desires a techne whose subject matter is arête."[9] Roochnik catalogues a large number of scholars who are in consensus around this point and at the same time further discriminates camps within that consensus. Some scholars argue that the "standard account" disappears in Plato's middle and late writings (often as a corollary to a theory about Plato's increasing maturity as a thinker in his own right, out from underneath Socrates's shadow), while others say the model of techne for moral excellence persists. Similarly, a fault line can be drawn between those who take it that techne is necessarily productive of some "work" apart from its own activity and if techne is much more expansive, including disciplines that don't yield an obvious "work" other than the practice of the techne itself (including perhaps skills like mathematics). Finally, there is disagreement over the extent of the analogy's relevance: Does Plato think moral knowledge is more or less exactly like other technai, or does he simply liken the imagined skill of moral excellence to other technai in limited respects?[10]

There is practical value in Roochnik's schema, though it should be noted that he provides it to offset his own idiosyncratic assertion that "*Plato rejects techne as a model of moral knowledge.*"[11] In this he is not entirely alone, however. We can enrich his schema and lay out some additional perspectives along a similar continuum. Throughout what follows we will stay oriented by the question of how techne relates to the question of human flourishing: What is it about work that contributes to or takes away from human well-being?

Depending on who you ask, techne is not a clue to the moral knowledge that is crucial to human well-being or it is a model for or a clue to the moral knowledge that is essential to human well-being, but no one would claim that it is identical to moral knowledge. Coming at the problem from the reverse direction, we might ask whether or not only moral knowledge or philosophical wisdom counts as knowledge at all according to Plato. Put another way, does the practitioner of techne have knowledge or just the philosopher?

A starting point toward addressing this question can be found in Plato's treatment of Socrates's account of his own philosophical mission. In the course of rebutting the charges brought against him by Meletus, Socrates reports in the *Apology* that his pursuit of insight into the many technai and those who practiced them was not just a matter of amateur interest but a component of his quest for wisdom. Responding to a friend's puzzling report of the Oracle of Delphi's judgment that Socrates was the wisest man of all, Socrates embarks on an effort to identify someone among his fellow citizens to prove the Oracle wrong, anyone whose wisdom was greater than his own (seeing as how, with his usual mixture of candor and irony, Socrates denies that he is wise at all and finds the Oracle's verdict utterly confounding).[12] The course of his investigation takes him first to an unnamed individual of reputed wisdom, only to discover that this reputation was unfounded. Endeavoring to proceed more systematically among the leading politicians of the city and making enemies of those whose pretenses to wisdom he unmasked all the while, Socrates discovers that there is an inverse relation between the highest reputation for wisdom and the presence of actual wisdom in all those he questioned.[13] Socrates next queried poets of all sorts only to conclude that "almost all the bystanders might have explained the poems better than their authors could," another sort of inverse relation, in this case between production and explanation. This observation in turn leads Socrates to surmise that "poets do not compose their poems with knowledge, but by some inborn talent and by inspiration" devoid of understanding, which nevertheless did not impede the poets from thinking "themselves very wise men in other respects, which they were not."[14]

The final group that Socrates says he interrogated were the craftsmen, "for," as he puts it, "I was conscious of knowing practically nothing, and I knew that I would find that they had knowledge of many fine things." Interestingly, Socrates names only the craftsmen as being those contemporaries whom he felt confident from the outset would possess wisdom. By contrast in this respect at least with the poets, "in this," he asserts, "I was not mistaken; they knew things I did not know and to that extent they were wiser than I."[15] At the same time, though, the craftsmen did in his judgment bear a similarity to the poets: "The good craftsmen seemed to me to have the same fault as the poets: each of them, because of his success at his craft, thought himself very wise in other most important pursuits and this error of theirs overshadowed the wisdom they had."[16]

To be perfectly clear then about the inferences that Socrates drew from what we have seen is a more than passing acquaintance with a multitude of technai, the great philosopher does conclude with ease that persons possessing techne are also in possession of some kind of knowledge, knowledge that Socrates himself lacks—this very limited expertise however induces the craftsmen to imagine themselves wise in other respects, not having to do with their own technical expertise, an error that Socrates claims casts a shadow on what they do know. The most basic point itself here is worth noting, for despite its apparent clarity, there are a host of commentators on Plato who deny that anyone but the philosopher has knowledge.[17]

Joel Martinez applies this insight to the argumentation of the *Republic* with productive results. Of particular importance is the connection between the way techne is discussed in the first and last books of Plato's longest dialogue. At both the beginning and the end of the dialogue, Plato affirms that one who possesses techne has knowledge of his or her own techne (though not, as we have seen, necessarily of anything else). In Book X, Socrates states plainly,

> It's wholly necessary, therefore, that a user of each thing has most experience of it and that he tell a maker which of his products performs well or badly in actual use ... Then doesn't the one who knows give instructions ... and doesn't the other rely on him in making them? ... Therefore, a maker—through associating with and having to listen to the one who knows—has right opinion about whether something he makes is fine or bad, but the one who knows is the user.[18]

Here again is a plain admission that the user of a craft product (in Socrates's example a flute-player who relates to the maker of flutes) has knowledge of his own techne and can counsel others to make products in accord with that knowledge (though the maker has only "right opinion" of such matters).

Similarly, in Book I, Socrates engages with the Sophist Thrasymachus in the opening debate over the question of justice, which drives the entire argumentation of the text. Justice is likened to the practice of a techne, and therefore techne becomes an important topic in need of precision. In defense of one of his claims, Thrasymachus introduces a "precise" or strict account of techne:

> I think that we express ourselves in words that, taken literally, do say that a doctor is in error, or an accountant, or a grammarian. But each of these, insofar as he is what we call him, never errs, so that, according to the precise account (and you are a stickler for precise accounts), no craftsman ever errs. It's when his knowledge fails him that he makes an error, and in regard to that error he is not a craftsman.[19]

Thrasymachus provides this specification because he is arguing that justice is nothing more than the advantage of the strong or those who are "rulers" in a given polis and furthermore that the content of this "justice" is simply whatever is to the advantage of those rulers in power.[20] In response, Socrates argues that if Thrasymachus is right to say that justice consists only of obeying the rulers when they rule to their own advantage (as opposed to that of the weak or the ruled) then he must also acknowledge that the rulers are not always correct about their own advantage and thus are liable to at least sometimes decree contrary to their own interests, in which case justice, if it is to remain founded in unconditional obedience to the rulers, will have turned into its opposite.[21]

Interestingly, Thrasymachus rejects outright a correction suggested by Cleitophon, who proposes what might seem to be the obvious qualification called for in the face of Socrates's contention, namely, that Thrasymachus specify that justice consists of what the rulers *believe* is conducive to their own advantage, even if sometimes they are mistaken about this point.[22] Despite the attraction of this modification, Thrasymachus refuses it and instead offers the "precise" or strict version quoted above to the effect that if the rulers are in error about what is genuinely to their own advantage then they are at that very moment failing to be true rulers. The point holds, Thrasymachus claims, for all practitioners of techne, including rulers and his further examples of doctors, accountants, and grammarians. Insofar as any of these is in error they are not, strictly speaking, practicing a techne, such that any true expert, insofar as he or she is an expert, cannot be in error.

Seizing upon this precise definition, Socrates proceeds to argue that each practitioner has an exact area of concern that is the object of his or her expertise: A doctor treats sick bodies as opposed to being a money-maker, while a captain rules over sailors as opposed to being himself a sailor.[23] Socrates is able to solicit Thrasymachus's agreement that in each case the techne itself, strictly considered, has no advantage for itself apart from the techne's own perfection, which is a point of contrast with the *objects* of each techne. Consistent with a pre-Platonic Greek tradition described above, Socrates maintains that technai correspond to needs or deficiencies; because the body is deficient and has needs, medicine was discovered and developed to address the body's needs.[24] No such corresponding need or deficiency can be found in the technai themselves, however; to continue with the example at hand, medicine itself is not deficient, that is to say, it is not in need of any additional techne for its own integrity. On this basis Socrates is able to conclude that "it isn't appropriate for any craft to seek what is to the advantage of anything except that of which it is the craft."[25] That this conclusion follows from the "precise" definition provided by Thrasymachus is emphasized by Socrates himself: "Since it [any techne] is itself correct, it is without either fault or impurity, as long as it is wholly and precisely the craft that it is. Consider this with the preciseness of language you mentioned."[26]

With this implication of the precise definition established, Socrates is able to defeat Thrasymachus's argument, though Thrasymachus himself resists conceding Socrates's final point, which follows naturally from his argument about the integrity of the technai. Medicine, to continue with the same example, seeks not its own advantage therefore but the advantage of the object with which it is concerned, namely, the sick body. Similarly, the horse-breeder precisely insofar as he is an expert in horse-breeding and practicing this techne, seeks the advantage of the horses that are his concern and not his own advantage.[27] Therefore, Socrates is able to assert, "No kind of knowledge seeks or orders what is advantageous to itself, then, but what is advantageous to the weaker, which is subject to it."[28] That this applies to ruling as well, Thrasymachus has to reluctantly admit: "No one in any position of rule, insofar as he is a ruler, seeks or orders what is advantageous to himself, but what is advantageous to his subjects; the ones of whom he is himself the craftsman."[29] Notice here that rule remains a techne, and like all other technai, rule concerns itself with the remediation of deficiencies in its object of concern, in this case, the subjects of rule; it is to their advantage that the techne of rule is ordered, not to the advantage of those who wield the power of rule, precisely insofar as those rulers are indeed genuine rulers with a true techne.[30]

The argument from here in an important sense turns in a new direction; its relevance for the debate about justice need not concern us, but for our purposes, we should track the further refinement that Socrates gives the precise definition of techne. Thrasymachus, speaking now out of pique and frustration with what he regards as Socrates's unbearable naivety, renews his cynical view of rule by ridiculing Socrates's assertion that every techne seeks only the advantage of its object of concern by reference to new examples. Thrasymachus counters Socrates by saying,

> You think that shepherds and cowherds seek the good of their sheep and cattle, and fatten them and take care of them, looking to something other than their master's good and their own. Moreover, you believe that rulers in cities—true rulers, that is—think about their subjects differently than one does about sheep, and that night and day they think of something besides their own advantage.[31]

Thrasymachus's point of course is that the shepherd looks to the advantage of the sheep only inasmuch as that advantage quite literally feeds another's advantage, namely, his own and his master's appetites. The shepherd rears sheep so they can make a fine meal, not because he is concerned with the sheep per se.

Yet this is exactly what Socrates goes on to rebut. Whatever additional advantage is to be gained by shepherding actually is not the concern of shepherding per se at all. Socrates insists—and this too follows directly from the "precise" definition of techne—that "every craft differ[s] from every other in having a different function."[32] This principle serves to distinguish every techne not only from every other but also from consequences that follow upon the practice of a techne, including both from profit and from accidental by-products that in the precise sense are associated with another techne. In practical terms, what Socrates establishes is that money-making is a distinct activity from the practice of medicine (even if practicing medicine earns money for its practitioner) and that medicine is concerned strictly with the health of the body and is thus different from sailing (even if sailing happens to make sailors healthy).[33] What Socrates thus proves is that again if we stay strictly focused on the practice of a techne itself then no benefit obtains to that practice other than the fulfillment of the aim of the practice and the advantage of its object.

Even when a practitioner of techne "works for nothing," therefore, "he still provides a benefit" because the work of any techne itself entails no supplemental benefit for itself or for its practitioner other than its own perfection and accrues no benefit for itself or its practitioner other than the advantage of its object.[34] Obviously other benefits can and do accrue to the practice of technai, including money-making and by-products of all sorts that are not essential to the techne in question, but again, Socrates has managed to reinforce his point "that no craft or rule provides for its own advantage, but, as we've been saying for some time, it provides and orders for its subject and aims at its advantage, that of the weaker, not of the stronger."[35] The latest consequences educed from the precise definition of techne are worth observing, because they establish a valuable point about Plato's attitude toward techne, which is the bedrock of what we would now call "work" in the lives of most ancient Athenians.

As Kenneth Knies has noted,

> The strict account of techne is strict because it forces us to abandon commonsense interpretations of what it means to "have a job." Normally, everyone speaks about technai as if they belong to people. Someone is a doctor or a cobbler because it is what she does. Her reasons for doing it, and doing it in the way she does, are only apparent when considered in the context of her personal motivations and the circumstances from which they arise. As against this ordinary way of speaking, the account considers doctors or cobblers exactly insofar as they are doctors and cobblers; it views the worker from the perspective of that which makes her a worker.[36]

As we have seen from our own examination of the text, according to Socrates's dispute with Thrasymachus, the practitioner of a techne is not, in the act of pursuing that techne, concerned with her own motivations apart from the aim of perfecting her techne or with any potential advantage or "side-benefit" either to herself or to the object of her techne apart from the reparation of what is deficient in said object.[37] In Knies's words, "the strict account of techne does not concern the motives behind a techne, but rather the kind of looking internal to the accomplishment of the techne itself."[38] At the minimum this implies that Plato views each techne as having its own independent integrity and value, quite apart from its usefulness or profit. A techne is worth practicing for itself, and it can be considered in itself with regard to its own perfection and without reference to its potential value in some other respect. That each techne has its own concern and its own internal good means that "one in the possession of the sewing techne does not look to the garment as something providing warmth, protection, or concealment. It is the wearer of the garment who looks to these things, and it is not the special business of the sewer to put herself in the wearer's place."[39]

For Knies, the integrity of the technai and their relatively limited area of concern imply that we have to revise the genealogy of city-states rehearsed by Socrates and his companions and summarized in the earlier section of this chapter. Recall that Socrates argued there with respect to the healthy city that citizens come together out of need; each individual finds him- or herself subject to a variety of needs, not all of which he or she can supply on his or her own resources but that can be satisfied by interaction with others. However, once on the brink of establishing the principle of justice, it becomes clear that while the polis may have arisen (experimentally at least in the conversation among Socrates and his interlocutors) from need, need is not the final meaning of the polis. In the course of entertaining a potential objection that the guardian class will be unhappy as a result of the austerity of their lives and the weight of their particular responsibilities, Socrates argues that the point of their shared exercise is not to concern themselves as founders of the ideal polis with the happiness of any class of their imagined society but with the happiness and flourishing of the whole.

This focus Socrates contrasts with what he takes to be the normal run of things in city-states (*poleis*), where the community is not ordinarily found to be at unity with itself. It would be a mistake, he argues, to furnish the guardians with luxuries and extra provisions, since these are the very additions that would cause them to cease being guardians. The interlocutors agree that if they wanted to dress farmers in fine raiment and allow them to spend all their time in feasting rather than working, then such a thing would be possible but not productive, inasmuch as then "a farmer wouldn't be a farmer, nor a potter a potter, and none of the others would keep to the patterns of work that give rise to a city."[40] So here again the sort of work that is being done is determinative of the role of the individual in the city, and each person is expected to keep diligently to their own practice. This policy must be consistently applied across all classes in the polis, in order to secure the well-being of all:

> If we are making true guardians, then, who are least likely to do evil to the city, and if the one who brought the charge is talking about farmers and banqueters who are happy as they would be at a festival rather than in a city, then he isn't talking about a city at all, but about something else. With this in mind, we should consider whether in setting up our guardians we are aiming to give them the greatest happiness, or whether—since our aim is to see that the city as a whole has the greatest happiness—we must compel and persuade the auxiliaries and guardians to follow our other policy and be the best possible craftsmen at their own work, and the same with all the others. In this way, with the whole city developing and being governed well, we must leave it to nature to provide each group with its share of happiness.[41]

Part of the nature of the polis is that it involves the coordination of various kinds of work, the harmonization of multiple valued technai. That is part of what it means to be a polis as opposed to a festival, where work is presumably suspended. The farmers and banqueters who are "happy" with feasting and indulgence would be fit participants for a festival but not fit citizens. For the sake of all the citizens and the coordination of their various activities, each must cultivate their own techne as assiduously as possible; all must be "the best possible craftsmen at their own work, and the same with all the others," underscoring yet again the intrinsic desirability of the pursuit of techne. As Knies puts it, "A true polis is not a need coordinating mechanism, but a vocational horizon. The coordination of technai serves to free vocational work from the material interest of life and allows it to become an end in itself."[42]

To support this contention, we might note further that this is also the reason why Socrates condemns both wealth and poverty, the extremes of which corrupt workers by promoting "luxury, idleness, and revolution" on the one hand and "slavishness, bad work, and revolution as well" on the other hand.[43] Most cities, Socrates points out, are actually not one but "two cities at war with one another, that of the poor and that of the rich, and each of these contains a great many."[44] If we keep in mind that the profit brought by the practice of any techne is irrelevant to the value of the techne itself, then the wealth brought about thereby is disqualified as a fit incentive for work and indeed condemned as a potential source of division. The stress on unity, both of the polis and of the soul (for which, don't forget, the polis is meant to be a correlate), accompanies both the beginning and the end of the conversation on work and its place in the polis.

Socrates very early on raises the question of whether one person will "do a better job if he practices many crafts or—since he's one person himself—if he practices one," and Adeimantus agrees immediately that it's better to practice one.[45] Similarly, at the end of this discussion, Socrates affirms that in the practice of one techne, "doing the one work that is his own," a person "will become not many but one, and the whole city will itself be naturally one, not many."[46] The principle of unity then that undergirds the city is not after all the panoply of human needs but justice, where that is identified with each individual or class or part of the soul doing its own respective job. There is then a very close tie between the practice of a techne and contribution toward the realization of justice. As Knies argues, this seems to go beyond the realm of the merely economic: "Each techne, no matter the nature of its product, renders a service and exercises a correlative power because it contributes to a thriving vocational life for all. The polis exists in order that each might be able to pursue her own work."[47]

Patrick Coby has argued along similar lines that while the city begins in a state of need, needs that are redressed by the practice of the various technai, that very practice ends up advancing virtues that play a key role in the overall health and flourishing of the citizens' common life. The technai as Plato consistently describes them are limited and therefore perfectible: They in and of themselves are geared toward their own optimal attainment. To be a technician in the true and strict sense is to be someone dedicated not just to the plying of the trade in question but to the best possible practice of it. All the technai on his reading are "forms of knowledge exhibited in their products: properly constructed homes and furniture, well-tailored clothing, all perfectly suited to the natural and limited needs of human beings."[48] The crafts then are not value-neutral but promote the moderation that is the hallmark of the artisan class and the perfection of the corresponding appetitive part of the individual soul. The mastery of their craft is itself what promotes the moderation of the craftspeople, fortifying them against preferring money-making to their own craft and instilling in them the love of what is fine and balanced and well-executed with a commensurate repulsion at the ugly and spoilt. As Coby puts it, "the craftsman who has mastered his art and knows its perfection will not prostitute it by creating inferior goods, especially if he is also supported by the institutions of a small, austere, and traditional society."[49]

In this way the craftsperson participates in their own characteristic (and admittedly indirect) fashion in the life of reason as fully lived only by the philosopher. By their mastery of and appreciation for beauty and the objects that reflect it, the craftsperson extends beyond the confines of their own individual life and the limit of their own craft and grasps something of the eternal perfections that the statesman embodies in law and political structures and the philosopher contemplates.[50] Coby concludes that the *Republic* then is largely about not just the philosopher's benefit from and to the ideal political order but also the benefits realized by all as a result of each doing their own respective work. He argues that the text intends to show

> what reason there is in artisans, in warriors, and in philosophers; further, that the principal hindrance to the liberation of reason lies with the passions and appetites, which must be disciplined; that they are disciplined insofar as each

individual "minds his own business" and practices his one art; and that by the skilled practice of an art the individual participates directly in the life of reason.[51]

So what we have established so far, at a bare minimum, is that techne is a constant theme of Plato's, that it is a form of knowledge for which Plato portrays Socrates as having respect and admiration, that strictly speaking every practitioner of techne is concerned only for its object's improvement and not for their own advancement or profit, establishing that the perfection of techne is a desirable project with internal and not merely external or instrumental value, and, finally, that techne's capacity to address need is the origin of political communities themselves though not their final meaning, which is found instead in the justice that results from every part of the polis doing its own particular work.

We have shown that techne is a kind of knowledge according to Plato. The next question we should return to is whether and to what extent techne might serve as a model or exemplar of the highest sort of knowledge, moral or philosophical, in which Plato depicts Socrates as being chiefly interested. It is clear that Socrates is interested in techne, believes it worthy of pursuit in its own right, and perhaps even thinks that the pursuit of its internal goods is essential to the flourishing of the just polis. But does this mean that the philosopher's knowledge is a kind of techne? Or is it simply *like* a techne? Or is it unlike techne altogether?

If we stay only in the vicinity of the material from Book IV of the *Republic* considered above, we find a telling passage, right after Socrates and Glaucon enumerate the "many kinds of knowledge in the city"[52] belonging to the different classes. By contrast to the knowledge possessed by carpenters and farmers, Socrates suggests there must be "some knowledge possessed by some of the citizens in the city we just founded that doesn't judge about any particular matter but about the city as a whole and the maintenance of good relations, both internally and with other cities."[53] This apparent analogy between knowledge of a given techne like carpentry or farming and a more general, comprehensive knowledge of the city's life as a whole and its internal unity and harmony seems to imply a comparison between techne belonging to a specific field and a techne that would concern human well-being as such. The passages cited above from the *Laches* and the *Apology* seem to suggest the same.[54] On this much there is widespread agreement, but from here on matters get more controversial.[55]

As Roochnik documents, the classic view is that the moral knowledge Plato depicts Socrates relentlessly pursuing has a strong relationship to techne. Let C. D. C. Reeve's argument[56] suffice as representative:

Wisdom is precisely a sort of techne—specifically, ethical techne—that ... constitutes a template of knowledge for Plato (as it did, indeed, for many of his contemporaries), and that, as a result, it sets a large part of the agenda of his epistemology and metaphysics. His use and critique of it, I want to suggest, marked the beginning of his construction of the ideal of knowledge represented by what he was probably the first to call philosophy.[57]

The details of Reeve's reconstruction need not detain us, but it is important to note two points. First, Reeve does not claim that Plato's desired ethical knowledge, or what he calls "craft-knowledge of virtue,"⁵⁸ is exactly like other technai. Near the conclusion of his paper he summarizes his account by saying that Platonic philosophy is a "craft-like science."⁵⁹ If we take Reeve then to be representative of a classic view that sees a strong association between techne and moral or philosophical knowledge, then we have to note that even here there is an attenuation of that association; Platonic philosophy is like a techne and is not (as Reeve explains at length)⁶⁰ exactly like any established kind of techne. Second, Reeve's account of "craft-knowledge of virtue" is a reconstruction, depending at least as much on what Plato does not say as on what he does say, and this is on his account partly attributable to the fact that Plato consistently depicts Socrates as denying that he is in possession of "the greater or more impressive craft-knowledge of ethics"⁶¹ and, by implication, tacitly conceding that no one is in possession of such knowledge. So even for Reeve, the putative techne of ethics toward which Plato is constantly gesturing has no known practitioners.

At the opposite end of the spectrum, so to speak, sits Roochnik's own denial that Plato uses techne as an analogy for philosophical knowledge at all. His conclusion is that Plato explores through the lens of techne

> the nature of the extraordinary moral knowledge he seeks. Nontechnical moral knowledge, which would make us happy, is not a theory. It is a Doric harmony of word and deed, a way of life spent seeking wisdom and urging others to do the same. It is a life spent turning a searching eye inward and therefore turning away from the external objects that become the subject matters of the ordinary technai.⁶²

Techne then on Roochnik's account is less an analogy and more a lens, through which what Plato espies is a possible nontechnical knowledge that is key to living well and bears no other similarity to the ordinary technai, the objects of which are indeed obstacles rather than helps to greater clarity about philosophical wisdom. Socrates's practice "takes knowledge," Roochnik asserts, but "not an abstract techne like arithmetic but a knowledge of how to direct a single individual to desire wisdom. Plato shows Socrates at work in his dialogues. And these, in and of themselves, represent his nontechnical knowledge."⁶³ Through detailed readings of five dialogues that pose an essential question about virtue and posit the possibility that the knowledge sought is the result of techne only to end in aporia, Roochnik argues that in each case virtue is indeed affirmed to be a kind of knowledge but equally that in each case the knowledge sought is not techne.⁶⁴ Even where the possibility of a "kingly techne" is tantalizingly raised in the *Euthydemus*, whatever comparison there might have been between philosophical knowledge and techne is vitiated by their heterogeneity: The kingly techne cannot be elucidated in terms of structure or specific subject matter; no result of its practice can be identified; discussion of it falls into a series of circularities.⁶⁵ This is not, however, to say that the conversation about kingly techne in the *Euthydemus* is without benefit.

Socrates's exhortation to philosophy according to Roochnik establishes that "a nontrivial form of knowledge" is at stake, and though Socrates cannot put forward a categorical imperative to pursue philosophy, he can, in a seemingly virtuously circular manner, encourage those inclined to self-knowledge to deepen this inclination.[66] Similarly, Roochnik reads the conversation in Book I of the *Republic* as equally "protrepric," using the techne analogy to persuade "Adeimantus that knowledge is good and should be sought, that is, the philosophical project is coherent and should be practiced."[67] The trouble with these assertions is that they seem to leave us with little to be content with from such a sprawling and voluminous engagement with the question of techne.[68] If the primary aim of the techne analogy in Plato's writings is to convince us that "knowledge is good and should be sought," then that goal could have been achieved by recourse to any number of analogies other than to techne. Roochnik would likely say that this is Plato's preferred analogy because it was the most readily recognized as paradigmatic for knowledge among his contemporary Athenians.[69] Even so, it's a comparatively small payoff for a prolonged perennial concern.

One reason for this result might be that there is an intrinsic difficulty for Plato in giving a technical (in the strict sense of the word, that is, based in techne) account of the philosophical life. For Roochnik, this difficulty is tied to what he called in another of his books the "tragedy of reason." Arguing in his conclusion to *Of Art and Wisdom* that the human being is for Plato fundamentally an erotic and therefore striving creature and further that Socrates is often presented by Plato as an expert in erotics (if indeed he can be said to have an expertise at all), Roochnik concludes that "the early Platonic dialogues express knowledge of, rather than theorize about, eros. Because they are dramas, they are the superb, even if strange, vehicles for the expression of nontechnical knowledge."[70] Because this erotic striving after philosophical wisdom is forever unfulfilled, however, Socrates "acknowledges he cannot prove knowledge is possible."[71] For this reason Roochnik rejects readings of Plato's middle dialogues guided by what he calls "theoretical optimism."[72] For Roochnik, that philosophical wisdom is not a techne means that Plato's enterprise is doomed to tragic frustration.[73]

Interestingly, as noted briefly above, Roochnik is not alone in asserting that for Plato philosophical wisdom is not a techne. Another scholar with whom he has some disagreement but largely appreciation it would seem,[74] D. C. Schindler, in his stimulating book on the *Republic*, flatly denies that philosophy can be a techne at all, but his reading might fall under Roochnik's judgment of "theoretical optimism," inasmuch as Schindler's overall interpretation is guided by a greater confidence in what he calls the ecstatic structure of reason and an illuminating insistence on the unique and absolute character of the form of the Good. "Every techne," Schindler writes, "aims at a particular good; that which aims at goodness itself—namely, philosophy—by definition cannot be a techne."[75] For Schindler, this conclusion follows from a proper appreciation for what might be the lodestar of his analysis, the unique character of goodness itself as opposed to the many and partial goods furnished by the cosmos and the realm of human experience. If philosophy were a techne, on his reading, then it would be reduced to the level of any other instrumental skill and would thereby be straightforwardly productive or useful. Citing the *Greater Hippias*, Schindler points out that there Socrates (facetiously) likens wisdom to "improvements in other skills," where constant refinement makes the contemporary practitioner almost certainly more adept than his predecessors.[76] As Schindler puts it,

Sophists claim to be "wiser" than the thinkers of the past, and in a technical sense they are no doubt right. But, notice, this makes wisdom a "skill" and makes it subservient to ends other than itself, i.e., practically useful. ... If wisdom receives its measure from something else, from some other human concern, it surrenders its absolute character and therefore its integrity.[77]

This is one of the key themes of Schindler's reading, that the Good itself stands above the welter of competing and specifically defined technai with their various objects of concern. If philosophy as the concern for the Good were to be structurally likened to any techne, then it would be reduced to a relative level:

Plato seems to suggest that if the "gratuitous" good is not fundamental, then "useful" relative goods will have sovereignty. Likewise, if there is no "useless" human activity that concerns the whole and the heart of things as such, then we are left with a series of relative skills. But, as we have suggested, relativity always implies an absolute reference point.[78]

That reference point is the form of the Good itself, which exceeds even the difference between the absolute and the relative as traditionally construed; the Good is so absolute as to realize its absoluteness not just in opposition to the relative but in surpassing the relative and being bound back to it. On Schindler's reading of Plato,

absolute goodness is not absolute unless it is also relative. Indeed, absoluteness and relativity cannot be simply juxtaposed to one another without making the absolute relative to the relative and therefore no longer absolute. Logically, while the relative is in some sense opposed to the absolute, the absolute is not in turn opposed to the relative, but inclusive of it.[79]

It is for this reason that he maintains with respect to techne, "The very same thing that makes philosophy absolutely good makes it something more than a technique."[80]

There are substantial similarities between Roochnik's and Schindler's arguments that philosophy cannot be a techne. Both scholars believe that philosophy's "useless" character is a testament to its inability to be squared with the techne-model.[81] Again referring to the absolute character of the Good and tying this expressly to the question of techne, Schindler argues,

Every techne, Socrates says in the beginning of the *Republic*, is ordered to an end that is different from itself. It is just this that makes the various technai both partial and relative. But the "art" that aims at the whole is itself necessarily its own end, and so there is no justification for it. This is what makes it useless.[82]

Both Roochnik and Schindler see the hallmark of philosophy as being exhibited by a kind of conformity between word and deed. Roochnik calls this a "Doric harmony" and says Plato uses the figure of Laches to dramatize it. From the beginning of the *Laches*, the titular character has praised the harmonization of logos and ergon, of word and deed. This harmony proves on Roochnik's reading to be more productive than any analogy to techne and a surer clue to what Plato means by moral knowledge. "The person with the moral knowledge Socrates seeks will suffer no gap between the possession and the good application of such knowledge. He will, in this sense … achieve a Doric harmony, an appropriate fit, of word and deed, a complete whole. The knowledge will be the good life well lived."[83] If this seems vague at first, Roochnik ties the point expressly to the dramatic logic of Plato's writings. Laches does not just talk passionately about an interest in courage; he exemplifies courage by persisting in the quest for knowledge despite the risks and thus harmonizes his words and deeds.[84] The dialogue form itself is uniquely suited to expressing nontechnical knowledge, to dramatizing the connection between word and deed. Far from it being the case that the dialogue format is somehow a pedagogical device or a provisional and imperfect form that could be discarded in favor of some more transparent form of writing, "it is essential to Platonic teaching. Moral knowledge is nontechnical. It is not reducible to a set of true propositions. It must embrace word and deed. And only the dialogue form can adequately explain it."[85]

Schindler too is emphatic about the fact that dialogue is indispensable for Plato's purposes, and he too ties it to Doric harmony, though he attributes this harmony preeminently to Socrates himself, whom he argues Plato depicted as uniquely realizing a consonance between word and deed. On Schindler's analysis, key to the epistemology of the *Republic* as a whole in fact is this intrinsic requirement on the part of the Good itself that its articulation cannot be merely argumentative but must be rooted in a life, which is why philosophy is never just argumentation (who excels at argument more than a sophist?[86]) but a lived demonstration.[87] The figure of Socrates provides just such a characterological demonstration, as he embodied philosophy itself for Plato. Speaking of the unique moment when in the cave allegory Plato the author inserts a clear reference to Socrates the historical figure "breaking in" to the narrative so to speak by descending into the cave, being ridiculed by his contemporaries for his apparent inability to debate matters in the law court, and then finally enraging them and dying at their hands for trying to free them from their chains, Schindler writes, "Socrates *says* that the philosopher must go down, but he in fact *is the very philosopher who goes down*. Socrates is known as one whose words and deeds 'match up.'"[88]

Finally, both think philosophy necessarily ends up being frustratingly defenseless, unproven, or without a systematic account of its own importance. Roochnik notices the apparent circularity of the hunt for moral knowledge in the *Euthydemus*, which he diagnoses as an implicit indication that the knowledge in question simply cannot be the product of linearly organized techne. What he calls nontechnical moral knowledge seems to have no object other than itself, other than the capacity to exhort others to philosophize. The "object" then of philosophy seems to be only its own propagation as self-knowledge. The basic premises on which an exhortation to philosophize, to pursue self-knowledge, would rest are themselves "undefended," deliberately leaving philosophy in a sense without the external motivations that attach to other technai[89] (the promise of riches perhaps or reputation?). Schindler too finds that for Plato philosophy is similarly defenseless.[90]

As a corollary, it should be noted that the Sophists' implicit answer to the question of what could coordinate all the various technai in the absence of something like the Good itself is perhaps money-making. Schindler poses and answers the question this way: "What, then, is the common 'useful' good unifying the relative benefits of the various technai? In the absence of philosophy, the useless devotion to the good, Plato suggests that the only alternative is the 'wage-earner's art.' Absent the good, mastery of this art becomes the supreme sign of wisdom."[91] Socrates ironically praises the Sophist Hippias for his "wisdom" as manifested in his ability to "make a lot of money from young people"[92] and again facetiously asserts that "the mark of being wise, I see, is when someone makes the most money."[93] Schindler astutely argues that the integrity and internal goods of the various technai are corrupted by money-making.[94]

So money-making could be a possible ersatz substitute for the Good as the one replacement for genuine wisdom that might coordinate all the technai and their various benefits. Absent such a motivation however, what could impel a person to philosophize? In Schindler's words, "so what need is there to get to the heart of things if it is, in fact, useless? There is, of course, no adequate response to be given to this question. Indeed, there cannot be because of the very nature of what is at stake."[95] All one can do is point out that if philosophy, impelled by the ecstatic character of reason, is the attempt to grasp the whole insofar as that is possible, then it is at once in a sense useless but in another sense absolutely indispensable, since it aspires to wisdom about the very nature of reality itself as a whole. Because it alone has this scope, no inducement or rationalization of its importance could possibly be appropriate to it. "Though the truth is defenseless, we could say it is so precisely because it needs no defense."[96]

It is telling perhaps that these pages in Schindler's discussion also define a significant disagreement between the two scholars. In the course of explaining exactly in what sense Plato views philosophy as defenseless or lacking in resources when it comes to advocating for its own usefulness, Schindler expressly departs from Roochnik's understanding of the matter. If philosophy is indeed in an important sense vulnerable, it seems especially so to the attacks of those who simply are not interested in the project of dialogue or truth-seeking, a paradox noted by Roochnik and Charles Griswold. Hence Plato's dialogues frequently seem to end in failure to convince or "win over" persons intransigent against "useless studies" due to their lack of interest "in truth for its own sake."[97] Schindler protests though against Griswold and Roochnik's fatalism on this point, because for him, "behind the wall is, however, not the last place Plato stations the philosopher, and this inevitable failure is not Plato's final word on reason."[98] The mistaken assumption he identifies behind their objections is that "*reason's primary aim is to persuade*, to such an extent that, if it fails to achieve this aim, its own integrity becomes suspect."[99] In opposition to this premise, Schindler rightly insists that the primary aim of reason is to seek the Good, which means that there is a fundamental divergence between learning the truth and being convinced of anything (even the truth), a divergence isomorphic to that between philosophy and rhetoric.[100] An equally important consequence of this view is that "winning" out over an opponent cannot be the philosopher's primary aim but only that of the sophist. If others are not convinced then this is not the fault of reason, which by its very nature does not avail itself of the inducements that accompany ordinary technai.[101]

Key to grasping this point is Plato's dependence on the dialogue form. A dialogue implies that the ultimate truth and reality of things is a shared project, not the private possession of the philosopher, no matter how gifted or insightful. To engage in the sort of polemics that were typical of the sophists is to lose the battle even if you win, for it is tantamount to reducing the absolute nature of the ultimate reality, the Good, to a relative question that could be subject to arbitration rather than to necessarily shared vision, a cooperative participatory project that dialogue uniquely expresses.[102] In Schindler's summation,

> the conflict that, in one respect, seems to present the failure of reason (viewed as an instrument of persuasion), actually, at another level, shows its supremacy (as that which makes fundamental truth manifest). Failure to convince becomes an occasion that manifests the truth in a more objective way. Thus, at the very limit of incommensurability in reason's confrontation with nonreason, Griswold and Roochnik, in different ways, end with the separation of two mutually impenetrable spheres, so to speak. But this, again, assumes reason has an individual or private structure, and so this final result proves the victory of sophistry.[103]

The true supremacy of philosophy cannot be assessed from the point of view of its competitive failure; quite the opposite, for failure at the relative level is a sign of victory at the level of the absolute, like the failure of the person who has been outside the cave to succeed at the trivial game-playing of the cave's prisoners.[104] This supremacy ultimately consists in the fact that philosophy takes as its object nothing less than the ultimate source and ground of reality itself, the form of the Good. In the totally comprehensive vision of philosophy, *all reality* must find its rightful place, and the coexistence of "two mutually impenetrable spheres" is an intolerable outcome, one that indeed surrenders the game to the sophist's agonistic view of reason as concerned only with the relative, with the private appropriation of whatever "truths" that can be capitalized upon financially, and the agonistic field of rhetorical battle. No wonder then that Schindler's final words on Roochnik are that "it is significant that Roochnik's final image of reason is a chastened 'hero' who must learn to content himself with his own 'game,' meaningful only for those within, and to surrender any aspirations to truth or universality."[105]

If we keep to the strongly comprehensive, universal view of reason that Schindler advocates, we might be able to unify the whole field of technai under the reality of the Good and exclude money-making as the crude ersatz substitute for this coordinating reality. Such a view would comport well with what we have seen already, that Plato views the variety of technai as positive goods, aiming at worthwhile internal benefits, and (according to the strict account) defined quite apart from the incentives of money-making or any other blandishment; his voracious interest in technai can be accounted for if we view him as finding all these human pursuits at home in the philosophical vision of complete universal comprehension (or at least aspiration to it). For all the scholars we have surveyed all too briefly, philosophy bears *some* relationship in Plato to techne, even if that relationship is inverse. The more classical line of Terrence Irwin or Reeve takes it that techne is strongly indicative of the nature of moral knowledge; Roochnik and Schindler deny that moral knowledge is techne, but even here, the nature of techne rightly understood is a sort of obverse to philosophy and thus the source of an indirect understanding of the moral knowledge Plato sought. All perhaps would agree that the exact shape of philosophy as Plato understands it by similarity or contrast to the practice of ordinary technai can be difficult to reconstruct.[106] It is clear though that what we do by way of our "jobs" is in some kind of relationship to what the practice of philosophy would consist in, no matter how exactly we parse that relationship. We have seen further that all technai involve knowledge, though clearly not the kind that is reserved for philosophy.

This matter of doing one's own work is an essential ingredient in the answer to the question that drives the dialogue as a whole: What is justice? And when it comes time to answer this question, Socrates invokes an analogy to techne to secure his point. Recall that Socrates introduced at first a healthy city, which occasioned the introduction of the many technai, since these serve human needs, and moreover, those needs are best addressed when each craftsman pursues the techne to which he is best suited, recognizing additionally that each practitioner of a techne will have needs in turn for the provisions of other practitioners. The plurality of craftsmen is by no means problematic for the healthy city but secures what seems to Socrates to be a somewhat idyllic social order of satisfying provisions and humble consolations. Not only that, in the healthy city Socrates and his interlocutors seem already to be on the threshold of defining justice. Once Socrates paints his charming picture of the healthy city he asks Adeimantus, "Where are justice and injustice to be found in it?," to which Adeimantus replies, "I have no idea, Socrates, unless it was somewhere in some need that these people have of one another."[107]

It is possible that this is the first intimation of a final conclusion we get only now, in Book IV, and just as the technai were connected to the posing of the question of justice and its first tentative answer, so too the technai return here. As Socrates puts it,

> Then the dream we had has been completely fulfilled—our suspicions that, with the help of some god, we had hit upon the origin and pattern of justice right at the beginning in founding our city ... Indeed, Glaucon, the principle that it is right for someone who is by nature a cobbler to practice cobblery and nothing else, for the carpenter to practice carpentry, and the same for the others is a sort of image of justice—that's why it's beneficial.[108]

At this pivotal moment then, the technai return once again, now as "a sort of image of justice," where the principle that each practitioner of a techne should adhere to his or her own job is a hint to the role that should be played by the parts of the soul to secure justice individually. Socrates's conclusion about justice is both like and unlike a techne (as is customary for his usage of this language):

> And in truth justice is, it seems, something of this sort. However, it isn't concerned with someone's doing his own externally, but with what is inside him, with what

is truly himself and his own. One who is just does not allow any part of himself to do the work of another part or allow the various classes within him to meddle with each other. He regulates well what is really his own and rules himself. He puts himself in order, is his own friend, and harmonizes the three parts of himself.[109]

For Plato, therefore, there is an important link between achieving the human good itself and performing a single definite task.

Rather than serve as an analogue for philosophical knowledge, it seems that the technai, being knowledge of a sort, but each one limited, are better understood as parts of knowledge. Plato's interest in the crafts of ordinary Greek workers is therefore actually *more* strongly motivated than simply as a basis for comparison with his own practice of philosophy. Plato thinks the crafts are an analogue for philosophy but not as a basis of simple comparison and not directly one to the other but indirectly. We have seen that Plato does affirm that people in possession of a craft have knowledge. The analogy in the *Republic* at any rate is not directly between the technai and knowledge but between the technai and justice. Because the technai are a kind of knowledge, and justice is a kind of virtue, the analogy is actually indirect rather than direct. As techne is to philosophical knowledge, so justice is to virtue. On that supposition, clarity about techne, a familiar and vital kind of knowledge, is helpful in defining justice—which comes about when a person does his own work—which in turn is key to virtue as a whole.[110]

Plato on Mimetic Arts

Another realm of technai remains to be examined, however, and it is one that is normally taken to be an area of human pursuit that Plato does *not* think is much to be esteemed or based in knowledge. That area of human activity is the imitative or fine arts, chiefly poetry and painting. Yet Schindler's view of reason as inherently ecstatic and all-embracing suggests that even here, in an arena of human activity that readers of Plato usually regard him as slighting, a place can be found in the flourishing philosophical life even for poetry and painting, as questionably allied with appearances as they seem to be at first reading. The suggestion from Schindler, that "we would need to show that the 'extraphilosophical' is in fact genuinely philosophical, and that it is all at the service, not of winning the argument and persuading one's opponent, but of making truth manifest," is the one we will follow here with his continued assistance.[111] The mimetic arts are the "extraphilosophical" devices in Plato's own philosophizing par excellence. It has frequently been observed that Plato at once seems to denigrate poetry while being himself arguably the greatest philosophical poet of all time. The way to resolve this apparent contradiction is to demonstrate how for Plato's theory of the universal scope of reason, even the "extraphilosophical" can be philosophical when it finds its place in the whole.

Practitioners of the mimetic arts were certainly important to the culture of Athens at Plato's time, and accordingly he treats poets and painters at some length in Book X of the *Republic*. Normally this section of Plato's single most important work is read strictly as a contribution to aesthetics, but it has to be considered as equally pertinent to his account of work in general. Furthermore, even when read only as a contribution to aesthetic theory, Book X of the *Republic* has been widely misunderstood. Let Desmond Lee's following introductory remarks from the Penguin edition serve as a prime example of this misunderstanding:

> This part has the appearance of an appendix, written to justify against anticipated or actual criticism the attack on the poets in Books II and III (Part III). It has sometimes been suggested that it should not be taken too seriously. But the claims made for the poets by Greek opinion were often extravagant. They treated the works of Homer and the poets as their Bible, and in Plato's *Ion* Homer is claimed as a teacher of everything from carpentry to morals and generalship. It is such claims that Plato has primarily in mind, but there is nothing to suggest that he is not serious, though he is often characteristically ironical; and the general contention in section I that poetry is illusion fits well into the scheme of the Divided Line.[112]

Unfortunately nearly everything said here is contestable. There is no chance at all that Book X of the *Republic* is an appendix; it has little direct relationship to the material on the poets in Books II and III, but if we read it as an integrated part of an overarching argument it finds its rightful place therein. A comparison between Homer and the Bible is inaccurate, and while Ion's claims on behalf of Homer are exaggerated, Plato in no way presents his views as representative or laudable. Quite to the contrary, Ion seems to be a figure of some fun. Lee is right though that this material should be taken seriously, for it does reward careful study. Such study I believe will conclusively show that Lee's choice of the word "illusion" in reference to poetry is highly prejudicial and that Socrates is more appreciative of poetry than he is normally taken to be.

Book X is often taken to be a series of three "arguments" to do with poetry, but rather what readers are presented with is a series of three potential problems followed by retractions or clarifications that surreptitiously resolve the problem. It must be kept in mind too that by this stage in the argument Socrates and his interlocutors have already conceded that their proposal for the ideal city was never meant to be implemented. As such, there is no reason to believe that the proposals put forward in Book X are somehow uniquely supposed to be implemented independently of all the other controversial proposals put forward in the whole of the *Republic*. On the contrary, this part of the text very much faces the contemporary reality of Athens, which precisely was not under the degree of social organization at first envisioned by Socrates and his interlocutors. Contemporary Athens is much taken with Homer as a pedagogical authority, and Athenians are surrounded by works of art that again are in no way under the degree of censorship entertained by the earlier part of the discussion in the *Republic*.

The first such assertion-followed-by-retraction concerns the nature of art; the second has to do with what the artist does or does not know; the last is about the effect of art on the soul. Book X opens with Socrates's repetition of his conviction that it was right to exclude poetry that is mimetic.[113] "Between ourselves," Socrates explains confidentially, 'for *you* won't denounce me to the tragic poets or any of the other imitative ones—all such poetry is likely to distort the thought [*dianoias*] of anyone who hears it, unless he has the knowledge of what it is really like, as a drug [*pharmakon*] to counteract it."[114] It is crucial to note the caveat that Socrates attaches to the end of his claim; he does this repeatedly in Book X, for what are arguably tactical reasons. Mimetic poetry, including but not limited to tragedy, is asserted by Socrates to be at risk of distorting thought *unless* one has the knowledge of what it is "really like." It is to that question that Socrates and his companions immediately turn: "Could you tell me what mimesis in general is? I don't entirely understand what sort of thing imitations are trying to be."[115]

So note carefully that the danger of mimetic poetry is that it is likely to distort thought unless the hearer has knowledge of what mimetic poetry is really like. Socrates and his companions then quite sensibly inquire after what mimesis is, and they agree to do so in keeping with their "usual procedure," according to which "we customarily hypothesize a single form in connection with each of the many things to which we apply the name."[116] In the examples immediately proposed, they agree that while there are many beds and many tables there are only two forms thereof, and the form in each case is that which is consulted by their "makers."[117] Here Plato uses the term demiourgos, and he has Socrates and his interlocutors agree that no demiourgos makes the form itself.[118] Socrates then raises the question of whether there could be a demiourgos who could make all the things that demiourgoi customarily make in their distinctive crafts. Glaucon agrees that if there were such a person he would be a "clever and wonderful fellow."[119] Socrates claims Glaucon is underestimating in fact, since such a person could in fact make not just the objects of crafts but plants, animals, the earth itself, the heavens, the gods, and indeed all heavenly bodies and things in Hades below the earth.[120] So the range of this hypothetical demiourgos is in fact not confined to artificial objects but encompasses the whole realm of physis and indeed the superlunary, sub-lunary, and subterranean worlds, a scope that Glaucon exclaims could only be attributable to one who was "amazingly clever."[121]

So what is it that seems stunning about this, Socrates asks. Is it that there is no way any demiourgos could do this at all? Or is that such a demiourgos would be "making" only in one sense while in another sense not making them? Leading Glaucon down the path of the second sort of inquiry, Socrates suggests that Glaucon himself could make all of them. The English translation misses this, but he actually uses the verbal form of "demiourgos" to assert that Glaucon could make all the things that he has just mentioned if he carried a mirror with him, suggesting that such effort would amount to practicing some kind of craft or trade. Glaucon concedes only that the product of this hypothetical trade would be phenomena, appearances but not "things themselves as they truly are."[122] This crucial recognition is what allows Socrates and Glaucon to agree that a painter belongs to this class of demiourgos; the painter "in a certain way" makes a bed, namely, by making an appearance of one.[123]

It is on the basis of this conclusion that Socrates begins to make a key distinction that leads quietly to the conclusion that a painter is in fact not a demiourgos at all. Even the carpenter makes *a* bed, not *the* bed, that is to say, the form of the bed (a point that Socrates raises again here without further elaboration since it has already been granted).[124] Using the same examples, then, Socrates proposes that they investigate what an imitator is. So far, they agree that there are three kinds of beds, the form of the bed, which is made by "a god," a bed made by a carpenter, and then the appearance of a bed made by a painter.[125] They further agree that the first two are "makers" of some kind.[126] But when Socrates asks Glaucon if a painter is also a demiourgos and a maker then Glaucon flatly denies it on the grounds that a painter relates by imitation to the works of the demiourgoi; the painter, he claims, imitates what the demiourgoi make.[127] The same holds for a tragedian as well, such that all imitators are alike in the essential thing, which is that in each case they imitate not the thing itself in nature but the erga of the demiourgoi.[128]

Furthermore, Socrates argues, the painter imitates the works of the demiourgos "as they appear," which is to say that the thing itself is imitated not as it is but as it appears. Continuing with the example of the bed, Socrates points out that with respect to the manner in which the bed made by the craftsman appears it can only do so perspectively, that is, from one angle at a time. Yet it is the same bed from every angle, that is, it is not a different bed, it only appears differently. Hence his conclusion that painting does not imitate "that which is as it is" but rather "that which appears as it appears."[129] If we wished to be a little freer with this rendering, we might say that Socrates's point is that the imitative arts provide us with appearance *as* appearance. If my son walks into the room and crosses into my line of sight, he appears to me. If I look at a photograph of my son, it is still he who appears, but he appears as an appearance rather than as himself in the flesh.

For this reason Socrates asserts that mimesis is "far removed from the truth" inasmuch as it captures only a profile of the things produced by craftsmanship, and this in turn according to Socrates explains "why it can produce everything."[130] Unlike the previous example of the mirror and the sum total of objects that a mirror can reflect, Socrates now stresses that a painter can paint a craftsman without knowing anything about the crafts that he is depicting. The example marks an odd shift: The prior list seemed intuitive enough and comprehensive in scope, which would be part of the point. Now Socrates says that "a painter can paint a cobbler, a carpenter, or any other craftsman, even though he knows nothing about these crafts."[131] Why a painter would wish to paint a carpenter is unexplained. Furthermore, the example seems inconsistent with the immediately prior argument that what painters imitate is not craftsmen but their "works." Presumably a painter would paint a house before he would paint the carpenter who built it. Finally, there is an interesting parallel here between the singularity of the form and the plurality of things that are created by craftsmen by reference to the form and the singularity of the craftsman's knowledge and the painter's putative knowledge of a great many different crafts.

The unusual change from object to craft itself or product to knowledge is actually a transition to Socrates's next point, which both is and is not a natural extension of the argument so far. It is not an extension insofar as the examples seem to have changed in a strange manner. It is an extension of it though insofar as it builds on a parallel that Socrates and his friends have already agreed upon, namely, that a tragedian is substantially the same as a poet, that is, both are practitioners of mimesis. Using the strange shift in emphasis from the works of craftsmen to the craftsmen themselves, Socrates is able to say,

> Whenever someone tells us that he has met a person who knows all the crafts as well as all the other things that anyone else knows and that his knowledge of any subject is more exact than any of theirs is, we must assume that we're talking to a simple-minded fellow who has apparently encountered some sort of magician or imitator and been deceived into thinking him omniscient and that the reason he has been deceived is that he himself can't distinguish between knowledge, ignorance, and imitation.[132]

It turns out this is the setup for a fairly predictable indictment of Homer. The deluded person in this example claims that he has met someone who knows all the crafts, but clearly, Socrates argues, this person is simple-minded and has been taken in by a Svengali because he himself is unable to distinguish between knowledge, ignorance, and imitation, which now seems to form a triad with the first two members being obvious opposites.

Who else could this Svengali be but Homer? Some unnamed people, Socrates claims, are of the view that poets know all crafts and all about human and divine affairs and that this knowledge explains their ability to produce fine poetry.[133] It is this assumption that Socrates proceeds to investigate. Isn't it possible, he wonders, that some people have encountered these skillful imitators and have failed to realize that their products are just imitations and thus at a remove from the form, and further that because they are at such a remove they are easy to produce without knowledge. Or is it really true that good poets do know about the things that they write about?[134]

Testing this latter possibility, Socrates asks if someone who could make both the thing imitated and images would prefer to be satisfied with producing images (*eidolon*) as his priority? Glaucon immediately agrees that no one would do so, and they further agree that if an imitator really "had knowledge of the things he imitates, he'd be much more serious about actions than about imitations of them" and would therefore prefer to "be the subject of a eulogy than the author of one," that is, pursue virtue rather than merely imitate the virtues.[135] The same person cannot command too many crafts; it is hard to excel at more than one, and this point seems to parallel again the unity of the form by contrast to the plurality of things. Part of what seems suspect about imitative arts is that they seem easy to command: A mirror is sufficient to produce images of any number of things that either nature or craftsmanship is required to produce. But if someone could produce the things in their very being why would they settle for producing their images? Only if they did not know the difference between a thing as it is and its image. Because the former is clearly superior, no one would knowingly pursue the latter.[136]

For that reason neither Homer nor any other poet can be regarded as a source of knowledge about any of the other crafts, keeping in mind that imitation is not the work of a demiourgos. The poet is not a doctor but at best an imitator of what doctors say, and no poet has ever actually healed anyone in the way a doctor manifestly can. Another reason for thinking that Homer and the other imitative poets are not philosophical types is that they founded no school or model for a way of life after the fashion of Pythagoras.[137] Had Homer been able to "educate people and make them better" and not just imitate, then people would have had a different attitude toward the rhapsodes who wandered the land reciting poetry. Rather than allow this peripateticism, Socrates asks rhetorically, "Wouldn't they have clung tighter to them than to gold and compelled them to live with them in their homes [oichoi]?"[138]

Bear in mind that the role of the demiourgos as being unattached to an oichos is being referenced here: As an imitator is not even a demiourgos and thus is not a household worker, if the poets had been regarded as genuinely knowledgeable and thus capable of enlisting disciples who could be improved by their pedagogical ability, then surely they would have been hailed as not only occasionally useful demiourgoi but as indispensable members of the household circle. This seems to indicate that in the same way a painter imitates a cobbler without knowing anything about cobbling itself, so too a poet "uses words and phrases to paint colored pictures of each of the crafts. He himself knows nothing about them, but he imitates them in such a way that others, as ignorant as he, who judge by words, will think he speaks extremely well." This shared ignorance is facilitated by "the natural charm of ... meter, rhythm, and harmony." The odd conclusion to this line of discussion is Socrates's somewhat surprising assertion that "if you strip a poet's works of their musical colorings and take them by themselves, I think you know what they look like."[139] Socrates and Glaucon immediately agree that without music poems are like the faces of young boys whose beauty has faded with age.[140] This is a strange claim, since without music poems are not poems at all. It is entirely unsurprising that "poetry" without music, that is, without that which makes poetry poetic, should be not unlike the looks of a formerly attractive boy from whom the bloom of youth has departed. Plato surely knows this, and one wonders what he is up to, particularly when we notice that the final phrase could be more readily translated as "how they appear [*phanesthai*]." Poetry is entirely concerned with how things appear, as we have already discovered, so stripping poetry of its mode of appearance and complaining about the result seems highly unusual, even for Plato.

The best way to read this odd assertion is as a sort of stopover to a larger, more nuanced conclusion, for which we still have to wait a moment. That this is a halfway point though is signaled by Socrates himself, who says, "Let's not leave the discussion of this point halfway, but examine it fully."[141] On my reading, the argument to this point is indeed truly only halfway finished. As I understand where this argument ends up, Plato has to hold that poetry could not withstand being stripped of its characteristic charms and remain what it is, but once we have seen where Plato is going I think he restores to us and to poetry itself those characteristic charms, with an important qualification (of which the first half of Book X is more or less comprised). When Plato rehabilitates poetry in an important sense, we will see that it can be appreciated for what it is by the philosopher who knows what it is and is aware of how it can both lead astray and yet be an indispensable part of his own philosophical work. If that is right, then poetry need not and should not be stripped of its music in order to be rightfully appreciated.

It is worth remembering at this pivot point though what has been established so far. We saw at the outset that Socrates issued a caution about the products of imitative art, which he warned were likely to draw astray those who don't know what they are. At this point in Book X though we have in fact learned what the products of imitative art are. The first of three assertions followed by a tacit retraction is at this point complete. The caution is that imitation is potentially dangerous to those who don't know what it is and thus have no pharmakon to combat its effects, but at this point the cause for worry has been blunted, inasmuch as we can and do know what imitation is and what it produces. The reader then is at this stage in fact equipped with an effective pharmakon.

What remains to be seen so far are the consequences of unchecked indulgence in imitation. To examine that point, Socrates actually reverses his previous prioritization of craftsman over crafted thing as the proper object of imitative artistry. Immediately after his exhortation that they not leave the conversation of this point half-finished, Socrates gets Glaucon to agree that "a painter paints reins and a mouth-bit," while a "cobbler and a metal-worker makes them."[142] Now once more it is the crafted object that commands the attention, not the demiourgoi who make them, but once more these alternatives are presented by both comparison and contrast to the painter. Though a painter does not know how the reins and mouth-bit have to be, it turns out neither do the makers. Only the horseman knows this, since he is the one who knows how to use reins and a mouth-bit.[143] With some rapidity, Socrates solicits Glaucon's agreement that this is true for all things: Three crafts correspond to each, that of use, that of making, and that of imitating.[144] This structure is perhaps related to the strict definition of techne expounded back in Book I; the maker is concerned only to pursue the craft itself, and only the user really concerns herself with the ultimate purpose or application of the techne's product. Recall that the shepherd looks after the sheep; what the owner does with the sheep is in fact not in the shepherd's narrow purview.

The most crucial element then is that of use, which is the foundation of "the virtue or excellence, the beauty and correctness of each manufactured item, living creature, and action."[145] The user is the one with knowledge who explains to the maker how the thing should be made, and the maker accepts the user's instructions. Because the maker has the benefit of the user's knowledge and is correctly steered by him, the maker can be said to have right opinion, while the painter lacks even right opinion as well as knowledge (as we have already seen), for the painter need not have any association with the user to produce his image.[146] Again these conclusions hold for both painters and poets and lead Socrates to assert that "an imitator has no worthwhile knowledge of the things he imitates, that imitation is a kind of game and not something to be taken seriously,"[147] inasmuch as the imitator is without accomplishment with respect to his subjects and their good or bad qualities but concerns himself only with "what appears fine or beautiful to the majority of people who know nothing."[148] Once again though if we keep the strict sense of techne in mind, the user and the maker can be fruitfully brought into a kind of companionship with one another, inasmuch as the maker is practicing his or her techne with a view only to the repairing of need by consultation with the form as the guide for that repair. What the user will do with the object in question falls outside of the maker's strict purview. Furthermore, it is worth bearing in mind that the "user" for Plato is not just a person who effectively deploys an item (as a modern way of thinking might have it) but is the one who truly regards the characteristic goodness of the object.[149] The user then is precisely not interested in instrumental value but the objective good of a thing that is only realizable in faithful practice with it.

Furthermore, yet once more at this stage of the argument the friends of Socrates are not among the ignorant majority; they know what appearance is, and they know that appearances are produced without knowledge. This conclusion is hardly inconsistent though with what Socrates argues elsewhere. For instance, at the end of the *Meno* Socrates (in my view deliberately) leads Meno into an impasse with regard to the challenge of education, arguing (in a purposeful mimicry of the sophists' pernicious habit) both that virtue can be taught and that it cannot. Having reached a point of irresolution, Socrates lamely concludes that statesmen must only follow the right course of action in their cities because they are under inspiration, not because they know what they are doing. In this respect statesmen are not unlike "soothsayers" and "prophets" and "poets," all of whom are "under the gods' influence and possession, as their speeches lead to success in many important matters, though they have no knowledge of what they are saying."[150]

Obviously lacking knowledge is not an enviable place to be according to Plato, but it bears remembering that knowledge is not the only source of good benefit. As Socrates has been discussing in the *Meno*, right opinion also produces a good result, but its defect is that it cannot do so reliably.[151] It's also wise to remember what Socrates said in the *Apology* about craftsmen. What he decided after discussing with craftsmen was that they knew their own craft but that this knowledge did not necessarily make them wise in the art of living well. In this regard they are like the poets, who again Socrates says he concluded from experience of conversation with them "do not compose their poems with knowledge, but by some inborn talent and by inspiration, like seers and prophets who also say many fine things without any understanding of what they say." [52] In like fashion, "the craftsmen seemed to me to have the same fault as the poets: each of them, because of his success at his craft, thought himself very wise in other most important pursuits, and this error of theirs overshadowed the wisdom they had."[153]

So the lack of knowledge by itself does not mean "fine things" cannot come of poetry or craft. It is a reason for caution on the part of the unwise, but those who are in the know are not misled by a fine product to the inference that it was produced by knowledge. It is for this reason perhaps that Socrates can mysteriously question the value of poetry when stripped of its music. Poetry lacking what makes it poetry would be a poor specimen indeed, but knowledge is not required to produce it. The danger is in imagining otherwise, falsely concluding that the poet knows whereof he speaks and thus is an authority on any subject except poetry.[154]

The effects then of this questionable practice of imitation remain to be described, and Socrates does so by courting the part of a person's soul that is easily misled by false perceptions, of which he gives a number of now classic examples (a stick appearing crooked in water).[155] In such cases we can thank the rational part of the soul and its ability to measure and weigh for correcting errors of appearance, which goes to show that the rational part of the soul is superior to the part that is deceived by false appearances.[156] As poetry and painting produce works that are far from the truth so too do they court the attention of the inferior part of the soul, such that "imitation is an inferior thing that consorts with another inferior thing to produce an inferior offspring."[157]

Not content in this case merely to settle for a possible analogy between painting and poetry, Socrates instead builds on previously established points to cinch the case. Earlier they agreed that the soul is filled with opposing impulses because it has different parts that can be at war with each other, but Socrates now adds, "I think we omitted some things then that we must now discuss."[158] Combining the prior point with another previously established claim, namely, that a decent man will bear loss more easily than other people,[159] Socrates continues to show that the decent man will not be entirely without grief but will rather be "measured in his response to pain."[160] His self-control will be more effective when he is in the presence of his equals, obeying more readily in the company of others than in solitude the rule of reason, which counsels equanimity, rather than the lure of experience, which is enticing.[161] Here again where there is conflict in the soul there is proof of two parts thereof. Of the four reasons Socrates gives as to why the law demands a moderate response to misfortune the last is most important: "Grief prevents the very thing we most need in such circumstances from coming into play as quickly as possible," to wit, deliberation, the capacity to accept what has happened and pursue the best response to it as reason determines, rather than to delay wise action with childish weeping and wailing.[162] The best part of the soul prefers this wiser course and pursues it, while the inferior part of the soul "leads us to dwell on our misfortunes and to lamentation."[163]

We are now ready then to confront the final reservation about imitation in its full development. An "excitable character admits of many multicolored imitations. But a rational and quiet character, which always remains pretty well the same, is neither easy to imitate nor easy to understand when imitated, especially not by a crowd consisting of all sorts of people gathered together at a theater festival."[164] The imitative poet is not "by nature related" to the part of the soul that rules an orderly and decent man, and his reputation depends on the tastes of the majority, so his ingenuity is not directed to satiating the better part of the soul but to the worse sort of character who is the easiest to imitate for a restless crowd.[165] It is only now that Socrates confidently identifies the painter and poet in this sense: Both sorts of imitative artist appeal to the lower part of the soul, and they can do so with such success that they are capable of corrupting even the best sort of person.[166] For when a real master like Homer depicts a hero in lamentation, "we enjoy it, give ourselves up to following it, sympathize with the hero, take his sufferings seriously, and praise as a good poet the one who affects us most in this way."[167] Conversely, when one experiences an actual loss, "the opposite happens. We pride ourselves if we are able to keep quiet and master our grief."[168] For this reason, it seems unreasonable to praise the work of the poet, which arouses our admiration and appreciation for action that we would not countenance in the course of an actual life.

The ultimate reservation then that Socrates presents is that poetic imitation has the capacity to corrupt its hearers because it provides pleasure in connection with the spectacle of suffering and lamentation, an artistic device that has real-life effects. "I suppose," Socrates demurs, "that only a few are able to figure out that enjoyment of other people's sufferings is necessarily transferred to our own and that the pitying part, if it is nourished and strengthened on the sufferings of others, won't be easily held in check when we ourselves suffer."[169] This is the danger of mimesis not only with respect to pitying and suffering but also to coarse indulgence in debased humor, sex, anger, and all other desires, pleasures, and pains that accompany action.[70] Here then is the final concern expressed by Socrates about mimesis. Because it is capable of acclimating the soul to indulge its least controlled and baser impulses and indeed to take pleasure in doing so, the mimetic arts must be carefully monitored. While admitting that "Homer is the most poetic of the tragedians and the first among them," nevertheless, the ideal city can only admit "hymns to the gods and eulogies to good people,"[171] presumably because these are edifying in content rather than apt to corrupt a good character.

One final time however we have a cryptic retraction. Reaffirming that they were right to banish poetry, Socrates nevertheless takes account of a potential objection that he and his friends might be "charged with a certain harshness and lack of sophistication."[172] Sensitive to such a possibility, Socrates concedes that poetry and philosophy have traditionally been at odds, and in view of this history, he invites poetry to make a defense of itself. "Nonetheless," he says to Glaucon, "if the poetry that aims at pleasure and imitation has any argument to bring forward that proves it ought to have a place in a well-governed city, we at least would be glad to admit it, for we are well aware of the charm it exercises."[173] Glaucon also agrees that the Muse is charming, so Socrates, again in what looks like a significant retraction, says, "isn't it just that such poetry should return from exile when it has successfully defended itself," a question to which Glaucon responds affirmatively.[174]

The interesting "catch" so to speak is that the poets themselves cannot offer this defense. What Socrates says we should allow is "its defenders, who aren't poets themselves but lovers of poetry, to speak in prose on its behalf and to show that it not only gives pleasure but is beneficial both to constitutions and to human life." Incredibly, Socrates concludes, "Indeed, we'll listen to them graciously, for we'd certainly profit if poetry were shown to be not only pleasant but also beneficial."[175] So this is a remarkable and indeed dramatic retraction, for poetry has been regarded as largely questionable up to this point. Now, quite to the contrary, should poetry be defended, then it will prove not just pleasant, as they have already agreed it is, but also beneficial and a source of profit. It remains the case that if poetry cannot so defend itself, Socrates and his friends will stay away from it as you might stay away from an attractive person whom it is best not to consort with.[176] Still, it's a stunning concession that poetry can be defended as worthwhile and to be included in the life of the wise man.

Who could provide the defense of poetry that would render it beneficial in this way? Who else but the philosopher? Who else but the participants in this very conversation? Recall that the initial conversation about poetry and its role in the ideal polis took place in Book III, before the climactic revelation of the form of the Good and its absolute status vis-à-vis the rest of reality. Socrates and his friends return to this topic with the benefit of having attained that height. If they "go back" as it were to the question of poetry and appearances, they do so having attained insight into the form of the Good as the source of all that is, including appearances, though of course those appearances are far from the Good. Nevertheless, they remain the Good's offspring, and their relative value is now in a position to be accurately assessed. Just as they began their conversation in Book I in a welter of confusion and conflicting appearances and opinions, so now they first attain knowledge of what appearance is, they agree that the products of imitation are not yielded by knowledge and so cannot hold moral authority, but they conclude that poetry is a source of pleasure certainly and benefit potentially, contingent upon whether it can be philosophically defended. In fact, the argument of the *Republic* as a whole, which begins in appearance, ascends to the form of the Good, and now returns to appearance, can be defensibly read as precisely the philosophical defense of the potential benefit of poetry that the book calls for.

The poet lacks these insights. In the best case the poetic imitator does not practice a demiurgic craft or have the knowledge that the user of the products of crafts possesses. In the worst case the poetic imitator simply manipulates appearances in order to appease the vulgar and unstable tastes of the crowd. The philosopher however uniquely knows what appearance is, that appearances are generated without knowledge, and that in view of these concerns the value of poetry will have to be carefully assessed before it is enjoyed.

That this is Socrates's final and genuinely appreciative point on the matter can be further demonstrated by what Schindler calls the ultimate "restoration of appearances" that takes place before the dialogue comes to an end.[177] Socrates and his friends decide that they have successfully praised the desirability of justice in itself, without recourse to threatened deterrents as punishments of injustice or promised rewards as incentives to righteousness. Possibly significantly, the interlocutors recall to mind that they specifically discussed how Homer and Hesiod praised justice in terms of its "rewards and reputations,"[178] which the younger men charged Socrates to avoid. The challenge they put to him then was to ignore the exhortations provided by their culture to heed the wisdom of Greece's teachers on the subject of justice and to praise it quite apart from the blandishments of Homer and Hesiod and the educational system based on them.

Having contented themselves that justice is to be preferred to injustice, regardless of whatever else may befall the human soul, Socrates asks his companions whether they will give him back what they had borrowed from him at the outset of this discussion. Socrates says that when the challenge to praise justice in itself was originally issued, they collectively stipulated that in order to prove the point, justice would have to be imagined as being completely without advantage or reward and injustice bedecked with every kind of advantage and honor. The thought experiment is not complete until justice can truly be praised as better than the life of wickedness even if the righteous life brings every kind of suffering and disgrace and the vicious person is covered in honors, wealth, and pleasure. Since this task has been accomplished by Socrates, though, he thinks it only fair here at the end of the argument that "the reputation justice in fact has among gods and humans be returned to it and that we agree that it does indeed have such a reputation and is entitled to carry off the prizes it gains for someone by making him seem just."[179]

Since justice has been proven to be best quite apart from reputation and prizes, now that the thought experiment has been concluded and the challenge of the younger men met, it is only fair that they agree that justice is in fact of good repute and carries with it certain rewards. Recalling that Homer and Hesiod have just been invoked as authorities who praise the reputation of justice, we can see in this agreement to restore the appearance of justice to justice itself as equally a qualified vindication of Greece's greatest poets. Their authority had to be placed in suspense for the argument to succeed, but having done so, their praise of justice in terms of reputation can now be restored as well.

Could this in fact be something like the defense of poetry that Plato and his friends agreed would have to be offered not by a poet but by a lover of poetry? It would seem so, inasmuch as the argument for justice has been won on strictly philosophical grounds. As such, the relative dignity of Homer and Hesiod's praise of justice can be reappraised as being on sure footing. Given the nature of the challenge to argue for the superiority of justice without the lure of such prizes and honors, Homer and Hesiod cannot be taken as authorities but must be "bracketed" as it were. Now however that we have a sound philosophical reason to believe that justice is genuinely superior to injustice, the philosophical soundness of their poetry at least on this score means that they can be readmitted to the conversation.

On an even wider level, we can read this final restoration of appearances as not just a defense of poetry (or at least the philosophically defensible elements of poems) but as a rehabilitation of appearance as such. If this is right, then the material on artistry in Book X is for yet another reason clearly not a mere appendix but is tied closely to the main concern of the entire book. By drawing this conclusion, I again follow Schindler's interpretation in placing central emphasis on the role of the Good in Plato's *Republic*. It is the form of the Good that uniquely stands as an absolute reality and thus one that binds together being and appearance in their very difference from one another. Because the Good occupies this unique role, we can read Book X as a final recapitulation of "poetry, and everything implied therein—namely, images, mythology, appearances, the senses, art, imitation, and the like."[180] If this reading is correct, then Plato's attitude toward the work of mimetic arts does not just happen to be ambivalent (as I hope to have shown so far), but it must be ambivalent in the true sense of the word, that is, not wishy-washy but genuinely two-sided.[181] As Schindler points out, the distinction between being and appearance is staged at the beginning and middle of the dialogue, so it's no surprise it returns here again at the end, and he returns to it in the same terms he has pursued throughout the text, namely, by reference to the question of what reality is like and how the soul should relate to what is really real. If the project of Platonic philosophy were to consist only of the disembodied intellectual contemplation of the forms, then any effort to communicate that very philosophy would be invalid: There would be no writing or speech or imagery at all, and of all of these Plato himself makes skillful and attractive use. That Plato does in fact have a more positive disposition toward appearance and those who traffic in it than it first seems is a result of the fact that for Plato the realm of appearance, far as it might be from the Good itself, is nevertheless the product of it and is itself in a qualified way therefore good.

If this is true for appearances, then how much more is techne elevated by this concluding study? It is surely important that Socrates ranks the maker above the imitator in this argument; if even the imitator's work can be qualifiedly praised, then surely all the much more so can the practitioner of techne also be appreciated in his or her proximity to the Good itself and as having a share in knowledge. As Schindler points out, while this is a bit more implicit in the *Republic* (and I hope my reading in Book X has done much to make that argument more explicit), in the

Timaeus the reader of Plato gets a more direct answer. Plato here for the one and only time in his writings raises the question of the origin of the universe, which he attributes to a divine craftsman. In fact, significantly for our study, he calls the divine craftsman a demiourgos. Speaking of the Demiourgos (if we can use the capital letter here for clarification), Plato writes, "Now why did he who framed this whole universe of becoming frame it? Let us state the reason why: He was good, and one who is good can never become jealous of anything. And so, being free of jealousy, he wanted everything to become as much like himself as possible."[182] So the forms are not actually the ultimate cause of all that is, from the highest to the least real, but goodness is, and the quality of that goodness is that it is not jealous, that is, that it declines to refuse to share itself. Plato thus affirms expressly that it is good that the realm of "becoming" (not being, note well) exists. The realm of becoming, of appearance, which the poet and artist work with, is one therefore that does not constitute a fall from goodness but a superabundance of goodness.[183] The philosopher is in a position to appreciate this point, and this is what makes it not just licit but essential for him to be an artist as well.[184]

This breakthrough should be less surprising in view of the fact that Socrates and his companions agreed earlier that a nonpoet would have to come to the defense of poetry. It may help too to recall that in Book VII, Plato gives us the immortal image of the cave, the one aspect of which that tends to stick in the mind of readers is the liberation of the prisoner and his emergence into the light of the sun outside. Yet this is far from where the indelible central image of the text ends. The summation of the lesson of the cave is immediately followed by an essential corollary. Socrates sums up by saying, "It is our task as founders, then, to compel the best natures to reach the study we said before is the most important, namely, to make the ascent and see the good."[185] The Good of course is symbolized by the sun, and the urgency of seeing it is the central thrust of the whole vignette heretofore. The very next sentence Socrates utters though is the following: "'But when they've made it and looked sufficiently, we mustn't allow them to do what they're allowed to do today.' 'What's that?' 'To stay there and refuse to go down again to the prisoners in the cave and share their labors and honors, whether they are of less worth or of greater.'"[186]

So as essential as the escape from the cave is, equally required is that the philosopher return to the cave and share in the labors of the prisoners, even though those labors have already been exposed as trivial and concerned only with appearances, whether those produced by the imitators or the practitioners of techne. Glaucon objects that this will make the philosophers unhappy, forcing them to live a life that is worse off in the cave as opposed to a better one outside the cave. Once more, the point of the philosophic life according to Plato is not to contemplate dreamily the forms but to take what that contemplation affords and return it to lived, embodied reality, immersed in the world of becoming and appearance.[187] Socrates's defense of his insistence is framed in terms of the realization of the good not for one group (like the philosophers themselves) but for the good of the whole.[188]

Because the Good is an absolute reality that unites all things in their differences, a true appreciation of the Good has to be comprehensive and fulsome. If the philosopher cannot see that the Good requires him to return to the cave to share in the labors of the prisoners, then he has not in fact *seen the Good*. To have truly seen the Good is to know oneself compelled to disseminate its goodness even further, not jealous for the Good as *per impossibile* the philosopher's own private property. It is not at all therefore an accident that the journey of the *Republic* ends in appearance, since the upward ascent of the philosopher out of the cave must be complemented by the return descent to the cave, where the philosopher has the ability to discern the difference between reality and appearance. This appreciation amounts to an appreciation for poetry, for the arts, and for the technai, inasmuch as Socrates says, addressing the imagined philosophers who have left the cave:

> Each of you in turn must go down to live in the common dwelling place of the others and grow accustomed to seeing in the dark. When you are used to it, you'll see vastly better than the people there. And because you've seen the truth about fine, just, and good things, you'll know each image for what it is and also that of which it is the image.[189]

Notice the express use of the term "image (*eidolon*)" in this context. While the poet and painter make images, the philosopher knows what is reality and what is appearance (much as the first point in Book X established) and thus can appreciate them both in their distinction and indeed make use of the latter with knowledge, skill, and sympathy.[190]

That the philosopher can and should do so is a consequence of the fact that he lives in the cave. The *Republic* ends in a study of appearance because it is the milieu of the philosopher, the one from which he departs and to which he returns. The philosopher does not live in the ideal city, nor, as we have seen, does Plato suggest that we should. Rather he dwells as a stranger in the realm of becoming who has seen what really is. Despite the ordinary interpretation of Plato as largely critical of artistry, we have I trust seen that if a philosopher is to do his work well, it can and perhaps must be done with the assistance of the mimetic arts.

Plato on Banausia

One category of human work remains to be examined, and that is the banausic trades. One might assume that for Plato what holds generally true of techne would hold equally true for the technai colloquially classed in the Greek mind as banausic, whose general nature we have already examined. Recall that Xenophon's Socrates expresses disdain for banausic trades and rejects them as unworthy activities for the nobleman. No one has explored in greater depth the role played by banausia in Plato's writings than Andrea Wilson Nightingale, whose *Spectacles of Truth in Classical Greek Philosophy. Theoria in Its Cultural Context* argues persuasively that banausia is a rhetorically loaded term for Plato and is used by him as a foil for his construction of the philosophical life as one of value and interest for free men, as opposed to other highly prized careers in ancient Athens, most especially engagement in political affairs.

The thrust of Nightingale's argument follows the development of *theoria* as a distinct cultural practice, which she maintains developed out of a pre-fourth-century milieu of conceptual categories not nearly as demarcated as they would be once Plato to a lesser extent but most especially Aristotle did the work of organization and distinction among different branches of science and practice. In her words, "the preplatonic thinkers did not conceptualize or formulate a 'spectator theory of knowledge,' nor did they privilege disinterested contemplation over practical or political activities. In fact, they did not even call themselves philosophers. They did of course engage in some forms of philosophical speculation, but this intellectual activity was not distinguished or detached from other forms of wisdom." Eventually of course all of this would be sorted out along the lines that are still familiar today: practical vs. theoretical, productive vs. "useless," technical vs. nontechnical.[191] Even the distinctions between the various *technai* were a product of the late fifth century BC and later.[192]

Let it first be noted that Nightingale sides with those who deny that philosophy is itself a *techne*: "The contemplative activity of *theoria*, then, appears to be neither acquisitive nor productive—indeed, it is not identified as a *techne* at all."[193] Like everyone else who has studied the question, Nightingale admits that Plato uses the "craft analogy" quite frequently, even sometimes appearing to conflate morally practical and technical activities, though also diverting away from the craft analogy, even if Plato never develops this divergence into a clear systematic account and all in all "never distinguished a faculty of moral reasoning distinct from *techne* and *theoria*."[194]

Yet it is apparent that Plato helped define theoria in part by juxtaposition with a form of techne that he knew would attract the universal condemnation of his peers: banausia. Nightingale situates this discussion in the course of her analysis of how Plato came to define and defend theoria by reference to a more generally approved cultural model; in its original meaning, a theoria was a journey abroad undertaken to witness an event, often of religious importance, and generally under the official patronage of the home polis though also assumed privately and then without express civic importance.[195] Because the destination of many such journeys was sometimes of pan-Hellenic character, the *theoros* or pilgrim retained his home identity while also being nudged toward a broader perspective.[196] Such a journey was regarded as risky in one sense, inasmuch as it entailed detachment from the norms of the community and exposure to foreign ways as well as the potential for those ways to be reintroduced into the home polis upon the pilgrim's return.[197] Such a reintroduction could be beneficial or corrupting, but for the relevant, Platonic conception, the return of the theoros to the home polis is a crucial component. The private theoros owes no one an account of his journey, but the official, civic theoros, whose journey is supported by public funds and who acts as an ambassador while abroad, would be required to report on his findings, which could be assessed for their likely effect on the home polis, for good or ill, by public representatives.[198]

Two features of this particular social practice lent themselves to being revised along philosophical lines. First of all, fourth-century philosophers thematized their own projects as having to do with the vision of truths or reality, and theoria was a matter of ritualized seeing; the theoros journeyed abroad with the express intention of taking in a spectacle, religious or political (or both, as they would have been in ancient Greece). As on a literal theoria, "philosophic *theoria* 'views' and apprehends objects that are identified as sacred and divine. In this activity, the 'spectating' operates outside of traditional social and ideological spheres. Like the *theoros* at religious festivals, the philosophic theorist ... completely detaches himself from his city—and, indeed, from the entire human world—and engages in activity that is impersonal, disinterested, and objective."[199] Second, pilgrimage away from the home polis to a pan-Hellenic space where a larger identity could be glimpsed and affirmed, with the possibility of gaining some beneficial insight that could be in the end returned to the home polis, afforded a model for a purely theoretical "space" that transcended local determinations: "Philosophic *theoria* operates in a sphere that completely transcends social and political life. In the activity of contemplation, the theorist rises above all earthly affairs—including his own individual human identity—in order to 'see' eternal and divine beings."[200] The question then of how this news would be received back home was as urgent for the philosophic theoros as for the literal one. For this and other reasons it is crucial to read the *Republic* as a whole journey, out of the cave and back again, with all the attendant complications and risks involved.

Indeed it is this feature of the *Republic*'s dramatization of the philosophic journey that attracts Nightingale's most sustained attention, and for this reason her account is in certain senses closely allied to that of Schindler, who also underscores emphatically the fact that the philosopher's journey does not terminate outside the cave but back inside.[201] Indeed the dialogue as a whole opens with a theoric event. The famous first lines reference this context plainly:

> I went down to the Piraeus yesterday with Glaucon, the son of Ariston. I wanted to say a prayer to the goddess, and I was also curious to see how they would manage the festival, since they were holding it for the first time. I thought the procession of the local residents was a fine one and that the one conducted by the Thracians was no less outstanding.[202]

The goddess is Bendis, a Thracian deity whose cult was of recent introduction, so the festival in question is honored by a Thracian delegation as well as by locals;[203] Socrates's judgment that both processions were equally admirable is not only a hint at his pan-Hellenism[204] but also an intimation of the ecumenism that endangered his reputation before the jury in Athens. The opening lines of course foreshadow the central image of the cave. Adeimantus tells Socrates that "there is to be a torch race on horseback for the goddess tonight" and that they can "look at it" after dinner and conversation.[205] The torches anticipate the shadows on the wall of the cave, cast by fire, and proleptically suggest that this festival is just another diversion in the cave, one that must be surmounted by a more objective "looking" than traditional theoria. Indeed, as Nightingale observes following Griswold, the anticipated return to a theoria of the festival for Bendis is never realized, supplanted as it is by a new, philosophic theoria shared by Socrates and his friends throughout the remainder of the dialogue.[206]

From beginning to end then, and most richly in the central books dwelling on the cave allegory, Plato defines philosophy (arguably for the first time as an independent discipline as opposed to a general term for overall intellectual cultivation) on the model of a theoria.[207] "We must remember that *theoria* in the traditional sense encompassed the entire journey from beginning to end: this included traveling abroad, seeing spectacles, and returning home."[208] Again, this emphasis on the entirety of the journey being preserved in the *Republic* is most helpful, and it allows us to incorporate the technai into a synthetic and holistic account of human work and flourishing. Keeping that in mind, we should further observe that this broad perspective on the work of theorizing includes on Nightingale's reading a productive dimension in Plato. Particularly in the final stage of the journey, the return, it is "clear that the contemplation of the Forms will lead to virtuous *praxis*," such that for Plato theoria involves both: "Contemplation and action are thus conceived as two distinct activities (in constant alternation) in the theoretical life: in contemplative activity, the philosopher is completely detached from, and blind to, the world; in practical activity, he acts within the world, using his knowledge of the Forms."[209]

The normal contemporary perspective on ancient theory is of course that it was strictly nonproductive and abstract, but Plato's wise man is not just a thinker but a doer, and he is so because of the transformation he undergoes as a result of his journey into the realm of objective truth and reality, again in parallel to a literal theoros, who learns of new things while abroad. "In philosophic *theoria*, this change is quite extreme: the theoretical philosopher becomes a sort of stranger to his own kind. According to Plato, *theoria* transforms the philosopher in such a way that he becomes wise, virtuous, and fully free," much more so than the literal theoros, who is freed from the conventions and norms of his home polis only provisionally.[210] The philosopher is truly free and remains so even upon return, where he is henceforth ill at ease in his own home.

How Plato explains this radical freedom is one of the central questions of this part of our study, for he contrasts it with the servile condition of the banausic worker. Normally such contrasts were deployed by the *aristoi* to distinguish themselves from their inferiors, but as Nightingale shows, Plato puts this slur to a different use that at once elevates his own calling to the philosophic life and retrenches the conventional distaste for banausic labor. Nightingale draws attention to two important passages, one from the *Symposium* and one from the *Theaetetus*.

In the former dialogue, Diotima, the woman Socrates hails as his instructor in the art of love, teaches Socrates that *Eros* is a *daimon* and thus neither a god nor a mortal but a being in between (*metaxu*) whose characteristic power (*dynamis*) is to mediate between the divine and the human realms:

> It is through this being [i.e. the intermediary called a *daimon*] that all intercourse and conversation takes place between the gods and men, whether they are awake or sleeping. And the person who is wise in this regard is a daemonic man, but the person who is wise in any other regard, whether in the realm of arts and sciences or manual labor, is a banausic man.[211]

A similar (perhaps even more wide-ranging) contrast between the genuinely wise and the banausic is made in the latter dialogue as well, where Socrates asserts,

> The god is in no way unjust, but is as just as it is possible to be, and there is nothing more similar to god than the man who becomes as just as possible. It is

concerning this activity that a man is revealed as truly clever or else worthless and cowardly. For the knowledge of this is wisdom and virtue in the true sense, and the ignorance of it is manifest folly and viciousness. All other things that appear to be cleverness and wisdom—whether their sphere is politics or the other arts—are vulgar or banausic.[212]

Finally, we might observe that the same term occurs with comparable opprobrium in the *Republic*, where Socrates accounts for the disrepute into which philosophy has fallen by arguing that those worthy of the philosophic life tend to be wooed away from it by the lure of power and wealth and by those who recognize the natural abilities of the would-be philosopher but seek to capitalize on those abilities for less lofty purposes; philosophy is thus left abandoned and exposed to the unworthy strivers who claim the philosophic life for themselves though they are nothing but crowd-pleasing sophists who package majority opinion as wisdom.[213] Socrates likens these pretenders to "a little bald-headed tinker who has come into some money and, having been just released from jail, has taken a bath, put on a new cloak, got himself up as a bridegroom, and is about to marry the boss's daughter because she is poor and abandoned."[214] Immediately before this passage there is an obvious parallel to what Xenophon's Socrates claimed about practitioners of banausic crafts, when Socrates condemns the pretenders to philosophy as having "souls [that] are cramped and spoiled by the mechanical nature of their work, in just the way that their bodies are mutilated by their crafts and labors."[215] The word translated here as "mechanical" is of course "banausic," and the word rendered "tinker" is a copper-worker or more generally a blacksmith working with any metal. As in Xenophon, the assertion is that banausic crafts ruin both body and soul.

So if we count the sophists as being included in this indictment from the *Republic*[216] then it seems that politicians and perhaps all other practitioners of technai (in the *Theaetetus*) as well as practitioners of all arts and sciences (from the *Symposium*) are as banausic as sophists and rhetoricians and just as lacking in philosophic wisdom. Plato then tars a wide swath with the banausic brush, and it is intended to be opprobrious, for banausia is tied not just to a category of literal work but to a host of associations that would resonate in the mind of fourth-century readers. In the first place, banausia is always servile, and the very term is used by Xenophon, Plato, and Aristotle almost exclusively and almost never by comic writers or orators, whose outlook would be more in tune with that of a wider audience.[217] For Plato, the servility of banausia is not just economic but seemingly moral. Socrates asks Glaucon late in the *Republic*, "Why do you think that the condition of a manual worker is despised? Or is it for any other reason than that, when the best part is naturally weak in someone, it can't rule the beasts within him but can only serve them and learn to flatter them?"[218] Here the single term "manual worker" answers for both practitioners of banausia and *chirotechnia* (hand-craft). The "beasts within him" are the representations that Socrates and Glaucon have agreed upon to symbolize the uncontrolled passions within the soul of the tyrant, such that the condition of the manual worker is linked through a litany of examples of different sorts of vices with the maximal injustice of the tyrannical soul.[219]

By contrast, as Oleson has observed, ordinary craftsmen and craftswomen were almost certainly proud of their work, even if it was "banausic," and cites for evidence the proliferation of references to occupations in ancient burial sites:

> Over half of the male names on tomb inscriptions at Korykos in Rough Cilicia are accompanied by an occupation, and the number of occupations totals 110. At least 85 occupations are named in various inscriptions and graffiti at Pompeii [and] over 200 on tombstones in Rome. ... These numbers imply self-identification and a certain amount of pride among craftsmen and the service professions.[220]

Evidence of this sort causes us to second, along with Nightingale, David Whitehead's verdict that banausia was a category constructed from the outside so to speak: "The 'definition' of a *banausos*, it seems, can only be articulated by someone outside *banausia*, and it varies as much with the position of the observer as that of the observed."[221] While adaptable for various purposes then, it is nevertheless the case that banausia was also consistently associated with the absence of leisure and thus unfitness for participation in political affairs.[222]

In short, to be banausic is to be unfree. Yet Plato is developing an even richer conception of freedom than the one required for participation in political affairs. In a brilliant reversal, as we saw from the passage from the *Theaetetus* above, it is the politicians themselves (among many others apparently) who are in Plato's judgment "banausic." Plato thus takes an insult that would be cavalierly used by the superior leisured classes against their inferiors and throws it back in their own teeth. Recall that for the model of philosophical theoria that Plato first articulated, the philosopher becomes "wise, virtuous, and fully free" in a way that even the ordinary theoros with his loosened relationship to political norms does not attain.[223] Because he is trying to define and defend a new form of life unrecognizable to his contemporaries, Plato engages the polemics of banausia to discredit rival conceptions of the good life. If indeed every form of life that is *not* philosophical is in the end banausic, it too is unfree and servile. In this respect the sophists and politicians are all alike: Crowd-pleasing and mercenary, they cater to the masses and give them what they want as if this were the result of genuine wisdom or done in view of what is truly best. By contrast, Socrates himself led by example: Eschewing involvement in political affairs, he declined to charge money from his "students" on the grounds that he had nothing to sell.[224] Socrates is thus beholden to none and precisely thereby is the archetypal philosopher and theorist, an outsider in his own city and consequently entirely free and untainted by even the hint of banausia.

Even though Socrates is the ultimate theorist then, his activity, which we have already seen is in the world of everyday appearances though it is guided and informed by appreciation of realities transcendent to that world, is not just speculative but also productive. The union of thinking and doing is more readily apparent in the *Timaeus*, which focuses on seeing itself rather than on the metaphor of the journey that takes the philosopher out of the cave and back again. Recall that in this dialogue Plato attributes the shaping of the cosmos to a divine Demiourgos. As Nightingale discovers, if we acknowledge the importance of the analogy here to craftsmanship, we will find that at the origin of all things according to Plato is not just a theoretical speculation on the part of the divine but a productive making, which puts craftsmanship at the origin and heart of the cosmos itself and thus once again sounds a more appreciative note on Plato's part for the work of productive making.

As the divine Demiurge is good and free of jealousy so should the philosopher be. Like the philosopher whose theoretical work according to Plato comprises both contemplative and active aspects, so too the divine Demiurge furnishes a model of activity comprising both contemplation and production to which the philosopher should aspire. In Nightingale's words, "In the *Timaeus*, humans [sic] souls must imitate a divine reason that is both contemplative and practical. On the one hand, divine reason contemplates the Forms, but the gods are makers and doers as well as theorizers."[225] Perhaps we should say that the gods are makers and doers as well as contemplators, for the point is that theoria in its Platonic version combines the theoretical and practical, which is why Socrates insists in the *Republic* that despite their reputation philosophers are indeed useful for the guidance of human affairs.[226] Continuing to engage the *Timaeus*'s claim that human souls "'together with *nous*' are the '*demiourgoi* of things that are beautiful and good,'"[227] Nightingale concludes,

> *Nous*, then, is not just a contemplative faculty but a demiourgic power in the physical cosmos. In fact, when the divine souls create mortal beings, they proceed by "imitating" the Demiurge's creative act. Plato places great emphasis on the productive, artistic nature of this activity: the gods mix and sift and knead and weld the elements. The creative activities of the divine souls, then, are directly connected with that of the Demiurge. Divine *nous* is, among other things, a productive power—that which makes order out of chaos.[228]

The terms for "mix" and "sift" and "knead" and "weld" emphasize the "hands-on" nature of the divine Demiurge's creative process. If the Demiurge is this involved in "earthy" productive activity then so too "in 'becoming like god,' then, the human soul must engage in contemplative, ethical, and productive activities. Indeed our task as human souls is to make of ourselves a cosmos."[229] This task is apparently born of familiarity with the wide manifold of productive human activities (as indicated from the outset of this discussion and by the quasi-technical terminology used to describe the divine Demiurge's activity in the *Timaeus*) and a proper appreciation for the role they play in the complete philosophical life, as well as a fitting admiration for the characteristic ways in which they reflect the absolute goodness at the heart of the cosmos itself and in the heart of the true philosophical theorist.

Conclusion: Plato on Work

The choice of Plato as a place to begin a study of work may seem a strange one if one takes the textbook approach to Western civilization's first great philosopher. On that simplistic view, Plato is disinterested in the particulars of human experience, the mundane realities with which workers are normally occupied, in favor of lofty ideals accessible only to theoretical philosophers. This view is in my judgment however just that, simplistic. Plato's technical vocabulary on the many technai he mentions implies that he made detailed examinations of various crafts and their practice by close familiarity with the people of Athens who undertook these many kinds of mundane work.

According to a familiar interpretation of Plato, he is more than casually interested in ordinary people's work because he finds in it a kind of analogy to the practice of philosophy as he is systematically articulating it. I have suggested that the analogy is in fact indirect: For Plato, as techne is to knowledge as a whole so justice is to virtue. This indirect analogy is further supported by my analysis of the contrast Socrates develops between his first proposed hypothetical city, the one dismissed by Glaucon as a "city of pigs," and the tripartite city that occupies the bulk of the conversation in the *Republic*, one that Socrates himself alarmingly calls "feverish" or "sick." The significance of the first, healthy, simple city is almost never acknowledged, simply because it seems to be set aside swiftly by the interlocutors. Because Socrates himself does something uncharacteristic at this point in the argument, namely, offer his unsolicited opinion, we should attend to this material with greater care. In the simple city the citizens do work; they are practitioners of various technai, and their needs are met satisfactorily by their dedicated labors. Having sketched this idyllic scenario, Socrates poses the question of where justice is to be found in the primitive community of workers he and his friends have established, and Adeimantus suggests that it must lie in the way the citizens interact with one another. It is at that point that Glaucon interrupts and diverts the conversation, suggesting that they should allow the citizens greater luxuries and niceties than the simple city affords.

While Socrates complies with this request, it is abundantly clear that he believes the simple city to be both sufficient for the needs of the conversation and preferable as an actual way to live. In fact, the friends are already on the cusp of an answer to the central question of the conversation, an answer that will now be delayed by scores of pages of discussion. Via a roundabout way, Socrates and the others will eventually conclude that justice is after all to do with the way that the citizens of a polis deal with one another. This much was evident though in a simple hypothetical city involving only workers, no warriors, and no rulers, again because the practice of techne is for Plato not just similar to wisdom but is profoundly tied to justice, and each is a part of their respective wholes. Ultimately it is through the work of the craftsmen and artisans that ordinary people participate in the full flourishing life that at its most developed is only lived by the philosopher. A society where ordinary people pursue their own work with integrity and without distraction seems to be close to an ideal community.

Even when pressed to adopt a more "realistic" view, Socrates will still insist that justice consists in everyone doing their own job, that is, everyone doing the best in their given area of expertise with as much dedication as possible and focused on the perfection of their own task rather than other inducements to excellence. The technai are good to pursue in themselves, like justice, and they aim at the attainment of a good that responds to a genuine human need. The friends have already agreed that it is best for the society if each worker does his or her own job, that each have one's own task and not interfere with the others'. At first this maxim is presented as a practical postulate, that is, as a wise proposal for the successful performance of work and no more. Having come around to the final answer about justice though, again through a long digression, this postulate is raised to the level of a philosophical principle. That each should have her own job is not just a matter of promoting the quality of work but of securing justice itself, inasmuch as justice proves to be the coordination of the parts of the city and the parts of the soul in an orderly harmony. In this respect then too the practice of techne is not just comparable to wisdom but essential to it. Because each techne addresses a genuine need, the practitioner thereof contributes to the well-being and flourishing of her neighbors.

Doing good and useful work thus becomes a kind of entry point at the mundane level for a more spiritual or philosophical work. In the *Apology*, Socrates tacitly revises each of the four cardinal virtues. When it comes to justice, he points out that he did not pursue this virtue by the characteristic means—a public life of political activity—but by privately exhorting each of his fellow Athenians to look after the quality of their own souls. "I shall not cease," Socrates vows to the jurors,

> to practice philosophy, to exhort you and in my usual way to point out to any one of you whom I happen to meet: Good Sir, you are an Athenian, a citizen of the greatest city with the greatest reputation for both wisdom and power; are you not ashamed of your eagerness to possess as much wealth, reputation and honors as possible, while you do not care for nor give thought to wisdom or truth, or the best possible state of your soul?[230]

Justice then arises in a community as a spontaneous consequence of each person looking after their own moral character individually. The average worker thus provides a model for a sort of self-cultivation of a more significant moral sort. Just as each person is meant to do their own work, so too for Plato is each person meant to "work" on themselves, to make of themselves a cosmos as Nightingale says. The practice of a craft is thus a kind of analogue to the philosophical life after all, not because techne is comparable in every particular to wisdom but because each person has one job to do, which can be understood on a mundane level as the need to stick to one's own area of expertise and the good that it promotes or on a deeper level as the summons to the cultivation of personal virtues. In this way the ordinary citizen who is not herself a philosopher or ruler nevertheless partakes in a limited way of the optimum form of life according to Plato. The philosopher alone fully contemplates the Good itself, while the craftsman sees the changeless qualities of beauty and balance and realizes them in her work. In this way each person doing their own job makes a vital contribution to the just and ordered nature of the whole society, which reason ideally rules by allowing each of its members as much involvement with the whole of wisdom and understanding as each is capable of realizing.

At the same time, there are limits to techne according to Plato. The technai are not philosophy itself, though they provide a more profound clue to it than previously perceived by most commentators. The trick to appreciating this intimate relation more fully is to track carefully Plato's use of the argument from analogy in *Republic* VI. There he uses the sun as a sort of springboard for the soul to gain provisional insight into the

Good, moving as it were from something known to something obscure. As diligent readers of the text have noticed however, the directionality of the analogy gets reversed once it becomes clear that the Good is the cause and source of all things and thus the ground of the intelligibility of the sun and the whole visible world. What was at the first regarded as known is now re-known so to speak as it is retroactively cast into a new light by relation to the Good that is at the origin of the whole. The relative realm of appearances is where we must begin, so Plato appeals to the familiar reality of human work in order to come to greater philosophic wisdom, which pertains not to some limited good (as the technai do) but to the Good itself. Having then shown though that the Good is the absolute source of all that is relative, the realm of limited goods becomes understood only by relation to the Good itself. Thus does philosophy for Plato ultimately show us what work is by relating techne to wisdom.

It does not follow however that we can then dispense with work. On the contrary, we require appearances and images to come to full understanding of reality. The Good is, if we understand it correctly, present in all its appearances and consequences, and it is only by virtue of this presence that we can move intellectually from the lesser to the greater, from the mundane reality of work to the heights of philosophic speculation. If work were not reflective of the Good, this ascent would be impossible. The analogy that Plato uses then is not accidental in the sense that it does not involve taking two realities that happen to have something arbitrary in common and placing them side by side for intellectual inspection. Quite the opposite. Work and philosophy do not happen to have comparable features; they are reflections of the same absolute reality that inheres in them and in all things.

The crafts include scores of tasks that we would call today "blue collar" at best, yet I think we can confidently say that for Plato their place of esteem is secure. We can be more sure of this conclusion when we realize that the *Republic* in a way ends where it began. Back in Book I, Socrates argued forcefully for what he called there a "strict" conception of techne according to which each and every techne is occupied with exactly one area of human need and the remediation of that need: Cobbling is about making shoes because our feet are vulnerable to cold and damage; construction is about building houses because we need shelter from the elements; farming is about providing food because we get hungry. The most salient point of the early argument about the "strict" conception of techne is that Socrates uses it to distinguish the practice of each and every techne from a frequently accompanying but nevertheless entirely different activity: making money. For Plato, no techne has anything intrinsically to do with money. No position could be more distant from that of the contemporary worker, for whom money is one of the chief motivations, if not the only motivation, for work.

According to Plato's argument, every form of work is about one and only one thing: its object of concern and the promotion of that object's advantage. So with respect to the argument between Socrates and Thrasymachus, and using their example, we can say that for Plato the shepherd is, insofar as she is a shepherd, exclusively concerned with the benefit of the sheep under her care. Contra Thrasymachus's objection that the shepherd looks to the good of the sheep only because the sheep is eventually bound for the shepherd's master's dinner table, the shepherd in point of fact is not mindful of the sheep's ultimate destination, only of the sheep's good.

What this means is that for Plato the practice of the technai affords internal goods, quite apart from the material advantages it offers. Naturally both in Plato's day and our own the practice of a techne usually brings with it a material benefit: Normally people get paid for their work. Nevertheless, this is according to Socrates an inessential connection. If a doctor is paid to practice medicine, then it happens to be the case according to his analysis that the doctor is simultaneously practicing two arts: medicine and money-making. Should she fail to practice medicine in the absence of payment, then we might be justified in questioning whether the person in question truly is a "real" doctor. At first this argument strikes us as strange, but I think it chimes with our intuitions even today. Suppose a doctor saved the life of a dying man on an airplane and then had the audacity to ask for compensation? We would be scandalized because we take it as incumbent upon a medical expert, as a medical expert, that they offer their services to those who need them urgently without expectation of financial recompense. That we arrange for financial recompense in the overwhelming majority of cases is a recognition not therefore of what is necessary for a doctor to be a doctor (or for any practitioner of any techne to be the expert she is) but of what justice and the working of a well-ordered society requires. We can therefore conclude that for Plato the doing of a job is worth doing for its own sake. Apart from whatever compensation it might provide, the practice of one's work is intrinsically desirable and worth pursuing for its own sake.

Because pursuit of a techne is itself valuable and promotes internal goods, the practice of the technai is itself conducive to virtue. Plato argues in the *Republic* that the artisans or the craftspeople in the ideal society will be marked by their temperance or moderation of desires, a virtue shared with the other classes in the same society. Because the technai are limited in scope and number, each to their own definitive good, they are in principle capable of near-perfectibility. Is it possible that the practice of the craft itself promotes the relevant virtue of moderation, and that the widespread commitment to temperance itself is, so to speak, contagious? What if moderation is not only needful for the right practice of the technai but is brought about by that right practice and thus is not the exclusive gift of the artisans themselves but also their gift to the entire society?[231]

This possibility is strongly implied at least by Socrates near the end of his discussion of the place of work in the polis. At first he and his interlocutors agree straightaway that each person will do best if they stick with one craft, as each person is herself one individual. This emphasis on the unity of both the individual soul and the polis (which, don't forget, are meant to correlate) is present at both the beginning and end of the long conversation on work and its place in the polis, but the relationship of unity *to* work has changed. Much later Socrates repeats the point that each person should have one craft but this time says this is so not because each person *is* one but because by practicing one a person *becomes* one. What this means is that by the practice of a craft a person comes into unity with herself, and the same holds true, Socrates says in this very same passage, of the city as well, that if each does her own work the city too will be one rather than many. This unity then is not merely the basis of the desirability of each person doing her own work: It is its consequence, and the consequence is felt not only in the individual's life but in the life of her community. It is for this reason then that Socrates in the same passage condemns the twin evils of wealth and poverty, the former of which promotes laziness and luxury and the latter of which fosters slavishness and shoddiness; both undermine the integrity of work and its products. Because of extremes in wealth Socrates asserts that most cities in fact are not one at all but two, the parts of which are at war with one another. The modest and devoted practice of the technai can help resolve these divisions.

The Greek idea of techne is commonly called "value-neutral," and there are ancient sources that can be cited in the centuries prior to Plato that seem to support this reading. However, the simple society that Plato sketches in the *Republic* and even the feverish society with its stratifications and corresponding virtues is arguably supported in virtue by the very functioning of the technai in an orderly and coordinated manner. This functioning will not be inherently interested in money, so the practice of the technai will be unimpeded by greed, motivated by the internal goods of the activity, and concerned only with the refinement of the practitioner's ability to bring about the most praiseworthy results. The technai then are not entirely value-neutral according to Plato but bring about their own characteristic virtue to the benefit not just of the objects produced by the work but to the whole society.

This salutary effect will be more easily realized of course in a society that fosters the sober, dedicated, and non-mercenary pursuit of the technai. In a political order where greed, blandishment, and self-indulgence are rampant, it will be harder for the workers to stay dedicated to their labors for their own sake and to the benefit of the work being done as opposed to from some other incentive. It should be noted that when the friends forsake the simple, healthy city for the feverish city Socrates says he does not mind doing so, in part because he says it will still be possible to see where justice *and* injustice arise in such a sick social order. While he inquired about the presence of justice in the simple city and solicited from Adeimantus the germ of an answer to this central question of the text, Socrates implies that where justice arises in the sick city is easy to see but just as easy to see where injustice comes from, while injustice is not as obvious in the simple city. What this in turn suggests is that the technai (which again are present in the simple city) are limited in the ways we have enumerated, so for their full flourishing they need coordination and promotion within a well-ordered social arrangement that will capacitate each of its members to pursue her own job. As Knies put it, the polis arises according to Socrates and his friends in the *Republic* out of need, but it finds its final meaning in its ability to facilitate the best sort of work being done by all the people who belong to the polis. The polis may be born in need, but its meaning is not exhausted by its ability to provide for those needs but in its promotion of each person's ability to pursue their own work.

This is one final reason why they insist that it is preferable if one person does one job each. In that case each person does one job that meets the needs of many others, and the same is true reciprocally for each of the social order's citizens. So Socrates contends unequivocally that it is people's indigence that drives them into congress with one another, or as he puts it in terms that become proverbial, necessity is the true mother of the invention of cities. Yet this is not the final destiny of the city. If the end goal is the liberation of a philosophical meaning to the practical principle that everyone do his or her own job, then the realization of justice is the real goal of the polis.²³² In the ancient world, the workers would have much more to do with one another than in a developed modern economy. In Plato's Athens, work was done to satisfy a human need presented by the workers' beneficiaries. In a modern economy work is done for compensation, and the market mediates relations of production and consumption, buying and selling. Money renders all products into commodities with equivalent valuation. Contemporary workers have a harder time envisioning what genuine human need they are serving and what contribution they are making to a just and harmonious social order rather than to a market's smooth operation.

Yet one basic lesson we can learn from Plato about work is that the best sort is so because it does furnish a genuine good that meets a real human need. Workers of today may do well to reflect on the extent to which they can say that about their job. Frequently today I suspect we think about work as merely instrumental, as externally good only for getting me things I need, not worth doing in itself. The extent to which a worker can affirm that her job is worth doing apart from any instrumental justification may again be a measure of how good a job really is today. Furthermore, a good form of work is one that will be motivated not by profit but by the contribution it makes to the justice of the whole community. Where justice rather than money is a worker's motivation, there is both the opportunity and even mandate for each citizen to do the best she can at her work. As Socrates himself puts it, "we must compel and persuade the auxiliaries and guardians to follow our other policy and be the best possible craftsmen at their own work, and the same with all the others. In this way, with the whole city developing and being governed well, we must leave it to nature to provide each group with its share of happiness."²³³

Part Two

The Middle Ages

One of the most important critical developments in recent historical scholarship on the Middle Ages has to be the thorough discrediting of the previously unquestioned characterization of the medieval period as the "dark ages." After an extended period during which modern prejudices cemented in such a way as to relegate the medieval period to a veritable backwater, widely regarded as having contributed nothing of much value to the progress of Western civilization—religiously, artistically, culturally, technologically, economically, scientifically, or politically—the old orthodoxy has been entirely demolished. The medieval period was substantially interesting for its contributions to the philosophy of work as well.

The pioneering work of French scholars like Richard Lefebvre des Noëttes,[1] followed shortly thereafter by Marc Bloch[2] and in later generations by Jacques LeGoff,[3] Jean Gimpel,[4] and Robert Fossier,[5] has come in for a wave of criticisms and reappraisals that have forced the current generation to regard their early claims for the dramatically more advanced character of medieval technology over that of the ancient world to be attenuated somewhat. Nevertheless, it is now universally acknowledged that the Middle Ages was an era of unprecedented technological development and urbanization, even if some of the first generation of French medieval historians overstated their claims.[6] The contrast between medieval and ancient social development is probably not as sharp as originally claimed by many in the early to mid-twentieth century but not negligible either.

Here we will follow the advice of George Ovitt, Jr., whose work will be a source of ongoing inspiration in this chapter. Ovitt writes, "In looking for the source of the medieval attitude toward the use of nature, one should examine religious views not with an eye toward finding the cause of a particular kind of behavior, but in order to recreate the context within which this behavior occurred."[7] To recreate this context we will proceed straightaway to the rehabilitation of work, which we find most thoroughly developed in the context of early monasticism. We will survey some major themes on this topic and then take stock of the philosophy of work intimated by St. Augustine, who wrote the late ancient world's only treatise devoted exclusively to the question of manual labor.

3

The Early Medieval Period

Work in Early Monasticism

Patrick Coby ends his study on the place of artisanship in Plato's *Republic* with the conclusion that while Plato successfully defends the value of justice for the philosophic soul he fails to provide compelling reasons for why the warrior or artisan should also be just in addition to brave and moderate, respectively. Recall that Coby successfully shows how in some limited way both the warrior and the artisan participate at least indirectly in the eternal verities that reason contemplates most perfectly in the person of the philosopher. The ability of craftspeople to create objects of beauty, and the knowledge that they have, which captures a part of wisdom, is their distinctive way of (however partially) living the life of reason and virtue. Without passing judgment on the merits of Coby's conclusion, I want to attend instead to his final speculation:

> Ultimately, it seems, the *Republic* fails in its defense of moral virtue in warriors and artisans. But its vindication of the philosopher's virtue shows what a successful defense would require: specifically a conception of divinity in which the divine is accessible by some instrument other than speculative reason; a godhead that does not await indifferently upon the ascent of the philosophical few, but which reaches down lovingly to every human being, and whose reception depends on the opening of the soul, for which the individual, through his virtue or his vice, is responsible. The conclusive and unassailable defense of moral virtue would therefore require a providential God whose dispensation of grace is made freely and to all. It would require, in other words, some combination of Platonic philosophy and Christian religion.[1]

I suggest that early monasticism was a laboratory for this exact idea. Combining Platonic thought with radical Christianity, the monks found a way to make the maximally spiritual life also a worker's life. Charles A. Metteer gives a helpful taxonomy of the purposes of work affirmed by early Egyptian monasticism, arguing that the architects of this form of life saw manual labor as a means for achieving self-sustenance, an effective weapon against temptation, a resource for the support of the needy, and a vital component in the monks' ascetic program.[2] Arthur T. Geoghegan meanwhile names three purposes: "The monks worked to acquire virtue, to support themselves, and to provide for others."[3] The exact place of labor was a source of some division between the cenobitic form of monastic practice associated with Pachomius's Upper Egyptian communities, which were populated by sometimes staggering numbers of men and women devoted to an expressly communal form of spiritual discipline, and the anchoritic form of monastic practice, normally associated with Antony in Lower Egypt, which was eremitic and thus stressed solitary life, interrupted only for corporate worship on the weekends. Both forms were of course devoted to poverty, chastity, and obedience to God as well as a spiritual superior. Work, perhaps unsurprisingly, permeated cenobitic practice, though it was not absent from the anchoritic life.

Work was certainly brought to a higher level of organization and diversity of aims in the Pachomian tradition. Palladius records the following in just one offshoot of Pachomius's original community at Tabennesi, the three hundred-strong monastery at Panopolis:

> (In the monastery I found fifteen tailors, seven smiths, four carpenters, twelve camel-drivers, and fifteen fullers.) But they work at every kind of craft and with their surplus output provide for the needs both of the women's convents and the prisons. ... One works on the land as a laborer, another in the garden, another at the forge, another in the bakery, another in the carpenter's shop, another weaving the big baskets, another in the tannery, another in the shoemaker's shop, another in the scriptorium, another weaving the young reeds.[4]

Similarly Jerome's personal witness of his time among the Pachomians testifies,

> The brothers of the same trade are assembled in one house under the direction of the same superior. For instance, those who weave linen are together, those who braid mats form one family, the tailors, carpenters, fullers, shoemakers are separately governed by their own priors. Every week they render an account of their labors to the superior of the monastery.[5]

All in all though, taking both eremitic and cenobitic communities into account, Metteer is able to provide a shocking number of sources for his assertion that "recent scholarship overwhelmingly defends the positive contribution of manual labor in early Egyptian monasticism," citing numerous accounts that clarify its role as "a fundamental aspect of monastic life" and as many more that explain its importance to the duty of "self-support."[6]

These rationalizations and the others Metteer and Geoghegan enumerate are present in various writings connected with anchoritic monasticism, with which we begin our survey. That manual labor should have been part of anchoritic life is not obvious; given that hermits were leaving the cities and the usual occupations of life in the world, there might be a question as to why they would seemingly return to such occupations having sought the purity of living alone in the desert. As Ovitt frames the question, "How does one reconcile monastic asceticism with worldly attitudes and material achievements?"[7] Indeed, as Birgit van den Hoven points out, that some ascetics rejected labor should not be regarded as disinclination or caprice on their part. Rather, these pious people vowed to obey a divine command and, moreover, their hands were not idle but constantly raised in prayer. They found a justification for their way of life in countless Bible texts, the best known of which are "Pray without ceasing" (1 Thess. 5:17) and "Mary hath chosen the good part" (Luke 10:42). Whoever understood these words to be a command could read in them that prayer was a duty and work "forbidden."[8]

These two texts are indeed under constant discussion in monastic sources. The former, the injunction of St. Paul to the Thessalonian church, inspired a long tradition of debate and discussion as to exactly how it was to be implemented, but was taken so seriously by all parties that it can be said without exaggeration that monastic life as a whole was largely motivated by an attempt to be faithful to this command. The latter is the conclusion to a short episode told in the Gospel of St. Luke of one of Jesus's visits to the Bethany home of his friends, the siblings Mary, Martha, and Lazarus. Mary sits at Jesus's feet and listens to his instruction, while Martha busies herself in the kitchen with the tasks necessary to show hospitality to their guest. When Martha appeals to Jesus to compel her sister to assist her, Jesus asserts that Mary has chosen the better path. This vignette came to be understood very early on as an allegory for the relationship between the contemplative and active lives, with the predominant interpretation being that despite the seemingly obvious conclusion that Mary's preference for contemplation is validated by Jesus himself above the preoccupation with worldly matters exhibited by Martha, the two are in some fashion complementary or both needful.

That this is so runs counter to van den Hoven's effort to depict two divergent (and, she seems to imply, equally promising) traditions in anchoritic monasticism, one of which embraced work and the other of which rejected it. The legacy of Scripture had always been ambivalent (in the most literal sense of that term) on the question of work, lending itself to either side of these discussions: On the one hand, there are counsels from Jesus himself exhorting believers to a kind of carelessness about self-sustenance and freedom from worry about provision of even basic needs. The appeal to imitate the simplicity and purity of the lilies and the birds in the Sermon on the Mount seems to stand in contrast with St. Paul's example of working for his own necessities. Paul, in the second letter to the Thessalonians, makes it clear that he as a spiritual worker is entitled to the support of the community, but his own decision, consciously pursued, was to practice his craft of tent-making so as to meet his own needs and thereby not be a burden to the community.[9]

The genius of early monasticism was to think these two heritages together. Naturally the monastic life is called foremost to prayer and contemplation, and this was the ideal to which all monks aspired, but at the same time, there was a keen awareness that a monk is still a human being. The goal to become like God was not inhibited by the limits of humanity.[10] According to one oft-reported apothegm that represents this balance, a young monk chided Silvanus, who was hard at work, with the counsel of Christ cited above: "Do not labor for the food which perishes. Mary has chosen the good part." Upon being so corrected, the old and wise Silvanus instructed his disciple Zacharias to give the young monk a book and retire him to his cell with no other provision. When the hour for the evening meal had come and gone, the young monk emerged and asked Silvanus if the brothers had eaten. When Silvanus replied that they had, the young monk inquired further as to why he was not called to supper, and Silvanus answered, "Because you are a spiritual man and do not need that kind of food. We, being carnal, want to eat, and that is why we work. But you have chosen the good portion and read the whole day long and you do not want to eat carnal food." Upon repenting of his folly, the young man receives the final verdict from Silvanus, "Mary needs Martha. It is really thanks to Martha that Mary is praised."[11]

From this anecdote van den Hoven concludes, "Work here is seen as unavoidable; there is no question of a deeper meaning or intrinsic value attached to work. We should, therefore, not be surprised to come across the view in other *apophthegmata* that you do not have to work much if you do not need much," and she cites examples accordingly. However, we could read this more positively as an appreciation if not for work itself than for the condition of humanity. The monks had an awareness of the world of spiritual beings neither divine nor human but angelic, both fallen and not. A monk is not an angel, as John the Dwarf learned. This example is especially valuable, because van den Hoven uses a story from John the Dwarf to argue for her contention that work was not especially valued among the anchorites. Conveniently though, she fails to cite the entire apothegm. She quotes John the Dwarf as having testified to his brother, "I should like to be free of all care, like the angels, who do not work, but ceaselessly offer worship to God."[12] Metteer supplies the complete story though, reversing van den Hoven's interpretation of it. After imitating the angels for a week by forgoing his daily tasks and withdrawing into solitude, John returned to his brother and knocked on the door of his cell only to receive the sarcastic reply, "John is become an angel and is no longer among men ... If thou art a man, thou must needs work again, so as to live."[13]

Furthermore, while the project of ascesis involved diminishing need and thereby requiring less work to furnish fewer necessities, this strategy is not incompatible with a largely positive view of work's spiritual benefit. Ascesis is no reflection on work as such; it is the path to sanctification, and travelers on this path will to some extent or another require work in order to sustain one's human life, even if that life needs little compared to others'. Van den Hoven cites approvingly Derwas J. Chitty's claim that "the true doctrine of the Eastern, Christian ascetics" was to "return to the state of Adam before the Fall."[14] True enough, but on this basis van den Hoven questions whether work should be as natural to the monk as prayer and meditation, implying that the answer is "not quite," or at least that it "is too quick and too easy" to conclude from this premise that "from the early beginnings until the present time work has had a high priority in monastic life."[15] If indeed the goal of monastic life is to return to an Edenic existence, then we must recognize that entailed in that very claim is some kind of work, since Adam had work to do *before* the Fall. Genesis 2:15 states, "The LORD God took the man, and put him into the garden of Eden to dress it and to keep it," so as all early Christian theologians acknowledged, even before the Fall, Adam in his state of created perfection had work to do.[16] The consequence of the Fall was not that human beings had to work but that their work became *difficult*. The judgment of God that falls upon Adam for his transgression is that "cursed is the ground for thy sake; in sorrow shalt thou eat of it all the days of thy life; Thorns also and thistles shall it bring forth to thee;

and thou shalt eat the herb of the field; In the sweat of thy face shalt thou eat bread."[17] This simple observation dispels a potential and potentially serious misunderstanding and assures us that at the very least the monks could not view labor as a consequence of the human being's fallen condition.[18]

For further illustration, we can turn as van den Hoven does to the sterling example of Antony. That Antony the first and paradigmatic anchorite, worked with his hands is reported early in the main source of information we have about his life, Athanasius's *The Life of Saint Antony*. In keeping with the tradition described above, Athanasius actually recounts that Antony was inspired by *both* Jesus's exhortation to be unconcerned about provision of one's own needs (which we have already encountered) and by Paul's declaration that one who will not work should not eat. This latter Scriptural sentiment, which comes from 2 Thessalonians 3:10, is almost certainly the most widely quoted Bible verse on labor in the monastic era, by a wide margin.[19] The context is Paul's reminder of his own behavior when he was ministering directly to the Thessalonian church. Paul asks the readers of his epistle to recall that when he was in Thessaloniki he "wrought with labor and travail night and day, that we might not be chargeable to any of you: Not because we have not power, but to make ourselves an ensample unto you to follow us. For even when we were with you, this we commanded you, that if any would not work, neither should he eat."[20] Paul raises his own example as the basis for dealing with reports he has received of idlers and "busybodies"[21] in their midst, people whom he commands "that with quietness they work, and eat their own bread."[22]

Once again, the teachings of both Jesus and Paul are unified in Antony's life and in Athanasius's chronicle thereof. In the space of just two pages, Athanasius cites the profound influence of each on his hero's ascetic existence. Recounting Antony's decision to commit to asceticism, Athanasius reports that his total obedience to Jesus's radical demand of the rich young ruler in Matthew 19 to sell all he had and give it to the poor was only secured when Antony heard in church the command of Jesus from the Sermon on the Mount to "be not solicitous for the morrow."[23] Thereupon, Athanasius writes, "he could not bear to wait longer, but went out and distributed those things also [the remaining proceeds from the sale of his family's land] to the poor. ... Then he himself devoted all his time to ascetic living."[24] After learning more deeply about ascetic practices from an elderly man well-practiced from youth in spiritual discipline, Antony determined to forsake everything of home and "to devote all his affections and all his energy to the continued practice of the ascetic life."[25]

Immediately after this decisive declaration, Athanasius gives his reader a short portrait of Antony's manner of living at this time. Interestingly, the very first descriptive point Athanasius chooses to relate is to do with work, which (startlingly) he mentions even before prayer and hearing of Scripture:

> He did manual labor, for he had heard that *he that is lazy, neither let him eat.* Some of his earnings he spent for bread and some he gave to the poor. He prayed constantly, having learnt that we must pray in private without cease. Again, he was so attentive at the reading of the Scripture lessons that nothing escaped him: he retained everything and so his memory served him in place of books.[26]

Antony then could be faithful to both Scriptural dimensions, responding to the call to abandon anxiety over future provision by selling his familial property and giving away the proceeds to the poor, and being obedient to the Pauline injunction to work for his own bread by supporting himself with effort in his ascetic style of life. Needless to say, Antony both reduced his necessities—eating only bread and salt and drinking only water[27]—and through work provided what little he needed.

Moreover, the conjoining of the imperatives to self-sustenance and charitable giving and support of others turns out to be entirely typical of monastic practice and reflection on work. As Metteer points out, on the most basic level, work was required to keep alive in the desert, and while the priority for the monks obviously had to be on the spiritual work of prayer and meditation, distraction from which was to be kept at an absolute minimum, nevertheless the most elemental rationalization for work was pure survival.[28] Metteer notices that there are in the monastic literature some odd but illustrative cases of monks whose progress in spiritual development was so advanced that their needs were miraculously supplied by God. Such anecdotes were useful to the anchorites, who were arguably especially vulnerable to pride in their ascetic accomplishments and less involved in organized corporate work.[29] Even in anchoritic communities then, the need for the sort of balance that Antony struck was widely acknowledged and practiced. All upheld the primacy of prayer and affirmed that God would provide while also insisting on a monk's contribution through labor to the project of self-sufficiency.[30] As Metteer puts it, "the Egyptian monks saw the need to maintain a balance between working for their sustenance and cultivating an awareness of their total dependence upon God. Whereas the former was a necessary activity, the latter was an indispensable element of faith."[31]

This necessity, as I have argued, was imposed by human limitations of which the monks were conscious and embraced, and as Metteer argues, by environmental realities: "The Egyptian desert was brutally unforgiving to those who refused to work. Rather than providing a haven from human need and everyday chores, the barrenness of the desert accentuated the basic necessities and duties of human life."[32] Under such conditions work was required for survival and, equally worth noting, little more than survival. As Ovitt points out, "the life of the desert was antithetical to productivity, and subsistence living, the assumed economy of the monastic community, makes excessive labor problematical, especially since the monk eschews trade, the amassing of objects, and the acquisition of money."[33] Both Metteer[34] and Geoghegan draw attention to the testimony of Jerome on this score, whose Epistle 125 reports that the monasteries would not even accept anyone unwilling to labor: "In Egypt the monasteries have made it a rule to receive none who are not willing to work; for they regard labor as necessary not only for the support of the body, but also for the salvation of the soul."[35]

As Geoghegan observes, "it is remarkable how often in Palladius' account of the Egyptian monks, and in other reports, too, special mention is made of the fact that the person described earned his living with his hands."[36] This was by no means exceptional; on the contrary, it is a constant refrain, and it is repeated to underscore time and again the monastic's "utter abhorrence of receiving support from another and their unswerving determination to earn their own sustenance until the end of their days," in some cases those days being quite numerous. The literature furnishes instances of men who worked into their eighties and on their deathbeds contented themselves that they had never, like St. Paul, "eaten another's bread for nothing."[37] Metteer gives examples as well of counsels that a monk be content with just this much self-sustenance and no more. Sozomen insisted that monks have no interest in stockpiling wealth or investing in anything other than the needs of the present, and Pachomius invoked Luke 12's cautionary parable of the rich man who stores up the excess produce of his land for future use, only to die in the night before he intended to begin enjoying his newfound security.[38] Metteer's summary captures the essentials:

> The writers of desert literature agreed that all monks—anchorites, semi-anchorites, and cenobites—needed to support themselves. Indeed, the harshness of the desert forced the monks to accept that God intended their spiritual regimens to include manual labor. Consequently, the relatively few accounts involving miraculous provisions were probably created either to emphasize the importance of asceticism, to embellish the memory of a great monk, or to protect a monk against the temptation of excessive labor.[39]

At the same time, while profit was out of the question in an Egyptian monastery and self-support achieved through hard work the most elementary goal, work also made possible a measure of charity for others in need. In van den Hoven's words, "in early Christian monastic literature, we regularly come across the belief that work should also serve our fellow-men. In other words, work is a vehicle for charity. A monk should produce more than is necessary for his own subsistence. Through the overproduction he could then obey the commandment to charity by giving alms to the poor." She cites the teaching of Poemen, who said, "As far as you can, do some manual work so as to be able to give alms."[40] Similarly Metteer contends that "serving others was a natural component of monastic life"[41] and "monks often helped others at great personal expense."[42] Archebius tripled his own workload so that he could pay off his mother's substantial debt, and Theodore of Enaton recollected that in his youth he would bake bread for six needy brothers before baking his own. All of these acts of care were capacitated by additional commitment to work, the only means a monk had to provide material relief for his own brothers or for laypeople in need. Metteer further cites Poemen's instructions to the brothers who sold goods at market:

> Seek not to sell it for more than it is worth, but rather if thou art vexed, be friend to him that would beat thee down, and sell it in peace. For when I myself have gone now and then to the market, I have never desired to please myself in the price of my work, and vex my brother, having this hope that my brother's gain will bring forth fruit.[43]

Numerous witnesses to charitable practice are compiled by William Herbert Mackean, who catalogues,

> Palaemon and his disciple Pachomius gave to the poor; the Pachomian monks provided for those in prison; and Schenoudi did much for those in want. Serapion

in the region of Arsinoitis distributed food to the needy, and boats full of food and clothing used to be sent to the poor of Alexandria; Apollo relieved large numbers in time of famine; Paesius and Isaias, sons of a merchant, on receiving their inheritance occupied themselves with work among the poor; relief was given to poor monasteries; and Cassian says that the monks not only relieve pilgrims and visitors but "actually collect an enormous store of provisions and food, and distribute it in the parts of Libya, which suffer from famine and barrenness, and also in the cities, to those who are pining away in the squalor of prison."[44]

These material acts of charity sometimes sat in tension alongside the monastic aspiration to *hesychia*, which was the spiritual tranquility with which ascetic achievement was rewarded.[45] Graham Gould argues that the term captured two main meanings, "first, solitude considered in itself, and second, an inward disposition of freedom from disturbance."[46] Gould goes on to show that not only is hesychia a calm that came from discipline and renunciation of the world and its cares, but it could also be the shape of a chosen way of monastic life. Some testimonies of early monks depict them as desirous of shaping their practices and behaviors around hesychia in a way that at least implies a corresponding diminution of relationship with others, even brother monks. It was said for example of Isaac that he achieved hesychia from participation in the Eucharist and immediately after dismissal from church would rush back to his cell, apparently spurning continued fellowship with the brothers.

> It happened that he was ill, and when the brothers heard they went to see him. When they were sitting they asked him, "Abba Isaac, why do you flee the brothers after the synaxis [the liturgical assembly]?" He said to them, "I do not flee the brothers, but the evil action of the demons. For if someone is holding a lamp, and stays standing in the open air, the lamp will be extinguished. Thus when we are enlightened by the holy offering, if we delay outside our cells our mind is darkened."[47]

In Isaac's case, zeal for the spiritual calm that came with Eucharistic devotion was worth preserving in solitude after the service had ended. Similarly, Moses complained to Macarius that he wished to live in hesychia and yet was being prevented by the brothers. Macarius replied that his peace was disturbed because out of kindness he could never turn anyone away, so he advised him to retreat even further into the desert, to Petra. As Gould demonstrates though, Moses remained renowned for his hospitality as well as for his love of undisturbed tranquility.[48]

The togetherness of the life of quiet withdrawal and charitable expansiveness is illustrated well in the following vignette:

> This is shown by ... the story of someone who visited him and Arsenius in turn, and found Moses welcoming and friendly, while Arsenius was silent and reserved, so that the brother found himself unable to speak freely. Here an old man prays to be told why it is that "the one flees in your name, while the other is welcoming in your name." He sees a vision of two boats, in one of which Arsenius is "sailing with

the Spirit of God in *hesychia*," while in the other he sees Moses with the angels of God, eating honey cakes.

The point of the story is that "several different ways of life were *equally* valuable,"[49] and Gould shows that in many cases one monk was reported to have walked many paths in the course of a long career in ascesis, sometimes preferring solitary prayer and contemplation, sometimes hospitality and charitable undertakings.[50] Another frequently reported story teaches the same lesson. Ovitt retells more completely a tale alluded to above by Mackean, namely,

> the story of Paesius and Isaias narrated by Palladius in the *Lausiac History*. Upon the death of their father, the two sons of a wealthy Spanish merchant decided to enter monastic life. They disagreed, however, as to the proper disposition of their inheritance: "One divided everything among monasteries, churches, and prisons. He then learned a trade so that he could be self-supporting and spent his time in ascetic practice and prayer." The other brother chose not to distribute his share of the inheritance, but instead built a monastery for himself and a few brethren. This brother took in and cared for strangers, invalids, the old, and the poor. After both brothers had died, various opinions were offered as to the comparative sanctity of their two ways of life. Finally, blessed Pambo, a great and holy hermit, offered the opinion that "both were perfect—one showed the work of Abraham, the other of Elias."[51]

Here again no choice is to be made as to the superiority of the comparatively solitary life of prayer in seclusion as opposed to the comparatively active communal life of service to others. Both are expressions of the same spiritual gifting. Ovitt also uses this story to remind his readers that the strictly solitary way was itself regarded as fraught with spiritual hazard, inasmuch as extremities in self-discipline could themselves be temptations to pride, and work, along with the tangible concern for others that work made possible, was regarded as a remedy for the dangers of self-indulgence.[52] Metteer concludes,

> Wise monks understood that their labor was essentially a service to God. This insight, however, did not clarify the role that service to others played in their monastic lives. Indeed, anchorites, semi-anchorites, and cenobites were frequently at odds on this issue. Their different orientations, however, were somewhat harmonized by the more balanced sayings of Poemen, Paesius and Isais, Nesteros, and Pambo, which emphasized equivalency of monastic movements, tolerance of different lifestyles, and respect for others.[53]

Gould draws a similar conclusion that the assembled sayings

> all show that the question of solitude *versus* interaction was keenly debated by the Desert Fathers. This is a fact of significance which shows that the *hesychia* chosen by some was put to the test and justified—it was not taken for granted. Not all of

these sayings imply that a life of *hesychia* is better than a life of interaction. In fact most of them go out of their way to avoid this suggestion, stressing the equal value of the two ways of life.[54]

Probably the single most important goal of manual labor for the monk was its contribution to the development of relevant virtues and its value as a component of an overall asceticism. In Metteer's judgment, "The writers of early Egyptian monasticism occasionally portrayed human work itself as having ascetical value. In some cases, the hardship associated with a monk's work was seen as an element of his askesis. In other instances, his labor was linked to the saving of his soul. Primarily, however, human work was considered a means of acquiring virtues."[55] Ovitt makes a similar point about the monastic expectation that work would improve the monk's soul.

The hermits worked alone to support themselves; the Pachomian monks worked cooperatively to support a broader constituency. In both cases there is little to suggest that his labor was purely penitential or deliberately nonproductive; and while there are some doubts expressed about the appropriateness of labor for those who have renounced the world, the judgment in the majority of cases suggests that productive labor is beneficial in both material and spiritual terms.[56]

Finally, Geoghegan summarizes the distinctiveness of the monastic view of work and echoes our contention above that the monastic view of labor in fact combined successfully the Pauline and Christological teachings.

Like St. Paul, they preached the worth of labor as a means of self-support and alms-giving. But it was from Christ's doctrine of self-denial that they derived their distinctive teaching on physical work. What distinguished their teaching on labor from that of their predecessors was their repeated emphasis on the ascetic value of work. For them manual labor was the daily cross to be carried in the footsteps of Christ.[57]

Metteer reports incidents in the sayings that boil down monasticism as a whole to a commitment to toil. According to John the Dwarf's description of a monk's life, a monk "is toil. The monk toils at all he does. That is what a monk is."[58] Less superlative perhaps but no less committed to the necessity of labor was the counsel of Pistamon that a monk should never give up manual labor, even if he can satisfy his needs through other means.[59] As we have seen, the goal of self-sustenance was an important one, but Pistamon's remarkable recommendation indicates that manual labor was valuable for its shaping of the spiritual life even when self-sustenance was achievable without it. At the extreme, the hardship of labor could be made even more burdensome than strictly required in order to enhance its ascetic value.[60] Geoghegan notes that in the community established by Pachomius, work went on even during the heat of the day, and monks at work were forbidden to sit during their labors unless permitted by the superior. Likewise, discussion of worldly matters among monks at work was forbidden, while talk of sacred subjects was allowed, and silence of course was always commendable.[61] Metteer cites an extraordinary vignette that vividly illustrates the monks' taking to heart of a quite literal, concrete interpretation of St. Paul's claim to the Corinthian church that "everyone shall receive his own reward according to his labor."[62] Apparently eschewing the thought that this sentiment applied only to spiritual struggle, an elderly monk walked twelve miles from the nearest fresh water.

> Every time he went to draw water he toiled and said, "What good is this labor? I will go and live close to the water." Saying this, he turned back and saw someone who was going with him and counting his steps and he asked, "Who are you?" He said, "I am the angel of the Lord, and I have been sent to count your steps and to give your reward." When he heard this, the old man was reassured and became more courageous, and he went and settled five miles farther off.[63]

More often though there are more modest cautions in the monastic literature against allowing workmanship to become an occasion for pride or personal satisfaction.[64] Metteer acknowledges that "while these examples strongly suggest that the Egyptian monks saw ordinary work as an indispensable aid in their pursuit of humility, their work-related attitudes could also lead them in the opposite direction."[65] He notes one instance of a monk who worked hard to make extra mats to impress Pachomius but earned a rebuke rather than praise.[66] Techniques were devised to make sure that monks were humble about their work. Pachomian communities would rotate monks through differing tasks,[67] a tactic that we might say ensured the very opposite of enhanced achievement and productivity secured by division of labor.[68] Speaking of the monastery of Pachomius, van den Hoven states that "for one week one house takes responsibility for organizing the work or performing the liturgy or preparing and serving meals. In this way specialisation is purposely avoided."[69] Ovitt cites Jerome's observation "that in the Pachomian communities the brothers had their work assignments shifted periodically so that they might learn to be 'ready and obedient' in everything and so that they might be more fully prepared to be employed in God's service."[70]

These practices were codified for all of Western Europe by the Rule of St. Benedict, which, in the words of Jonathan Malesic, "prescribes a division of labor that would forestall rank-and-file monks from identifying themselves too closely with any one work task."[71] Supervision of the kitchen for instance fell to two capable brothers, but they only did the job for one year. Workers carrying out specific duties under their supervision did so on a weekly rotation. The job of reading aloud to other monks also rotated. Some special tasks, like that of the cellarer or the abbot (obviously), required specialization and prolonged commitment to one job, but expertise was largely discouraged in monastic rules, and under no circumstances could one's work be an occasion for self-satisfaction or lack of humility. In the words of Benedict,

> If there are artisans in the monastery, they are to practice their craft [*artes*] with all humility, but only with the abbot's permission. If one of them becomes puffed up by his skillfulness in his craft, and feels that he is conferring something on the monastery, he is to be removed from practicing his craft and not allowed to resume it unless, after manifesting his humility, he is so ordered by the abbot.[72]

By reflecting on such tactics and their purpose, Malesic concludes,

> In the monastery, expertise can be a dangerous impediment to the health of the community and the spiritual development of the individual. A skilled artisan invests himself or herself in their craft. The danger in this investment is that the artisan will identify himself or herself with the work, and the pleasures of the craft will overtake the purpose for which the craft is being done.[73]

That purpose is of course primarily spiritual.[74] It is for this reason that the actual tasks performed by monks were of a sort to allow for quiet, meditation, the recitation of psalms, and discussion of sacred matters. In Pachomius's communities, if a new monk had worked a trade before entering the monastery, he could continue to do so within, provided that the work met the general expectations of humility and service to others rather than self-congratulation and profit. The untrained could be assigned to learn simple tasks or to work in farming and gardening.[75] St. Euthymius, who laid down monastic rules for the communities of Palestine, had learned basket-weaving, following the example of his predecessors, and recommended it to the monks under his supervision because of "its sedentary and noiseless character," which "conformed nicely to a life of contemplation and quiet."[76] In support of her point that work served the purpose of prayer, van den Hoven points out,

> The classic form of work for the anchorites was that for which the basic materials were at hand, which was easy to learn, and which assured the monks of an unconcerned, though modest, existence. The twining of ropes and the making of baskets and mats met these requirements. John the Persian wove linen, Poemen made rope, Silvanus threaded peas, and John the Dwarf and Megethius wove baskets.[77]

The same sorts of considerations motivated the Pachomian communities: "mat- and rope-making, certain forms of outdoor labour, the making of dough—these are all relatively simple, rather mechanical occupations which do not distract the thoughts of the monks and which combine well with the *meditatio* [contemplation of Scripture]."[78] Jerome made several recommendations in his Letter 125 to Rusticus, who aspired to the monastic life: "weaving, gardening, irrigation, apple growing, beekeeping ('so you might learn from these tiny creatures how to structure a monastery and order a kingdom'), fishing, and book copying."[79] As Ovitt observes, though, in the same letter Jerome exhorts Rusticus to "never take his eye off his book" and memorize the entire Psalter, so clearly none of these labors he thought could interfere with the primary task of spiritual devotion and ascesis. He concludes, "It seems likely that what Jerome was actually advocating was a mixture of prayer, reading, and labor—precisely the trio of monastic activities recommended by the majority of monastic Rules," and this seems reasonable inasmuch as Jerome himself both worked with his hands and worked diligently in his library.[80]

Metteer organizes a number of anecdotes from the desert under the headings of obedience, charity, and humility. Specifying the ascetic project and the cultivation of the virtues in this way allows us to see that work contributed to each of these excellences. Recognizing that strict obedience to a spiritual director was difficult for most novices, the superiors would use the assignment of work to accustom a new monk to unflinching obedience and submission, even when asked to perform the same tasks repeatedly without complaint or objection or, at the most extreme, even when given a strictly impossible task.[81] As we have seen to some degree already, work also made charity possible and, in some cases, meant forgoing the material benefit of one's own labors.[82] Finally, undertaking the labors normally associated with the poor and overburdened elements of society meant that the monk gained humility, by not despising exertion and lowly employment.[83] As Ovitt puts it, "Christianity was a religion for the humble, and … unlike the pagan sects it displaced, it did not disdain manual labor or associate work with the shame of slavery. Indeed, labor was a sign of humility and was practiced by the monks for precisely this reason."[84]

Here perhaps it is worthwhile to pause and offer some summary remarks about the transformation of the character of work in early monasticism. The point just made by Ovitt seems worth dwelling on, that under the inspiration of St. Paul and Tertullian among others, the early Christian ascetics deliberately embraced, as essential to their way of life, the daily practice of manual labor, an activity previously regarded as at best to be held in low esteem by elite culture and at worst as the domain of slaves. It is often claimed in the critical literature that work was prized by the monks "only" as a means to an end. Work for the monks lacked, in van den Hoven's judgment, "positive religious sanction."[85] Similarly, LeGoff writes that while the early church developed "a spiritual approach to labor, a veritable theology of work" based in St. Paul's writings (and once more, 2 Thessalonians 3:10 is cited) and the works of the early Fathers, centuries went by without this theology being developed or implemented effectively. In his view, rather than the later Middle Ages dignifying work by adopting the characteristic activity of the lowly to show that Christianity was a religion that refused pride and embraced what the world contemned, "labor was thus discredited by association with the baseness of the class that monopolized toil [that is, the peasant laborers, not the monks who freely devoted themselves to work]. The Church explained the serf's lowly condition as that of society's scapegoat, invoking man's servitude to sin."[86]

LeGoff then reads this later denigration of work (which as we have seen is contradicted by the monastic model) back into Benedictine spirituality and practice. "In this connection," he asserts,

> there should be no mistaking the position of Saint Benedict and Benedictine spirituality with regard to labor. The Benedictine Rule imposes labor on monks in two forms, manual and intellectual, and both are penitences, in conformity with the ideology of the time. In the Benedictine mind during the early Middle Ages, both labor's spirituality, which was merely a penitential instrument, and its theology, according to which labor was a consequence of original sin, had only negative value, as it were.[87]

LeGoff reaffirms this perceived tie in his mind between monastic labor and penitence by arguing in the same vein that "the meaning of this monastic labor was above all penitential. Because manual labor was connected with the Fall, the divine curse, and penitence, the monks, as professional penitents, penitents by vocation, penitents par excellence, had to set an example of mortification."[88]

LeGoff's claim that labor was closely associated with the Fall can surely be challenged on the basis of the many witnesses we have canvassed so far. An explicit thematic connection between the Fall and labor does not seem to appear with much frequency in the monastic literature, and we know that Christian theologians agreed that only the difficulty of work was consequent upon the Fall, not work itself. The picture he paints therefore is rather needlessly dour. Despite his rather negative verdict, LeGoff concedes that "the simple fact that the highest type of Christian perfection, the monk, engaged in labor caused a part of the social and spiritual prestige of the practitioner to reflect on the activity of work. The spectacle of the monk at labor impressed his contemporaries in its favor. The monk's self-humiliation in labor raised labor in general esteem."[89]

It is this final concession that I think is perhaps most important. For while all commentators tend to agree that work was not the final end of monastic life it did find an important place therein, and at the least we can say that work was thereby ennobled. We must keep in mind that while work might have been subordinate to the ultimate goal of monastic living, that form of life was not held to be just one among others by the medieval mind. To be a monk was indeed to strive for "the highest type of Christian perfection"; it was to realize as far as possible the overriding goal of all Christian living, the sanctification of the whole person, mind and body. So the aim of the monk was nothing less than the superlative aim of his or her entire religious orientation, one that also permeated his or her society and culture and, insofar as it did not, was judged wanting by the monk on that very, most important, score. To say further that manual labor was a necessary component of such a life was thereby to dignify it to a higher degree than Western culture had generally affirmed heretofore.

Suggesting that work was not praised "in itself" or had only a "negative" value compared to the highest aim of human life as the Christian early medieval West conceived it would be like arguing that for Plato geometry had only a negative value or was not valued in itself compared to philosophy. That may be, but for Plato philosophy was the royal road to the happy life and to the human condition fully realized in all its splendor, and geometry was necessary to be a proper philosopher and thereby attain the human good. That it was required for such a lofty aim is no insult, and this holds true all the more when we remember that manual labor of the sort pursued by the monks was not just inessential to, but was almost entirely alien from, the ancient world's views of what constituted the highest and happiest life. The monk is the medieval counterpoint in many ways to the ancient sage, who would have never viewed manual labor as a component of his own formation, education, and moral improvement.[90]

We should also keep in mind that this process of formation and improvement was one that was never complete. If work played a role in it, it did so not just provisionally but continually, inasmuch as the process of sanctification is itself never drawn to a close (perhaps not even in death). Speaking of obedience specifically, Metteer makes a point that holds for the cultivation of all virtues, which he calls "a permanent way of life that had value in itself, and not merely a means to an end that could be set aside once formation in the monastic life was accomplished."[91] If work was instrumental in the promotion of obedience, humility, and charity, then while it may play a subordinate role in the development of sanctity and ascesis, it played it to the end and could not be disposed of at any point any more than the cultivation of virtue itself could be regarded as achieved once and for all. It is Ovitt who seems to capture the required sensitivity when he judges that "if the purpose of labor was the creation of a self-sufficient monastic economy, the primary byproduct of this economic purpose was the creation of an environment that fostered self-effacement, obedience, and the 'repose of the spirit.'"[92] This was indeed the goal of the monastic life, such that we can admit that "the legacy, then, of the first ascetics and the first monastic theorists favored manual labor, but always as a means to a spiritual end."[93]

Two other points are worth bearing in mind. First, as Susanna Barsella has argued, expanding the points made so far, the monastic ambition combined the theological potential of human production in imitation of God's creation by drawing on the innumerable metaphors in Scripture of God as a maker or builder or even a potter or a farmer and the ethical and political meditations of the classical world on the nature of work.[94] The product of this combination was in her estimation "a revaluation of work as a fundamental element in the economy of salvation. Set within the eschatological perspective established by the Incarnation and Redemption, in the Fathers' thought work became an instrument of human cooperation with Christ in the edification of the Christian community."[95] Barsella develops this point profitably, underscoring the theological horizon of the monastic enterprise, an aspect of their theory and practice of labor that is often omitted or misunderstood by historians or economists or social theorists who examine these issues.

For Barsella, the civic, communal nature of the monastic effort must be appreciated to grasp the topic of work properly as it was treated by the early church, which concerned itself not just with the salvation of individual souls but with the creation of a new society ordered around Christian precepts. She locates the first contribution to this unique combination in St. Paul, who in her view does not just extol work to combat idleness but values its benefit to the community. Once again, Paul can be read as a contributor to the Platonic tradition by reason of this tight link between just work and promotion of a healthy social order. According to his proto-theology of work, all Christians become cooperators with Christ by imitating him, and in the same chapter from 2 Thessalonians that we have seen referenced time and again Paul presents himself and his commitment to work as a model for Christian imitation.[96]

> The Early Fathers, inspired by Paul's principle of imitation extended to the ministers of the Church and also as heirs to the philosophical tradition, developed an idea of work in which these strands of thought combined. As ancient philosophy had seen in the *techne* [sic] the engine moving human beings to work toward the full realization of their potentialities in whatever art they practiced and in so doing they laid the foundations of the ideal polis; likewise, the Church made work the ethical leverage to accomplish attainment of likeness with God and contribute to the building of the Christian community.[97]

This point is all the more important to acknowledge if we keep in mind that for the early Middle Ages the individual was an imperfect being who could only realize his or her full spiritual development in community, whether monastic or otherwise. The centrality of the civic and political concern evinced by the builders of monastic communities, and the place of work in the building up of those communities, should not be minimized.[98]

As we have seen, work for the monk was a means of adopting the virtue of humility by taking on tasks formerly regarded as the exclusive and demeaning province of slaves, the itinerant, and the impoverished. Barsella thinks the truth is even deeper, that "Christianity not only tried to give dignity to certain forms of manual work because of their symbolic and theological value in terms of servitude and humility, but also engaged in an ideological effort to define work as *poiesis* that allows for participation and cooperation in Christ's redemptive work," such that poiesis itself almost becomes redemptive.[99] The example she develops is that of St. Basil, who she argues transformed the very nature of poiesis in a new theological direction. Drawing on Aristotle's familiar distinction between productions that exist apart from the act of their making (works of architecture, sculpted or woven articles) and productions that exist only in the act of their making (dance, music), Basil shifts the grounds of this distinction from the origin of the existence of the product (which was the basis on which Aristotle distinguished products of artifice from products of nature, his primary interest) to the end for which the product is made, where that end is understood to be the appreciative contemplation of the product.

In this sense Basil realizes a realignment of the very meaning of production, which he reorients around the aim of contemplating the excellence of the producer. Basil thus analogizes the faithful Christian's admiration for the work of God to that of an appreciative critic for a work of art and thereby links a philosophical point to a theological one. The argument is clear in Basil's *Hexameron*, where he says,

> In the case of the productive arts, the work remains, as that of architecture, carpentry, metalwork, weaving and of as many such arts as, even if the craftsman is not present, ably manifest in themselves the artistic processes of thoughts, and make it possible for you to admire the architect from his work, as well as the metal worker and the weaver.[100]

The parallel then is that just as a worker who produces a product separate from the process that produced it can be admired for his craftsmanship even when he is not present, since the work itself testifies to his skill, so in the same way God can be admired by the faithful appreciator of his divine creative work. Barsella concludes,

> This passage shows how Basil re-read the relationship between the artisans/ artists and their products in light of Creation and illustrates an example of theological reading of the *techne* [sic] in light of the incommensurable parallel between human and divine *poiesis*. As in Aristotle, all specific ends, either of action or production, found their ultimate meaning in the highest end of human happiness and, in political terms, in the common good of the *polis*, so in Basil

and the Fathers any specific end related to *praxis* or *poiesis* was subsumed into the highest end of salvation,[101]

both individual and communal.

Notice though that praxis and poiesis are not merely subsumed into the highest end of salvation. That point we have established already, and with the agreement of many commentators. Barsella though amplifies the point by showing that not only was the ultimate horizon to which production belonged one of paramount importance (a point that we have already made and that we think should temper the criticism that work for the early Middle Ages was "merely" a means to an end) but also that that very horizon of eschatological salvation *transformed* the meaning of production itself. By working in imitation of the practices of the lowly, the monks not only disciplined themselves but reinterpreted the very nature of work, by situating it in an eschatological horizon and thus making of it something that contributed to the divine project to redeem the entire world.

Contra LeGoff, who read Benedict as prescribing manual and intellectual labor as a sort of twofold penitence and for no other reason, Barsella maintains that Basil's teaching on the contemplation of the worker's ability via the appreciation of his or her work inspired a view of manual and intellectual labor as complementary on the ground of their twinned ambitions to support a community of divine imitators. Basil's instruction found its way almost verbatim into Ambrose's *Hexameron* and into Augustine and ultimately Benedict, whose Rule reflects "this positive vision of work involving both body and mind."[102] Benedict's Rule, on her argument, advocates for manual and intellectual work not out of penitence but out of appreciation for the work of God; the Rule stresses "the importance of manual work to foster humility and social ethics in the community. Monasteries represented an attempt to build an ideal Christian *poleis* [sic] where the members worked in continuity with the divine exemplar [of] work" in order to "fashion a lifestyle coherent with evangelical values" and express "the cohesion and functioning of these institutions."[103]

A similar transformation takes place in John Chrysostom, who in his own way revaluates what is meant by techne in general by arguing that almsgiving is a techne. We have seen already that work was valued because it made charity to the needy possible, but Chrysostom goes even further than this, considering "almsgiving not as a by-product of work but work in and of itself."[104] He makes this point in one of his homilies on Matthew, where he preached in an aside on charitable almsgiving,

> Almsgiving is a kind of art [ars, techne], having its workshop in Heaven, and for its teacher, not man, but God. … Almsgiving is an art, and better than all arts. For if the peculiarity of art is to issue in something useful, and nothing is more useful than almsgiving, very evidently this is both an art, and better than all arts. For it makes for us not shoes, nor doth it weave garments, nor build houses that are of clay; but it procures life everlasting, and snatches us from the hands of death, and in either life shows us glorious, and builds the mansions that are in Heaven, and those eternal tabernacles.[105]

Using rhetoric that would have been commonplace in the ancient Greek setting, appealing to the usefulness of the products of techne as definitive of the nature of techne itself, Chrysostom here in revolutionary fashion posits the giving of alms as a techne and indeed not just any techne but the best. Like any techne, almsgiving can be taught by a master, but in this case the teacher is no human authority but God himself, and the workshop where this techne is learned is not on earth but in heaven. Almsgiving, Chrysostom claims, is useful like any techne, but it is queen of the technai because it produces something of ultimate usefulness, the blessedness of eternal life and a place in paradise. Chrysostom thus has expanded the notion of "usefulness" well beyond its classical conception, such that it is no longer simply appreciation for the true good of a thing, and certainly not only of instrumental value, but worthiness as esteemed by a Christian theological value system and the potential contribution that can be made to the work of nothing less than salvation. Barsella concludes that the distinction between action and production, so precious to Aristotle, is minimized in this vision, which prizes above all "the community in which evangelical values can (and should) be realized."[106]

The criterion of "usefulness" has been daringly reinvented by Chrysostom, according to which both action and production as classically conceived "are evaluated in terms of their instrumental value in realizing the good of the community."[107] The key moments that Barsella identifies (admittedly not in the monastic literature per se, but shedding light on the question of early medieval thought on work) indicate not just a recontextualization of the purpose of work; they point to a transfiguration of its potential character. Techne, as Chrysostom and Basil discuss it, is simply not the same thing as Plato and Aristotle had in mind. By resituating its classic qualities—productivity, usefulness, teachable mastery—in the Christian horizon, these Church Fathers pushed toward a new understanding of work as an eschatological project, one that could make a vital contribution to the building of Christian community on earth as in heaven and secure the highest possible goods of human life.

The second and final point to keep in mind is provided by Malesic, who argues that the penultimate status of work in monastic communities was by design; commentators who raise the point that work was not of ultimate importance to the monks sometimes seem to think that it thereby fails to meet some imaginary burden. Malesic though situates work properly by simply underscoring not just the purpose of promoting it (which we have seen explained fully) but the point of promoting it just to the extent that monastic views of labor did (and Malesic relies principally on Benedict here).[108] Malesic puts his central claim this way:

> I argue that within the rule there are several mechanisms to encourage monastics to detach themselves from their required manual labor so that they do not identify their earthly purpose with their work. Rather, the monastery is a workshop for the formation of the monastics as persons oriented toward holiness. Work, though important, can inhibit the attainment of their overall form of life, so it is imperative to develop disciplines that limit the person's self-investment in work.[109]

Rather than increase the weight human beings place on work and expand their expectations of what can be meaningfully derived from it, the monks instead suggest that by limiting the place of work in the development of a spiritual life that work has precisely such a limited role to play in a life dedicated to more exalted aims. Van den Hoven, for one, seems to disparage the monastic work ethic with the recognition that the work done by the monks consisted of "simple, rather mechanical occupations" and implies that this was a reason to infer that monasticism did not regard work as highly as an observer might think. Malesic would likely agree but would argue that by limiting work to a matter of repeating simple routines they successfully managed to regard it just as highly as it merited and no more. According to his reading,

> Work must be kept within strict limits so that it does not become an end in itself. Work is good, and it is better than wayward idleness, but it is not among the highest goods for the person. If work can be limited, then it should be, so that the worker can invest more of himself or herself in higher activities.[110]

Malesic's interpretation of the twinned Pauline command to work for one's own bread and Christ's instruction to look to the birds of the air and imitate their example of devout unconcern is that these two principles do not in the monastic understanding form a contradiction but open a space, a space in which work can be preserved as a good while not being overvalued.[111]

When concentrating on Benedict in particular, Malesic notices the predominance of work-related metaphors used by the Rule, the upshot of which is that the monk works for and under God (as Chrysostom said of the almsgiver) while both the matter and the aim of the monk's work are in fact nothing other than his or her own self.[112] To use Malesic's terminology, the monastic ethos therefore prizes the subjective goods imparted by labor (self-renunciation, devotion, hope, virtues that Benedict calls "the tools of the spiritual craft")[113] rather than the objective goods (economic security). It is in this context that Benedict orders the rotation of monks through different jobs and the other tactical strategies canvassed above. Similarly, time itself was ordered, with the emphasis on prayer, which was sufficiently more important than work that monks were obligated to abandon the latter without delay when the time came for the former.[114] In these respects work was bounded by both physical and spiritual needs and imperatives. Clearly then work was no curse, but neither was it overprized. As Malesic puts it, if work is itself an ascesis, then because it was not the most important element thereof, work had to itself submit to an ascesis. For Benedict, work was always to be done moderately, was not to be over-burdensome or requiring heroic effort, and was to be apportioned based on the abilities of the workers. In this fashion work was not allowed to become an end in itself, not because work was not viewed favorably but because it was always to be respected as a spiritual opportunity for, and not a replacement of, self-development. For Malesic, "considering monastic asceticism can help illuminate the fact that work is an *askesis*. The most basic assumption of monasticism is that our repeated bodily actions form us spiritually. The monastic's product, produced in cooperation with divine grace, is his or her own more perfect self."[115]

That conclusion is a fit one with which to end this part of our study. That this is the truth of the monastic life was recognized centuries ago by one of its most distinguished architects, none other than St. Augustine, to whom we now turn, who wrote in his *Confessions* a declaration that could stand as the motto of monastic life and work as a whole: "O Lord, I am working hard in this field, and the field of my labors is my own self."[116]

Augustine on Work

Rudolph Arbesmann rightly points out that "Saint Augustine of Hippo is the only author of antiquity from whose pen we have a treatise on manual labor, to wit, his precious little work entitled *De opere monachorum*."[117] This treatise was an occasional piece, written at the request of Aurelius, a personal friend of Augustine's who was serving as bishop of Carthage at the time.[118] The case Augustine makes in favor of monks doing manual labor was pressed against a group of monks under Aurelius's authority in Carthage, who had agitated him by their refusal to do manual labor and provide for their own needs, citing instead their devotion to strictly spiritual labors.[119] It would be too much then to say that this short work was written by Augustine because he had a spontaneous interest in the subject of monastic labor as such, though before 400, when he composed *The Work of Monks*, he had already written his own monastic rule, which would prove enduringly valuable to the formation of Western monasticism up to the present day, so it was not a subject of which he was ignorant. Even so, Kenneth Steinhauser cautions that while

> Augustine's *On the Work of Monks* is considered by many the only piece of literature from Christian antiquity dedicated entirely to the topic of human labor ... in spite of its title a careful reading of the treatise reveals that human work is actually a secondary concern. Augustine presents no theoretical definition of work. He does not deal with the origin of work. He does not develop a theology of work.[120]

One of the striking things about *The Work of Monks* is how little it depends on the commonplace rationalizations for monastic labor that we have gleaned from our study so far. Augustine rarely appeals to the value of work as a promoter of virtue, as a resource for almsgiving, or as a means of self-sustenance. Certainly a major reason for this absence of customary rationales is Augustine's scanty familiarity with anything written in Greek, in which the early compendia of monastic sayings were composed.[121] Augustine notoriously admitted his distaste for Greek as a student,[122] and the extent to which he knew the language well enough to read deeply in Greek sources has been frequently disputed.[123] Pierre Courcelle's treatment of this question is arguably the most extensive. Chiding other scholars for failing to take in the entirety of the corpus and paying insufficient attention to the question of chronology, Courcelle advances the argument that Augustine's earliest works show rudimentary knowledge of Greek, retained from school days, while his later works, especially those dedicated to the controversy with Pelagius, give evidence of increasing, mature facility with the language, though even at this later stage, Augustine's knowledge of Greek remained bookish, and at no time could he rival a titanic Hellenist like Jerome.[124] Of Greek works on monastic life only two major texts we can be sure would have been familiar to him, the *Historia monachorum in Aegypto*, translated by Rufinus of Aquileia,[125] and Athanasius's *The Life of Saint Antony*, translated by Evagrius of Antioch.[126] As Berthold Altaner observes, Augustine borrowed an incident from the life of John of Lycopolis for his "On the Care of the Dead," which is found only in the *Historia monachorum in Aegypto*, so we can be certain of his familiarity with this report of monastic life at least.[127] Finally, as Maria Doerfler reminds us, the development of monasticism in North Africa was still quite young at this stage. According to Augustine's own recollection, in the year 400 monasteries were still new additions to the landscape around Carthage.[128] Yet *The Work of Monks* perhaps had its most profound influence on that very monastic movement in its earliest phase of development, by steering the course of monastic legislation for the whole of medieval Europe and beyond.[129]

Instead of depending on commonplace defenses of the value of work for monastic life, Augustine's argumentative agenda in *The Work of Monks* is entirely exegetical.[130] I have already suggested that monastic rationalizations for manual labor attempted in practice to reconcile the teachings of Jesus, who seems to exhort his followers to a life of unconcern for material needs and their provision, and Paul, who counsels the Thessalonians that all should work for their own bread. We can read *The Work of Monks* as laying out with unparalleled amplitude and detail this very reconciliation and thereby supplying the Scripturally reasoned theoretical case for what the monks practiced. According to Barsella's helpful summary of the argument,

> First he demonstrated that manual work was Paul's precept set forth both in his epistles and by the example of his own life. Then he showed that the Gospel's passages the monks misinterpreted to cover their idleness were compatible with Paul's teachings. In this way, Augustine designed a self-contained system where the spiritual and the literal senses of the Epistles and the Gospel were harmonized and enlightened each other.[131]

The nonworking monks against whom Augustine addressed his critique had an exegesis of their own.

> They assert that when the Apostle says: "If any man will not work, neither let him eat," he does not refer to bodily labor at which farmers or artisans work. For, they maintain, St. Paul's attitude cannot be in contradiction to the Gospel where our Lord Himself says: "Therefore I say to you, do not be anxious for your life, what you shall eat; nor yet for your body, what you shall put on." . . They say: "Behold the passage where the Lord bids us to be free from care in regard to our food and clothing. How, then, can the Apostle, opposing the direction of the Lord, command us to be solicitous about what we are to eat and drink and wherewith we are to be clothed and thus burden us with the arts [*artibus*], the cares, and the labors [*laboribus*] of workmen?"[132]

The nonworking monks then imagine themselves as being faithful to both Jesus and Paul, by taking no thought for the morrow as Jesus commands and busying themselves instead with spiritual labors of prayer, recitation of psalms and hymn-singing, and mutual edification, activities that they regard as fulfilling the Pauline mandate.[133] Augustine wastes no time in reversing these significations. Arguing that Jesus frequently spoke in "parables and similitudes" while Paul never used figurative language but rather expressed himself "literally rather than figuratively, as is evident from almost all the statements in his Epistles," Augustine wonders whether it would make much more sense to interpret the (figurative) words of Christ as an exhortation to freedom from spiritual anxiety and those of Paul as a (literal) directive concerning bodily work rather than spiritual labor.[134] Further attacking his opponents for the selectivity of their reading of Paul, as if he had only written this one sentence on work, Augustine immediately turns to the context of Paul's command.[135] The surrounding verses prove that Paul was in fact entitled by his spiritual labor to receive recompense from the Christian community, but he declined to do so, thus pointing his reader toward his true view of the value of manual labor both by his words and by his deeds.[136] Augustine is confident that "the blessed Apostle Paul wished the servants of God to perform manual labor which would merit a great spiritual reward, and to do this without seeking food and clothing from anybody, but to procure these commodities for themselves by their own work."[137] If this is correct, then Augustine has to further demonstrate that the Gospel teachings do not conflict with Paul's teaching. He too then has a task of exegetical harmonization before him, but it will arrive at the opposite conclusion to that of the nonworking monks.

Conceding that all "servants of God" have the privilege of being supported by the Christian community to which they minister, Augustine underscores that this policy was "permitted but not ordered," which is the grounds on which Paul abstained from drawing his livelihood from the generosity of the community and instead worked with his hands.[138] The servant of God *may* derive her livelihood from the support of the faithful but does not *have* to do so, as Paul shows by his decision, together with Barnabas, to "not use their privilege because they judged it more feasible to direct those funds to the Church, in view of the weakness of the faithful in those regions where they preached."[139] This was a pragmatic decision, one they were free to undertake given the circumstances and motivated by a desire to remove any obstacle to the spread of the Gospel. In keeping with a broad and recurrent typically Pauline and paradoxical theme, Augustine reads the Apostle as having with respect to manual labor made himself a slave though he is free.[140] Though Paul does not have to work he does so anyway in order that he may more faithfully propagate the Gospel. In this as in other ways, Paul says he became weak that he might win the weak over to Christ, "suffering with" the community "to the extent that he was unwilling to accept what was due him by the Lord's direction lest he should seem to be putting a price on the Gospel and lest he should thus, by becoming an object of suspicion among the ignorant, hinder the progress of the word of God."[141]

Augustine then imagines a potential interlocutor asking what sort of work Paul must have done. For Augustine the question is immaterial. What is crucial is that Paul worked with his hands and supported himself from the wages earned by his labor.[142]

Augustine's answer though provides another clue to the way he thought about work. For here Augustine says he is confident that Paul "was neither a thief nor a robber, neither a charioteer nor a hunter, neither an actor nor a gambler, but that innocently and honorably he performed such labors as are suitable for human occupation, such as the work of carpenters, builders, shoemakers, farmers, and similar trades."[143] We will see in the next part of our discussion that Augustine's thoughts on work were innovative in part because he substantially enlarged the scope of human activities that could be deemed honorable and worthy of pursuit. Here he discounts a handful of jobs that are inherently disrespectable: criminal activities and the sordid business of acting and chariot-driving,[144] and he endorses farming and the humblest sorts of crafts. This is consistent with his general theory that no part of creation is inherently bad but becomes so by misuse. As we will see, Augustine applies this thinking to work as well, and here in *The Work of Monks* we have an anticipation of the point. Augustine condemns outright only very few occupations and by and large thinks that most work can be respectable if done well. "Respectability," in fact, he argues, "does not belittle what is scorned by those who desire to be called honorable but who do not wish to be so."[145] This is an important development in the moral assessment of work. Much labor that society scorns is in fact respectable, according to Augustine. Those who disdain menial trades are in his judgment mere posers when it comes to honor; the truly honorable dignify their work, even if it is of the kind that is generally despised.

For this reason Augustine confidently concludes that Paul would have had the same attitude: "The Apostle would not refuse to perform any rustic labor or to engage in any workman's craft."[146] Who, Augustine rhetorically asks, would malign Paul for the kind of work he chose to engage in? "If persons should suggest the Jews, their patriarchs tended flocks; if the Greeks whom we call pagans, they considered cobblers as quite respectable philosophers; if the Church of God, that just man, chosen to be an example of conjugal and perpetual virginity to whom the Virgin Mary who bore Christ was espoused, was a carpenter."[147] So regardless of religious horizon—Jewish, pagan, Christian—Augustine's point is that no major existing cultural tradition in late antiquity should find Paul's dedication to manual work objectionable. As we have seen, Augustine's confidence might be misplaced, particularly in the case of the pagan Greeks, but it is possible he has a specific instance in mind: Simon the Shoemaker, who was reputed to be a conversation partner with Socrates.[148] Little is known for certain about this personage (some question his very existence), but he is featured in Cynic philosophy.[149] Diogenes Laertius claims he was the first to write Socratic dialogues, which accurately recorded their conversations, though these have all been lost if indeed they existed in the first place.[150]

For our purposes, the most relevant point is that Simon came to be appreciated by at least a strand of Cynic philosophy for his refusal to accept the patronage of Pericles and thus, he feared, forfeit his ability to speak forthrightly (*parrhesia*) and his consequent decision to remain a cobbler. Simon was thus appreciated as the paradigmatic example of the self-sufficiency (*autarkeia*) prized by Cynics.[151] Speaking of autarkeia, John Sellars writes, "Simon is said to have exhibited this Cynic trait, reducing his material needs to a minimum and providing for those left by way of his shoemaking."[152] Interestingly, this is precisely the point on which Augustine praises Paul: Paul worked to support himself so as not to be beholden to anyone and so as not to compromise the integrity of the Gospel.[153] If Augustine is specifically thinking of Simon the Shoemaker as the cobbler who was also a respectable philosopher, then the parallel is surely deliberate and illuminating, as he recasts Paul as a Christian Simon who preferred humble work to compromise.[154]

In sum, Augustine is rather more expansive than any of his predecessors when it comes to what sort of work can be honorable. With characteristic pith he announces a principle that must be regarded as almost revolutionary: "Whatever work men perform without guilt and trickery is good."[155] Here the ethical criterion has shifted entirely from the type of work that merited honor to the manner in which work was done as the source of its honor or lack thereof. As Barsella expresses this key point, for Augustine, "no profession should be condemned in and of itself, for what matters is how it is performed. Only man, not an activity on its own merits, can be good or bad. In this way Augustine introduced a principle of subjective moral responsibility with respect to work."[156]

Augustine implicitly expands on this point in the next chapter. He asserts,

> For it is one thing to do manual work with a free mind, as a workman does if he be not dishonest, avaricious, or greedy for personal profit, but it is another matter to occupy one's mind with the pursuit of riches without expending bodily labor, as do business men, administrators, or overseers, for, in attending to their duty, they work with care, not with their hands, and hence they occupy their minds with the anxiety of possessing.[157]

For this reason we can agree with Barsella that Augustine in fact generally prefers manual labor: It is less apt to be misused for greedy personal gain.[158] The honest workman labors with a free mind (the Latin *animus* could just as easily, and perhaps preferably, be translated as "soul"), while the worker who does not use his hands has his mind burdened by "care" (again, a better translation would be "concern," as *cura* in Latin does not mean "care" in the sense of "feel fond toward" but in the sense of "have concern for," as in, "have no care for the morrow"). Once more, the distinction between how the work is done, with free or with occupied soul, is more important than what sort of work is done. If business and management are here slighted by Augustine, it is not because there is anything inherently wrong with these pursuits but because they are more likely to burden the worker's soul than to lighten it. Yet another reason to prefer manual labor according to Augustine is that it is compatible with prayer and recitation of psalms, such that he can ask, with some sarcasm, what it is that the nonworking monks imagine themselves to be freeing up their time for that they can't also do while working.[159]

The culmination of Augustine's argument consists in an elaborate *reductio ad absurdum*: If the nonworking monks truly wish to take Christ's teaching literally to be like the birds of the air, who neither sow nor reap nor gather into barns, then, he says, they should do so in all things. In a series of ever-increasingly accusatory questions, Augustine points out how inconsistent the nonworking monks are in their imitation of the birds. "Why do they take from the labors of others, hide away, and save what they may draw upon for daily use? Why, finally, do they grind or cook the grain? Birds do not act thus."[160] "Birds do not act thus" becomes a repeated refrain for Augustine's final diatribe. Birds don't make bread; birds don't make other birds serve them to meet their needs; bird's don't cook food at times of year when the harvest is otherwise unpalatable.[161] The final conclusion of the argument is a masterful (apparent) dilemma: "Those who, from a perverse interpretation of the Gospel, strive to discredit such clear precepts of the Apostle either should not take thought for the morrow like birds of the air or they should obey the Apostle as sons of God; in truth, they should do both because both are compatible."[162] So Augustine secures his principal exegetical goal, to harmonize the teachings of Jesus and of Paul, to demonstrate that in fact "it is possible to pass one's life in manual labor without acting contrary to the Gospel or to the similitude of the birds of the air."[163] The monk can and should work to supply his own needs without violating the spirit of the Sermon on the Mount, and if he truly wishes on the contrary to follow the most literal interpretation of the Sermon on the Mount, then he would find that he would fail absurdly.

The practical conclusion of *The Work of Monks* is underpinned by another of Jesus's famous dilemmas: "You cannot serve God and mammon."[164] The prohibition against being anxious for the needs of life does not proscribe effort expended in order to secure required goods, but it does proscribe devotion to mammon. This means that a hypothetical preacher of the Gospel, who might imagine herself serving God through her spiritual labor while serving mammon through her worldly labor, the latter presumably supporting the former, is bound to fail. Augustine contends on the basis of Matthew 6:24 "that this cannot be done." The truth of such a hypothetical case would be that one "who preaches the Gospel for his own needs is convicted of serving mammon, not God, even though God may make use of the preacher, in a way he does not know of, for the progress of others."[165] On this scenario, the preacher who is motivated by the satisfaction of need is vitiating the Gospel they imagine themselves serving. Whatever good they realize, Augustine claims, is due to God, who of course could use the preaching to good effect, but that would be despite, rather than because of, the excellence of the preacher, which is compromised by their misconduct. It is possible to be a monk and yet "serve mammon" if the monk's motivation is questionable.[166]

The reverse holds true though as well. It is possible to do manual labor and yet serve God. The counsel not to be anxious is not given "to forbid the procuring of what the monks need in order to live respectably, but so that they may not fix their attention on these commodities in preaching the Gospel, and with them in mind, do whatever they are commanded."[167] The monks are exhorted not to total indifference and passivity toward things that satisfy needs but to non-attachment to those things, all of which have God as their ultimate source and provider in any event. The dutiful monk declares therefore,

> It is by His gift that we are able to do what we do, and ... while we live on this earth, we live by His bounty, since He has made our existence possible. For that reason, we are not anxious about the necessities of life, because, when we can perform these labors, He feeds and clothes us as men in general are fed and clothed. When,

however, we are not able to work, then He feeds and clothes us just as the birds are fed and the lilies clothed, since we are of more value than they.[168]

The things the monks need to sustain their own lives cannot be the motivation for why they work, nor can they attribute the attaining of those needful things to their own effort. Again it is a matter of the way in which work is conducted that is most important, or what Augustine here calls the "intention for which something is done." This intention is symbolized earlier in the Sermon on the Mount by the "eye," which Jesus says is the lamp of the body, and he again proposes a dilemma: "If thy eye be sound, thy whole body will be full of light. But if thy eye be evil, thy whole body will be full of darkness," a pronouncement that Augustine glosses as meaning that our deeds are "such as the intention which prompted them has been,"[169] that is, the goodness or badness of an act proceeds largely from its subjective motivation. As we will see in due course, this principle is the bedrock of Augustine's broader philosophical and theological engagement with work, which we turn now to explain more fully.

At the time that he wrote *The Work of Monks*, Augustine had already meditated deeply on the mystery of creation, and work was a part of that study. As Michael Fiedrowicz points out, as early as 388 or 389 Augustine had already written his first commentary on Genesis and then produced a second, unfinished one in 393–395. The last three books of the storied *Confessions* are a commentary on Genesis as well, and the final *Literal Commentary on Genesis* was written over the course of about fifteen years from 401 to 416,[170] so *The Work of Monks* was written with the relationship of work to creation already well established in Augustine's mind and bound to occupy his attention for some years to come. As Fiedrowicz notes, Augustine's interest in creation was existential in emphasis. For Augustine, a fuller appreciation of the meaning of creation as he interpreted it entailed the aim of harmonization with creation and thus with the purposes of the creator. Rebuking the aspirations of the classical world, Augustine instead saw that "the true greatness of human beings does not consist in the supposed autonomy of an individual who makes himself the ultimate norm" but rather that "creation by its very nature involved relations" both with other creatures and with God.[171]

This hermeneutic principle applies equally to the specific question of work as it was an element of creation. Inasmuch as the Genesis account is also an "origin story" of the sort we have seen told by Plato, it too serves a similar purpose for Augustine's thinking on work. The origin of humankind is for him just as revelatory of the nature of work as it is for many other classical writers whose views they present partially in the frame of an origin story about humanity and the human arts and crafts.[172] Augustine does not depart from the consensus position of the early church that work was intended to be part of human life, even in its created perfection. Addressing the question of work in paradise, Augustine begins his treatment of this subject in *The Literal Meaning of Genesis* with characteristic rhetorical flourish and power. Taking note of the verse from Genesis 2 that says God placed the man he had made in the garden "for working and guarding," Augustine inquires after what could be meant by "working": "The Lord, surely, did not wish the first man to work at agriculture, did he? Is it not simply incredible that he should have condemned him to hard labor before sin?"[173]

His reply to his own sardonic question is intriguing, for Augustine does not straightforwardly introduce here the datum that might be most natural to expect, namely, that the difficulty of labor was a product of sin and fallenness and was not therefore, by implication, part of the experience of labor before the Fall. Instead, he turns attention to the present rewards and joys of agricultural labor, arguing from thence backward as it were to the conclusion that since agricultural work provides many joys now, then a fortiori they must have been even more impressive in the prelapsarian condition. Was Adam then condemned to hard labor? Augustine admits,

> Certainly we would judge it to be so had we never seen how some people till the fields with such pleasure, such uplift of spirit, that it is a severe punishment for them to be called away from that to anything else. So then whatever delights there are to be found in agriculture, they were of course far and away more complete at that time when neither earth nor sky was putting any difficulty in the way.[174]

Again the form of the argument is remarkable, for it would be most expedient (and perhaps more convincing) one might imagine to raise the doctrinal point that work itself was not a result of the commission of sin but only its difficulty and use that theological point as the basis for arguing that Adam was not in fact sentenced to hard labor in his Edenic condition. Yet Augustine rests on something like empirical observation of the current reality and expatiates upon the beauties of farming with lofty praise:

> What greater or more wonderful spectacle can there be, after all, or when is human reason more able after a fashion to converse with "The Nature of Things," than when after seeds have been sown, cuttings potted, shrubs planted out, graftings made, each root and seed is questioned, so to say, on what its inner vital force can or cannot do, what helps and what hinders it, what is the range of the inner, invisible power of its own numerical formula, what that of the care bestowed on it from outside?[175]

As we have seen, farming has always been praised by Western thinkers, and Augustine is effusive;[176] he emphasizes here the ability of agricultural work to promote the speculative appreciation of nature. This is particularly evident in his reference to "The Nature of Things," which the translator wisely notes is almost certainly intended to be an allusion to the Epicurean poem of Lucretius bearing the same name. Augustine here is subtly jabbing at some of his pagan opponents, promoting the providential character of the Christian God over the random machinations of Epicurean cosmology. Agriculture thus bespeaks not just nature but nature as created by a loving divine father, for inspection of seeds, shrubs, cuttings, and roots allows the farmer to perceive that "*neither the one who plants is anything nor the one who waters, but the one who gives the growth, God*, because the work and skill applied from the outside is applied by one who also was nonetheless created and is being governed and directed invisibly by God."[177]

The quote from 1 Corinthians introduces Augustine's other primary theme when it comes to the question of work in its perfect created form. Given the somewhat exaggerated depiction of the enticements of agricultural work, which furnish uplift of spirit, and the extrapolation that such enticements would have been all the more irresistible in Eden itself, Augustine concludes that for Adam, "there was no stress of wearisome toil but pure exhilaration of spirit, when things which God had created flourished in more luxuriant abundance with the help of human work."[178] Augustine's account of Edenic labor actually couples human effort with divine provision, such that the result of the conjoining would exceed in scope the capacity of either alone. Human agency actually enhances divine creation, and the praise that would redound to God would be likewise expanded, when work was done by means of human reason only "as much as would satisfy its willing spirit, not as much as it would be reluctantly forced to do by the wants of the body."[179]

Augustine's vision of the original state of humanity acknowledges that bodily needs would have to be met, but he denies that these would be the motivation for work; rather the will would be in command, and work would be pursued not to supply what was wanting but for the joy of it. Augustine affirms more than once in *The Literal Meaning of Genesis*, in an ongoing but oblique critique of the classical ideal, that even the intellectual life of the human being is benefited by work in an ideal condition: "The man of course was put in Paradise in order to work this same paradise," he asserts, "by cultivating it in a way that was not painfully laborious but simply delightful, furnishing the sensible and observant mind with the most important reminders and useful advice."[180] In the summary words of Carol Harrison, "here then is a portrait of man at his most noble, freely practising an art which affords him pleasure and delight, exercises the body, engages with nature and lifts the mind to spiritual thoughts. It is the ideal portrait of man at work, a work undertaken not through obligation or necessity but freely, and with spiritual profit."[181]

That God is the one who gives growth remains true, for divine providence is in operation across the entirety of the universe itself, awaiting human beings' cooperative cultivation. In continuing this argument Augustine deploys a surprising image: "From this the eye of the mind can now be raised up to the universe itself as if it were all some huge tree, and in this too will be discovered the same twin functioning of providence, partly through natural, partly through voluntary activity."[182] The universe as a whole, then, can be likened to a natural organism, a tree, that thrives partly because within all things "is working the hidden management of God, by which he also gives growth to trees and herbs" and partly because human beings are at work in God's creation, the result of which is that "signs are given, taught and learned, fields cultivated, communities administered, arts and skills practiced, and whatever else is done."[183] Human accomplishments then contribute to and expand upon the created order, which was ordained for the sake of justice and when neglected falls into ruin. Again using the metaphor of a tree, Augustine argues that "agriculture acts from the outside to ensure the effectiveness of what nature is busy with on the inside," such that human effort complements and promotes the natural tendency toward flourishing rightly instituted and ordered by God. Therefore it can in no way be scandalous to "believe that the man was set up in Paradise to work at agriculture, not in servile toil, but with genuine pleasure and uplift of spirit," a calling ennobled by its participation in the very flowering of creation.

As Harrison further observes, the choice of gardening as the occupation to illustrate noble deployment of effort implies a critique of the classical ideal. The Romans prized the notion of *otium*, leisured withdrawal from worldly concerns, but this was normally undertaken for its value in contributing to the philosophical or contemplative life. That Augustine makes of gardening the characteristic activity of an ideal existence that otherwise resembles the cultured ideal of otium suggests "an implicit criticism of the classical ideal, or at least a desire to broaden it out to include in man's pre-fallen condition other aspects of life worthy to be counted as free, leisure work."[184] As Harrison rightly argues, this widened scope of what might be counted as potentially included in a worthwhile human life also seems to include the practice of diverse arts, governance of human families and communities, and education.[185] Given the reality of the Fall, of course, these tasks become matters of drudgery, and tasks like governance and education, like agriculture, become matters of unavoidable necessity rather than free exuberance.[186] As noted above, though, Augustine is content to base some of his reasoning on the blessings and benefits of work even as it exists in the current fallen state of affairs. For him, even within the reality of fallen humanity, the ideal sort of work is not entirely unattainable, even for those who pursued occupations widely regarded in ancient and early medieval societies as menial or undignified.

> The occupations pursued by the "silent majority" were recognized and accepted as useful and good by Augustine so long as they were conducted with integrity and honesty. He tends to favour manual work for precisely this reason: it was much less likely to present a man with the dilemmas and temptations which those engaged in trade and business frequently had to face, and kept his mind free from worldly preoccupations in order to dwell on more spiritual matters.[187]

Augustine's positive assessment of honest work is also supported by a lengthy and effusive discourse in praise of the diversity and usefulness of the plurality and scope of human productive activities in *The City of God*. This passage from Augustine's mammoth and influential work occurs in the context of his grateful meditation on the many blessings afforded by God to human beings *despite* their fallen condition and is worth quoting at length:

> For besides the arts [*artes*] of living rightly and at last attaining immortal happiness—which are called virtues, and are given only by the grace of God that is in Christ to the sons of the promise and of the kingdom—has not human ingenuity [*humano ingenio*] discovered and exploited all our numerous and important techniques [*artes*], some of which supply our needs, while others are for mere pleasure? And is not this mental, this rational drive, even when it seeks satisfaction in things superfluous, nay more, in things dangerous and suicidal, a witness to the excellence of its natural endowment, thanks to which it had the ability, whether to discover, to be taught, or to exploit these arts?
>
> What marvellous, stupendous results has human industry [*industria humana*] achieved in the production of clothing and buildings! What progress in agriculture and in navigation! What imagination and elaboration it has

employed in producing all kinds of vases, and also in the varieties of statues and paintings! How marvellous, in theatres, to those who sit as spectators, how incredible to those who merely hear the report, are the compositions and performances contrived by men! What great inventions for capturing, killing and taming irrational animals! Against even human beings all the many kinds of poison, weapons, engines of war! And how many drugs and remedies it has discovered to preserve and restore men's health! How many seasonings and appetizers it has found to increase the pleasure of eating! What a number, what variety of signs for conveying thought and persuading men, among which words and letters are most important! What ornaments of speech to delight the mind, what abundance of all kinds of poetry! What musical instruments, what modes of song have been devised to soothe the ears! What skill in measuring and reckoning! With what acuteness have the courses and laws of the heavenly bodies been grasped! With what enormous knowledge of worldly things have men filled their minds! Who could describe this, especially if we wished not to gather everything in one pile, but to dwell on each several topic?

Finally, who could estimate the great talent of philosophers and heretics displayed in defending errors and untruth? For we are speaking now about the natural capacity of the human mind with which this mortal life is endowed, not about the faith and way of truth by which that immortal life is obtained.[188]

Notice first that Augustine calls it an "art" (*ars*) to live rightly and thereby secure salvation via the infused grace of God that alone bestows virtue and that he uses the same term to name the arts (here translated as "techniques") discovered by human ingenuity to supply need or to furnish pleasure to human life. Even when this skill is directed toward ends that are superfluous or even dangerous, the mundane arts belong to the same genus as the art of living in accord with supernaturally endowed virtue, and they are thus testimony to human ingenuity. Augustine's subsequent catalogue—progressing from mundane productive arts like those that provide the basic necessities of clothing and shelter through agriculture and navigation to the fine arts—as some commentators have noticed, seems to be organized according to an implicit hierarchy, which culminates in language, music, and astronomy, some of the most spiritual of the disciplines.[189] The final entry is devoted to philosophy, which remains admirable for the "talent" it involves, again even when directed toward the blameworthy end of defending falsehood. The final caveat Augustine gives is worth attending to, for it clarifies the spirit of this passage against a misunderstanding that has arisen. Augustine qualifies his praise by reminding his reader that "we are speaking now about the natural capacity of the human mind with which this mortal life is endowed" and "not about the faith and the way of truth by which that immortal life is obtained." This conclusion naturally pairs with Augustine's opening remark, which expressly sets aside the art of living rightly and turns to a consideration of the arts that are not essentially oriented toward the good. In this respect Augustine's survey is wholly consistent with the classical tradition, but the bookends assure us that the horizon is a thoroughly Christian one, in which the diverse human arts have a place, though of course not the ultimate place.

This framing is also entirely consistent with the context of this passage, which falls very near the end of the work as a whole. The heading for chapter XXIV reads "Of the good things with which the Creator has filled even this condemned life."[190] This is worth bearing in mind, for this section of the text follows after two chapters wherein Augustine has already rehearsed at length "the miseries and evils to which the human race is subject as a result of the first sin, and from which no one is freed except through the grace of Christ" (chapter XXII)[191] and "the troubles which (in addition to the evils common to the good and the bad) belong especially to the distress of the righteous" (chapter XXIII).[192] It should be clear, then, that Augustine has already chronicled the many ills of human existence, and he now turns his attention to underscoring the blessings and benefits of human life that remain estimable and worthy of attention even amid the fallen condition of humanity and the world as a whole. Augustine is in the above long passage focusing on the available goods discernible within the practice of the arts, even when those practices can be undertaken for less than salutary ends. He has already been more than clear about the ills of human life, and now he is accentuating the positive: He writes,

> Now I plan to speak of the good gifts of God which he has conferred, or still is conferring, even on our corrupted and condemned nature. For in condemning he did not take away from that nature everything which he had given, otherwise it would not exist at all. Nor did he release it from his power, even when he subjected it to the devil as a punishment—for not even the devil himself is banished from his rule.[193]

Among these gifts Augustine addresses not only the crafts but also the joy of fecundity and family life,[194] the beauty of nature,[195] and the elegance and functionality of the human body.[196] Augustine therefore is closing on a high note so to speak in anticipation of the few remaining chapters of *The City of God*, which defend the most hope-imparting and forward-looking Christian doctrines: the resurrection of the body and the beatific vision.[197]

The reason this is important to bring up is that this passage in praise of the human arts has lately been misrepresented as a piece of irony. Elspeth Whitney, for one, not only rightly notes that this passage "remained a touchstone for attitudes about crafts through the thirteenth century"[198] but also claims that "the mood of this account of the arts is one of ambivalence and paradox."[199] She acknowledges that Augustine is treating the arts and sciences in a Christian context, but she places more weight on its classical heritage, which she traces to Cicero's praise of crafts in Book II of his *De natura deorum*.[200] Whitney asserts that the Roman Stoic's spokesman Balbus represents Cicero's own view that "technological arts are a product of human reason well and properly used," making the *De natura deorum* "one of the most positive statements on technology in classical literature."[201] Yet Cicero's purpose in praising crafts is quite different from Augustine's. The culmination of Balbus's encomium is: "I think that my exposition of these matters has been sufficient to prove how widely man's nature surpasses all other living creatures; and this should make it clear that neither such a confirmation and arrangement of the members nor such power of mind and intellect can possibly have been created by chance."[202] This is Balbus's conclusion because he is trying to counter the arguments of the Epicureans, who espouse the view that the gods are uninterested in human life and make no provision for it.[203] For Augustine, that God is providentially invested in human affairs is a given, and his description of the value and beauty of human craftsmanship serves the purpose of assuring his reader of the reality and pervasiveness of that providential concern even in a fallen world. For this reason Kevin Greene's observation on the parallelism between this passage from *The City of God* and from Cicero's *De natura deorum* is quite salient. Following Maurice Testard, Greene argues further that "similar parallels might be found between the evils Augustine has enumerated in Chapter 22 above, and those described by Cicero's sceptic in the last book of his work. Characteristically, Cicero gives the last word to his sceptic, while Augustine reverses the order."[204] This reversal is not at all unimportant but rather establishes even further the priority that Augustine is currently laying on the value of crafts and his distance from Cicero.[205]

Whitney's contention that Augustine "finds technology to be an expression of the 'natural genius' of man but *at the same time*, to be 'superfluous, perilous and pernicious'"[206] cannot be sustained. For Augustine precisely does not claim that technology is superfluous and dangerous "*at the same time*" as it is an expression of the natural genius of humanity but rather that *even* when its application is superfluous and dangerous it *nevertheless* remains an expression of the natural genius of humanity. Recall: "And is not this mental, this rational drive, even when it seeks satisfaction in things superfluous, nay more, in things dangerous and suicidal, a witness to the excellence of its natural endowment, thanks to which it had the ability, whether to discover, to be taught, or to exploit these arts?"[207] Nothing in the quoted passage suggests that Augustine views technological activity as always and necessarily superfluous and dangerous but only that it sometimes can be, and when it is, it is still a testament to human ingenuity if not to human wisdom.

Whitney argues further,

> Although some commentators have taken both the introduction and catalogue of arts at face value as straightforward praise of the ingenuity and power of the human intellect, in fact Augustine's tone is heavily ironic. His subject is the condition of our mortal life, which, he carefully points out, is divorced from faith, truth and eternal life, and which he describes elsewhere in the same chapter as depraved and condemned to sin. His list of the arts, it should be noted, includes heresy, theatrical spectacles, traps, poisons, weapons and war machines.[208]

How to respond to this claim should be clear from what has been said so far. Augustine's subject is indeed this mortal life, but his purpose is to elucidate the signs of divine grace within that life, obscured as they may be, even under the auspices of questionable aims and pursuits. The truly objectionable elements of human existence have already been extensively treated by him in the previous two chapters, though it could be admitted that Augustine rarely misses a chance to point out that human affairs are "depraved and condemned to sin." Augustine does not include these items out of a sense of irony (or at least not one more ironic than what is customary for him), nor is his praise of crafts insincere.[209]

That Augustine is in a way customarily ironic should be understood as a function of his bedrock metaphysical outlook, which some commentators do not seem to grasp. For Augustine, an essential part of his rejection of the Manichean system of belief of which he was a provisional member for some years is his eventual affirmation of the fundamental goodness of all existing things. Rejecting Manichean dualism meant the need to explain the origin and meaning of evil, if it were not to be understood as a positively existing principle in the universe. In the philosophically densest part of his autobiographical narration of his own conversion in Book VII of his storied *Confessions*, Augustine put the problem to himself this way: "Though I said and firmly held that the Lord God was incorruptible and unalterable and in no way changeable, the true God who made not only our souls but our bodies also, and not only our souls and bodies but all things whatsoever, as yet I did not see, clear and unravelled, what was the cause of evil."[210] The acknowledgment even at this stage of some perplexity in Augustine's young mind that God is the creator not only of the human soul but also of the human body already constitutes a major step forward in his intellectual and spiritual itinerary. According to the Manichean system to which he had hitherto been committed (if only half-heartedly and with eventually greatly diminished enthusiasm) for nearly a decade, the source of evil was to be located in dense matter, and the cause of specifically human evildoing was the body. Yet now Augustine has at least come far enough along the path to admit that the body is not an alien, hostile entity but created by the same supreme God who made the soul.

Augustine's signal breakthrough was, significantly for our purposes, precipitated by his full recognition of the consequences of the orthodox Christian doctrine of creation. That all things were created by the God who is nothing less than "Goodness itself"[211] implies that all of creation is itself good. Considering the whole range of created entities ranked by varying degrees of goodness with God as the supreme Goodness itself at their summit, Augustine remembers of this stage in his journey that "I said 'Here is God, and here is what God has created; and God is good, mightily and incomparably better than all these; but of His goodness He created them good ... Where then is evil, and what is its source, and how has it crept into the creation?'"[212] The answer to this metaphysical dilemma revolutionized Augustine's personal spirituality and exercised staggering influence on Western philosophy and theology for centuries to come.

Considering the conspectus of creation, Augustine came to see that entities enjoyed varying degrees of goodness to the exact degree that they enjoyed varying degrees of being: "Then I thought upon those other things that are less than You, and I saw that they neither absolutely are nor yet totally are not: they are, in as much as they are from You: they are not, in as much as they are not what You are."[213] All things that God has created are less good than God himself, to varying degrees, according to the share of potential excellences their natures make possible, from the highest spiritual entities like angels down to the lowest material, nonliving things. Considered as such, nothing is inherently metaphysically evil because it has been created for the sake of some good, no matter how small, by the God who is Goodness itself.

For this reason, Augustine recalls,

It became clear to me that corruptible things are good. If they were supremely good they could not be corrupted, but also if they were not good at all they could not be corrupted: if they were supremely good they would be incorruptible, if they were in no way good there would be nothing in them that might corrupt. For corruption damages; and unless it diminished goodness, it would not damage. Thus either corruption does no damage, which is impossible or—and this is the certain proof of it—all things that are corrupted are deprived of some goodness. But if they were deprived of all goodness, they would be totally without being.[214]

Only God is incapable of being corrupted or damaged by way of harming some good that belongs to God. All other beings, having been created by God, are good to a relative degree and are therefore capable of being corrupted or having their characteristic good damaged. When that takes place, the being in question suffers some loss of a good that it should otherwise possess; this is what it means to be corrupted on Augustine's schema. But something that had lost all available goods, something that had been utterly corrupted, would not possess any being at all, that is, it would not exist. So all things, insofar as they exist, are also to that same extent good or possessed of some—however minimal—degree of goodness that reflects—however imperfectly— the consummate goodness of their divine creator. Thus was Augustine able to famously and influentially claim that "to You, then, evil utterly is not—and not only to You, but to Your whole creation likewise, evil is not,"[215] that is to say, evil is nonexistence. Evil is "not a substance";[216] it is *no thing* at all; it is nothing.

The upshot of this incredibly important metaphysical point is that all things then are touched by a fundamental and decisive ambivalence, in the precise sense of that term. Nothing that is can be wholly evil, but everything that is, is partially so. Nothing is as it should be, though all things that are, are at least somewhat good. The crucial ethical corollary then to this metaphysical doctrine is that nothing created is inherently bad, but everything created can be turned to a bad purpose. Metaphysically speaking, all things are good insofar as they are at all, such that ethically speaking, only the misuse or improper love of things makes them bad for the one who so misuses them or loves them improperly. As Augustine puts it in one of his dialogues,

> The very same things are used in different ways by different people; some use them badly and others use them well ... one who uses these things rightly shows that they are good, although not good for himself. For those things do not make the one who uses them good or better; in fact, they become good by being put to good use ... Since this is the case, you must realize that we should not find fault with silver and gold because of the greedy, or food because of gluttons, or wine because of drunkards, or womanly beauty because of fornicators and adulterers, and so on, especially since you know that fire can be used to heal and bread to poison.[217]

That fire can be used to heal and bread to poison is not an incidental observation in Augustine's work; it is a fundamental principle of his metaphysics and ethics, and it is this principle that underlies what Whitney and van den Hoven mistakenly read as his irony when it comes to his praise of crafts, or again, which they regard as special, local, irony rather than a function of Augustine's entire philosophical and theological outlook. Bread and fire are in themselves unobjectionable; it's their misuse that causes harm and constitutes sin, not anything about themselves per se. So of course, all human crafts and activities are capable of misuse—the same ingenuity that devises medicine is also adept at poison; the same talent for engineering buildings can craft machines of war for the destruction of the same. There is nothing especially ironic about Augustine's ambivalence (again in the strict sense of the term) in regard to human craftsmanship or nothing more ironic than his ambivalence about the goodness of all created things, all of which are subject to misuse and therefore corruption and corrupting influence. All created things are subject to a simultaneous, twofold form of appraisal, according to which their intended created goodness must be praised, while their corruption or degree of imperfection must be accurately assessed and condemned. The two go hand in hand: "If we condemn something," Augustine explains, "it is only because of some flaw that it has. But we cannot condemn a flaw in something without thereby praising the nature in which the flaw is present."[218] It is according to this logic that Augustine also assesses the many human crafts that he catalogues in *The City of God*.

Nowhere is this logic more vividly illustrated in Augustine's writings than in the celebrated incident of the youthful pear tree theft in the *Confessions*, which provides the last element necessary for an appreciation of some of the fundamental Augustinian commitments that underpin his philosophy of work. The key to understanding the difference between right and wrong use of created things, and therefore between righteousness and sin, is love. After recounting the famous purloining of the pears during his wayward youth, Augustine steps back from this recollection and considers its meaning in light of his mature understanding of sin. He muses,

> There is an appeal to the eye in beautiful things, in gold and silver and all such; the sense of touch has its own powerful pleasures; and the other senses find qualities in things united to them. Worldly success has its glory, and the power to command and to overcome; and from this springs the thirst for revenge. But in our quest of all these things, we must not depart from You, or deviate from Your law. This life we live here below has its own attractiveness, grounded in the measure of beauty it has and its harmony with the beauty of all lesser things. The bond of human friendship is admirable, holding many souls as one. Yet in the enjoyment of all such things we commit sin if through immoderate inclination to them—for though they are good, they are of the lowest order of good—things higher and better are forgotten, even You, O Lord our God, and Your Truth and Your Law. These lower things have their delights but not such as my God has, for He made them all.[219]

Again it is possible to discern in this brief summary a loose hierarchy, beginning with the objects appropriate to the bodily senses, proceeding to worldly glory and friendship, culminating in divine truth, divine law, and the divine nature itself. Much as in the passage in praise of crafts from *The City of God*, occasional reminders of the potential hazards occasioned by these goods are sprinkled in: Friendship unites souls but can be an opportunity for sin (as it was for Augustine himself as he recollects his adolescence, and indeed friendship with unworthy peers is part of the setting for his theft of the pears recounted in this very section) while earthly power can be a source of the lust for revenge. Yet here we have Augustine's first mention of what he thinks is the true source of sin, in and among all created goods: immoderate inclination. It is because of love gone wrong, a literal dis-order in our affections, that we sin, not because of any given created thing per se.

> Now when we ask why this or that particular evil act was done, it is normal to assume that it could not have been done save through the desire of gaining or the fear of losing some one of these lower goods. For they have their own charm and their own beauty, though compared with the higher values of heaven they are poor and mean enough. Such a man has committed a murder. Why? He wanted the other man's wife or his property; or he had chosen robbery as a means of livelihood; or he feared to lose this or that through his victim's act; or he had been wronged and was aflame for vengeance.[220]

For Augustine sin is always motivated by a preference for lower things over higher things: The man who spends time at the bar instead of at home with his family loves alcohol more than his wife and children; the man who robs another loves money more than his fellow human being; the traitor loves his own private gain over comradeship. In all such instances, human beings are perversely seeking genuine goods, for, like Plato, Augustine thinks we all genuinely want good things, but he thinks we go astray when we prefer lesser goods to higher ones like God and God's divine law and will. It is that law and will that has fixed the order of things, ordaining that money is to be valued less than friendship, which is to be valued in turn less than God's own self. So every sinner is misguidedly seeking the ultimate good in the panoply of lesser, relative goods that creation lavishly affords but only according to an unalterable ranking of highest being and goodness to lowest.

Augustine concludes,

> Thus the soul is guilty of fornication, when she turns from You and seeks from any other source what she will find pure and without taint unless she returns to You. Thus even those who go from You and stand up against You are still perversely imitating You. But by the mere fact of their imitation, they declare that You are the creator of all that is, and that there is nowhere for them to go where You are not.[221]

It is with these core principles of Augustinian thought that we should interpret a final passage that both Arbesmann and Harrison seize upon as illustrative of Augustine's considered verdict on the value of work.[222] In "The Excellence of Widowhood," Augustine writes of the spiritual disciplines that are pursued by consecrated widows: almsgiving, fasting and keeping vigils, meditation on the Scriptures; all these he claims

> that seem laborious, are changed into spiritual pleasures. The labors of those who love are never tiresome, but they are even a source of pleasure as in the case of hunters, fowlers, fisherman [sic], grape harvesters, bankers, and persons who amuse themselves at some game. What matters is that the work be enjoyed.

There is either no weariness in work that is loved, or the weariness itself is loved. If pleasure is found in such activities as capturing a wild animal, filling a cup or purse, or throwing a ball, think of the shame and grief we ought to feel if we do not find pleasure in the exercises for attaining God.[223]

Here is perhaps the clearest articulation Augustine could give of his view that work, like all things, is motivated by and gets its dignity from love. Love makes even difficult labor a spiritual pleasure. Even in the mundane cases he cites of the hunter, the fowler, the fisherman, the farmer, and, most controversially, the banker, "What matters is that the work be enjoyed." Where this love is present, either work is not wearying or the weariness consequent upon work is itself loved, caught up in the attitude of the worker toward her task. As Harrison puts it, "this is a reminder that, for Augustine, it is in love, above all, that God's redemptive grace makes itself felt and makes possible the free action of man's fallen will, even in contexts which might otherwise be regarded as necessitated by the Fall."[224]

So, not only did Augustine provide the most comprehensive exegetical defense of the obligation to work, but he also perhaps could be argued to have at least tacitly given the most comprehensive theoretical articulation of the place work should have in the Christian life. While he was, as we have seen, not familiar with the vast bulk of monastic literature that has come down to our moment in Western civilization, he nevertheless captured with conceptual clarity a point that was made above about monastic labor, namely, that it was to be practiced in a manner helpful for, but always subordinate to, the main goal of sanctification. To use Augustinian terminology, work should be loved just to the degree that it is worthy of love. It is not ultimate to be sure, but like all created things, it shares in a degree of goodness that ought not to be spurned or misused by devoting more dedication to it than it merits. Augustine affirms that there are few careers that are inherently vicious and instead prosecutes the case, consistent with his overall metaphysical and ethical teaching, that the value of *work* comes down to the rightly ordered loves of the *worker*. It is not the job that makes one bad or good, but a good person uses and loves the job well.

4

The Late Medieval Period

Beginning around the twelfth century Europe underwent an unprecedented level of urbanization and economic growth. Heretofore we have seen, as Ovitt helpfully reminds us, that work in the medieval period has been considered as an important but subordinate element of the spiritual life, which is of course the highest priority for a professed monastic in particular but for Christian societies at large. "That work should be seen primarily as a means of creating wealth, or of altering the material world to serve human needs, or as an outlet for human creativity … simply was not considered."[1] These candidates for what work might mean to human beings would have to wait for a later stage in history, one that Ovitt suggests begins in the twelfth century. It was during this period that agriculture flourished and there was explosive growth in the use of water- and wind-harnessing technologies, which carried the benefit of maximizing energy efficiency while relieving laborers of their livelihoods and thereby reorganizing a variety of work forces.[2] The extension of regular trade routes both within the continent and to the Middle East precipitated further innovations in banking and commerce, including official minting of coinage and the invention of letters of credit.[3] Such developments in the financial sphere enabled for the first time the paying of money to settle obligations that previously had been matters of commodity exchange, a transition that Ovitt defensibly identifies as "a stage in the separation of the worker from the products of his or her work," a significant disruption to "traditional forms of social interaction."[4]

At the same time, the church was solidifying its position and defining its role with respect to secular authorities (with which it was in constant conflict). There was also an outburst of reform among monastic communities and the founding of new orders like the Cistercians and Carthusians, each of whom ended up giving very different answers to the questions of work and wealth but which were alike in that their "charters and practice specifically addressed the issues of labor and the wealth it created."[5] That being said, Brian Stock's counsel on this point is important to keep in mind: During this era of considerable development and upheaval, while the nature of activity and contemplation was a frequent topic of discussion, outside theological and monastic circles the relationship of work and leisure as a whole is still not yet thematically taken up.[6] We will consider the destiny of the Augustinian inheritance as it found expression in Bernard of Clairvaux's account of the complementarity of the active and contemplative lives and Theophilus Presbyter's *The Various Arts*.

Bernard of Clairvaux and the Cistercians

Founded in 1098 as a reform effort, the example of the Cistercians is frequently held up as a case study in the collision of monastic ideals and new economic realities. Specifically motivated by a desire to repudiate the wealth and worldliness of the Cluniac monasteries, founder Robert of Molesme (soon to be outshone by Bernard, who came first to the original community at Cîteaux but was soon dispatched to their daughter house—Clairvaux) insisted that the communities be founded away from population centers and eschew sources of income like tenancies, bequests, and fees for the use of mills so the monks could devote themselves to pure adherence to the Rule of St. Benedict. Thus did the Cistercians acquire notoriety for their effectiveness at clearing previously inarable land, draining swamps, and improving wilderness.[7] Yet the Cistercians discovered that the old ideal of humble self-sustenance was not achievable. Not every monk could say the divine office and work with sufficient energy to realize the goal of self-sufficiency. At Cluny, the monks solved this problem by employing peasant laborers, who had no real connection to the monastery other than as paid employees. The Cistercians instead proposed the creation of a "lay brotherhood," a sort of second-tier group of men that took the same vows as the monks but did the work needed for the community's well-being, freeing the full members to say the daily office. As Ovitt documents, this process simply continued apace, with further and further practical distance being opened up between the original Benedictine ideal that Robert of Molesme sought to restore and the actual daily life of the late twelfth-century Cistercian monk, who by this time did not work at all but found his monastery not merely self-sufficient but, indeed, rich, despite the original intent of the order.[8]

This might be called the now "standard" view of the history of the Cistercians' engagement with work. We should complement it briefly by examining the Cistercians' own advocacy of work as an element of the spiritual life, for this will shed light on the ideal to which they at least aspired.[9] It is advisable I think to consider the Cistercians' story, because it gives expression to a late ambition to preserve and carry forward the early monastic legacy on labor, one that puts into practice the Augustinian tradition, which found itself being challenged by the Thomistic inheritance from Aristotle as well as by changing economic, political, and ecclesiastical realities.

Christopher J. Holdsworth provides a valuable examination of the ideals to which the early Cistercian reformers aspired, concluding that with some unanimity "they read the rule [of Benedict] to mean that manual work was a proper activity for a monk and that a monastery should attempt to live by the fruit of its own labour."[10] Citing the standard narrative according to which the Cistercians developed (though did not invent) lay brotherhood with unprecedented success and thereby advanced economically well beyond their original ambitions, Holdsworth poses the more interesting question of what effect work had on Cistercian spirituality.[11] The picture he paints is remarkably consistent with the logic of the early Desert Fathers and Mothers. Manual labor for the Cistercians followed naturally upon the embrace of poverty, since they had given up their worldly goods to enter monastic life and now needed to supply their own needs so as to be free for whatever Christ, who had given up all for them, might call them to do. Like their predecessors they invoked the usefulness of manual labor for the supplying of alms for others in need. Again with remarkable consistency with the tradition they argued that prayer and meditation could be performed while occupied with mundane tasks.

Of particular note, and perhaps particularly Cistercian, is the emphasis on what Holdsworth calls "the alternance of work and contemplation, as a kind of rhythm which would enable the soul to come closer to God."[12] Citing both Bernard himself and Gilbert of Hoyland, who continued the former's sermon series on the Song of Songs, Holdsworth points out their use of the term "vicissitudo" for this characteristic rhythm, which Gilbert calls "blessed" and also applies to the dynamic of love between the soul and God that itself forms the heart of the Song.[13] Though he does not use the same terminology, Stock too seems to pick up on the alternation or, as he puts it, "dialectical movement, discernible in Bernard's style as well as in his thought" that shuttles between related pairs in Bernard's writings, the most significant of which for our purposes is between action and contemplation.[14] For Bernard, the life of the monk, the most complete spiritual life, alternates between these two, holding them together without conflation.[15] As Matthew the Precentor of Rievaulx wrote to a friend with regard to Cistercian practices, and again evidencing this logic of alternation or vicissitudo, "so, at certain regular times work gives place to contemplation and contemplation to work, so that contemplation does not impede work, nor work disrupt contemplation."[16]

As Stock rightly points out, this makes work for Bernard an element of an ongoing, rhythmic process of sanctification that plays out between the poles of cognitive intellect and affective sensation and experience, which leads to learning and in turn reconfirms what has been learned.[17] It is this oscillation that Stock argues lies at the basis of Bernard's "philosophy of action or of work," the first principle of which Bernard takes from 1 Corinthians 7:29–31, where St. Paul says,

> But this I say, brethren, the time is short: it remaineth, that both they that have wives be as though they had none; And they that weep, as though they wept not; and they that rejoice, as though they rejoiced not; and they that buy, as though they possessed not; And they that use this world, as not abusing it: for the fashion of this world passeth away.

It is this final phrase, using the world as if not using it, that should draw our attention. Stock does not make this point, but it is easy to see in Bernard's handling of this paradoxical Pauline exhortation a radicalization of Augustine's posture toward the world. For Bernard, the world, the body, and mundane activity must be used for spiritual profit, which requires a sort of using without using, or use without cleaving to material and mundane things. "Thus the material components of man and his world, in Bernard's theology, are not merely the debased reminders of original sin; they are quasi-technological *instrumenta* through the correct application of which he may again raise himself up. Human labor and human tools are in part the preconditions for salvation."[18]

Bernard takes the view that manual arts and manual labor can serve as part of an overall program of redemption. To be clear, for Bernard they do not have to be part of such a program, but they are no impediment to it. Bernard makes this plain when he says,

> All ignorance does not damn; rather, an innumerable number of things exist of which one may be ignorant without a diminished possibility of salvation. For example, if you do not know the mechanical arts, either that of the carpenter or the mason ... what impediment would there be to your spiritual health? Even without all those arts which are called liberal ... how many men have been saved, giving satisfaction in their ways of life and their works?[19]

Stock is correct that Bernard is by no means condemning the study or practice of mechanical or liberal arts; he is simply stating that they do not amount to salvation.[20] For Bernard, all learning must be actuated in charity for it to be genuinely useful.[21] Once more, this is a continual process for Bernard,[22] one that may involve various fields of learning, even the mechanical arts, as having "an active role in the pursuit of charity," the true goal of all sanctification.[23] According to Stock's thorough analysis, which sounds entirely Augustinian,

> In Bernard's rephrasing of the Pauline "utentes hoc mundo tamquam non utentes," one has, in a nutshell, the theology of work which is developed in various directions throughout the sermons. The problem is the fundamental ambivalence of man before the material universe of which he is, in part, a product, and which he in turn must appropriate to himself if he is to achieve his spiritual goals. The goals, of course, are entirely spiritual. Therefore, although we must continually labor, our labor may be useless for attaining grace, which can only be bestowed from above. We must use this world, and those below us, the *servi et pecora*, must work for us, even though what we achieve may be without reward. We must fill up the time because the time is short.[24]

Bernard is explicit in his endorsement of manual work as conducive to the development of charity. His occasional sermon "Concerning Six Spiritual Water Pots" provides an allegorical interpretation of the six urns filled with water by the servants at the wedding in Cana where Jesus performed his first miracle according to the Gospel of John, by turning the urns' contents to choice wine.[25] For Bernard, each of the six water pots, which recall those used in the Jewish ritual of purification, symbolizes a different observance, the fulfillment of which contributes to spiritual refinement. According to Bernard, "these six are silence, psalmody, vigils, fasting, manual work, purity of the flesh."[26] Obviously the fifth interests us. "If you seek to know whether it purifies in some way, then you can easily find many [examples]. Still, to pass over most because I strive for brevity, let this alone [show] how worthy of proclamation and how much a grace it is: Who would not respect living one's life by one's own labor and desiring nothing from anyone?"[27] Lest any of his hearers imagine he is being rhetorical, Bernard right away draws on the familiar verses to the Thessalonians, bolstering his case from the example and teachings of St. Paul himself.[28] Bernard claims that St. Paul insisted on these points with such care because "like a good and diligent shepherd, he foresaw this as most expedient for salvation of the flock."[29]

Even for the advanced contemplative, there can be no leaving off of the life of virtuous activity. In Sermon 46 on the Song of Songs, Bernard memorably likens good works to flowers that strew the bed of the lovers. "Perhaps you too long for the repose of contemplation," Bernard says to his hearers, "and you do well; only do not forget the flowers with which you read the bed of the bride is strewn. Therefore you must take care to surround yours with the flowers of good works, with the practice of virtues, that precede holy contemplation as the flower precedes the fruit."[30] Once again underscoring that Rachel and Leah must both have their claims on the monk's affection, Bernard condemns the effort to circumvent good works in favor of seizing contemplation without effort. "But it is a perversion of order to demand the reward before it is earned, to take food and not to work, for the Apostle says: 'If anyone will not work, let him not eat.'"[31] Here the Pauline injunction clearly refers not to manual labor as such but to the practice of good works and the development of virtues. So Bernard is capable of putting St. Paul to good use in support of both literal manual labor (as above in the sermon on the six water pots) and the doing of good deeds as a sort of spiritual "work" that is indispensable to the process of sanctification.[32]

To cite another much more poignant example, in one of his sermons Bernard digressed to lionize a departed brother, Gerard, whom he praises for his discipline and spiritual giftedness. Furthermore, though Gerard

> was not acquainted with literature ... [he] possessed the sense of one who discovers letters: and he had an illuminating spirit. He did not reveal himself to be small in the greatest tasks but rather greatest in the smallest. In the buildings, fields, gardens, water-works, indeed, in all the skills and jobs of the peasants—was there anything, I say, in this kind of activity which would have escaped Gerard's ability? With ease he was the master of the stone-masons, carpenters, gardeners, shoemakers and weavers.[33]

In this touching vignette, we perceive Bernard's estimation for the finished character of one who had progressed far along the path of spiritual perfection, which was in no way in tension with mastery of various crafts and labors. Indeed, these practices were quite at home in the life of one who is clearly a sort of ideal monk by Bernard's lights.[34]

The ideal of Cistercian labor, however imperfectly it may have been realized, was upheld against the excesses of the Cluniac community to powerful and even occasionally hilarious effect by the monk Idung of Prüfening in his "A Dialogue between a Cluniac and a Cistercian."[35] Written with the zeal of a convert, in this imagined dialogue Idung defends himself and his order with wit and verve. He had been a lay brother among the Cluniacs for ten years and then entered a Cistercian monastery, convinced that the latter's adherence to Benedict's Rule was more in keeping with its original intent.[36] At first attacked by his Cluniac interlocutor for abandoning his order and thereby breaking his vow of stability, that is, the promise to remain tied to a community, Idung, speaking through the anonymous Cistercian, defends his decision against the unnamed Cluniac on the grounds that what matters in a monastic's life is not the particular house to which he is pledged but adherence to the Rule.³⁷ So while the dialogue is imaginary, the issues at hand are not, and indeed they so concerned Idung personally that in his dedication of the dialogue to the abbess Kunigunde of Niedermunster he asserts that he "penned this *Dialogue* with the express purpose that, through the reasons and authoritative evidence collected in it, it may serve as my legal counsel and defense against those who accuse and censure me."³⁸

The Cistercian and the Cluniac waste no time in broadening their argument beyond the autobiographical details of Idung's own transfer of monastic residence, and the question of manual labor comes up repeatedly as a bone of contention. It was widely known that by this time in medieval Europe the Cluniac Benedictines had all but ceased to do any manual labor and instead preferred to think of themselves as devoted exclusively to *opus Dei*, the work of God, that is, saying the daily office and worshipping.³⁹ This is the nub of one of the Cistercian's very first attacks on the Cluniac, who has slighted him with fancy poetical words.

> It does not surprise me that when you were insulting me you made use of the words of poets, because to you and to others of your Order, poetic imagery is so pleasing that you make a study of it, you pore over it and you even teach it during the times which St Benedict intended and decreed should be set aside for spiritual reading and for manual labor.⁴⁰

The Cluniac attempts to rebut this charge by saying that they read secular books in order to better understand Scripture and that they use spiritual reading and prayer to reinforce each other. "As yours is an active Order," the Cluniac continues, "you have chosen to do manual labor with Martha, so ours is a contemplative because we chose holy leisure with Mary. Because, as Christ bears witness, Mary chose the better part, there is no doubt in my mind but that our Order is more worthy than yours."⁴¹

This opening debate on work is sidelined for several pages of digression, but when they get back to the topic, the Cistercian reminds the Cluniac that he disagrees with the latter's interpretation of Scripture on the issue of Jesus's apparent preference for Mary over Martha.⁴² Yet even this discussion is delayed in favor of the Cistercian's lengthy inveighing against the numerous luxuries at Cluny: their love of "beautiful paintings, beautiful bas-reliefs, carved [in ivory usually] and each embossed with gold, beautiful and costly cloaks, beautiful hanging tapestries painted in different colors, beautiful and costly [stained glass] windows, blue-colored sheet glass, copes and chasubles with golden orphreys, chalices of gold and precious stones, books illuminated with gold leaf,"⁴³ bells so heavy that their ringers are caused physical injury,⁴⁴ unmanly singing of "new and frolicsome songs on your new and unauthorized feast days,"⁴⁵ and the wearing of breeches.⁴⁶

When the issue of manual labor is finally revisited, rather than turn back to Scripture the Cistercian cites Ambrose, Jerome, Cassian's *Institutes* on acedia, and Augustine's *The Work of Monks* to further besmirch "the idea of leisure as you have propounded it in your Customary."⁴⁷ In fact it is only with the help of a long citation from *The Work of Monks* that the Cistercian returns to the initial discussion of labor in connection with Scripture. Returning to the question of monastic labor, the Cistercian accuses the Cluniac anew: "But above all else, by doing as you have done—contrary to the precept of the Rule and to the precept of the Apostle [Paul, surely, and almost certainly the second epistle to the Thessalonians]—you have stolen the time for manual labor."[48] It is then that the Cistercian quotes at length from *The Work of Monks*; the Cluniac professes total ignorance of the text, precipitating the need for the Cistercian to give a precis of its contents and the occasion of its writing. Only then does the Cistercian return to the case of Mary and Martha. "Have you noted the righteous zeal with which St Augustine inveighs against, and by the fact that he does inveigh proceeds against, that inactivity of yours which you say you chose with Mary? Would to heaven it were with Mary!"[49]

The reason the Cluniacs' inactivity is not in fact with Mary is that, according to the Cistercian, they do not actually want to imitate Mary properly. Like her, the Cistercian argues, the Cluniac should be quiet and direct his whole attention to the word of God when it is spoken through the mouths of his superiors. "During the hours designated in the Rule for manual labor, you should obey the Apostle and your Rule."[50] The Cluniac protests that as he understands Augustine's teaching, the monk is being exhorted to pray and sing during manual labor, but what then, he asks, would become of "the prolonged prostration of the whole body, which cannot very well be made at manual labor."[51] To this objection the Cistercian counters that prolonged prostrations are warrantless and contrary to the decrees of the Fathers, that they are less beneficial than the singing of psalms and praying during work would be,[52] and, in any case, that they run the risk of putting monks to sleep.[53]

The debate is renewed pages later, when the Cistercian moves again to prove his case that "manual labor is a furtherance rather than a hindrance to contemplatives," among whom of course the Cluniac numbers himself.[54] This time the Cistercian helps himself with a lengthy quotation from Cassian, who recounts the example of Abba Paul, "the most experienced of the Fathers,"[55] who kept himself busy with weaving palm leaves even though he had all the food he needed from his garden and every year burned all his work, "thereby proving that without manual labor a monk cannot persevere in his place nor attain the heights of perfection."[56] The Cluniac concedes that "we do not work in the garden or in the fields" but objects that his order is not thereby idle, because "some read and some work with their hands." With typical sarcasm, the Cistercian replies snippily, "I know these idle works of yours."[57] He condemns Cluniac labors as "idle" because they are not pertinent to salvation, in the same way that words that fail to edify are idle prattle; grinding gold dust for illumination for instance is in the end idle because it indulges a taste for luxury, and the Cluniacs on his charge neglect the appointed times for labor anyway, so what useful labors they do engage in are performed in contradiction to the precepts of the Rule.[58]

The Cluniac rightly perceives that the Cistercian is by implication upholding their own labors as useful, an implication that the Cistercian confirms: "We put great effort into farming which God created and instituted. We all work in common, we [choir monks], our laybrothers and our hired hands, each according to his own capability, and we all make our living in common by our labor."[59] The Cluniac retorts that these efforts are not labor at all "but recreation and a frittering-away of the passing day."⁶⁰ Dismissing this calumny, the Cistercian insists that while the Prior sees to it in conformity with the Rule that those who are fainthearted not be overburdened with labor, nevertheless the great majority of Cistercian monks sing Psalms amidst their manual labors and suffer remorse for their fellow men while they work, which does in fact provide their bread, just as Benedict intended, whereupon the Cluniac changes the subject: "You have talked enough about manual labor."⁶¹ Even so, in the final pages the Cistercian gets in his last word, a word—significantly—on love. "If you were to love the work prescribed in our Rule, it would become to you a labor of love."⁶² Here in the final pages of Idung's dialogue then, the voice of Augustine still rings out, calling the monastic laborer to love the work and thereby find in it no burden but joy and blessing.

There is a telling remark though before this final summation that should be noted. Harping on the need for self-denial and the embrace of manual labor for the discipline of body and soul, the Cistercian at one stage of his argument cites a number of authorities who teach that monks should eat only the simplest and cheapest foods. In response, the Cluniac laments that "these rules of the holy Fathers are not well suited to the modern monk's lack of stamina; they have more delicate bodies than our holy Fathers the monks had in the good old days."⁶³ The very idea of there having been "good old days" in the monastic tradition is a new one. Some of the momentous changes in high medieval European society had the effect of reorganizing the relationship between church and state and codifying a delineation of social classes between dedicated functions exercised by the nobility, by the clerisy, and by the workers. Part of the Cluniac's wistfulness may be attributed to a dawning sense that a monk's life simply cannot be as spiritually and physically taxing as it might have been in days past. Working with one's hands is no longer a monk's job but someone else's, and the monks have their own calling, which no longer need include hardship like physical labor. This is especially possible in light of generally advancing economic conditions, flourishing trade, and increasing urban prosperity.

By the same token, the Cluniac's admission is of a piece with the general trend toward redefinition of the practice of spiritual life. In Ovitt's summation of the literature of this period,

> what emerges from these texts is the sense that during the twelfth century, Christian theoreticians of culture attempted to fashion a pluralistic view of society and of social obligations, one that insisted on the primacy of the solitary spiritual life but also acknowledged that more public forms of spirituality, and a greater variety of professional occupations, could be integrated into the church.⁶⁴

This broadening of perspective though, as we have seen from the "Dialogue," meant also that a variety of viewpoints on monastic labor were now under consideration. The consensus of the past, of the "good old days," had been undermined, as the "Dialogue" illustrates: The question of manual labor for monks was for the first time up for debate. Moreover, the ideal that was once universally upheld was now receding into the mist of nostalgia. The exemplars of old, who belonged to the "good old days," simply were not taken to be models for contemporary imitation but distant appreciation. In Ovitt's judgment, "manual labor, once an integral part of every devout life, becomes by the mid-twelfth century part of hagiography, an act of extraordinary devotion whose practice defines a religious ideal that, we may infer, is no longer the norm."65

This verdict is confirmed by another mid-twelfth-century text, the anonymously composed *Libellus de diversis ordinibus*, which stands at the opposite pole from Idung's polemicism. With deftly organized irenicism, the *Libellus* arranges the various monastic orders along a continuum from solitary to living in the world and by charism, linking each with an Old and New Testament prototype. The author thereby tacitly argues that the most important distinctions in monastic life were not between orders but between the spiritual tendencies and emphases shared by each, such that the strict observance had most in common with other strict observances, not with looser practices within the order itself, which might admit a range of expressions.66 The purpose of the work is decidedly affirmative where Idung is combative—the point is that, taken together, all the orders and their respective tendencies have a role to play in the kingdom of God, and each contributes to that project with its own particular kind of value.67

This appreciation of diversity within the monastic orders extends even to the question of manual labor, as Ovitt notices. The author of the *Libellus* asserts in the chapter on canons who live close to human communities that "prayer is much helped by those who minister to us in external things, for it can hardly be offered if he who wishes to become perfect in prayer has also to occupy his mind with external matters and corporeal labours."68 Here it is flatly stated, rather than argued, that prayer is interfered with by manual labor, the exact reverse of the case pressed by the Cistercian, by Bernard himself, and the consensus position of the early monastics. The author of the *Libellus* puts this thesis forward as if it were in no way controversial.

Continuing in this vein, the author writes,

> If anyone should be disturbed that many canons among those who, I say, live next to men do not work with their hands, we can first reply briefly with what the apostle said: "For bodily exercise is profitable to little, but godliness is profitable to all things." For when he says bodily exercise profits little, he shows that it is worth something, but not so much that he would impose more than this precept on anyone or would judge anyone who does not work physically to be inferior.69

Here the author turns the Apostle Paul against himself it would seem. Obviously this verse has come up before, and everyone essentially agrees and always has that godliness is to be preferred to bodily exertion, yet it has generally been customary to read the full counsel of Paul as praising bodily exertion as a *part* of the spiritual effort toward godliness. Drawing the conclusion that this verse alone from St. Paul implies that the apostle would not have judged anyone who does not work physically to be inferior, the author of the *Libellus* overreaches quite a bit. Rather than praise those who work outdoors, esteem is directed toward those canons who prefer to remain in the cloister, going out as little as possible. If the cloistered canons

> also wish to do some work with their hands, I declare this to be good, and I consider that idleness should be denied to them as it is to others, saying with the apostle: "If any man will not work, neither let him eat." I understand that this was said not

only of manual labour but of all work suitable for men of the church, that he who does nothing shall not eat. That life is to be judged blessed, which keeps within the cloister, sequesters itself to a certain degree from worldly affairs, and extends itself into heavenly ones. And let not him who works with his hands vaunt himself above the man who works seated, since there is labour in both.[70]

So when the key passage from 2 Thessalonians is finally broached, the author again without any trace of controversy interprets St. Paul to have been referring not to manual work expressly but to any work whatsoever, and not only is the cloistered life to be judged superior, those monks who do work with their hands are enjoined not to regard their nonworking peers as inferior to them for this reason. Ovitt claims that "this is the first interpretation of the oft-quoted verse from 2 Thessalonians 3:10 to assert that labor need not be physical in order to be blessed."[71] This might be overstating it a bit, but he is right that it flatly contradicts the Rule of St. Benedict. Furthermore, he is correct to say that "'work suitable for men of the church,' implies, of course, that manual labor is not always suitable for monks and canons and that, more broadly different forms of work are better suited to different classes of men and women."[72] This assumption that different tasks are appropriate to different people becomes increasingly widespread. We find it, for example, in the work on the division of the sciences by Robert Kilwardby, whose thirteenth-century *De ortu scientiarum* declared openly that "physical activity is more suited to insignificant and common people, the peace of meditation and study to the noble elite; in this way, everyone has an occupation fitting his station of life."[73] The very idea that one could have such a station, that one could be fit for certain kinds of work and not for others, is a radical departure.

Theophilus Presbyter

No discussion of medieval work can be complete without a treatment of Theophilus Presbyter's *De diversis artibus*. The only systematic, thematic treatment of artistic craftsmanship in the Middle Ages, Theophilus's handbook is not a miscellany or compendium of recipes and procedures that compiles without any organizational logic any and all tidbits of technical knowledge but a disciplined selection of techniques for the production of art objects needed to fit a church for divine worship.[74] Though Theophilus clearly favored metallurgy (the subject of Book III, the longest) and was probably most expert therein, he includes painting (Book I) and stained glass (Book II) as equally valuable crafts for the artist to master. A monk, a priest, and an adept craftsman, Theophilus's descriptions of how to go about working in various media are clearly the product of extensive direct experience. (Theophilus is clearly aware, for example, of the many things that can go wrong in workmanship and how to guard against mishaps.)[75] Theophilus embodies an ideal: He was a spiritual man who was also a workman.

Like Bernard of Clairvaux, he presents his arts as part of an overall program for the restoration of not just human knowledge but the redemption of all of mankind. Unlike

Plato though, he never speaks of the origin of the arts as grounded in human need; as far as Theophilus is concerned the arts that he covers in his book are there for the worship of God. In C. R. Dodwell's words, *The Various Arts* presents

> in detail the considered conclusions that a mature and educated artist has reached about his work: what place it takes in the universal order of things and what its relationship is to his religion. His skill he sees, above all else, as a gift of God, but it is also, in a more subtle way, an inheritance of those qualities which Man possessed in full measure before the Fall and which can still be used to reflect something of the essential purpose of Man—the praise of God.[76]

Each of his three books features a prologue, which lays out the most philosophically and theologically valuable material, while the bulk of the text is descriptive of various craft procedures, which are obviously of mostly historical interest but do provide valuable insights into Theophilus's attitudes toward the practice of artistry.

Theophilus opens with a wish for those "who are willing to avoid and spurn idleness and the shiftlessness of the mind by the useful occupation of their hands and the agreeable contemplation of new things, the recompense of a heavenly reward!"[77] Several points bear mentioning right at the outset. First, notice that Theophilus repudiates idleness (*desidiam*) and shiftlessness of mind (*animique vagationem*), vices against which the monk has always been on guard. The antidote he immediately prescribes is "useful occupation of their hands" (*utili manuum occupatione*), but note well that craftwork does not simply engage the body but also entails "contemplation of new things" (*novitatum meditatione*), such that from the very beginning of the book Theophilus signals the togetherness of work and thought, body and mind. Finally, his invocation of a hope for heavenly reward for all those who might benefit from the practice of their bodies and minds in devotion to the arts suggests that not only is artistry not a hindrance to the project of salvation but may be a help to it.

Insofar as Theophilus has an "origin story" regarding the arts, he tells it in full consonance with the Scriptural account of creation, to which he proceeds:

> In the account of the creation of the world, we read that man was created in the image and likeness of God and was animated by the Divine breath, breathed into him. By the eminence of such distinction, he was placed above the other living creatures, so that, capable of reason, he acquired participation in the wisdom and skill of the Divine Intelligence [*divinae prudentiae consilii ingeniique mereretur participium*], and, endowed with free will, was subject only to the will of his Creator, and revered His sovereignty.[78]

The practice of the arts then for Theophilus is rooted in the original gift of reason, the capacity by which human beings participate in the wisdom and skill of God's own intellect. In fact, the verb "mereretur" could be translated even more significantly as "merited" or "had a right to," a phrasing that might be preferred given where Theophilus is going with his argument.

The Fall, of course, disturbed this participation in divine intellect, robbing humanity of their immortality, but not, it would seem, of all their capacity to continue to participate in divine intelligence. Humankind, though deceived by the devil and impaired in their abilities, nevertheless "transmitted to later posterity the distinction of wisdom [*scientiae*] and intelligence [*intellegentiae*], that whoever will contribute both care [*curam*] and concern [*sollicitudinemque*] is able to attain a capacity for all arts and skills [*totius artis ingeniique*], as if by hereditary right [*quasi hereditario iure*]."[79] So even despite our fallen condition, we are still able to possess some wisdom and intelligence, such that *all* arts and skills can be obtained as if they belonged to us by hereditary right. Notice the powerful parallelism in Theophilus's argument: Just as prelapsarian man enjoyed participation in the wisdom and skill of divine "intelligence," so too does "intelligence" survive in fallen human posterity, such that the image and likeness of God is not fully destroyed but only partially obscured. Similarly, just as human beings "had a right to" participate therein, so too can that "right" be recovered as if it had never been lost in the first place.

Furthermore, "skill" is referred to first in connection with God's own *consilii ingeniique* and then again in connection with human *artis ingeniique*. The grammatical connection makes a strong tie in Theophilus's presentation between the current practice of art and skill and the original gift of such abilities to humanity in its perfect, created condition. Finally, notice that "both care and concern" are required in order to realize this full recovery of the original endowment to human nature of the capacity to participate in divine intellect. "*Cura*" and "*sollicitudo*" are two of Theophilus's watchwords, for he is forever stressing that successful artistry depends vitally on diligence, attention, concern, and taking care.

That these two key concepts are joined here with several other favorites—*prudentia, consilium, ingenium, scientia, intelligentia*—suggests further that the practical need for care and concern is closely tied to the traditionally theoretical notions of knowledge, wisdom, and deliberation. In fact, as John van Engen argues, we could see in this parallelism an even stronger and entirely innovative claim on Theophilus's part. Theophilus is extending the range of what traditionally counted as evidence of human likeness to God. In van Engen's words, "whereas most Latin-speaking theologians designated 'rationality,' often together with related components of man's mind such as the 'memory' or the 'will,' as the common and abiding property of man's image-likeness to God, Theophilus extended the notion of 'rationality' to include as well the mental faculties necessary for the craftsman."[80]

This residual ability to practice arts and crafts was sustained by "human skill" (*intentionem humana*) according to Theophilus, providing "profit and pleasure" until it could be fulfilled in the Christian era, at which point the capacities for art and skill reached their true and proper end, not profit and pleasure, but the right worship of God.[81] For this reason, Theophilus argues, we ought not to neglect what has been bequeathed to us by our forebears, to whom he attributes "wise foresight," as if anticipating the Christian era, and again he speaks of this endowment as an inheritance (*hereditarium*), using the same term as before to imply that the capacity for artistry is a surviving bequest of creation itself and therefore must not be neglected. Once again though, he makes it clear that this will involve work: "What God has given man as an inheritance, let man strive and work [*laboret*] with all eagerness to obtain."[82] The inheritance cannot simply be received but must be attained, and having been attained, it is equally incumbent upon us to give thanks to God from whom it comes and to share that knowledge with others.

Indeed, this is precisely the position in which Theophilus finds himself, the beneficiary of divine grace and long experience in the arts, and this is what motivates him to write his book.

> Fearful of incurring this judgment, I, an unworthy and frail mortal of little consequence, freely offer to all, who wish to learn with humility, what has freely been given me by the Divine condescension, which gives to all in abundance and holds it against no man. I exhort them to recognise God's favour towards me and to appreciate His generosity, and I would have them know that they can be quite sure that the same things are at hand for themselves if they will add their own labour [*operam*].[83]

This theme is a constant for Theophilus: Mastery of the arts is possible thanks to the gracious provision of God and the dedication of the human being to careful and thoughtful work.

Interestingly, Theophilus counsels against work that is unnecessarily hard or circuitous. Just as it is wicked to take by theft, so it is lazy and foolish according to Theophilus to fail to strive after what is rightfully our inheritance (*hereditarium* again). This means that the dedicated student of the arts will not spurn "useful and precious things, simply because your native earth has produced them for you of its own accord or unexpectedly." It may be, Theophilus seems to say, that what is needful is near at hand, and it would be as ridiculous to ignore those gifts as it would be for a merchant to find a treasure in the ground and fail to pick it up and keep it.[84] Theophilus admits that it is customary for people to value "precious things that are sought with much toil [*multo sudore*: literally 'much sweat'] and acquired at great expense," but he nevertheless asserts that equal or even greater care (*custodia*) should be shown for valuable things that can be had for nothing. Therefore, Theophilus concludes,

> In so far as those things are offered freely, for which many at the greatest peril of life plough the sea waves compelled to endure hunger and cold, or which others, wearied with long servitude [*servitute*] in the schools and not exhausted by the desire of learning, only acquire with intolerable labour [*labore*]—be eager and anxious to look at this little work on the various arts, read it through with a retentive memory, and cherish it with a warm affection.[85]

The pearl then of great price is none other than Theophilus's own accumulated wisdom and practical experience.[35] It has come into the hands of his reader without the expenditure of the reader's own labor, but it is the product of Theophilus's own, and the only recompense he hopes for "the labour of instruction" he has invested is that his reader will pray for God to have mercy on him, for, as he maintains, he has kept nothing back as his own private prized possession and has not sought his own benefit but rather "ministered to the necessities of the many and had regard to their advantage."⁸⁷

Similar themes are reiterated in the preface to Book II, where Theophilus again addresses his reader with the hope that the first book has caused him to realize "how much honour and advantage there is in eschewing idleness [*otium*] and in spurning laziness and sloth [*inertiam desideamque*]."⁸⁸ Citing the book of Ecclesiastes's declaration that "he that increaseth knowledge increaseth labour," Theophilus gives this sentiment an unusual interpretation. Couched as it is in a lengthy lament for the "vanity" of life and human pursuits, this epigram is normally understood to be a lament for the difficulties imposed by learning, which in the world-weary view of the eponymous Teacher burden rather than relieve. Theophilus though interprets this passage much more positively: If you think about it, Theophilus writes, you "will be able to observe how much progress of the soul and body results thereby."⁸⁹

The addition of labor is not a matter of glum resignation but joyful acceptance, for abandonment to "idleness [*otio*] and irresponsibility" is a gateway sin, so to speak, leading on to even worse vices. By contrast, dedication to labor and self-discipline improve, notice, both soul and body, for "God is mindful of the humble and quiet man, working [*operantem*] in silence in the name of the Lord, obedient to the precept of Blessed Paul the Apostle: 'but rather let him labour, working with his hands the thing which is good that he may have to give to him that needeth.' "⁹⁰ The Pauline precept is familiar certainly, but it is uniquely tied by Theophilus to a counterintuitive citation from Solomon (the traditional author of Ecclesiastes and builder of the Jerusalem temple), a reference that might help explain Theophilus's reference to "the temple of holy wisdom,"⁹¹ his image here for the colored sanctuary that is the church and its painted and stained glass elements.⁹²

Temple imagery returns in the prologue to Book III, only this time the reference is David, who originally purposed to build a sanctuary for God to dwell in, rather than Solomon, his son who was graced with the favor of actually building the temple at Jerusalem. In telling this story, Theophilus again engages in some sophisticated and surprising exegesis. Rehearsing the merits of King David, and citing his utterance in Psalm 26, "Lord, I have loved the beauty of Thy House," Theophilus admits that it is possible to give this verse a strictly spiritual interpretation: "It is true that a man of such authority and such great intellect may have meant by that House the habitation of the heavenly court, in which God presides over hymning choirs of angels in inestimable glory."⁹³ He in addition concedes that David may have meant by this "the refuge of a devoted breast and pure heart where truly God dwells."⁹⁴

So when David speaks of the house of God, Theophilus is prepared to allow at least two "spiritualizing" understandings of this sentiment, such that the "house" of God could be understood to be the heavenly court or the heart of the person who loves God. Yet, Theophilus insists that "it is certain that he desired the embellishment of the material [*materialis*] House of God, which is the place of prayer," for David desired to build just such a material house and bequeathed to his son Solomon all the gold, silver, bronze, and iron needed to build it. Again notice the material and earthly quality here: David's story and example prove that not only is there no shame in honoring God with a material house, it is praiseworthy and needful to do so and has biblical sanction besides.⁹⁵

That sanction is further strengthened by the tie Theophilus makes from David back to Moses, claiming that the King had read the Lawgiver's exploits in the book of Exodus, where Moses was commanded by God to build the tabernacle and had chosen "masters of the work [*operum magistros*], and had filled them with the spirit of wisdom [*sapientiae*] and understanding [*intellegentiae*] and knowledge in all learning [*scientiae in omni doctrina*] for contriving and making works in gold and silver, bronze, gems, wood and in art of every kind" in order to carry out that commandment.[96] The reference is to Bezaleel and Aholiab, whom God commissioned to make all the furnishings required for the tabernacle and empowered with the "spirit of God, in wisdom, and in understanding, and in knowledge, and in all manner of workmanship, To devise cunning works, to work in gold, and in silver, and in brass, And in cutting of stones, to set them, and in carving of timber, to work in all manner of workmanship."[97]

As Heidi C. Gearhart has noted, this is the one time that Theophilus mentions a "model artist" as an exemplar, though he does not do so by name (by strange contrast to Exodus's assertion that God called Bezaleel "by name"[98]), and she argues that he does so because he wants to focus on Bezaleel's skill as a function of his endowment by the Holy Spirit, not on his individual character or the rhetorical value of his example.[99] In something of a departure from Augustine, who denied that the "spirit" that animated Bezaleel's creativity was the one and only Holy Spirit,[100] Theophilus insists that the Holy Spirit indeed is the author of artistic ability, and that David recognized this, for "he had discerned that God delighted in embellishment [*ornatu*] of this kind, the execution of which He assigned to the power and guidance of the Holy Spirit, and he believed that nothing of this kind could be endeavoured without His inspiration."[101]

Just as David recognized the work of the Holy Spirit in Bezaleel, and believed that the Holy Spirit's influence was needed for the building of the temple, so too does Theophilus acknowledge the work of the Holy Spirit in his own experience and exhorts his reader to be convinced of the same: "When you have adorned His House with such embellishment [*ornasti*] and with such variety of work, you will not doubt, but believe with a full faith, that your heart has been filled with the Spirit of God."[102] That Spirit Theophilus declines according to seven graces: wisdom, understanding, counsel, fortitude, knowledge, godliness, and the fear of the Lord. The list is the same as what is found in Augustine's commentary on the Sermon on the Mount, but, inexplicably, the order is exactly reversed.[103]

The important point here, as Gearhart indicates, is that for Theophilus the work of an artist, whether Bezaleel or his own or that of his reader, "is the operation of the Holy Spirit on earth, a physical manifestation of that presence."[104] This makes Theophilus's the highest possible view of artistry encountered so far in Western thought. It is this sense of high calling that explains why Theophilus is so meticulous, why he constantly stresses that the work of the artist must be done with care, concern, and, most especially, diligence.[105] As Gearhart persuasively argues, for Theophilus, the high calling of the artist moralizes skill itself, showing that aesthetic labor is in no way alien to the spiritual life but rather that every element of artistic practice depends on rationality, free choice, and the perfection of virtue.[106] Theophilus's work thus stands as a noble capstone to a venerable tradition. At the same time, it is important to acknowledge that this tradition is also at its end. As van Engen observes, "Within a few decades lay professionals took over the craftsman's art so completely that monastic craftsmen were the exception in the latter Middle Ages, and at the same time universities came to replace the monastic schools which had predominated in the early Middle Ages."[107]

Part Three

The Modern Era

5

Petrarch

One regrettable consequence of the otherwise laudable and voluminous scholarship on the question of labor in the Middle Ages is that it leaves out the Renaissance. A converse problem is inherited from the scholarly tradition that does focus on the Renaissance, which does not neglect the Middle Ages but impugns the medieval period, sometimes due to ignorance but often it would seem with contempt. This pattern was set in motion not only by the founding text of Renaissance scholarship generally, Jacob Burckhardt's *The Civilization of the Renaissance in Italy*, but also by writers in the Renaissance itself, who sought to establish their own self-consciousness as modern people by denigrating their own heritage. Interestingly, the class of Renaissance scholars least likely to distance themselves from the medieval period were the philosophers, the same significant group of players all but omitted by Burckhardt.[1] Burckhardt's one-sided account cast the Renaissance as a period of unprecedented activity and grasping of the possibilities of the active as opposed to the contemplative life, thereby leaving out all the most significant advocates of the contemplative life, who remained fairly conservative on the question of the supremacy of philosophy and theology over the other arts and sciences.

Moreover, Burckhardt's distaste for the medieval church and the orders of knowing and doing that it organized and cemented causes him to overlook the obviously religious character of Renaissance thought, which too remained by and large fairly conservative. As Ernst Cassirer argued, "It was precisely the Scholastic character of Renaissance philosophy that made it impossible to distinguish between philosophical and religious issues. The most significant and far-reaching works of philosophy in the Quattrocento are and remain essentially theology."[2] In the same vein, Paul Oskar Kristeller, in his *Renaissance Philosophy and the Mediaeval Tradition*, takes to task a historian who claimed that "the Renaissance is the Middle Ages minus God" for having "pronounced an unfair value judgment, in addition to committing a factual mistake."[3] Finally, Charles Trinkaus passes a sound verdict when he writes,

> Renaissance studies have suffered even more from the Renaissance's own myth ... Now it seems as though the men of the Renaissance who gave us that name of the Middle Ages have, by their distortions or memory-lapses or simple ignorance—or much more likely their disgust with the more traditional scholastic and logistic professions and intellectuals of their own day—also created our modern partisanship and rivalry between Renaissance scholars and medievalists.[4]

His summation of the matter is worth keeping in mind going forward: "I do not see how any conception of man that could have viability in the Renaissance could avoid a theological motivation, and, conversely, what is significant about humanist religious thought is its anthropocentric character."[5]

Most contemporary scholars simply do not study both the Renaissance and the Middle Ages with the same level of commitment, and so similarities are often unnoticed. Certainly the old stereotype of the Renaissance as singularly illumined in contrast to the backwardness of the Middle Ages has gone by the wayside, and rightly so.[6] Trinkaus perhaps supplies us with one of the best capsule expressions of the aims of Renaissance humanists: "to arrive at a definition of the nature, condition and destiny of man within the inherited framework of the Christian faith."[7] This is surely true of Petrarch, with whom most surveys of Italian Renaissance humanism correctly begin.[8] Petrarch is the first major exponent in his tradition of the dignity of human nature, and as Trinkaus has explained, there are a few reasons why this notion came to the fore, though again, it was not without medieval precedent. The question of the unique dignity of the human being had been addressed at least obliquely in a few traditions of medieval speculative writing: the hexameral literature; the thinking inspired by John Scotus Eriugena's innovative attempt to resynthesize Platonism and Christian theology and his translations of Dionysius the Pseudo-Areopagite and Gregory of Nyssa's *De opificio hominis*; the genre of writings on the misery of human life, which was often paired with praise for the nobility of human nature; and the Scholastic tradition, which constantly took up the dignity of the human in commentaries on Peter Lombard's *Sentences*, Book II, Questions XVI and XVII.[9]

The theme came into its own though in Italian Renaissance culture because it also had antecedents in pagan antiquity, the great field of interest for humanists like Petrarch, who was convinced that at least in some respects "antique rhetoric, poetry, history, and philosophy were not in conflict with Christianity but could actually strengthen religion."[10] Furthermore, human dignity was frequently tied by the humanists to free will and its active exercise, and here again Petrarchian humanism exalted these powers as hallmarks of human dignity. Moreover, acknowledging the dignity of the human person could be full-throated while also admitting that the human being, while an exalted creature, is nevertheless of relative import and subject to praise or blame based on whether she ascends to the heavens or debases herself to the level of the beasts.

As Trinkaus points out, praise and blame and the estimation of human character in the eyes of critical contemporaries, awaiting posterity, and even eternity, is the very vocabulary of the rhetoric so admired by the humanists. Finally, given that urban civilization was expanding rapidly in Northern Italy, and these developments rested uneasily alongside a medieval tradition emphasizing ascetic withdrawal from the world, the trope of dignity could make sense both of flourishing human energy and creative activity as well as the human being's capacity for contemplation and spiritual elevation, the superiority of which Petrarch and his comrades upheld, even while according significant respect to humanity's active enterprises.[11]

What is new and noteworthy in Renaissance thinking is the intensity of lay piety, a shifting of the theological heft of the culture from the Scholastic heritage (by now widely viewed as bloated with jargon and tedious and irrelevant logic-chopping) onto a fervent scholarly class that held tightly to the Christian faith but sought in the classics—and not just the pagans of Greek and Roman antiquity but the Church fathers of the first four centuries AD—the basis for a revivification of that faith. The humanists' interest in rhetoric, for instance, was what we would now call existential, inasmuch as they pursued it in search of a means by which to persuade and exhort their audiences to rededicated piety, a task for which the aridity of the late Middle Ages had left them poorly equipped.[12] Petrarch exemplified this new situation as none other. Intensely religious, he nevertheless spurned Scholasticism and sought to redeploy the rhetorical and communicative power of the ancient philosophers and early medieval theologians in the service of building up a lay spirituality with genuine vigor and consolatory power.[13]

Petrarch's singular contribution to our discussion so far may be that he linked the Christian life with all its struggles to a new conception of the self as a deep and divided well of inwardness; this possibility was always present in Augustine, to whom Petrarch perhaps owes his deepest (confessed) debt,[14] but Petrarch's own self, which is clearly the theater from which and for which he performs all his varied writings, is one that is incipiently modern, at a remove from the traditional consolations of Christian metaphysics and Scholastic theologizing.

Petrarch's most popular work during his lifetime and for years after,[15] all but forgotten today, was *Remedies for Fortune Fair and Foul*, a two-volume compendium of counsel—often sarcastic and even hilarious—voiced by "Reason" in a series of one-sided conversations with "Hope," "Joy," "Sorrow," and "Fear." As the name suggests, Petrarch is concerned to address both putative good fortune and to limit its potentially corrupting influence, and bad fortune, subordinating it to the calm that comes from wise and reasoned counsel. In format, the book reads almost like a medieval miscellany, a compendium of recipes and prescriptions, but the aim throughout is not to instruct the reader toward the securement of any external outcome but to remedy the self as it confronts decidedly this-worldly challenges.

When it comes to the issue of work, the *Remedies* is full of exhortation to labor and toil, generally as a means of combating ill fortune. It is invoked in the first volume on fair fortune only twice with any substance, as a guard against the enticements of "Leisure and Rest" (Dialogue 21) and "Tranquility" (Dialogue 90). In the former dialogue, Reason hails leisure and rest as "two of the most welcome goods in human life, provided that immoderate use does not turn them into the gravest of ills." When Joy boasts, "I enjoy the most delightful leisure," Reason issues a corrective: "You should say 'I use the most delightful leisure.' Here on this earth nothing can be enjoyed, but many things can be used—thus says the salutary doctrine." The doctrine in question is surely Augustine's, who distinguished between the "use" and "enjoyment" of earthly goods and argued that the righteous make use of the world to enjoy God while the wicked make use of God to enjoy the world.[16]

From the outset then, leisure is an unquestioned good, but in true Augustinian fashion, one that can easily be misused and result in harm. Leisure is not to be enjoyed as if unqualifiedly excellent but used to higher purposes. Petrarch, through the voice of Reason, goes on to clarify by drawing a distinction between two kinds of leisure:

One which is active, full of work even when at ease, and concerned with honest efforts. Nothing is sweeter than this. The other kind is sluggish and dull, wholly given to repose. Nothing is more detestable, nothing more similar to the grave. And thus the first kind produces often great attainments, useful to the world and bringing glory to its authors; but the second brings nothing, save inglorious torpor and numb stupefaction. The first is fit for the philosophically minded, the second for dullards given to their bellies and snoring, who seek to eat and sleep without interruption.[17]

The recovery of the notion of otium is not unprecedented in Petrarch, but his appreciation for it (which we will see continued in other works) is characteristic of his retrieval of classical sources. Consistent with the Stoic and Christian traditions, leisure is of course not idleness, which is universally decried, but occupation with noble and uplifting tasks. This leisure Petrarch calls active, wholesome, and sweet, while warning against the laziness that otium always makes possible though certainly not inevitable. Philosophers take advantage of the opportunity for otium, while the dull indulge themselves in it, even though sleep, Reason asserts with the support of poets, is a kind of brother to death. Even when "all chores [are] pushed aside," Reason cautions against too much of this "pleasant slumber."[18] "Toil," Reason advises, "is the material cause of virtue and glory. Who rejects toil, rejects these too. Conversely, too much sleep is the material cause of crime and infamy, which drives many headlong toward eternal slumber."[19]

In the second part of the *Remedies*, work appears in a more provincial capacity, as a potential ally in the battle against misfortunes of various kinds. When Sorrow complains about being born from ignoble stock, Reason urges, "then strive for a noble end! Beginnings mean toil; the fruit comes at the end."[20] Similarly, in Dialogue 9 on "Hard Times," Sorrow complains that "harsh Fortune has robbed me of all I had." Echoing Boethius, Reason retorts that fortune can only take away what is hers to begin with, such that Sorrow's complaint is an old but ill-founded one. "No one can deprive you of the necessities of life, because there is hardly anything without which a person cannot live well," where "living well" is understood naturally to mean living without luxuries and indulgences but with only what is absolutely needful being supplied: "But there are only very few things needed to support or alleviate man's natural requirements. If wanting, they can be readily supplied by doing some light work with your tongue or with your hands. Virtue is satisfied by very little, vice by nothing ever."[21] Fortune's advice then is to work for what is really necessary and not give way to greed and excess, which can never be satisfied in any event and which can only complain over the loss of things that could not be held securely in the first place.

By contrast, goods that cannot be taken away are to be preferred, because the business of scrabbling for goods under the control of fortune is a sucker's game. Reason says, "All the stratagems and weapons, which you think are yours, are in the hands of your enemy. She holds the hilt, and the point is aimed at you. If you want my advice, do not bother with any of this, do something else, and apply your mind to pursuits which are not governed by Fortune."[22] In support of this advice, Reason cites the example of Aristippus, who upon being shipwrecked off the coast of Rhodes found himself stripped of clothes and all other goods of fortune. Exploring his new setting, he espied geometrical figures traced in the sand and called out to his companions: "Be of good cheer; we are not in a deserted region; I see the tracks of men." Thereupon he and his mates discovered a city where Aristippus impressed the local philosophers with his learning and acquired the goods he needed from their new hosts.

The moral of the story according to Aristippus is that the wise will "provide for your children goods that will not perish in a shipwreck—that turmoil, be it now on sea, on land, or due to warfare, cannot ever take away from them."[23] These things having been secured, the lesser goods can be had with a bit of work and initiative. Reason cites numerous examples of philosophers and poets who were unashamed to work, sometimes with the reward of eventual success attributable to hard work, often undignified. If such a multitude of examples does not convince, Reason caps them off with an appeal to the "Lord of Heaven himself. He was poor, so that by His example He might teach that such poverty is the way by which to hasten gaining the true riches. He, I say, by Whose grace kings reign, was born poor, lived poor, and died naked—He to Whom all the elements obey."[24]

Dialogue 56 on "Difficulties and Hard Work" is by now predictable in its contents. Against Sorrow's grievances about being overwhelmed by difficulties, Reason flatly insists that "there is no glory without toil" and that "work is the seat of virtue, leisure that of pleasures. Without work, nothing is praiseworthy, nothing outstanding." Again Reason is well-supplied with examples from myth and ancient Roman history, including Hercules, Ulysses, the Scipios, Pompey, Julius Caesar, and unnamed poets and philosophers as well as artisans. "Just look at all kinds of people," proclaims Reason, "and you will find that wherever there is much reputation there is much toil."[25] To be beneficial, Reason contends, hard work must be protracted and a source of continual challenge and stimulation. Only then can it serve as a remedy for the ills of life, as it "purges and cleans out those infected by repose. It is obvious that it cures the mind, prevents the springing up of vices, and pulls out those that have taken root."[26] According to Reason, our "arts" are to be work and virtue, two things that are never separated and both of which have to be undertaken with the long view, focusing on the goal and enduring present difficulties for the sake of eventual reward.[27] Toil is not so great an ill as weak and vicious humans suppose,[28] and at least twice Reason cites the oft-quoted verse from Job—"Man is born to labor"—as proof that it is our lot.[29]

Petrarch's complete view of the role of work and leisure in human life is given expression in his edifying little work *On Religious Leisure*. From the title alone (*De otio religioso*), we can appreciate that this is an effort to retrieve the classic concept of otium and assign it a new meaning fit for Renaissance Christendom. Written after a visit to his brother Gherardo, who had joined the Carthusian monastery at Montrieux as an avowed but non-cloistered monk, Petrarch dedicated this work to Gherardo and his companions, all of whom were killed by the Black Death in 1348.[30] In the first pages, Petrarch confesses himself to be "a sinful man who is tired, and ignorant, and overwhelmed with care," but he writes the book to discharge a debt of gratitude for the spiritual refreshment and intellectual stimulation he received in the company of the monks.[31] Petrarch's leitmotif is Psalm 46:10: "Be still, and know that I am God." As he himself emphasizes, at the heart of this passage, in the Latin Vulgate, are two imperatives, "*vacate et videte*," which Petrarch says he believes together encapsulate "the course of your whole life, all your hope, all your motivation, and your final destiny."[32] The translator of *On Religious Leisure* renders this verse as "take time and see (that I am God)," in order to chime with Petrarch's own exegesis, which stresses the literalism of "seeing" God and the need to actively "take time," to dedicate time, freed from other mundane pressures, for this vision. As Ivan Illich argued in connection with his reading of Hugh of St. Victor's influential text *Didascalicon*, "vacate" is a term rich with significations and was even a technical term of great import for any monk. "Rufinus," he points out, "was the first to define the monk as someone 'who in solitude makes himself free for God alone,' *solus soli Deo vacans*."[33] Illich goes on to show that the verb, as used by early Christian writers, means to have been set free, where the emphasis is on the active taking up of a new liberty, to be engaged in "a new way of life."[34] Just as Hugh used this word to signify the embrace of otium for religious activity and flight from worldly distraction, so too Petrarch dusts off this usage.

In so doing he rejects Aristotle's claim that "we do not take time now so that we may have time in the future." The translation here is a little idiosyncratic, forced a bit in order to establish the required parallelism to Petrarch's reading of Psalm 46:10. Another more intuitive rendering would be "we deny ourselves leisure so that we can be at leisure."[35] Aristotle's point here is that we work in order to enjoy the benefit of leisure, not the other way around. Yet Petrarch argues that in view of "the labor of farmers," "the worry of merchants," "the long nights spent by scholars," "the sweat of artisans," and all "humanity's struggles,"[36] this is not really true; we imagine through our work we will attain our goal and then rest, but not so. "According to Aristotelian teaching, they do not take time so that they may someday have time; that is, they work so that they may rest, and they work intensely so that they may enjoy a little rest; no truly, so they may have no rest at all; even more truly, so that they may work even more."[37] Sounding for all the world like the eponymous writer of Ecclesiastes, Petrarch concludes,

> Certainly when one has labored greatly for a long time, whether he arrives at his destination or not, his labor only increases, and his worries double. The joy of success for which one has hoped usually leads to an accumulation of worries no less than does the pain of failure. So we should say more properly that they do not take time now, and therefore they will never have any time at all.[38]

Petrarch's argument about the distraction of labor seems to be that, contrary to Aristotle's generalization, it tends to lead to more exertion rather than less, and that if one will not then *deliberately* take time, that is, dedicate time to the spiritual life, then one never will. To take time and see God is something that cannot be "postponed" so to speak but is always a matter of immediacy, something that must be prioritized lest it find itself not at second place in the order of priorities but in no place at all. The goal then is to be like the Carthusians, for whom rest in the present is a priority that anticipates the eternal rest of the blessed: "'Take time': this means there is rest in the present; 'know' means there will be eternal repose. Take time on earth, and you will know in heaven."[39] The experience of the monks is then the exact opposite of the logic that governs worldly work: "Among other people labor creates more labor; among you, however, rest creates rest."[40] Just as there is a self-perpetuating cycle of work leading to more work, so too rest in the present builds on itself, generating yet more rest, which Petrarch calls "a goal which untiring and resolute minds ought to have worked toward through their whole lives. No labor would have appeared heavy if it had resulted in something so enjoyable as rest."[41]

He returns to this theme later in the text, and blending the language of Jesus from the Sermon on the Mount and that of St. Paul from 1 Corinthians 3 about how humans labor but only God gives growth,[42] Petrarch suggests that the pagan ethicists of classical antiquity labored for the incomplete reward of virtue so that Christians can rest in the full truth of revelation. This relationship of work to rest that he teases out at the beginning of the text at the individual level proves by the end of the text to apply to the historical level as well, binding antiquity to Christian civilization in their very distinction. He apostrophizes,

> O great philosophers and hard-working men, whose natural intelligence overwhelms us, look at how we have overtaken you in grace and free blessings. You have labored, but look at how we now rest. You have planted, but look at how we now harvest. You have sought, but look at how we now find. It is neither your fault nor our merit, but only the favor of God which has done this.[43]

The lesson for today then is

> short and not difficult. You are not commanded to fight, to sail, to plow, to be ambitious, to accumulate gold, fame, vain knowledge, all instruments of desire. They are useless, harmful, lethal. They are costly. They are sought with labor. Once attained, they do not satisfy us. When lost, they torture us. Having to be guarded, they worry us. In their midst we are never at peace: everywhere there is fear, everywhere there is labor.[44]

The one thing needful is to take time, which costs nothing and yet issues in the superlative reward: the vision of God. This second part of the imperative, in fact, Petrarch argues at this point is not so much another command but the result of obedience to the first, and no one can excuse themselves from failing to follow the first, inasmuch as taking time is within the reach of all people.[45]

In typical Petrarchian fashion though, we have only ourselves to blame for perverse failure on this score, which we seem wantonly to crave. Citing Augustine's *Of True Religion*, Petrarch's favorite book of his favorite thinker, to the effect that "the friends of this world so fear to be separated from its embrace that nothing for them is more laborious than not to work," Petrarch rues that we sabotage our own rest with insistence on scattered activity. The worst consequence of this self-undermining is that it is reflected in eternity. Just as the monks rest now to seek God and so prepare themselves for the everlasting beatific vision, so too does the frenzied striver win for herself an eternity of occupation. Petrarch again enlists both Christians and pagans, in this case Augustine and Virgil, as having seen that the life we choose here is also the life with which we will be saddled in eternity. We choose our own reward or punishment in the life to come.[46]

> Whole and fresh, the very same person, not someone else, he will still live for this very purpose of being tortured without end and of working for eternity, with his wish fulfilled and no reason to complain. It shall be said to him: Why are you sad, "why do you gnash your teeth," or why do you weep? You have found what you were seeking. You have acquired what you wanted. You were afraid to take time and to rest. Now work! You have no need here ever to seek labor or fear rest.[47]

Sounding like another Augustine, Petrarch sums this book together with his *The Life of Solitude* as having "one conclusion, that it is the badge of mortal madness which rejoices more in work than in the enjoyment of work."[48] Obviously the religious leisure that Petrarch commends as the hallmark of the Carthusians' practice is not freedom from activity but occupation with higher things, the work of God to which monks were always called. Imagining a potential interlocutor's objection—"'From which of our concerns, my friend, shall we take our rest?' It is surely not right for those who profess to fight for Christ to rest from all that has to be done"—Petrarch makes his understanding of religious rest plain: "I am not encouraging you to inactivity, but rather just to be at leisure, and that for religious purposes."[49] Demetrio S. Yocum notices in fact that the seeds of this clarification are planted even earlier in the book and, significantly, in the context of Petrarch's own autobiographical recollection of his visit among the monks. He remembers,

> I scarcely had the chance to look upon your venerable faces. Never was a day shorter, a night faster. While I was contemplating your most holy hermitage and shrine, while I wondered at your devoted silence and angelic singing, while I admired you, all together at times and at times individually, and while (as is natural to humanity) I embraced my beloved brother, my sweetest treasure whom I had entrusted to you, and while I took pleasure in the conversation I had so much wanted with my best and only brother, the whole brief time fled by me without my realizing it. I had no opportunity to put words together and to collect my thoughts.[50]

So apart from the brevity of Petrarch's visit, it would seem that in some sense the monks' religious leisure is also a kind of busyness, so much so that Petrarch was occupied to the point of not noticing how quickly the time was passing. The time was in its way quite full, as Petrarch mentions contemplation, silence, singing, corporate and individual prayer, and conversation, the true monastic occupations, as impressing him with their own demands, so different from those of the world, but nevertheless also "filling" so to speak the brief time spent at Montrieux. Yocum uses the term *otium negotiosum* to describe this leisure that is also active and fertile as opposed to inert laziness.[51] Petrarch says that amid all this sacred activity he had no chance to even collect his thoughts or put his words together, which is why he writes the book later, in order to gather his thoughts and words at a temporal and spatial remove from the monastery.

As Yocum persuasively documents though, for the Carthusians, writing was the most cherished form of manual labor a monk could do, and so Petrarch here is taking up not a merely scholarly or literary task but is extending and reinventing the Carthusians' own preferred manual labor as part of his own lay practice. They called it "silent preaching" or preaching done with the hand, and they viewed it as being a form of physical effort (keeping in mind that this was before movable type or even the widespread use of paper) and as having spiritual benefits first for the writer himself, then for the reader.[52] Book-making was thus the Carthusians' foremost apostolate and was considered by them "an essential component of their *otium negotiosum* and another way to pray, often involving the recitation of mental or vocal prayers."[53] Second to book-making was gardening, which was as we have seen a pursuit common to many monastic orders but Yocum argues reached a high point of sophistication among the Carthusians, who developed a rich symbolism around gardening.[54] These two activities found their way into Petrarch's own spiritual life, for he was a notorious devourer of books and kept a garden in each of the many places he lived.[55]

Less noticed than the active leisure of the monks though is its obverse, which is characteristic perhaps of the proto-modernity of Petrarch's time, which he is inventing as much as he is reflecting. For all the busyness of worldly occupations, there is a kind of stultifying torpor beneath all the activity; lurking behind it there is an otium in its worse sense, the negative connotation that persists in our word "otiose." Perhaps we could call this *negotium otiosus*. This conjunction of hyperactivity with dulled sensibility is the "mortal madness" Petrarch spoke of above that rejoices in work precisely where work is not loved and enjoyed in the Augustinian sense. Work for work's sake is the incipiently modern and harried mirror image of the monks' religious leisure.

It has been well said that Petrarch wrote for himself principally.[56] If we keep that in mind, we can understand *On Religious Leisure* as not so much an exhortation to the Carthusians to maintain their precious way of life—a commitment about which he does not seem to be in any real doubt[57]—but as a reminder to himself to incorporate the monastic way of life into his own scholar's existence and to avoid the enticements of worldly, sterile busyness. An element of this self-motivation is his periodic insistence to the monks and to himself that externals do not suffice for the securing of religious leisure. The monks are not necessarily safe from temptation in the monastery, Petrarch cautions,[58] which again conversely implies that religious leisure is not impossible for one outside the monastery. This too is an innovation on the classic schema of otium, which for the early Latins required physical retirement to the country for its enjoyment. Petrarch's peace is inward, not dependent on externals.[59] It is his way of appropriating for himself, as always on his own personal terms, the legacy of the monastic tradition, for which no modern writer will show the same intense admiration.[60] He combined in his own person the rhythmic alternation of work and leisure celebrated by a long monastic tradition and now transposed from a harmonious society to the peace of one man's inner life. This transformation, a shift away from the monastery as the scene of privileged work, and even away from the sacred groves of academe, would reach a point of unprecedented pitch in the watershed thinking of Martin Luther.

6

Martin Luther

Martin Luther, the one-time Augustinian monk who catalyzed the Reformation in continental Europe, wrote an avalanche of commentaries, sermons, and treatises, scattered across the wide swath of which is a surprisingly high number of engagements with the subject of work. In fact, "work," understood as labor in the restricted sense of tasks appointed for the securing of goods necessary for life, becomes in Luther's voluminous writings a kind of metonym for "works," understood as humanly undertaken efforts to cooperate with the divine plan of salvation, the efficacy of which and necessity for the justification of the Christian believer in the eyes of God were at the center of Luther's polemic against the papacy and the entire Roman church's understanding of the economy of salvation. As early as 1520, just one year after the publication of the famous 95 theses, Luther wrote three short works that together constituted a powerful broadside against the imposing edifice of the Roman Catholic Church: *Address to the Christian Nobility of the German Nation, On the Babylonian Captivity of the Church*, and *On the Freedom of a Christian*.

As noticed by one of its translators, it was the last of these three that was the least inflammatory against the church, the most positive in terms of its concrete proposals for what the Christian life ought to look like, and the most influential.[1] The key Lutheran doctrine of justification by faith here received its first thoroughgoing explanation. In brief, *On the Freedom of a Christian* argues,

> Through God's gracious gift of faith, Christians required no acts or works to make them righteous or to save them. They were thus free of the chains of constant religious action or ritual required by the medieval church. They were also free of fear and death. This did not mean that Christians should not do good works or serve their neighbors, or that they were free to do whatever they liked. Luther argued that the very love they had for God, who had freed them, also bound them to act according to His will.[2]

This paradox is at the heart of the *Freedom* treatise, given pithiest expression by Luther at the outset of the work and repeated frequently like a refrain throughout: "A Christian is a free lord of all things and is subject to no one. A Christian is a dutiful servant in all things and is subject to everyone." The inspiration is, as is true for so much of Luther's writings, St. Paul, as Luther himself immediately admits: "These two conclusions are clear from St. Paul, in 1 Corinthians 9: 'I am free in all things and have made myself a servant of everyone.' Likewise in Romans 13: 'You shall owe no one anything, except that you love one another.' Yet love is dutiful and subject to that which is loved."[3] The tension between these two Pauline claims, that the believer is at once free and sovereign and bound and servile, is reconciled by Luther in his theory that

> every Christian has a double nature; a spiritual and a physical. In regard to the soul, he is called a spiritual, new, internal man; in regard to flesh and blood, he is called a physical, old, and external man. And it is because of these differences that, as I have just said, he is mentioned in the Scriptures both in terms of freedom and servitude, one directly contrary to another.[4]

For the inner person, external states of affairs and appurtenances do not affect the quality of the soul. In Luther's summation,

> no external thing, of whatever name, can make [a Christian] either free or pious; for his piety and freedom, or, on the other hand, his wickedness and imprisonment, are neither physical nor external. How does it help the soul if the body is unbound, fresh, and healthy, and eats, drinks, and lives however it likes? On the other hand, how does it damage the soul if the body is imprisoned, sick, and feeble, and hungers, thirsts, and suffers against its wishes? None of these things reach the soul, either to free or imprison her, or to make her pious or evil.[5]

Because all such externals are a matter of spiritual or moral indifference,

> it is no help for the soul if the body puts on holy garments, as do the priests and clergy; nor if the body is in churches and holy places; nor if it is occupied with holy matters; nor if it physically prays, fasts, goes on a pilgrimage, and does every good work that might only ever happen through and in the body.[6]

Conversely, all such "works" are potentially compatible with a person being "a hypocrite and a fraud," since evil persons with corrupt souls can just as easily undertake such outward actions and behaviors without improvement to the soul. Furthermore, wearing unholy garments, visiting profane places, eating and drinking in the normal manner rather than fasting, declining to go on pilgrimage, and generally omitting all such allegedly pious outward acts do not necessarily do any harm to the soul. So, Luther concludes, something else must account for the piety and freedom of the Christian soul, and that something else is conformity with the gospel message, "the word of God preached by Christ," which is of utmost and utterly decisive importance, inasmuch as "the soul can dispense with everything but the word of God, and without the word of God nothing can help her."[7]

For this reason, according to Luther, the only needful "work and exercise of all Christians should rightly be that they establish the word and Christ within themselves, continuously exercising and strengthening such a faith. For no other work can make a Christian." For support of this dramatic claim, Luther cites Jesus himself, from John 6, when the Pharisees inquire after what sort of works they should be doing to be in right standing before God. Christ's answer is straightforward, and it seems to underwrite Luther's contention rather neatly: "The only divine work is that you believe in the One whom God has sent."[8] The question then predictably arises as to what use the many "laws, commandments, works, estates, and ways"[9] laid down by Scripture might serve. If the only work required is faith, then why do there seem to be so many different works called for in the Bible? Luther's answer again follows Paul closely, especially the argument of the letter to the Galatians.

The Scripture, he argues, contains both commandments and promises. The former are meant to point up our own incapacity to meet the demands of God for holiness of life, which in turn drives the individual, now deprived of any illusion about their own worthiness or ability to deliver themselves from damnation, to seek out the consolation afforded solely by the promises of God. "Now when a man has learned of and perceived his own incapacity from the commandments, he will be fearful about how to satisfy the commandments; for the commandments must be fulfilled, or he will be damned. Thus he is rightly humbled and reduced to nothing in his own eyes, and finds nothing within himself that might make him pious."[10] Needless to say, a person's own works, no matter how apparently pious they may seem to the outside observer, are fully included in this indictment; works cannot make one pious and thus justified, because no one is capable of unerringly amassing a sufficient quantity of good works to merit salvation. All hope is not lost, however.

> But then the other word, the divine promise or assurance, appears and says: If you will fulfill all commandments and be free of all your wicked desires and sin (as the commandments oblige and require), then behold, believe in Christ, in whom, I assure you, is all grace, righteousness, peace, and freedom. ... For what is impossible for you to achieve through all the works of the commandments—which are necessarily numerous, and yet useless—will be easy and quick for you through faith. ... Thus the assurances of God give what the commandments require, and accomplish what the commandments decree.[11]

For this reason the work of salvation is attributable solely and in full to God's divine initiative. It is God that lays down the commandments in the first place and God that realizes their fulfillment uniquely in the life of Jesus Christ. Faith in him therefore is the only so-called "work" required of the believer,

> and no works are required to make him pious; and if he requires no further works, then he is certainly released from all commandments and laws; if he is released, then he is certainly free. That is Christian freedom: faith alone, which does not lead us to live in idleness or do wickedness, but instead means that we require no works to obtain piety and salvation.[12]

Let this then suffice for an explanation of in what sense, according to Luther, the true Christian is free and thus subject to no one. Christian freedom consists in liberation from the burden of the commandments, which no one can faultlessly discharge. Yet even here, it should be noted carefully, Luther hastens to add that Christian freedom is not license for idleness or for wickedness. It is not a pretext for the believer to do whatever she pleases or to excuse herself from a certain kind of "working." Accounting more fully for this point will explain how the Christian is also simultaneously subject to everyone, which is the second major principle around which the *Freedom* treatise is organized.

Faith alone justifies and suffices for the soul's salvation, but as Luther admits, this might occasion an obvious question: If faith suffices for salvation, then why are good works compulsory at all? Why couldn't a believer content herself with her faith and assurance of salvation by faith alone and abstain from any additional efforts in the direction of Christian virtue? Luther's answer is that this otiose conclusion is blocked by the fact that we are not "completely spiritual and internal" persons and will not be prior to Judgment Day. While we live this mundane and temporal life, Luther insists, we are called to servanthood and "must do all manner of things," though the things he has in mind sort out into two main categories: rulership over the body and devotion to others. Inasmuch as the believer "still remains on earth during this physical life and must rule his own body and interact with people," it is at this point, Luther pithily asserts, that "now works begin."[13]

Interestingly, Luther seems from the outset to think of "labors" (*Arbeiten*) as a chief instance of the sort of "works" (*Werke*) that are required of a Christian. Luther mandates that the Christian believer, despite being fully justified by faith, even so "must not be idle; indeed, his body must be disciplined and trained with fasts, vigils, labors, and with every reasonable correction, such that it becomes obedient and in conformity to the internal man and to faith, rather than that it hinder or resist them, as is its way when it is not constrained."[14] Echoing Paul's rueful meditation in Romans 7 on the division of the will he experienced, between the warring impulses toward good and evil within his own self, Luther generalizes Paul's own self-report, arguing that while the internal person is united with God through faith in Christ and gratitude for his saving work, in whose service he finds nothing but freedom and joy and love, there remains a "recalcitrant will"[15] at work even in the free and joyful believer that seeks only to please the world and flatter its demands. Work then is required to bring this rebellious will to heel, and not just work in the general sense of pious deeds but work in the sense of labor, which Luther practically conflates with the broader sense: for him, clearly, work is a form of works.

The crucial qualification of course is that works are not to be done out of the false expectation that they have power to save or to make the believer pious and acceptable before God. The motivation for doing good works changes in the life of the faithful person, who performs good works not because she is hoping that they will justify her before God in the absence of faith but "in the opinion that thereby the body is made obedient and purified of its evil passions."[16] Similarly, the mood one might say in which works are done changes for the believer. No longer does she do good works out of a panicked anxiety to mollify God but instead "gratuitously and freely out of love, in order to please God; thereby not seeking or attempting anything else from them, than that they please God."[17]

Works, one might say, now flow from the believing person in a free and spontaneous manner rather than being assumed as a burdensome requirement to establish right relationship with the divine. The faithful person is already in right relationship with God and does good works not in order to curry favor or divert divine wrath but simply as tokens of her love for God. It is only in this spirit that a faithful person "can determine the manner and have the discretion to mortify his own body, for he may fast, perform vigils, and labor insofar as he sees it necessary for his body in order to subdue its wantonness."[18] Luther leaves the extent and character of such self-mortifying disciplines very much up to the decision of the individual, but he consistently over the course of his career cautions against extravagant overindulgence of the sort he took himself to be guilty of throughout his life in the monastery.[19] Beginning in this work and on many future occasions to which we will turn soon, Luther will again and again insist that idleness is to be avoided at all costs, that good works are required of the believer, and that labor, even or perhaps especially of the most humble sort, is a paramount instance of the good works that are indicative of faith and expected of the person of faith.

That this is so is demonstrated by Luther's choice of analogies to illustrate his point in the immediately following paragraph. Intriguingly his first such choice is "the work of Adam and Eve in paradise." Citing Genesis 2, Luther, like so many medieval theologians before him, notices that "God placed the man He had created in paradise, so that he should labor and tend [*bearbeiten und heten*] the same."[20] Unlike his predecessors, Luther seems to assume that Eve would have worked in paradise as well. Also innovative is Luther's conflation of this sort of work—which in the Middle Ages tended to be read as a straightforward reference to work as labor and was thus the source of a new appreciation for labor as being biblically based and mandated—with work in the sense of any faith-motivated act of Christian virtue. Luther reads Adam's (and Eve's presumably) work as not just a reference to labor but as a metonym for good works as a whole.[21] "Now Adam was created by God as pious and good, without sin, such that he did not need to become pious and justified through his labors and tending. Yet so that he did not go idle, God gave him something to do: plant, cultivate, and safeguard paradise."[22]

For Luther, this familiar point does not just provide scriptural warrant for the importance and dignity of avoiding idleness and doing labors; it is exemplary of the nature of good works as a whole and their intended relationship to faith. Medieval commentators were unanimous in their estimation that this verse proved that Adam had work to do even in a perfected state and that therefore his labors would have been easy and pleasant prior to the Fall. Though we have no reason to think he would dispute it, Luther does not emphasize this point here, stressing instead that Adam's labors in paradise would have had the character and quality that *all* good works should have in the perfectly realized human life. Luther does not emphasize that Adam's labors were easy or pleasant but rather that they

> were purely free works, done for no other purpose than solely to please God and not in order to gain the piety which he already had, and which naturally would also have been inherited by all of us. The works of a believing man are like this; through his faith he is once again placed in paradise and created anew. No work is required to make him pious; instead, solely to please God, he is ordered to do

such free work so that he does not go idle and in order to exercise and safeguard his body.[23]

Uniquely for Luther, Adam's paradisal labor is not just a clue to what role work might play in the complete Christian life, especially that of a monk, or an indication that work can be rewarding and joyful; it is the preeminent example of how all good works should be motivated and in what spirit performed. Faith restores the human being to paradise on earth, where work becomes not just pleasant (though it would stand to reason that it would be) but freely motivated by a desire to please God with no ulterior motive. That Adam's work prevents idleness and fortifies his bodily constitution is a more traditional point; the radical point that Luther makes about Adam's Edenic labor is that it would have been freely performed as a function of Adam's righteousness, not as effortful attempts to secure righteousness. Luther's interpretation of Adam's work in the Garden is thus entirely Lutheran.

He turns again, intriguingly for our purposes, to the language of work in another illustration of this dynamic. Keying off of Jesus's pronouncement in Matthew 7 that "an evil tree bears no good fruit" and, conversely, "a good tree bears no evil fruit," Luther interprets this to mean that a person's deeds do not contribute to their character but that the truth is the other way around: A person's character issues in deeds that are produced in accord with that character. The tree precedes the fruit, such that the fruit does not make the tree good or bad but vice versa. "So too," Luther contends, "must a man first be pious or evil as a person before he does good or evil works; his works make him neither good nor evil, rather he does good or evil works."[24]

It is this priority of character before deed that completely reverses a position Luther detected in Aristotle and on the basis of which (among many other objections) deplored him and his influence on Christian theology. Very early on in the second book of the *Nicomachean Ethics*, Aristotle declares that virtues are acquired by performance of activity, such that "we become just by doing what is just, temperate by doing what is temperate, and brave by doing brave deeds."[25] This Aristotelian principle drew Luther's ire as early as 1517's *Disputation against Scholastic Theology*. There, once again referring to Matthew 7 on good and bad trees, Luther put forward the thesis that "a human being, being a bad tree, can only will and do evil." The subsequent thesis, which is directly entailed by this one, is that "it is false to state that one's inclination is free to choose between either of two opposites. Indeed, the inclination is not free, but captive."[26]

A fascinating (for our purposes) point of further comparison, not obvious to the casual reader, is that both Aristotle and Luther appeal to the example of crafts or trades to support their otherwise completely divergent views. According to Aristotle, virtues and *technai* are exactly the same in this respect. Speaking of the virtues, and how they arise as a result of activities that support them, Aristotle expressly analogizes them to the *technai*, saying that both come about because we practice the relevant activities: "This is like the case of the arts, for that which we are to perform by art after learning, we first learn by performing, e.g., we become builders by building and lyre-players by playing the lyre."[27] Curiously, Luther also uses the example of craftsmanship but gives it the exactly opposite meaning. Luther writes,

We see the same thing in all trades. A good or evil carpenter makes an evil or good house. No work makes a master craftsman, whatever the work may be, but as the master is, so too is his work. The work of man is the same; how he stands in faith or unbelief determines if his works are good or evil, not the other way around, that how his works stand determine if he is pious or believing. Just as works do not make one believing, neither do they make one pious; but just as faith makes one pious, so it also makes one do good works.[28]

For Aristotle, the activity characteristic of a given *techne*, repeatedly undertaken, makes one into a master practitioner of that *techne*; for Luther (who presumably is not invoking the analogy for its value in determining how people actually practically become builders or carpenters), only a good carpenter can build a good house, such that the quality of the work doesn't so much contribute to the acquisition of the corresponding ability as the converse.

All this so far, however, as Luther himself concedes, only touches on good works in general and particularly those done for the benefit and exertion of one's own body. Yet we do not live alone but among others, and to those others the Christian also has responsibilities. Citing Paul's exhortation to the Philippian church "that you would completely gladden my heart by henceforth wanting to be of one mind, each one bearing love toward the other, each one serving the other, and everyone paying heed not to himself or to his own affairs, but to others,"[29] Luther argues that the Christian life, which should take this Pauline mandate to heart, thereby demands that "all works should be directed toward the good of the neighbor, because everyone has enough for himself in his faith, and all other works and life are superfluous for him, so he may thereby serve his neighbor freely out of love."[30] As examples of such works, Luther refers to Luke 2, where the Virgin Mary dutifully observes purification rituals after the birth of Jesus even though she was not impure; Paul's consent to Timothy's circumcision, which quieted potential objections to the Gospel even though observance of the ceremonial law was not necessary for Timothy's salvation; and Matthew 17's report of Jesus's miraculous provision of tax money neither he nor Peter was obligated to pay but that they paid in order to avoid scandal. In every instance, the point is that the believer's submission to the expectation of a righteous work is freely undertaken as an expression of faith and service to others, not as a matter of compulsion or adherence to law.[31]

This should be the model, Luther further maintains, for all Christian institutions. Despite his ferocious criticisms of monasticism and the clergy of his day, Luther suggests that they can serve a useful purpose if their work is pursued in conformity with the scriptural examples he has just cited. "Thus all works by priests, monasteries, and religious foundations should also be done the same way, such that each one does the work of his estate or order only to please another and to rule his own body. They should also provide and be an example to others, who also need to constrain their bodies."[32] Again this is an unusually complimentary concession for Luther to make, that the clergy and the monks could in principle at least serve as inspirational examples if they undertook genuine self-discipline and properly motivated good works. More typical of his style is his concern that "few foundation churches, monasteries, altars, masses, and testaments are Christian; nor are the fasting and prayers specially made to a number of saints." Much of the time, Luther fears, these works are undertaken out of a self-interested but vain hope that they will expiate sin. His advice on the contrary is, "if you wish to make an endowment, pray, or fast, do it not with the thought that you will do something good for yourself, but give it away freely so that other people may enjoy it. And if you do it for their good, then you are a proper Christian."[33] The implication then is that the exact same sorts of external "works"—praying, fasting, bequests—can be either good or bad, again depending on the faith of the individual undertaking them. The same principle, we shall see, holds true of work in the more limited sense.

Surveying Luther's copious writings on labor specifically, we find that the points laid out for the first time in *On the Freedom of a Christian* recur frequently, and we can take note of new and more elaborate developments in Luther's thinking on this subject as well. Many such developments occur, unsurprisingly, in Luther's commentaries on Scripture. Most frequently cited by Luther is Genesis 3:19, while 2 Thessalonians 3:10 comes up frequently (but not perhaps as often as one might have guessed given Luther's early years as an Augustinian monk and a devoted student of Paul), and he wrote a commentary on Ecclesiastes that also afforded the opportunity to speak about work. We observed above that in *On the Freedom of a Christian* Luther declined to exploit Genesis 3:19 to put forward the classic claim that this verse enjoins work as a duty, but he does clearly think that this verse teaches that all people are enjoined to labor: "For in Adam we are all condemned to labor, as God says in Genesis 3[:19], 'In the sweat of your face you shall eat your bread,' and Job 5[:7], 'As the bird is born to fly, so man is born to work.'"[34] In his lectures on Genesis, Luther echoes this straightforward point and generally presses a primitivist interpretation of the Genesis era. When he comes to verse 19 (here translated as "In the sweat of your face you will eat your bread"[35]), he argues that the tasks of today "are far more difficult in our age than they were in the beginning. Even where there is a sure prospect of food, we see how hard it is to hold the household to their duties,"[36] a state of affairs he attributes to "the perversity of people."[37] Although Adam too, Luther alleges, had his share of difficulty in domestic labor, as he lived long enough to witness his son Cain kill his brother, in this respect he is both the progenitor and exemplar of a pervasive human predicament: "There ought," Luther argues, "to be no one who does not feel this sweat."[38] Those who don't he suspects of being "papists" devoted not to hard work but to their "own pleasures and idleness" and thereby exploiting the "wealth produced by the labor of others."[39]

That is not to say though that all work should be of the same sort. Without benefit of transition, Luther raises the question of whether "we all ought to be farmers or at least work with our hands, as some foolishly maintained when the Gospel was first proclaimed."[40] Luther here has in mind his contemporary and sometime rival Andreas Carlstadt, who abandoned academia and bought a farm under the conviction that radical fidelity to the Gospel required preachers and scholars to give up their positions and adopt the work of the common folk. Luther condemned this move, insisting that Carlstadt had in essence given up his calling. In an autobiographical note, he insists that he would find it more pleasant and easier "to be in the garden, to dig with a hoe, and to turn the ground with a spade" than to do the work of a pastor. Extending his own personal opinion that "work on the farm does not compare with this strenuous exertion of ours," Luther decisively repudiates a giant swath of monastic thought and practice, claiming that "we must utterly reject the opinion of those who maintain that only manual labor may be called work."

Interestingly Luther makes his case by citing verses from Jesus and Paul that in monastic writings were used to prove a very different point. Luther quotes Luke 10:5-7: "'When you enter a house,' says He (Luke 10:5-7), 'first say: "Peace be to this house," eating and drinking what they have; for the laborer is worthy of his hire.'" Luther interprets this to mean that "Here the Lord takes the bread from the table of those who hear the Word of God and gives it to the teachers," such that the command of Christ amounts to the saying "that those who teach should have the benefit of the labor of others." Luther also cites 1 Corinthians 9:14: "'He who teaches the Gospel should also live by the Gospel.' And in support of this statement he (St. Paul) also quotes the command of the Law (Deut. 25:4): 'You shall not muzzle the mouth of the ox that treads out the corn.'"[41] That ministers of the Gospel were entitled to support from the church was uncontroversial, as we have seen. At least as far back as Augustine it was agreed that ministers should not have to work for their support apart from their Gospel labors, even if Paul himself sometimes did. These verses supported that point, by carving out a form of religious life that was not subject to the general injunction to work, an injunction for many centuries laid even upon monks. Luther's point though is a bit different: Based on these verses, he does not draw the conclusion that ministers of the Gospel are not required to work but rather that active pastoral ministry already *is work*.

"These and similar passages show clearly that the sweat of the face is of many kinds," Luther concludes.[42] Carlstadt is mistaken to think himself obliged to do manual labor; if he is a true pastor he already has a job to do, and as we will see, for Luther it is fitting that each person stay with the calling he has been given. As he declares later on in the same lecture, "each individual must be convinced that he should not abandon the position into which God has placed him."[43] Inspired again by Paul, this time in his first letter to the Corinthians (7:20: "Let every man abide in the same calling wherein he was called"), this sentiment takes on the weight of unshakable principle in Luther's writings. Scripture then as he reads it does not afford a justification for why pastors should not have to work—it teaches that pastors are already workers and that they should not abandon their post.

Luther is also required to exegete 2 Thessalonians 3:10 in a somewhat original way. In his lectures on 1 Timothy, Luther condemns the "Enthusiasts" who insisted on the agrarian way of life. Against them he proclaims that he is already in effect at work in the country as a minister of the Gospel.

> The Waldensian preachers are compelled to be workmen and provide for themselves. "If anyone will not work, let him not eat," we read in Thessalonians (2 Thess. 3:10). I interpret "work" as understanding, as working in the Word, as I mentioned earlier. We work, and we work in the Word. To minister the Word is also work. Paul does not order Timothy to become a farmer.[44]

Let no one think that the sectarians have Paul on their side on this score. In order to combat an impulse afoot in the wake of his own reforms, Luther has to condemn Carlstadt's and the Waldensians' invocation of the familiar Pauline injunction on work. In this case though the more "radical" reformers extend the Augustinian argument to themselves as ministers of the Gospel, making the duty to labor with the hands truly comprehensive in scope. Luther takes the tack though that ministry is already work, and that if Paul wanted Timothy to farm he would have ordered him to do so.

Continuing on with the reading from his lectures on Genesis, Luther then insists work is of different kinds and retrieves the traditional threefold structure of medieval society, though he gives it a more expansive set of applications. Of the three forms of work he writes, "the first is that of the farmers or householders; the second is that of the officers of the state; and the third is that of the teachers in the church."[45] Contours of the familiar medieval division between workers, warriors, and prayers are discernible underneath this framework.[46] There are those who do manual work and maintain households, those who serve the body politic, and those who work on behalf of the church, and in each case Luther seems to have a somewhat wider conception of who fits into each category. The "officers of the state" are not just knights but all those who have political positions; pastors and servants of the church are not just (in keeping with Reformation developments Luther himself in many cases instigated) ordained clerics or dedicated religious; and everyone in some way or another has a household to be concerned with, which anticipates another point we will see recur in our study: For Luther, these categories do not exclude one another. A holder of a civic office or a pastor could also be (again, for the first time as of the Reformation) a husband and father.

In keeping though with a much more traditional outlook, Luther is hopelessly romantic about farming. He confidently proclaims that the "best-situated" of the three classes is the farmers, and he cites Virgil's *Georgics* for his support: "Exceedingly happy if they realized their blessings!"[47] Conceding that "they are plagued with hard labor," Luther nevertheless insists that the farmer's "labor is seasoned with matchless pleasure, as daily the new and wonderful sight of the creatures impresses itself upon their eyes." By contrast, the labors of civil servants and pastors are much heavier, if indeed the holder of such a position seeks to discharge it responsibly and takes care to do the job well. Obviously, he allows, if someone in such a position neglects their actual duties, then being so well-placed makes for a comfortable path in life. For the conscientious however, "in both state and church, on the other hand, there are daily dangers and countless burdens," such that "in one single day these people work and sweat more than a farmer does in an entire month, if you consider the vastness of their work and its various dangers."[48]

Luther develops this thought at some length, using the Emperor Maximilian as his example of a political ruler overwhelmed with his responsibilities, so much so that "he never had enough leisure for taking food. And so at times he was compelled to get away from his tasks and to hide in the forests, where he went hunting," a recourse that Luther defends as a matter of necessity for the overtaxed ruler rather than a self-indulgent pleasure. Because of the weight of political responsibility, Luther again contrasts the lot of the officeholder with that of the farmer: "Now what plowing or digging or other farm labors will you liken to the labor which the governing of such a large empire calls for? Therefore they are called kings and princes as a mark of their dignity, when in truth kings and princes are the most wretched of all servants."[49] He makes a comparable contrast between farm labor and pastoral work, this time using Augustine as his example. "We say the same thing about the worry of a pastor, which must be considered so much the greater because the duties he performs are the more important."[50] Here Luther has primarily in mind the protracted combat the great church father took up against a host of heretics and pagans.

On the strength of these examples Luther determines that it is

> the utmost stupidity for the enthusiasts to insist on manual labor, which is useful for strengthening the body, when, by contrast, these very great labors in the state and church wear out the body and drain off all vitality, as it were, from its innermost centers. We should, therefore, differentiate between degrees of hard work. The hard work in connection with a household is great; greater is that connected with the state; and greatest is that in connection with the church.[51]

The only people who don't work hard—and this is a running polemic for Luther—are "the pope, the cardinals, and the whole pack of wicked men who use up great wealth, although they do no work and are concerned only with their bellies and their leisure."[52] It is to this group that Luther maintains Paul's classic teaching in 2 Thessalonians—"He who does not work should not eat"—most especially applies. In a precise reversal of the early medieval consensus, that it is to the workers of the church that this verse alone does *not* apply, Luther says the ones to whom it *most* applies are the church hierarchy, starting with the pope himself. "But to work in the church means to preach, administer the Sacraments, contend with the enthusiasts, remove offenses, edify the godly, etc.," and those who actually do this work are worthy of their recompense.[53]

Adam's case is an interesting and apparently unique one, because Luther sees the father of the human race as having held all three offices, which makes his life

> as the initiator of sin … worse than ours, if we appraise it correctly. Where we work hard, each one in his own station, Adam was compelled to exert himself in the hard work of the household, of the state, and of the church all by himself. As long as he lived, he alone held all these positions among his descendants. He supported his family, ruled it, and trained it in godliness; he was a father, king, and priest. And experience teaches how each one of these positions abounds in grief and dangers.[54]

If each form of life and work has its own attendant grievances, Adam experienced all of them compounded, as he was master of a household, held political power, and functioned as the intermediary between his family and God.

That work is difficult Luther frequently admits, and he cites this difficulty on more than one occasion as the primary reason he thinks people are disposed to avoid the responsibilities that attach to the various estates or offices that people occupy. Nevertheless, he repeatedly invokes Genesis 3:19 against the human disposition to laziness and underscores that God has enjoined a duty to labor upon all. Typical remarks on this theme come up in one of Luther's sermons on John chapter 14. Referring to the first epistle of John in his exposition on the Gospel, Luther cites the "lust of the flesh" as one of the ruling powers of the world and provides his understanding of what this means:

> The expression "lust of the flesh" means that the world seeks and strives solely for things that serve the comfort and well-being of the flesh, which is loath to undergo any toil, unpleasantness, or discomfort, although man is ordained to earn his bread in the sweat of his face (Gen. 3:19). Everyone wants to be exempt from this and tries only to be free from it, to live a life of ease and comfort, untrammeled and unrestrained. This is apparent in all walks of life, high and low.[55]

As illustrations of the "walks" of life he has in mind Luther offers a husband who prefers consorting with prostitutes to his own wife and a magistrate who shifts the burden of his office onto others and milks his position for his own benefit and enrichment. In this context then Luther mentions the first two estates—household and political office—but omits church leadership. Nevertheless, the general point seems to remain:

> All aspire to advance in life and to attain high position. But when they obtain this and feel the labor and the worry it involves, they soon grow weary and stop their efforts; for they sought only pleasure and ease. It is similar in the state of matrimony. All seek its pleasure and enjoyment; but when they do not find this in marriage, they resent it. This also applies to other positions and stations in life.[56]

Luther has a keen psychological sense for this particular form of dissatisfaction, which has a rather contemporary flavor to it. Readers today are bound to feel a pang of self-recognition in Luther's often wry but apposite observations on how readily people become annoyed with the positions they themselves have sought out in life.

> He who wants to administer his office properly and in a God-pleasing manner will soon find what danger and difficulty this entails, and he will often join in the world's chorus of lament that life is hard and miserable. He will soon exclaim: "Who would have believed that this involves so much labor? Oh, if I were only done with it!" Yes, my dear man, if you did not want this, you should have kept away from it in the first place. Who would not like to harvest nothing but joy, pleasure, or honor and sit on top?[57]

This temptation to despair over one's position is one that Luther himself experienced. In a sermon preached on the Seventeenth Sunday after Trinity, Luther makes a similar observation about how people easily become discouraged by the burdens of responsibility and hard work:

> Before they get to the top rung, everyone is eager for the top job. But once these individuals come into an office and are expected to carry out its duties, they end

up "sitting on the job." Anyone who took the office with the intent of doing what is right and serving his constituents faithfully will soon find the work too much. He very soon becomes disillusioned and weary, and, at the very least, he will think, even if he doesn't say it aloud, What the devil, who gave me this job?[58]

Again Luther thinks this dangerous disillusionment pertains to all the stations of life. How easy it is for a young woman or man, he says, to be unaware of all the difficulties that attend marriage and therefore unrealistic about what is entailed by it and to find themselves mutually unhappy as a result of the rude confrontation with reality that awaits them. With respect to political leadership, Luther imagines an average citizen not satisfied with his calling but imagining that he would like to be mayor:

> But if that happens and he becomes mayor, inheriting the stress, the work, and the trouble, then he says, To the devil with this position! I'm ready to chuck it. That's what it means to have an office. To be on top is no frolic or bunny dance. It entails work and stress, so that no one in his right mind would actively seek it.[59]

The same is true of church work, according to Paul's statement in 1 Timothy 3:21 that "If a man desire the office of a bishop, he desireth a good work."[60] Luther is careful to specify that this cannot mean that one is entitled to an extravagant lifestyle but to the true nobility of service to others, whether in the capacity of a "bishop, pastor, or schoolteacher, provided he has the discipline and capacity for the task. It is commendable, Paul is saying, if someone desires to be of service to people. But if you want the position only for self-glorification, you are a lazy lout, of service to no one, seeking only your own gain, glory, and self-indulgence."[61] Luther himself admits that his own work has sometimes seemed burdensome enough that he too has been tempted to be rid of it.

> I myself must confess, if I were to bare my heart, that the same thought has come to me, Oh, why did not the Lord God raise up someone else to be preacher to the German people? Because the lukewarm spirit is so great, the work too much, the maliciousness and thanklessness of the people so overwhelming, that flesh and blood can scarcely tolerate it but becomes morose and impatient, ready to chuck it and be free of it once and for all.[62]

But this attitude is no good for either Luther himself or Christians in general, and here Luther explicitly connects the difficulty of work with the hardship of the Christian life.

> For he who cannot endure unpleasantness in his position and dislikes work will find the exalted office of being a Christian even less tolerable. If he cannot suffer petty vexations in his position, what will he do when he is asked to enter the lists against death, the world, and the devil for Christ's sake? Therefore being a Christian implies that one does not love what the world loves; one must love even minor offices in order to bear the physical discomforts and hardships they involve.[63]

So once again for Luther work in the ordinary sense is keyed to a theological theme: If one cannot faithfully discharge the difficult tasks that belong to their job in the mundane sense, then there is little reason to believe that they could bear up under the demands of the Christian life, which calls for rigor, self-discipline, and endurance against even more profound and universal challenges: death, the world, and the devil. If a Christian is to defeat these enemies then she not only has to put up with the "petty vexations" that belong to her appointed tasks but even has to *love* minor offices, which will evidently not be glamorous, easy, or rewarding.

Part of the reason why a Christian is called to faithful and dutiful execution of appointed labors is not just the plain witness of Scripture as Luther sees it but also his vision of how God is at work within human effort and striving. This is a complex point, because Luther at various times writes confidently about a correlation between effort and reward when it comes to work, sometimes seeming sure that God rewards hard work, but at other times he admits that there is no apparent correlation between effort and reward, and that even or perhaps especially in such circumstances Christians are called to persevere in the work that belongs to their particular station in life. We have seen already the danger of dissatisfaction or discouragement that attends work, and we have seen that Luther criticized the officials of the church hierarchy for their corruption, decadence, and idleness, but there is another danger inherent in our attitude toward work, and that is anxiety or concern.

This idea is broached in some detail by Luther in his "Exposition of Psalm 127, for the Christians at Riga in Livonia." The first verse of Psalm 127 is: "Except the Lord build the house, they labour in vain that build it," and Luther interprets this opening declaration as pertaining mainly to household management and the vicissitudes that attend the establishment of house and home. He points out that experience seems to suggest a high degree of unpredictability when it comes to the relationship of effort to success in such areas; many people start off married life with plenty of money but soon lose it; others manage very well without much money. "Reason and the world," he argues, "think that married life and the making of a home ought to proceed as they intend; they try to determine things by their own decisions and actions, as if their work could take care of everything."[64]

A glance at the common run of things though shows that this is just not so, and the reason it is not so is because God is alone the source of reward and blessing, and at least sometimes God "disrupts marriage and household management, and turns them so strangely topsy-turvy."[65] Solomon (to whom Luther attributes Psalm 127), he claims, wants to refute the wisdom of the world and point to God as the true source of all good things. This is why God turns things topsy-turvy, to furnish "an assault on unbelief, to bring to shame the arrogance of reason with all works and cleverness, and to constrain them to believe."[66] Frequently then the outcome of our labors does not seem to be a straightforward or rational result of the effort invested in our work, but for Luther this is simply evidence that unless God builds the house, human labor is in vain. Here is the core of a paradoxical set of teachings that we find Luther affirming again and again in their very tension: A person must work, but only God rewards work. Labor is necessary for blessing and reward but not sufficient for it.

Luther's key summation of this doctrine is worth quoting at length:

We are not to understand from this that God forbids us to work. Man must and ought to work, ascribing his sustenance and the fullness of his house, however, not to his own labor but solely to the goodness and blessing of God. For where men ascribe these things to their own labor, there covetousness and anxiety quickly arise, and they hope by much labor to acquire much. But then there is this contradiction, namely, that some people labor prodigiously, yet scarcely have enough to eat, while others are slower and more relaxed in their work, and wealth pours in on them. All this is because God wants the glory, as the one who alone gives the growth [1 Corinthians 3:6–7]. For if you should till the soil faithfully for a hundred years and do all the work in the world, you couldn't bring forth from the earth even a single stalk; but God without any of your labor, while you sleep, produces from that tiny kernel a stalk with as many kernels on it as he wills.[67]

There are a number of points here that require some attention. First, Luther reiterates that work is by no means forbidden, that this verse does not proscribe work. On the next page he once again uses Genesis 3:19 as proof that "God commanded Adam to eat his bread in the sweat of his face [Gen. 3:19]. God wills that man should work, and without work He will give him nothing."[68] The point is that within our very work, which we must regard as incumbent upon us, we must not simultaneously attribute whatever success or benefit might be yielded in connection with that work to the work itself but only to God. The same teaching Luther detects in Deuteronomy 8:17, where Moses counsels the people of Israel against imagining that their blessings have been secured by their own effort. "For when wealth abounds, the godless heart of man feels: 'I have wrought these things with my own efforts.' Nor does it notice that these are simply blessings of God sometimes through our efforts, sometimes without our efforts, but never from our efforts and always given out of His free mercy."[69] Humility is called for in the face of the unstable correlation between effort and reward, an instability that is providentially ordered. The phrase "sometimes through our efforts, sometimes without our efforts, but never from our efforts" captures this Lutheran ambivalence nicely. The godly person then will work but will do so without pretending that their work is the source of whatever good that work yields (or at least appears to yield).

> Otherwise we may think that our possessions have been produced by our powers or efforts; or, as he says here, we may think that "we have achieved this wealth" by the strength and vigor of our hand. But we are to remember the Lord God, that it is He Himself who grants the powers for achieving this wealth, not through our merit but because He has promised to do so.[70]

Besides humility, another ethical consequence implied by this tension is freedom from anxiety and concern. As Luther observed above, whenever we attribute success to our own efforts, there is a temptation not only to self-congratulation but also to anxiety, since people convinced of the efficacy of their own effort aspire to amass much wealth as a result of much hard work. Yet we have seen already that Luther is convinced that these two things do not necessarily go hand in hand. He plainly calls this a "contradiction," that some can work hard and reap little benefit, while others seem to gain much without trying. This contradiction is the result of God's desire to secure glory for himself as the author and dispenser of all good things. There is perhaps a parallel here to the gratuitousness of divine grace: Just as God freely dispenses grace without our doing good works (while also mandating the performance of good works), so too God freely dispenses material and tangible blessings and is capable of doing so without our effort at all while nevertheless expecting effort from us. In Luther's agricultural example, God can make the crops grow without us plowing or sowing; conversely, we can plow and sow as much as we like, but if God does not make the crops grow then they won't, regardless of how much work we do.

Luther reads Solomon as offering further support for this notion in Ecclesiastes and its famous declaration that "the race is not to the swift nor the battle to the strong nor bread to the wise nor riches to the intelligent nor favor to the men of skill; but time and chance happen to them all."[71] That the race goes not to the swift means that success or failure does not ultimately depend upon the person, regardless of how many gifts they may enjoy. The strong are sometimes defeated by the weak, the many overcome by the few. On Luther's account, this insight applies to any execution of an appointed office, which means that in every case

> I cannot determine the outcome or the success, regardless of how much I may labor. You simply do what is your duty, and the Lord will find His appointed time to make use of your labor. We cannot make any judgments about these matters; we ought to labor, but not to prescribe the end and the outcome of our work.[72]

Because there is an irreducible misalignment here, one that almost seems to inject an element of arbitrariness into our daily effort, there is no sense at all in a faithful Christian worrying about the outcome of their labors. Anxiety and concern are only in order where control is available, and Luther is fairly clear that we are not in control of the outcome of our own labors.

Returning to his exposition of Psalm 127, Luther maintains that Solomon sanctions work but rejects worry and covetousness.

> This is as if he were to say: Man must work, but that work is in vain if it stands alone and thinks it can sustain itself. Work cannot do this; God must do it. Therefore work in such a manner that your labor is not in vain. Your labor is in vain when you worry, and rely on your own efforts to sustain yourself. It behooves you to labor, but your sustenance and the maintenance of your household belong to God alone.[73]

For this reason, Luther advises that we keep labor and sustenance far apart in our minds, indeed as far apart as "heaven and earth or God and man."[74] His reasoning seems to be that labor and the expected result of labor, the fruitful outcomes toward which our labors are consistently directed, simply do not have as close an association as we would hope. If God correlates these two—labor and result—then so be it, but that the matter is in God's hands means it should not burden our minds unduly.

To be sure, sometimes Luther speaks as if we do have reason to believe that God will reward our effort,[75] and he even finds passages from Solomon that seem to indicate as much.

> In the Proverbs of Solomon we often read how the lazy are punished because they will not work. Solomon says, "A slack hand causes poverty, but industrious hands bring riches" [Proverbs 10:4]. This and similar sayings sound as if our sustenance depended on our labor; though he says in the same passage [Proverbs 10:22], as also in this psalm [127:1], that it depends on God's blessing.[76]

Even so, Luther on balance teaches that we should be prepared for anything and, having dutifully done all we can, we should renounce anxiety and trust in God's gracious provision.

Naturally Matthew 6 is a key passage for Luther on this point. The birds of the air to which Christ gestures as a model for the freedom from anxiety that should characterize Christian faith Luther says "perform their tasks" but "do no work from which they gain sustenance."[77] The birds have activities that are characteristic of and expected of them, but these activities are not the ones that furnish them with their necessities. It is God who provided them with the food they need, which they had to discover but which they did not create.

> Similarly, man must necessarily work and busy himself at something. At the same time, however, he must know that it is something other than his labor which furnishes him sustenance; it is the divine blessing. Because God gives him nothing unless he works, it may seem as if it is his labor which sustains him; just as the little birds neither sow nor reap, but they would certainly die of hunger if they did not fly about to seek their food. The fact that they find food, however, is not due to their own labor, but to God's goodness.[78]

The same is true for human beings, who depend on divine provision of everything needful for life, such that "all our labor is nothing more than the finding and collecting of God's gifts; it is quite unable to create or preserve anything."[79] With this wisdom Luther attributes to Solomon the solution to one of the most vexing universal afflictions of humanity: the problem of "how to feed our poor stomachs."[80] Taking all worldly proposals and rejecting them outright, Solomon shows how labor is in vain when directed toward self-sustenance and deluded about its own efficacy, a state of affairs that only brings about further anxiety, arrogance, and lack of faith. We are to take up an occupation that will keep us busy, free of worry, and "place everything in God's keeping."[81]

One of the more memorable images that Luther uses in connection with this idea is of human effort as a "mask" under which God is operating in disguise. As he puts it in his lectures on Deuteronomy, "He uses our effort as a mask under which He blesses us and dispenses His gifts, so that there is a place for faith. Otherwise we may think that our possessions have been produced by our powers or efforts."[82] The image of the mask is connected to Luther's retrieval of the structure from Augustine and carried forward by Bernard of Clairvaux[83] of "using without using" or using earthly things for spiritual profit while not adhering to them unduly. At the very outset of his commentary on Ecclesiastes Luther repudiates the erroneous interpretation that Solomon herein condemns creation and worldly things as inherently bad. Invoking the goodness of creation as taught by Genesis, Luther counters this misreading by saying, "God has made all things to be good and to be useful for some human purpose. What is being condemned in this book, therefore, is not the creatures but the depraved affection and desire of us men, who are not content with the creatures of God that we have and with their use."[84]

The proper way to despise the world is not to dispense with its goods but to live "in the midst of these things" without being "carried away by his affection for them."[85] To honor this Augustinian principle is tantamount to seeing through worldly things and operations as just so many "masks" concealing the divine hand at work in human affairs. Referring to God's commandment to the people of Israel to at once take up arms into the land to possess it yet at the same time not to trust in the strength of their own weapons, Luther shows that the condition of being so armed is just a mask in the sense that it provides cover for what is not their own action or effort but God's effort via human means. To thus make use of worldly things and procedures while not being reliant upon them is to know the truth behind the mask. "Yes, if someone knows that the power and wisdom of God are of such a sort, he trusts wholly, not in the mask of God but in the Word behind the mask; and he can and does perform wonders, yes, everything, in the Lord."[86]

There is an existential corollary to this important point. If we can see the masks of God for what they are, then we avoid despair, because we recognize that God can act on our behalf either with or without our cooperation being adequate to the task at hand. "So it will come about that he [the believer] walks on, free and safe in the midst of presumption and despair, and does not tempt God while he has what he needs; again, he does not despair if what he needs is lacking."[87] Speaking elsewhere directly about the prohibition against putting God to the test in this way, Luther argues that God can bring about salvation whether the means of deliverance is at hand or not, such that "one must use things, but one must not trust in them. Only in God should one trust, whether that which you may use is at hand or lacking."[88] This trust is difficult when work seems unrewarding, but Luther exhorts his readers to remain faithful to their charge and execute their duties in confidence that they are performing the will of God.

Recalling the instance from Scripture where Peter spends a night fishing with no yield, Luther admits that life is a test, and that "when we experience what Peter did, that is, toil all night catching nothing, we tend to become anxious, start to grumble, and become so discouraged that we're ready to run away from it all."[89] Like Peter, though, whom Jesus commands to throw out his net despite the fact that he has spent hours in fruitless labor, and who then does so only to haul in a massive load of fish, Luther advises everyone to persist in their task even when it seems hopeless, because the work has a divine warrant and will eventually yield fruit.

> If you are a pastor engaged in preaching and teaching your people, and the response hasn't been all that great, don't be dismayed and diverted. Say to yourself: God has

ordered me to proclaim his Word, and that's what I'll continue to do. If it doesn't always prosper, God knows why; if my work does thrive, it pleases both him and me. The same attitude should prevail in any other of life's callings."[90]

Like Peter, we too have an assurance that even in the face of difficulty the station in life we occupy with its attendant responsibilities is worth doing and will yield fruit, all the while remaining untroubled by the timing or quantity of that yield.

The opposite attitude would be one that sticks too closely to love of earthly things and relies upon them for deliverance; this attitude, though, leads to despair: "The godless, however, are puffed up by the property that is on hand; and when this is gone, they are downcast, because they grasp only the mask of things."[91] To grasp only the mask is to see the surface, which only ever ambiguously betrays the divine hand at work. Our striving is required because God has decreed that we are to assist him in his work, though our work is strictly speaking not needed for him to accomplish his purposes. As Luther puts it in his commentary on the Psalms, "God could easily give you grain and fruit without your plowing and planting. But He does not want to do so. Neither does He want your plowing and planting alone to give you grain and fruit; but you are to plow and plant and then ask His blessing."[92] This conviction extends to "all our work to God—whether in the fields, in the garden, in the city, in the house, in war, or in government," which in every case Luther calls "the masks of God, behind which He wants to remain concealed and do all things."[93] There is consolation and encouragement to be had when one discerns that the outwardly mundane circumstances of their work situation are in fact disguises for God's own work in the world and that human workers are ultimately cooperating with the divine worker just by assiduously attending to their given tasks. To see through the mask is to discern that what we do in our jobs on earth has a heavenly significance and that this significance is grasped precisely when we see through the worldly circumstances of our jobs for what they are, that is, we see them precisely as a mask and nothing more.

According to Luther, confidence also comes from knowledge that God has ordained certain stations for people to occupy. We have seen already that he largely adopts the threefold medieval scheme and makes it his own. He puts this scheme to even further use by demonstrating that the stations God has established for people's faithful occupancy are bases for trusting in the dignity of the station to which the Christian believer has been assigned and the importance of holding to that station. One important discussion of this idea occurs in Luther's commentary on 1 Peter 3, where the apostle calls for one mind among all believers. For this sort of unity to be preserved, Luther argues, Christians must have one shared conviction about what is right and good, but that this unity will necessarily entail different kinds of work. "We cannot all do work of the same kind. Everyone must do his or her own kind of work. A man's work is different from that of a woman, a servant's from that of the master, etc. It is stupid to teach that we should all do the same kind of work, as those foolish preachers have taught."[94]

On the contrary, Luther holds that the only avenue to unity of mind in the Christian community is if everyone does their own assigned work; the unity that results spontaneously is precisely that born of adherence to the principle that everyone should do their own assigned work. In this way Luther picks up the originally Platonic theme of each person's attentiveness to their own task of moral self-improvement, resulting in the coordinated justice of the whole community. Vying over what sort of work is best has been the hallmark of medieval church history, with orders arguing that their own charism was superior to all the others and squabbling over which station is the most exalted: This is precisely disharmony in Luther's judgment, not unity at all. The cure is to assure everyone that

> before God no work is better than the other, but that through faith they are all alike, then the hearts would have remained in harmony, and we would all be of like mind and say: "Before God the bishop's order or position is no better than that of the common man. Nor is the position of a nun better than that of a married woman, and so in positions of all kinds."[95]

If everyone correctly regards her own work as in no way inferior to that of another, then unity results, because disunity comes about only when one class of person haughtily looks down upon the others as inferior.

Instead we should affirm the goodness of the station into which God has assigned us, recognizing that it is our own and thus good for us and ought not to be abandoned lightly (or perhaps not at all). This is the key to lightening the burdens that work imposes upon us and rightly discharging our specific duties. Adherence to the particularities of our own station "calls us away from alien anxieties to our own business."[96] This too is part of Solomon's wisdom in Ecclesiastes as Luther understands it. Solomon, he claims,

> wants you to do your duty happily in accordance with your assigned task and to leave other things to other people. He wants us to enjoy our pleasure when it is present, not as the wicked do, nor grieve when it is absent but bear it with equanimity. You should, he says, have a happy spirit and an active body, but in such a way that you abide in your assigned place.[97]

Unfortunately, it seems characteristically human that just as we easily become dissatisfied and discouraged with our lot, so too we are frequently inclined to meddle with others' work, thereby doing neither their work nor our own appointed work well.[98]

Luther could be read as preaching a fairly quietistic and static view of social structuring, but at the same time, it should be noted that a person's station is conceived rather broadly to encompass in one dimension all their domestic responsibilities, which for the vast majority of people not also engaged in civic or religious business probably entails their job as well. There is thus no reason to think that Luther would automatically approve of any particular expression of an estate or station, or that he would insist a person keep any particular job, but he does recognize that there will be particular offices that admit of greater or lesser degrees of importance. He admits that "in temporal affairs there will be those who hold stations of honor and power. We cannot all be the same," but we are to be content with our situation, neither scrabbling for honors to which we are not entitled nor envying the benefits of someone else's station, provided they are faithful occupants thereof.[99] It cannot be wrong, Luther asserts, merely to be in a position of earthly power and honor, but it is wrong to seek one's own glory or to forsake one's duty.

Abandonment of one's own station, whether high or low, is doubly unfortunate in that all stations, properly understood, are directed not toward the benefit of the officeholder but to the benefit of others. That they be executed well is crucially important, because God has ordained them for good use, and that use redounds to the help of others. In keeping with the Platonic heritage, dutiful work at one's station is not for one's own benefit but for the benefit of others. This proper use of stations also has its own appropriate sort of concern, which Luther distinguishes from the blameworthy anxiety that we have seen has no place in faithful Christian life. "Concern about making a living" as Luther puts it is not a temptation but a virtue in the eyes of the world; it is service to Mammon, which "means thinking only about this life, about how to get rich here and how to accumulate and increase our money and property, as though we were going to stay here forever."[100] This is not the same as taking due interest in how to secure what we require for life; much less is it the same as taking due interest in your God-given responsibilities, and once more Luther gives examples from household management, political authority, and pastoral care. These concerns he calls "official," which are not the same as self-seeking greed because they are ordered toward the advantage of those whom they serve. In fact, Luther goes so far as to say that official concern is hindered by self-seeking greed.[101]

There is an assurance that comes with faithful attendance to the duties appropriate to one's station if we are convinced that these things come from God; then the duties of our work are done to and for God. "Therefore," Luther preaches on one occasion,

> with all his effort and labor a person can have all that is good, joy in the heart and a good conscience, because he knows that his work and labor are a service pleasing to God; also, things need not become a grind for him if he thus resigns himself to his service and calling. For there can be no greater joy than knowing that our life and deeds are a service to God.[102]

The peace and consolation that come from this knowledge Luther says ought to be worth the price of the wealth of the world, and yet we can have it free of charge if only we remain in our calling and do what it requires of us. Fidelity to the tasks also elevates the job, no matter how menial, because even the lowliest station is one that God has instituted and that we thus can be sure is worth doing even if it does not yield many earthly rewards.

This is yet another dimension of meaning that Luther reads out of Jesus's declaration that "Every sound tree bears good fruit, but the bad tree bears evil fruit."[103] Here he links this idea to the quality of the station, not the quality of the individual human being, as he did in *On the Freedom of a Christian*. If the station is good, as Luther now argues, then right actions done in accord with that station by a person faithfully working within it must be good as well. Luther advises,

> Learn to look at your station on the basis of this statement and draw this conclusion from it: "Thank God, I know now that I am in a good and blessed station, one that

pleases God. Though it may be annoying to my flesh and contain a great deal that is troubling and disgusting, I shall cheerfully put up with all that. Here I have the comfort that Christ says: 'A sound tree bears good fruit.' He says this about every station that is grounded in the Word of God, though it may be despised and decried by the world and the special saints."[104]

Conversely, the condemnation of the evil tree Luther sees as a reason to cast further aspersion on the monastic orders, which outwardly seem to have all the good fruit one might want, but which are highly open to question according to Luther inasmuch as the monastic way of life is *not* ordained by God as a proper station, and thus no good can come from it.[105]

What this lack of sanction means is that we are not reliable judges of what sort of work is most estimable. The world sees the monk as inherently pious, and the world despises the man who hauls manure. But it is the latter in Luther's judgment who is more worthy of respect. "When a pious hired man is hauling a wagonload of manure to the field, he is actually hauling a wagonload of precious figs and grapes—but in the sight of God, not in our own sight, since we do not believe, so that everyone gets tired of his station and goes staring at another one."[106] In the sight of God all stations are equally dignified, which means that outward distinctions fail. If being a faithful Christian does not entail undertaking extreme, visible acts of piety, in the monastic fashion, then what sort of distinctive activities should be undertaken by Christians? If these people really do love even the lowliest and smallest offices and their attendant tasks, then what makes them special?

> Judged by such common tasks as those performed by father and mother, child, servant, husband or wife, the heathen would fare better than we. Therefore we must have something different and out of the ordinary—something beyond what the common man does, as, for instance, entering a cloister, lying on the ground, wearing a hair shirt, or praying day and night without ceasing. Such works they call a holy life and Christian fruit. And they are quick to deduce from this that rearing children, doing domestic work, etc., is not a holy life.[107]

Yet this conclusion is utterly unwarranted. Even Luther himself admits that of course the outward works of monasticism with its show of piety *appear* more impressive than the humdrum labors of an ordinary worker like a farmer or a maid. The point is that the quality of the work comes not from such externals but from the inner faith of the worker and her right relationship to God; if this is in good order then she is, to continue the metaphor, a good tree that cannot help but bear good fruit. This is true "even if it were something more menial than when a farm hand loads and hauls manure."[108] Despite outward appearances, then, there is, Luther affirms, a great difference between a menial task done by a heathen and done by one who remains in Christ and is animated by faith in him, and this difference holds "even if the work is completely identical."[109]

This radicalized Augustinian thesis is not mitigated by the fact, which Luther concedes, that a true Christian's work is not as "striking" as that of a monk, since the workaday Christian confines himself to the ordinary tasks that come up in everyday life. The trouble is that the world is unable to see that these are works performed by a new person in Christ. Therefore one and the same work becomes different even in one and the same person, depending on whether it is performed before or after he has come to faith in Christ.[110]

The quality and character of work then depend utterly on the orientation of the worker toward or away from Christ. Luther countenances no value one way or the other to the work considered "as such"; in fact, there may be no such thing on his scheme as the work as such, only whether it is judged or commended. Luther boldly declares that years of daily mass, abstinence, and self-mortification, while perhaps qualifying as "great and arduous tasks," amount strictly to "nothing" if they are not done in a spirit of faith, while the lowly tasks of a faithful maid, done in no way outstandingly in comparison to other similar labors, amount to "precious gems." Luther's obvious conclusion is that "the point is to judge the work by the motive behind it, not by the kind of work it is. What is done—whether great or small, much or little—is not important."[111]

This is why Luther can flatly assert that "there is no distinction among works."[112] To an unprecedented degree, Luther elevates the most humble and menial sort of labor, dignifying it as being not just on an equal footing with the officially religious life but in many cases obviously superior to it, at least where monasticism—which, keep in mind, served for centuries as the unquestioned highest standard of calling to which a Christian could aspire—is concerned. "I must esteem everything as good and must approve of the kind of work everyone does, provided that it is not a sin in itself."[113] Again Luther's example contrasts the excellence of a believing woman's calling to marriage with the haughtiness of a monk, and he expressly declares the former superior to the latter. Prior to Luther, no Christian theologian went this far to affirm the value of ordinary labor or to denigrate monasticism in relation to other forms of work.[114] In one of his sermons Luther straightforwardly preaches that "when a maid cooks, washes, sweeps, and does other housework it is looked down upon as trivial. But since there is a command from God for this, such trivial work cannot but be extolled as a service to God, surpassing by far all the holiness and austere life of all monks and nuns."[115]

In conclusion, we might say that Luther has not secularized labor, but he has laicized it. Work is still very much invested with theological significance: Work is a mask of God's operation in the world; work is a duty for Christians, including pastors and teachers, who are workers in the same sense that a farmer is; and all sorts of work, including that of the lowly and of women, is equally dignified in the sight of God if not in the estimation of the world. By contrast to a thinker as proximate to his own time as Petrarch, monastic labor is no longer normative or an example for lay imitation. Quite to the contrary, monks practice a station that is not authorized by God, and while they make a great show of piety in the world, their works are corrupt at their basis and thus irredeemable. Luther's works then thus mark a significant transformation in Western theological attitudes about work.

7

John Ruskin

A neglected contribution to this study can be found in the eclectic writings of John Ruskin, who turned from a celebrated career as a noted art critic and exposed himself to public ridicule by writing on the social ills of his day. Like his far more famous contemporary Karl Marx (whom he never mentioned in thousands of pages of writing), he was profoundly disturbed by the conditions of the working class in the rapidly industrializing economies of Europe, believed in the dignity of human labor of all sorts, and was trenchantly opposed to the doctrines of political economy. Unlike Marx, Ruskin was not a socialist or a revolutionary[1] (quite to the contrary, in the opening of the first chapter of his memoir he called himself a "violent Tory of the old school"[2]), was not romantic about work and did not anticipate its eventual decline or disappearance, and based his arguments on Christian theology and classical thought (he read Plato almost every day and was constantly steeped in the Bible and Christian theology).[3]

Ruskin was at first known only as an art critic, easily one of the most accomplished of his day, whose reputation rested on the multivolume *Modern Painters*, *The Stones of Venice*, and *The Seven Lamps of Architecture* (a medium he celebrated as most disclosive of the public character of a nation and its people).[4] His turn from these subjects to political economy was in his own account morally motivated: He felt he could no longer pursue subjects that amounted to matters of luxury when economic injustices were so conspicuous and widespread.

Ruskin claimed no special expertise in political economy as a result of conventional schooling in the subject but relied on his own critical and observational acumen, much as he had with art,[5] and he expressly compared his abilities in both areas. His engagement with social and economic theory though, as he himself admitted, was unconventional. In the preface to "A Joy for Ever" he claimed that "The statement of economical principles given in the text, though I know that most, if not all, of them are accepted by existing authorities on the science, are not supported by references, because I have never read any author on political economy except Adam Smith, twenty years ago."[6] This lack of customary background in the subject matter however was no impediment according to Ruskin, who, referring to his own admission of lack of education in political economy, nevertheless boasted,

I have investigated this subject as deeply, and as long, as my own special subject of art; and the principles of political economy which I have stated in those lectures are as sure as the principles of Euclid. Foolish readers doubted their certainty because I told them I had "never read any books on Political Economy." Did they suppose I had got my knowledge of art by reading books?[7]

Reconstructing Ruskin's views on work is a challenge, because his writings are occasional and discursive, and his engagements with various subjects to do with economy and society are scattered across any number of voluminous writings. As F. W. Roe summarizes Ruskin's style when it comes to political economy, "his writings on society and the laws by which men live are to be found not in one or two volumes, but in a dozen. They are, moreover, in the highest degree discursive—'desultory talk,' Ruskin once aptly called them,—'unprogressive inlets' of thought, he described them on another occasion."[8] Still, critics have sought to find a unifying thread to Ruskin's rambling but always impassioned writings. Roe points to some passages from *The Seven Lamps of Architecture* as the earliest anticipation of which direction Ruskin's examination of political economy would take him, wherein Ruskin made a strong connection between the character and quality of architecture and the health and happiness of the workers who produced it. "I believe," Ruskin wrote, "the right question to ask respecting all ornament is simply this: was it done with enjoyment—was the carver happy while he was about it?"[9] This glimmer took more fulsome expression in Ruskin's famous chapter on Gothic architecture from *The Stones of Venice*, which Roe calls "one of the most convincing and most eloquent statements of the fundamental principles of social reform written in the nineteenth century."[10]

The key principle Roe identifies herein is Ruskin's conviction that "happiness in labor is the right of every worker, from gifted genius to humblest toiler,"[11] a happiness that the art critic found on rough but exuberant display in Gothic architecture and absent from the products of art and labor in his own time and place. What Gothic architecture accomplishes is a kind of perfection of imperfection; to paraphrase, it declines to make the perfect the enemy of the good and harmonizes the honest efforts of the many into a whole that is not perfect after its kind but evinces a beauty that Ruskin does not hesitate to call savage. In this the Gothic style incarnates a Christian truth of great value to Ruskin, the imperfection and imperfectability of the human being. By contrast to the ancient world, where slavery made it possible to press great masses of human beings into serving the "perfect" aim of their overlords, medieval Christianity abolishes slavery and recognizes "in small things as well as great, the individual value of every soul. But it not only recognizes its value; it confesses its imperfection, in only bestowing dignity upon the acknowledgement of unworthiness," an acknowledgment that "the Christian makes daily and hourly, contemplating the fact of it without fear, as tending, in the end, to God's greater glory."[12]

The Gothic style put this self-awareness to best use, such that for Ruskin "it is, perhaps, the principal admirableness of the Gothic schools of architecture, that they thus receive the results of the labour of inferior minds; and out of fragments full of imperfection, and betraying that imperfection in every touch, indulgently raise up a stately and unaccusable whole."[13] Speaking particularly of manual laborers, Ruskin argues that the Gothic builders understood that workers have varying levels of ability and accomplishment and yet made a place for all to contribute, taking the rough with the smooth and putting it to good overall effect in a single coordinated project. In this historical setting Ruskin sees a lesson for his own day, and he argues that even now workers cannot be strengthened in their abilities unless their weaknesses are accepted as well

> and unless we prize and honour them in their perfection above the best and most perfect manual skill. And this is what we have to do with all our labourers; to look for the *thoughtful* part of them, and get that out of them, whatever we lose for it, whatever faults and errors we are obliged to take with it. For the best that is in them cannot manifest itself, but in company with much error.[14]

As Roe indicates, in the background here is Ruskin's condemnation at the outset of this chapter of modern industrial manufacturing techniques, which he claims (in a fashion entirely reminiscent of Marx) degrade man into a machine.[15] Ruskin's point is that the worker, no matter how crude his ability, in order to be human in his work, must be allowed to be precisely human and not a mere mechanism for churning out perfectly formed objects, which, after all, a machine can do better than a person. Ruskin's example later in this same chapter is of the manufacture of glass beads.

> Glass beads are utterly unnecessary, and there is no design or thought employed in their manufacture. They are formed by first drawing out the glass into rods; these rods are chopped up into fragments of the size of beads by the human hand, and the fragments are then rounded in the furnace. The men who chop up the rods sit at their work all day, their hands vibrating with a perpetual and exquisitely timed palsy, and the beads dropping beneath their vibration like hail. Neither they, nor the men who draw out the rods or fuse the fragments, have the smallest occasion for the use of any single human faculty.[16]

By contrast, allowing for a measure of imperfection and soliciting the active mental engagement and reflection of even a manual worker makes the worker into a human participant in his own activity.

There is here, according to a severe logic that we will see is utterly characteristic of Ruskin, "a stern choice" to be made: "You must either make a tool of the creature, or a man of him. You cannot make both. Men were not intended to work with the accuracy of tools, to be precise and perfect in all their actions," and if this is the goal, as it is of modern manufacture, then Ruskin contends that you cannot help but "unhumanize" the worker, making all her attention and strength devolve into the automatic and repetitive production of her "mean act."

> On the other hand, if you will make a man of the working creature, you cannot make a tool. Let him but begin to imagine, to think, to try to do anything worth doing; and the engine-turned precision is lost at once. Out come all his roughness, all his dullness, all his incapability; shame upon shame, failure upon failure, pause

after pause: but out comes the whole majesty of him also; and we know the height of it only when we see the clouds settling upon him.[17]

This is the grandeur of the Gothic according to Ruskin, and he advises that critics of its simplicity and rudeness properly perceive that these homely features are precisely "signs of the life and liberty of every workman who struck the stone; a freedom of thought, and rank in scale of being, such as no laws, no charters, no charities can secure; but which it must be the first aim of all Europe at this day to regain for her children."[18] Gothic architecture took decades to build, so it expresses flexible adaptability to the needs of the moment and the spontaneous variation of its successive contributors. The Gothic era forged a specifically Christian unity wherein art and society were indistinguishable and together redeemed the imperfections of both life and work.

Such a unity is sorely lacking as far as Ruskin is concerned in the Europe of his day. Instead, he unfavorably contrasts the simple and authentic and above all free and satisfying labor of the past with the technically more polished but ultimately servile labor of the time. The trade has not in his estimation been for the better. It is not that the workers are starving but that "they have no pleasure in the work by which they make their bread, and therefore look to wealth as the only means of pleasure."[19] The trouble with today's work is that it is not satisfying in that deep human way that Ruskin glimpses in the medieval cathedral. Finding work unfulfilling, the worker looks for other sources of consolation, in wealth, which, as we will see, Ruskin also excoriates and dissociates entirely from labor itself. Also in line with Marx's critique are Ruskin's strong words on the division of labor, which he too emphasizes has a human cost above all.

> We have much studied and much perfected, of late, the great civilized invention of the division of labour; only we give it a false name. It is not, truly speaking, the labour that is divided; but the men:—Divided into mere segments of men—broken into small fragments and crumbs of life; so that all the little piece of intelligence that is left in a man is not enough to make a pin, or a nail, but exhausts itself in making the point of a pin or the head of a nail.[20]

The example of making pins is not accidentally chosen. This is Adam Smith's famous illustration of the division of labor from *The Wealth of Nations*. In chapter I of Book I Smith uses the example of making pins to illustrate how many more pins can be produced by a number of workers each doing one part of the overall job of pin-making—drawing the wire, straightening it, cutting it, filing it to a point, grinding the other end to receive the head—than can be produced by the same number of workers each making pins from the start of the process to the finish, inclusive of course of each of the above separately enumerated tasks. Ruskin uses this classic example to raise an objection to the division of labor, which he admits is more efficient than doing the whole job from beginning to end: "Now it is a good and desirable thing, truly, to make many pins in a day; but if we could only see with what crystal sand their points were polished,—sand of human soul, much to be magnified before it can be discerned for what it is—we should think there might be some loss in it also."[21]

The loss is a human one, for while industrial England manufactures cotton, steel, sugar, pottery, and much more besides, Ruskin is concerned that the one thing that is not made in his country's economy is human beings: "to brighten, to strengthen, to refine, or to form a single living spirit, never enters into our estimate of advantages." The only way to correct this deficiency, Ruskin maintains, is

> by a right understanding, on the part of all classes, of what kinds of labour are good for men, raising them, and making them happy; by a determined sacrifice of such convenience, or beauty, or cheapness as is to be got only by the degradation of the workman; and by equally determined demand for the products and results of healthy and ennobling labour.[22]

Here indeed is in capsule form some of what will prove to be perennial issues for Ruskin's ongoing career as a social critic. He consistently will insist upon the need for decent, honest, and rewarding work for all people, regardless of class and profession, and that such work be properly recompensed by society. Furthermore, as he eschews all revolutionary fervor, he will continually insist that the economic decisions that contribute to the exploitation and undervaluing of genuine labor are in the hands of those who make them, and that each person is responsible on his or her own to refuse the products of diminished labor offered for reduced prices in the name of greater ease and affordability and to invest instead in products of true worth that duly remunerate the laborers who made them.

We will see the extent to which and detail with which Ruskin elaborates these fundamental principles of his thinking about labor as we proceed through his later writings, but the first such occasion is here in the context of *The Stones of Venice*, where Ruskin lays down three "rules" that in spirit if not in exact wording will echo throughout much else of what he writes more directly on the subject of political economy (remembering that the work at hand is ostensibly devoted to architecture, not philosophy of work). How, Ruskin asks himself at this point, is the average consumer to regulate her purchasing behavior, directing her resources only to those products worth her expenditure and of genuine value to the worker whose labor made them? "Easily" is his answer,

> by the observance of three broad and simple rules: 1. Never encourage the manufacture of any article not absolutely necessary, in the production of which *Invention* has no share. 2. Never demand an exact finish for its own sake, but only for some practical or noble end. 3. Never encourage imitation or copying of any kind, except for the sake of preserving records of great works.[23]

For our purposes, it is the first of these that is the most interesting and to which Ruskin immediately turns in *The Stones of Venice*, and it is at this point that Ruskin introduces the observation above about glass beads, the manufacture of which he condemns as requiring no actual human involvement but only repetitive mechanical gestures. Now though the ferocity of his moral energy is made clear: Given that the process by which glass beads are made is degrading to the workers who make them, "every young lady, therefore, who buys glass beads is engaged in the slave-trade, and in a much more cruel one than that which we have so long been endeavouring to put down."[24] This sort of language is by no means unusual for Ruskin. It clarifies what he takes to be the seriousness of the issues at hand: It is our economic decision-making, the consequences of our own choices as to what to purchase and at what price, that implicates us in a hugely weighty moral matter, nothing less than the perpetuation or suppression of an invidious and commonplace form of slavery. Ruskin, though, is both hopeful that individuals' aggregated choices in the marketplace can affect change and firm that such conscientious decisions are morally imperative whether they result in such societal improvements or not. In a lecture from 1853 he made this point in a particularly straightforward way:

> Now let us remember, that every farthing we spend on objects of art has influence over men's minds and spirits, far more than over their bodies. By the purchase of every print which hangs on your walls, of every cup out of which you drink, and every table off which you eat your bread, you are educating a mass of men in one way or another. You are either employing them healthily or unwholesomely; you are making them lead happy or unhappy lives; you are leading them to look at Nature, and to love her—to think, to feel, to enjoy—or you are blinding them to Nature, and keeping them bound, like beasts of burden, in mechanical and monotonous employments.[25]

Speaking of such employments, before departing from *The Stones of Venice* and thus from one of Ruskin's earliest commentaries on the nature of work, let us take stock of what he says here at this early stage about the nature of mechanical work. Imagining an objection from a potential interlocutor, Ruskin asks himself what would be wrong with the artist capable of unique, humane, and therefore somewhat imperfect design being set to the intellectual task of planning the work and thus being "made a gentleman" while the execution of the design be relegated to "common workmen" for perfection in finish and technique.[26] There is a twofold wrong in fact. Ruskin says that behind such thinking stand two mistaken assumptions: "first, that one man's thoughts can be, or ought to be, executed by another man's hands; the second, that manual labour is a degradation, when it is governed by intellect."[27] The first assumption is not of immediate interest to us or to Ruskin in the context of the present argument, though he acknowledges that architecture is arguably unique among the arts in *requiring* a master planner and many workers to implement the plan, but this he holds is the exception that proves the rule, which is that no one's thoughts can be successfully expressed by another.[28]

The second assumption is the more important, and Ruskin targets it for criticism, condemning both the hatred of manual labor that is genuinely guided by intellect and the mindless celebration of manual labor as an end in itself. Throughout his writings on work, Ruskin attempts to avoid these two extremes, both honoring manual labor when it is done by a worker whose hand is guided by her head and condemning as truly servile and wretched manual labor that does not draw on any of the worker's intellectual resources. Thus does he attempt to avoid sentimental romanticism while nevertheless subjecting to criticism the culturally ingrained habit of separating head from hand. "We are always in these days endeavouring to separate the two," he grouses.

> We want one man to be always thinking, and another to be always working, and we call one a gentleman, and the other an operative; whereas the workman ought often to be thinking, and the thinker often to be working, and both should be gentlemen, in the best sense. As it is, we make both ungentle, the one envying, the other despising, his brother; and the mass of society is made up of morbid thinkers, and miserable workers.[29]

It should be noted that Ruskin thinks a certain hierarchy in society is inevitable and that strict equality is impossible, so he often refers to ways in which people differ in character and ability and means while refusing these things as the legitimate bases of rigid social distinctions.[30] Hence here his insistence that everyone should be a "gentleman" in the best sense, that is, a human being educated in moral and aesthetic sensibility.[31] Such education bears in Ruskin's view a necessary connection to labor. "The first condition of education, the thing you are all crying out for, is being put to wholesome and useful work."[32]

Ruskin's holistic theory of education lurks in the background of his contention that head and hand belong together and thus that education should include intellectual and manual activity. Employing a rhetorical reversal typical of Ruskin's style, he quipped in *The Stones of Venice*, "Now it is only by labour that thought can be made healthy, and only by thought that labour can be made happy, and the two cannot be separated *with impunity*."[33] It is perhaps also this holistic view of education and of the human being as such that also accounts for a sort of unity to Ruskin's seemingly disparate subjects of interest. It is the same discipline, sensitivity, and moral sensibility that is appropriate to both art and work, both of which are in his mind quite public projects with social and moral implications. Because of this coimplication Ruskin goes so far as to maintain, and here he is not without precedent,

> It would be well if all of us were good handicraftsmen in some kind, and the dishonour of manual labour done away with altogether; so that though there should still be a trenchant distinction of race between nobles and commoners, there should not, among the latter, be a trenchant distinction of employment, as between idle and working men, or between men of liberal and illiberal professions. All professions should be liberal, and there should be less pride felt in peculiarity of employment, and more in excellence of achievement.[34]

This echoes Ruskin's claim above that inequality is unavoidable but that divisions within society should not be arbitrarily imposed but follow upon the earned rewards of labor, of whatever form it might be. Correlate to that claim is his insistence that all labor be honored and properly remunerated, a point to which we will shortly return. Everyone he maintains, much as the monastic tradition all the way up through Petrarch at least did, should practice some kind of manual work, and the customary division between the liberal and the illiberal should be abolished. Pursuant to such an agenda,

Ruskin asserts that any master of her craft ought to be both willing and able to do the hardest work that belongs to her expertise, such that a painter should prepare her own colors and an architect hew stones in the mason's yard.[35] The only work-related distinction that Ruskin countenances is gradation of "experience and skill, and the authority and wealth which these must naturally and justly obtain."[36]

It bears mentioning though that for Ruskin there are some forms of work that are irredeemable. Some kinds of labor seem to have no intrinsic relationship to the knowledge (which is certainly not cerebral only, as we have seen) that is an essential ingredient of happy and fulfilling work. Interestingly, classicist that he is, Ruskin invokes the ancient category of the banausic and updates his condemnation of it to his own time. In his *Lectures on Art* he advised that dependence on manufacturing "needing the help of fire" be reduced to an absolute minimum, and he quotes the words of Xenophon's *Oeconomicus* in support of his view. "Nothing," he counseled, "may ever be made of iron that can as effectually be made of wood or stone; and nothing moved by steam that can be as effectually moved by natural forces. And observe, that for all mechanical effort required for social life and in cities, water power is infinitely more than enough."[37] For those who would maintain the contrary, Ruskin points out that there is already a dramatic inconsistency between the promised rewards of industrialization and the material benefits actually enjoyed by the common people: "Though England is deafened with spinning wheels, her people have not clothes—though she is black with digging of fuel, they die of cold—and though she has sold her soul for gain, they die of hunger."[38] If industrial manufacture were so indispensable for the nation's forward progress, then why aren't the benefits of this alleged progress obvious to all? If mechanization makes for cheaper, more widely available clothing, for example, why are so many poor people so ill-clad? For Ruskin, this is a state of affairs incompatible with justice, with so-called progress, and with any artistry worthy of the name.[39]

Rectifying such fundamental injustices is the basic task of political economy, and at the heart of Ruskin's political economy is work. In a word, Ruskin holds that society and the economy should be based on two ordinances: "That every man shall do good work for his bread: and secondly, that every man shall have good bread for his work."[40] These sound like two ways of saying the same thing, but they are not. In fact, Ruskin's brief diagnosis for the ills of his society is that the two ordinances do not in fact go hand in hand though they most definitely should. In short, Ruskin consistently maintains that work is required for human beings but that human beings frequently do their best to shirk it themselves and to deny the proper reward for the work of others. So what appears to be a tautology in fact is not; the sad truth of the human condition is that work is the source of a great many goods but that we habitually seek to have our reward without work and to deny others the reward of their work (these latter two crimes, in fact, are the ones that go hand in hand). So let us consider Ruskin's thoughts on both of these ordinances, beginning with the first.

He repeatedly affirms, throughout his career, that both the laws of nature and of God have ordained it that work is required for reward. In *The Two Paths*, he writes, "The law of nature is, that a certain quantity of work is necessary to produce a certain quantity of good, of any kind whatever. If you want knowledge, you must toil for it: if food, you must toil for it: and if pleasure, you must toil for it."[41] In keeping then with the Platonic tradition with which he firmly allied himself, work for Ruskin is not just about the acquisition of external goods but the means of self-improvement and key to flourishing as a whole person. Not only do the laws of nature mandate this constant association, but so too, as we remarked above, does the law of God. As an impassioned Christian moralist, Ruskin is deeply indebted to the wisdom of Scripture and the tradition of Christian thought to establish this point, which he does with prophetic fervor. We should not be surprised then to find that constant touchstones for Ruskin, as for the monks, are 2 Thessalonians 3:10 and Genesis 3:19, though in his hands these familiar passages take on new emphases.

While Ruskin insists on the importance of work, and even its divine mandate, he always admits that it is difficult, and that some degree or another of resistance to the application of effort is definitive of work. It is for this reason that his cannot be considered a naïve view, though he often grounds his sobriety about work in the words of Scripture, without thereby asserting the heterodox opinion that work is only associated with man's fallen condition. "Of all hand work whatsoever," he opined in *The Crown of Wild Olive*, "necessary for the maintenance of life, those old words, 'In the sweat of thy face thou shalt eat bread,' indicate that the inherent nature of it is one of calamity; and that the ground, cursed for our sake, casts also some shadow of degradation into our contest with its thorn and its thistle."[42] When he comes closest to giving a definition of work, Ruskin emphasizes this dimension of difficulty, though again without calling work cursed as such. In *Munera Pulveris* he said,

> I have already defined Labour to be the Contest of the life of man with an opposite. Literally, it is the quantity of "Lapse," loss, or failure of human life, caused by any effort. ... Labour is the *suffering* in effort. It is the negative quantity, or quantity of de-feat, which has to be counted against every Feat, and of de-fect, which has to be counted against every Fact, or Deed of men. In brief, it is "that quantity of our toil which we die in."[43]

Work then is by necessity depleting, such that it even contributes to our death and eventuates in it. At the same time, labor can be said to be for Ruskin a sort of expenditure or investment of life itself, such that work is linked to life and its self-promotion and self-expression. Work is thus never to be avoided, but it must be recognized that as a source of value, work nevertheless resists effort and provides difficulty while yielding gains that can only be hard won.[44] As Supritha Rajan has noted, the implication of this view is profound: "Since we sacrifice a portion of our lives in labor, labor's value is absolute and insubstitutable."[45] Ruskin's view of labor is clear-eyed but overall positive in a way that Smith's is not.[46] Ruskin can declare a formula like "Government and co-operation are in all things the Laws of Life; Anarchy and competition the Laws of Death"[47] because he is thinking of labor as an ingredient of individual and social flourishing that is self-perpetuating and *alive*.

Not clear from the immediate context but plain when turning to the original source of this slogan in *Modern Painters* is Ruskin's elaborate parallelism between art or society and nature, individual and whole. Speaking of composition with respect to painting (and again this should be a clue to us for how Ruskin thought art and society related), he defines it as the "help of everything in the picture by everything else" and invites his reader to dwell on what is meant by "help," a concept he restricts to animate things. Removal of one part of an inanimate thing does not damage the remainder, but removal of one part of an animate thing (and clearly he has in mind here both literally animate things like plants and animals but also paintings and social bodies that "live" only by this same logic he is articulating) damages the whole.[48] This is because in living things its components do not merely consist with one another but actively help one another. By a creative etymology, Ruskin connects the notion of "help" to "holy" and draws a relationship between the holiness of a thing and its life and mutual help.

> Life and consistency, then, both expressing one character (namely, helpfulness of a higher or lower order), the Maker of all creatures and things "by whom all creatures live and all things consist," is essentially and for ever the Helpful One, or in softer Saxon, the "Holy" One. The word has no other ultimate meaning: Helpful, harmless, undefiled: "living" or "Lord of life." ... A pure or holy state of anything, therefore, is that in which all its parts are helpful or consistent. ... The highest and first law of the universe—and the other name of life is, therefore, "help."[49]

The opposite of holiness, help, and life is separation, competition, and death.

Work has a central role to play in this dynamic, inasmuch as properly exercised it is a foremost example of the help that is essential to flourishing human community and improperly exercised is a harbinger of death. The word "competition" here surely is meant to stir echoes of Smith. Ruskin's opposed view connects labor as the basis of value with its operation within a horizon of the absolute value that is life itself. "If life is holy," as Rajan concludes, "the labor as the expenditure of bodily energies is also holy."[50] This is why Ruskin can say, in one of his more famous phrases, that "THERE IS NO WEALTH BUT LIFE," because for him all value comes down to what promotes life and allows it to flourish.[51] Note here too that the cooperative dimension remains fully in force, and this is a truism for both individuals and societies: "That country is the richest which nourishes the greatest number of noble and happy human beings; that man is richest who, having perfected the functions of his own life to the utmost, has also the widest helpful influence, both personal, and by means of his possessions, over the lives of others."[52] Here again we see the logic of "help" reinscribed at the socioeconomic level. Furthermore, the polemic against competition-based capitalism is also present, again at the level of the economy, and here stated with considerable sharpness. Ruskin himself concedes that his is "a strange political economy; the only one, nevertheless, that ever was or can be: all political economy founded on self-interest being but the fulfillment of that which once brought schism into the Policy of angels, and ruin into the Economy of heaven."[53]

Work is thus at the very basis of other human goods available only in a healthy society. This point too Ruskin associates with Genesis 3:19, where the mandate to earn bread by the sweat of the face is linked to the recognition that "Dust thou art, and unto dust shalt thou return." This grim reality, Ruskin says, is the first truth we have to learn of ourselves; and to till the earth out of which we were taken, our first duty: in that labour, and in the relations which it establishes between us and the lower animals, are founded the conditions of our highest faculties and felicities: and without that labour, neither reason, art, nor peace, are possible to man."[54]

For work to play this positive foundational role however, to function as "help" within and among a human society and to contribute to its flourishing and holiness in Ruskin's sense, it must be the case that work is rewarded, that labor brings good bread. This principle Ruskin constantly ties to the old familiar refrain from Paul's second epistle to the Thessalonians.

In keeping with his emphasis on personal accountability for the sufficiency (and not luxury) of one's own means and the needs of others, Ruskin issues this challenge to his readers in *Sesame and Lilies*: "Whatever our station in life may be, at this crisis, those of us who mean to fulfil our duty ought first to live on as little as we can; and, secondly, to do all the wholesome work for it we can, and to spend all we can spare in doing all the sure good we can."[55] The first way such a duty to do good to others expresses itself is in the humble and humane imperative to supply the basic need for food.[56] Ruskin is militant that this duty cannot be limited by convenient qualifications: "The order to us is not to feed the deserving hungry, nor the industrious hungry, nor the amiable and well-intentioned hungry, but simply to feed the hungry."[57]

At the same time, the unrestricted nature of this moral duty does not in his mind conflict with the Pauline imperative on labor. "It is quite true, infallibly true, that if any man will not work, neither should he eat."[58] The primary interest held out by Ruskin's adoption of this maxim though is his turning of it away from the typical target: Rather than stress the apparent implication that the lazy are responsible for their own poverty in Lockean fashion,[59] Ruskin uses this Scripture to press home the obligation of the wealthy to have genuinely earned their means through their own labors rather than their appropriation of the labors of others (which we will see is a perennial concern of his). The question then for Ruskin's readers in view of 2 Thessalonians 3:10 is not so much whether they have enough to eat but whether what they have has been earned through real work: "Every time you sit down to your dinner, ladies and gentlemen, say solemnly, before you ask a blessing, 'How much work have I done to-day for my dinner?'" This is the first order of business according to Ruskin, such that even before compelling the inveterate vagabond to work for his dinner a society should make sure that there is plenty to go around and that famine is an impossibility, a goal he thinks well in reach of a civilized nation.[60]

Sharpening that same arrow against an audience that he presumes regards itself as Christian (though he repeatedly expresses his disappointment and annoyance with a nation that institutionalizes "systematic disobedience to the first principles of its professed religion"[61]), Ruskin baldly asserts,

> All true Christianity is known—as its Master was—in breaking of bread, and all false Christianity in stealing it. Let the clergyman only apply—with impartial and level sweep—to his congregation the great pastoral order: "The man that will not

work, neither should he eat;" and be resolute in requiring each member of his flock to tell him *what*—day by day—they do to earn their dinners;—and he will find an entirely new view of life and its sacraments open upon him and them.[62]

The boldness of this sweeping claim is entirely Ruskinian, as is the acerbity of the subsequent indictment of his coreligionists, as we will see momentarily. Again for Ruskin the primary purpose of 2 Thessalonians 3:10 is not to convict the idleness of the poor but the contentedness of the rich. If the clergy were truly interested in the meaning of Paul's counsel they would wield it against their own parishioners to ensure that their resources were truly and honestly well-earned. The promised consequence is a dramatic one: Ruskin claims that not only will both clergy and laity find by way of fidelity to Paul's order a new view of life but even of the sacraments.[63]

For this reason we might say that Ruskin is the first to interpret 2 Thessalonians 3:10 as principally about our responsibilities to others and their work rather than primarily about a responsibility we have to ourselves. That latter obligation Ruskin takes for granted. He succinctly asserts that "the first necessity of all economical government is to secure the unquestioned and unquestionable working of the great law of Property—that a man who works for a thing shall be allowed to get it, keep it, and consume it, in peace."[64] Work is needful, it is the only rightful basis of any assertion to property rights, and rightfully secured property is not to be disturbed. Yet 2 Thessalonians 3:10 in Ruskin's handling is less about the mandate of the worker to diligently labor or the right of the worker to the fruits of her own effort and more about the imperative she has to ensure that other workers enjoy the same privilege.

Ruskin's real barb is yet to come however. The corollary to Ruskin's insistence that everyone work for their bread is his constant conviction that most people, even in allegedly Christian England, gain their bread by means that he is unafraid to condemn as tantamount to theft and fraud.

> For the man who is not—day by day—doing work which will earn his dinner, must be stealing his dinner; and the actual fact is, that the great mass of men calling themselves Christians do actually live by robbing the poor of their bread, and by no other trade whatsoever; and the simple examination of the mode of the produce and consumption of European food—who digs for it, and who eats it—will prove that to any honest human soul.[65]

This theme broaches the second bedrock principle of Ruskin's political economy. We have seen how emphatically he insists on the necessity and prerogatives of labor; the companion principle is no less forceful. Just as honest labor is entitled to its recompense, so is recompense required for honest labor. This principle of course has widespread notional acceptance, but Ruskin argues that it is rarely upheld in practice. There are a number of ways in which people enrich themselves without their own labor and by chiseling others out of the reward of theirs.

It is worth observing at the outset that Ruskin believes it is impossible to be wealthy through honest and actual work. In *Munera Pulveris* he contends, "No man can become largely rich by his personal toil. The work of his own hands, wisely directed, will indeed always maintain himself and his family, and make fitting provision for his age. *But it is only by the discovery of some method of taxing the labour of others that he can become opulent.*"⁶⁶ Similarly, he will maintain that "large fortunes cannot honestly be made by the work of any one man's hand or head."⁶⁷ At this point in *Time and Tide*, Ruskin says that there are only three ways to make vast fortunes, none of which counts as actual work: "(1.) By obtaining command over the labour of multitudes of other men, and taxing it for our own profit. (2.) By treasure-trove,—as of mines, useful vegetable products and the like,—in circumstances putting them under our own exclusive control. (3.) By speculation, (commercial gambling)"⁶⁸ The first two Ruskin says are generally legal and sometimes acceptable, while the third is always detrimental, inasmuch as in this arena one man's profit is necessarily another man's loss, and there is no benefit to the community at all, only the extravagant enrichment of the select few. Furthermore, speculation aims not at the remediation of genuine needs but at gain for the sake of it and thereby generates

> imaginary necessities and popular desires, in order to gather its temporary profit from the supply of them. So that not only the persons who lend their money to it will be finally robbed, but the work done with their money will be, for the most part, useless, and thus the entire body of the public injured as well as the persons concerned in the transaction.⁶⁹

Speculation and indulgence in luxuries both attract Ruskin's severest condemnations, but there are even more commonplace and widely practiced forms of fraudulence and exploitation. It is to this more pedestrian but pervasive abrogation of the rights of labor to which Ruskin attributes the majority of his society's economic ills:

> By far the greater part of the suffering and crime which exist at this moment in civilized Europe, arises simply from people not understanding this truism—not knowing that produce or wealth is eternally connected by the laws of heaven and earth with resolute labour; but hoping in some way to cheat or abrogate this everlasting law of life, and to feed where they have not furrowed, and be warm where they have not woven. I repeat, nearly all our misery and crime result from this one misapprehension.⁷⁰

We have seen already that Ruskin insists on the moral necessity of work on the grounds of both reason and revelation, and it is equally true that he thinks most injustice stems from avoidance of this necessity and the effort to take advantage of others' work while doing as little as possible of our own.

A frequently employed means of achieving this evasion is by purchasing goods on the cheap, a practice that Ruskin contemns in the strongest possible terms and once more calls on individuals to take pains to avoid.

> Whenever we buy such goods, remember we are stealing somebody's labour. Don't let us mince the matter. I say, in plain Saxon,—taking from him the proper reward of his work, and putting it into our own pocket. You know well enough that the

thing could not have been offered you at that price, unless distress of some kind had forced the producer to part with it. You take advantage of this distress, and you force as much out of him as you can under the circumstances.[71]

Ruskin retains his penchant for colorful comparisons when he analogizes the purchasing of cheap goods to the medieval use of the thumbscrew to extort property. The method has become more supposedly humane, "but the fact of extortion remains precisely the same."[72] To those who would plead that the unconsciousness of such casual actions must mitigate their blameworthiness, Ruskin retorts, "The question is one of responsibilities only, not of facts. The definite result of all our modern haste to be rich is assuredly, and constantly, the murder of a certain number of persons by our hands every year."[73]

The strong language is testimony to Ruskin's passion on this front. The two predominant concerns foremost in his mind are luxurious and wasteful spending and hasty and heedless acquisition. These are the two most ordinary and yet most heinous forms of theft and exploitation, and the moral stakes here could not be higher in Ruskin's mind:

> Wherever and whenever men are endeavouring to *make money hastily*, and to avoid the labour which Providence has appointed to be the only source of honourable profit;—and also wherever and whenever they permit themselves to *spend it luxuriously*, without reflecting how far they are misguiding the labour of others;—there and then, in either case, they are literally and infallibly causing, for their own benefit or their own pleasure, a certain annual number of human deaths; that, therefore, the choice given to every man born into this world is, simply, whether he will be a labourer or an assassin; and that whosoever has not his hand on the Stilt of the plough, hast it on the Hilt of the dagger.[74]

Economic activity can be fair and just according to Ruskin, when exchanges are genuinely mutually advantageous and each participant's labor is properly compensated. Yet for this just arrangement to take place is the simplest matter, of no great intellectual or ethical sophistication, and wherever exchange is fair, profit is excluded on principle. Profit is only justly realizable as a product of one's own labor or, in an unjust scenario, wherein one person takes advantage of another. Ruskin's example in *Unto This Last* is of one man who grows corn and another who makes shovels. If each works at his respective labor then small measures of corn become larger and one shovel is joined by others as a result of each worker's industry. If the corn farmer wants a shovel and the shovel man is hungry, then an equitable arrangement is possible, but there is, strictly speaking, no profit on such terms because neither the farmer nor the ironmonger has realized a gain over the other; quite to the contrary, both have benefited.[75] Political economy however assigns the name of profit to what in Ruskin's mind is in fact ruthless capitalization of one's own advantage over another's disadvantage. Thus it is contrary to "the laws both of matter and motion" to secure "universal acquisition of this kind. Profit, or material gain, is attainable only by construction or by discovery; not by exchange."[76]

Therefore there can be no science of exchange, as any such "science" would be in Ruskin's judgment utterly nugatory and in fact resting upon nescience, inasmuch as ignorance on the part of one participant in an unjust economic exchange and a corresponding willingness on the part of another participant to leverage the other's ignorance is required in order to sustain such a fundamentally unjust interchange. Ruskin's example is illustrative of situations he thinks take place every day, thousands of times a day: "If I can exchange a needle with a savage for a diamond, my power of doing so depends either on the savage's ignorance of social arrangements in Europe, or on his want of power to take advantage of them, by selling the diamond to any one else for more needles." In the absence of such an advantage there can be no profit attained: "So far, therefore, as the science of exchange relates to the advantage of one of the exchanging persons only, it is founded on the ignorance or incapacity of the opposite person. Where these vanish, it also vanishes."[77]

Ruskin himself has to confess that it is impossible to overcome the endemic drive to wealth and will to exploitation that seems built into the modern economy, so once more he calls upon each to at least do her part in whatever small way is available. In the face of overwhelming injustice, "we may at least labour for a system of greater honesty and kindness in the minor commerce of our daily life; since the great dishonesty of the great buyers and sellers is nothing more than the natural growth and outcome from the little dishonesty of the little buyers and sellers."[78] If it is indeed the case that the large-scale injustices of buying and selling are simply the concatenation of millions of small-scale decisions, then there is reason to believe that there is some small efficacy to the pursuit of justice in matters to do with work and its reward.

> Every person who tries to buy an article for less than its proper value, or who tries to sell it at more than its proper value—every consumer who keeps a tradesman waiting for his money, and every tradesman who bribes a consumer to extravagance by credit, is helping forward, according to his own measure of power, a system of baseless and dishonourable commerce, and forcing his country down into poverty and shame.[79]

These petty but nonetheless consequential crimes at least can be avoided by persons of goodwill who have the sensitivity to realize the consequence of their actions and the resolution to guide their actions by honest and rather homely principles. Not only does Ruskin insist that such mundane practices can have a beneficial effect but that they are far more effective than ambitious philanthropic schemes and complicated theories. "And people of moderate means and average powers of mind would do far more real good by merely carrying out stern principles of justice and honesty in common matters of trade, than by the most ingenious schemes of extended philanthropy, or vociferous declarations of theological doctrine."[80]

Many of Ruskin's often-repeated themes come together in a sort of brief manifesto from *Time and Tide*:

> There are three things to which man is born—labour, sorrow, and joy. Each of these three things has its baseness and its nobleness. There is base labour, and

noble labour. There is base sorrow, and noble sorrow. There is base joy, and noble joy. But you must not think to avoid the corruption of these things by doing without the things themselves. Nor can any life be right that has not all three. Labour without joy is base. Labour without sorrow is base. Sorrow without labour is base. Joy without labour is base.[81]

First of all, Ruskin continues a classically Augustinian tradition when he puts forward that a thing of value cannot be dismissed because it is susceptible to corruption, and it is this latter only that should be despised and rejected. Work is among the fundamental goods of life, and while it can be debased, it ought not to be refused on that grounds, only the debased forms of it. Second, Ruskin remains candid in his admission that work brings both sorrow and joy. Without sorrow, labor would be as debased as it would be without joy. For Ruskin, work always has this twofold character, exhibiting difficulty even when maximally rewarding. Third and finally, joy purchased without labor is debased, as it is always blameworthy in Ruskin's eyes for gain to be claimed without effort.

This compact statement of principles implies that there is a distinction between noble and base forms of work, and that is so according to Ruskin, so we should conclude this study by considering what sorts of features the best work exhibits in his estimation. We have seen already that some forms of work he regards as irredeemable, and we know that he objects to commonplace but nonetheless venal practices that defraud workers of their rightful benefits. What is it that makes good work noble? As usual, Ruskin's comments are fragmentary and scattered. In the first address that comprises *The Crown of Wild Olive* however, he focuses on work and helpfully stipulates that all praiseworthy work must exhibit three qualities: "It must be honest, useful, and cheerful."[82]

Ruskin again expresses a typical surprise and chagrin with his contemporaries: While the English temperament warms to nothing more affectionately than fair play, absence of fair work seems not to scandalize at all, even though cheating has far greater moment in matters of labor and trade than it does in sport and games.[83] The first order of business then for the workmen of Victorian England is "to be true to yourselves and to us who would help you. We can do nothing for you, nor you for yourselves, without honesty. Get that, you get all; without that, your suffrages, your reforms, your freed-trade measures, your institutions of science, are all in vain."[84]

Second, if work is useful, its difficulty is not burdensome. Recalling a proposal as old as Augustine at least, Ruskin maintains that if work is achieving something worthwhile, then the worker won't mind it even if it is difficult.[85] What the worker should object to in her work is not its difficulty but its being wasted: "Of all wastes, the greatest waste that you can commit is the waste of labour."[86] With characteristic hyperbole, Ruskin responds to an imagined objection that this claim is overstated by doubling down: Not only is the waste of people's labor the worst sort of waste it is tantamount to slowly murdering the worker with the oppressive conviction of her own efforts' worthlessness. Recalling Marx's famous objections against the alienation and expropriation of the worker,[87] Ruskin includes the confiscation of the products of her labor and the thwarting of her creative energies in a litany of grievances against the waste of human labor and—what is the same—human life:

> If you put him to base labour, if you bind his thoughts, if you blind his eyes, if you blunt his hopes, if you steal his joys, if you stunt his body, and blast his soul, and at last leave him not so much as strength to reap the poor fruit of his degradation, but gather that for yourself, and dismiss him to the grave, when you have done with him, having, so far as in you lay, made the walls of that grave everlasting ... this you think is no waste, and no sin![88]

Finally, with respect to work's cheerfulness, Ruskin says it should evince the cheerfulness of a child. Departing immediately from this thought and exhorting his listeners to take this one charge home with them if they forget all else, Ruskin points out that everyone in his audience has been taught to pray the Lord's Prayer, which includes the phrase "Thy kingdom come."[89] Comparing the mockery of praying this petition without sincerity with the mockery of Christ by the Roman soldiers, Ruskin demands that praying for the coming of God's kingdom in seriousness must also entail working for it. Moreover, no one, we learn from the words of Jesus himself, enters into the kingdom of God unless they become like a child.[90] So it stands to reason that to work for the kingdom of God is to work with the cheerfulness of a child. The child, in turn, has three qualities relevant to the way in which workers should do their work well. The child is modest, knows that she does not know everything, and thus is always ready to learn. The child is also faithful and trusts in the wisdom and goodwill of her superiors.[91] Finally, a child is loving and returns love readily, looking for opportunities to help and grateful to be of use in even small things. The cheerfulness typical of children and illustrative of the best qualities of a devoted worker rests on these three qualities. Invoking yet another *locus classicus* from the New Testament, Ruskin asserts that this is the character of the great worker: "Taking no thought for the morrow; taking thought only for the duty of the day; trusting somebody else to take care of to-morrow; knowing indeed what labour is, but not what sorrow is; and always ready for play—beautiful play. For lovely human play is like the play of the Sun. There's a worker for you."[92]

In his provocative and illustrative writings, Ruskin accommodates a specifically modern expectation that work afford subjective consolations or gratifications into a classically Augustinian Christian Neoplatonic ontology of human action. Ruskin's primary inspirations, as we have seen, are Platonism and Christian theology. Consider, for example, a passage that appeared in the original edition of the pages studied above from *The Crown of Wild Olive*. "Wise work is, briefly," Ruskin wrote, "work *with* God. Foolish work is work *against* God. And work done with God, which He will help, may be briefly described as 'Putting in Order'—that is, enforcing God's law of order, spiritual and material, over men and things."[93] The appeal to a notion of work with or against God of course refers to the specifically religious horizon of Ruskin's thought, and the invocation of order is classically Platonist. His interest in these perennial themes is further evidenced by his appeals to creation theology and monastic tradition. In a fascinating passage that anticipates environmental considerations as well as sociopolitical concerns, Ruskin uses the days of creation as indications of what divine and noble work should look like and by inference how bad work in a way inverts the work of creation. Writing in *Fors Clavigera*, Ruskin reiterates his frequent argument:

> Neither almsgiving nor praying, therefore, not psalmsinging ... have anything to do with "good work," or God's work. But it is not so very difficult to discover what that work is. You keep the Sabbath, in imitation of God's rest. Do, by all manner of means, if you like; and keep also the rest of the week in imitation of God's work.[94]

To flesh out this sketch, Ruskin alludes to the work of each of the six days of creation as models for what good work should entail and what the opposite would be as well. The analogy is straightforward in Ruskin's mind: "if Man be made in God's image, much more is Man's work made to be in the image of God's work."[95]

So, for instance, if light is the creation of the first day, then good work will consist in "letting in light where there was darkness; as especially into poor rooms and back streets" while "the correspondent Diabolic work is putting a tax on windows, and blocking out the sun's light with smoke."[96] The second day implies that good work is keeping the waters pure rather than polluting them;[97] the third day implies a duty to plant and care for trees rather than clear-cutting them and converting good land to waste; and in a strikingly contemporary argument, Ruskin says the establishment of times and seasons suggests that we are to guide the rhythms of our lives by the seasons rather than overusing artificial light to blot out the stars and eating hothouse strawberries and peas out of season.[98]

In the same spirit, Ruskin praises the monastic attitude toward work, especially the program of St. Benedict. The details of Ruskin's engagement with the Benedictine tradition cannot completely be reproduced here, but suffice it to say that in *Valle Crucis* Ruskin sees in Benedict the beginning of a proud and precious heritage that united work in the world with architectural innovation that contributed as well to beauty as to sanctity. Ruskin seizes on the miracle of the child Benedict mending his nurse's corn-sieve as an exemplary moment in his life and ministry, analogous to Hercules's battle with the Nemean lion.[99] The reason this is so illustrative is that for Benedict the corn and the tools used to harvest it are alike sacred, a homely verdict that Ruskin charmingly contrasts to the unworldly idiosyncrasy of Benedict's monastic forebears, who according to him "had gone mad, in great numbers,—had lived on blackberries, and scratched themselves virulently with the thorns of them,—had let their hair and nails grow too long,—had worn unbecoming old rags and mats,—had been often very dirty, and almost always, as far as other people could judge, very miserable."[100] This history of repellent oddity Ruskin says Benedict rejected in favor of the determination that "Christian men ought not to be hermits, but actively helpful members of society: that they are to live by their own labour, and to feed other people by it to the best of their power."[101]

Thanks to the profound influence of the Platonic and Christian traditions, Ruskin is a hierarchical thinker, and he is a holistic one, who sees the beauty and intelligibility of art and society as ultimately one, expressions of a single ontological whole, embroidered and internally organized with everyone and everything in its place. The place of the human being in this order is to do the best work, a form of effort that at once enhances and drains human life, and in doing so promotes both loveliness and justice—for Ruskin aesthetics and ethics go hand in hand.

> The real "good work" is, with respect to men, to enforce justice, and with respect to things, to enforce tidiness, and fruitfulness. And against these two great human deeds, justice and order, there are perpetually two great demons contending,—the devil of iniquity, or inequity, and the devil of disorder, or of death; for death is only consummation of disorder. You have to fight these two fiends daily.[102]

We have seen that for Ruskin in this daily battle the most effective combatant is the individual, upon whose shoulders he places a substantial burden of responsibility. This is part of the reason why Ruskin was regarded in his day and in our own as a notorious Utopian, and he is short on concrete proposals for changing the economic and labor practices of a society at large rather than just one's personal economic behavior.[103] Nevertheless, Ruskin regards work and the individual's responsibilities around labor as so central as to merit its being a sort of metonym for the basic moral obligation of the human person. Ruskin exploits a kind of double meaning to the phrase "work iniquity" from the King James Version's translation of the portion of the Sermon on the Mount contained in Matthew 7. In that chapter Jesus warns his listeners that "Not every one that saith unto me, Lord, Lord, shall enter into the kingdom of heaven; but he that doeth the will of my Father which is in heaven." This is a quintessential warning against hypocrisy, which, as we have seen, is a significant criticism that Ruskin lodges against his own supposedly Christian society. In the original context, Jesus cautions that he will not acknowledge all those who verbally hail him as lord if they have not in fact done the will of God the Father. This is true even for those who claim that they have done miracles, prophesied, or exorcised devils in the name of Jesus.[104] The performance of these marvelous deeds in the name of Christ is no guarantee against judgment, for Jesus affirms, "I will profess unto them, I never knew you: depart from me, ye that work iniquity."[105] So the point of the passage, and Ruskin obviously has this in mind, is that even someone who claims to believe in the message of Jesus Christ can be judged by him to have worked iniquity rather than righteousness if their deeds are wanting. Ruskin draws the natural conclusion:

> So far as you don't fight against the fiend of iniquity, you work for him. You "work iniquity," and the judgment upon you, for all your "Lord, Lord's," will be "Depart from me, ye that work iniquity." And so far as you do not resist the fiend of disorder, you work disorder, and you yourself do the work of Death, which is sin, and has for its wages, Death himself."[106]

Ever the moralist, for Ruskin the need to work is ever present, and the category of what counts as "work" extends to a whole range of aesthetically and ethically significant choices. The only question for Ruskin is whether we will work righteousness or work iniquity.

8

Simone Weil

An extraordinary and unique contribution to the philosophy of work comes from the inimitable Simone Weil, a person who expressed her thought by her deeds as much as by her words. Weil combined a passion for Platonism with an unofficial Christianity (she was never baptized) and an ambivalent borrowing from Marx, a blend of influences distilled most potently in her writings on labor. As a philosopher and not a social scientist, it has been accurately noted that for Weil "labor is not presented as a social category. Rather, it is envisaged as the activity through which the form of the human condition is discovered."[1] For Weil, work occupies a pivotal, though not comprehensive, place in human reality. It is the site where body and soul, spirit and matter, meet in a relationship of mutual resistance and yet also productivity. Weil wrote on this dialectic of labor in some of her earliest manuscripts.

> Work expresses the opposition of soul and matter. But not only this opposition; otherwise no work would succeed. Work, inasmuch as it arises from an intention of the soul and ends in a reflection conforming to this intention, expresses the union of soul and matter; it expresses the opposition, not in that sometimes work does not succeed, but in that work can always not succeed, as it's composed of a series of changes independent of each other.[2]

On Weil's analysis, work arises from thought, though work itself, when in operation, excludes or overcomes thought, at least momentarily. This interplay is what makes it so that the soul and matter are not *just* opposed in work, though they are; they are also united at the same time, inasmuch as the soul exerts its power over matter in work, and this very exertion depends on the resistance of matter to soul, without which matter makes no sense at all. Work can fail because the attainment of its end always depends on the success of a variety of intervening procedures and tactics. It is in this sense that soul and matter are in opposition. For Weil, "If one considers man taken as an individual, one can see in him two species of activity, and two only. He can form ideas, and that is thought; he can indirectly transform impressions, or in other words, voluntarily change matter, and that is work."[3]

There are two and only two distinctly human activities, thinking and working. These two are at once irreducible to one another and yet are also bound together in a dialectical knot that nothing it would seem can cut. In the closest thing to a definition that we get in this manuscript, Weil calls work the voluntary alteration of matter, an alteration that always takes place again incrementally. The intermediary or mediating character of work is an important part of Weil's account. For her, work is not exhaustive of human action, in part because action can include a great many spontaneous or immediate responses to the environment, while work to be work relies on indirection, and the more complicated the work, the more intermediary steps and procedures are entailed by the task. Weil's example here is of lifting a heavy weight by means of a winch. In such an operation, "the arrival of the object at the desired height does not follow my desire directly, but by intermediary movements, such as the formation of knots, turns of a crank; these movements are decomposed into as many parts as we like, and in each of these parts of the work the matter does not know what it is useful for."[4]

As she stipulates here again, indirection is an essential quality of work. Work for Weil only proceeds through intermediary stages, achieving its aim not straightforwardly but by operationalized steps like the movements constitutive of raising the weight. If it were not possible for us to work in this way, then the soul would have no power over the world at all. We are however capable of a species of activity that is spontaneous and immediate and thus not work. In fact, immediate movements are the ones that Weil claims "are related to life itself, and can be produced without thought."[5] These movements are fleeter than any thought, and they are the basis of our awareness of our own embodiment. Weil considers the example of a runner: "The runner thinks: 'I am going to jump,' or 'I have jumped,' never: 'I am jumping.'"[6] In this way for Weil there is a "thoughtless" component to spontaneous lived action. The runner can be conscious of an intent or an accomplishment but in the moment of lived action is not, strictly speaking, *thinking* about what she is *doing*. It is because of this structure that thinking and working can be at once opposed and fruitfully cooperative. In another helpful contrast, Weil discusses how "it happens that, seeing a fruit, I extend my arm, pick it, eat it, without even knowing it." This unreflective or unthinking series of actions is "only spontaneous movement of the living body." By contrast, if I see a beautiful but unreachable rose, "I think, 'I know someone who this rose would please'" and form an intention to pick it that cannot be fulfilled without work.

In the former case, "This kind of action is not work, and it's not even action. For as long as the movements of the living body, which by the inexplicable union of the soul and body, accompany each of my desires, find themselves sufficient to accomplish these same desires, the mind, attentive only to its thoughts, never turns toward work."[7] In the latter case, "The idea of matter begins with work, begins when, for example, I climb on the embankment where the rose is, making with my legs movements that have no relation with the admiration that the rose inspires in me."[8] Work is required to overcome the resistance of matter, to accomplish the intermediate steps that intrude between intention and achievement.[9] In fact, in what could be read as an actual challenge to the Platonic understanding of techne, and this is surprising perhaps because Weil is such a thoroughgoing Platonist, she claims that it is the end in view that is determinative of the meaning of work, not the need that motivates it.[10] This departure can be understood as a consequence of Weil's more expansive understanding of work. As in the example of picking the rose, it is enough that the rose is not in my hand the moment I form an intention to pick it to prove that the action required in this case to secure the aim in mind is in fact work.[11]

In the same manuscript, Weil affirms that "work is thus universal in essence" because work is properly human, and it comprises movements that are not born directly of the setting of action but are nested within each other one might say, in a series of entailments by which one action primes the next, in conformity with the laws of matter and in view of the proposed end.[12] At the same time, it should be reinforced that work is not comprehensive for Weil; there are plenty of actions that barely merit the name and certainly don't deserve to be called work. Aside from these, however, work seems to govern an admittedly wide range of human undertakings. Another way of thinking about the scope of work in Weil's thinking is in terms of its relationship to necessity. "The philosophy of work is *materialism*. Action that encounters an obstacle gives us *matter*. Matter is something that imposes an unavoidable order to our actions."[13] To work is to encounter resistance, or, put another way, it is to encounter necessity. At one stage in fact Weil flatly declares that "the real includes a contact with necessity," and this is what makes reality real.[14] Once more, though, to encounter necessity is not to be defeated by it. That is because while in one sense thought is excluded by action (as in the case of the runner, who precisely does not think about jumping in the act of jumping), in another sense it is bound intimately to action. "If the idea of necessity appears for the first time at the stage of work," Weil writes, "freedom also appears there."[15]

Matter and necessity afford resistance to thinking and acting, but this very resistance is what allows the opportunity for action, as if matter were a springboard rather than just an obstacle. This is why thought and action are also not just opposed but bound together in a more complicated manner than first appears. That relationship is one of true liberty, which Weil asserts "is not defined by a relationship between desire and satisfaction, but by a relationship between thought and action; the absolutely free man would be he whose very action proceeded from a preliminary judgement concerning the end which he set himself and the sequence of means suitable for attaining this end."[16] As we have seen, effort and distance are crucial elements of Weil's philosophy of labor, and it must be underscored that these are definitive of labor for her and by no means the automatic source of an objectionable oppression or insurmountable difficulty. They are both obstruction and opportunity. As James Gordon Calder puts it,

> We cannot escape from necessity in the form of the completely conditional character of our existence. The whole of our life activity is subject to the inescapable dominion of labour as effort. Effort is the distance that separates every desire from its satisfaction. However, contrary to the stance of modern liberalism, for Simone Weil this is not the source of oppression in human life.[17]

Because the ideal of liberty entails the bond of thought and action, materialism, on Weil's paradoxical analysis, does not exclude mind but in fact *requires* it.[18] "Everything is matter, except *thought*, which grasps necessity. Materialism is inconceivable without the notion of mind."[19] So in work I encounter necessity, but it is thought that grasps necessity as what it is and responds constructively in thought to that encounter, which, as we have seen, is not a barrier but a provocation. Thought is thus dialectically excluded by work and vice versa, but there is no strict and final opposition between the two. "To exist, for me, is to act; but there is only one way for mind to act, and that is to think. There is no thinking and working; work is no less thought than reflection. It is no less an absolute act of mind."[20] Mind is thus implicated in work, while at the same time the two have to exclude each other in such a way as to never be coincident. As Weil puts it elsewhere, "We are, by work, separated from ourselves. But not working is not enough to deliver us from this separation. First of all, as soon as we are active, we are working."[21] We are separated from ourselves in work because the two fundamental activities of the human person find themselves coordinated, one might say, in work but never overlapping.[22]

This conclusion is in part certainly attributable to Weil's own personal experience. Not content to simply opine on these matters, Weil committed herself to acquiring direct experience of what it is like to work. She expressly rejected the potential appeal of a monastic model of labor, writing, "There is no need for a new Franciscan order. The monk's order and the convent are a barrier. The new *élite* must be a part of the mass and in direct contact with it."[23] In keeping with that verdict, Weil pushed herself into difficult labors in three factory jobs from December of 1934 to August of 1935, living off modest wages in a rented room in a working-class neighborhood.[24] Her *Factory Journal* is a chronicle of these difficult months. Weil's diary is a record of her constant battles with fatigue, migraine headaches, hunger, and a soul-crushing inability to think brought on by long hours of repetitive, mechanical work.[25] Weil was thus personally acquainted with the sort of working conditions that were such a concern to Ruskin, though she puts her own emphases into her reflection on the character of contemporary working conditions.

For instance, in her "Reflections Concerning the Causes of Liberty and Social Oppression," she writes, "Technical progress and mass production reduce manual workers more and more to a passive role; in increasing proportion and to an ever greater extent they arrive at a form of labour that enables them to carry out the necessary movements without understanding their connection with the final result."[26] Here thus we find something distinctive about Weil's view of work injected into what might otherwise be a fairly straightforward analysis of the alienation of labor. Because for her the intermediate nature of work is such a major part of what makes labor what it is, the form of "alienation" (if we can call it that) that concerns her is that modern work renders the worker passive because she is stranded at one intermediary stage of an overall working process that has intervening stages before her and will be picked up again after her by additional steps in a progress that extends in both directions without her knowledge or ability to control. Mechanized labor is thus effective but at the same time thoughtless for the worker who executes one part of it in any given work process.[27]

Similarly, Weil laments that the working system of any given industrial concern has become so vast that no one human mind really could try to understand every step within and every component of an enormous mechanism, such that "the social function most essentially connected with the individual, that which consists in co-ordinating, managing, deciding, is beyond any individual's capacity and becomes to a certain extent collective and, as it were, anonymous."[28] The divorce of action and thought in modern mechanized work is also a particularly Weilian point, reflecting once more one of her basic principles underpinning her philosophy of labor as a whole. Calder quotes Goethe's *Faust* as having been of interest to Weil on this score: "To end the greatest work designed, a thousand hands need but one mind." For Weil, as Calder understands her, this slogan bespeaks an important truth about manual labor in a factory setting. Thought and action have to be thoroughly dirempted in order for work on a certain scale to be accomplished. "The fact that thought and action can be separated into the distinct functions of command and obedience constitutes the necessary condition for human activity upon a certain scale."[29]

All work requires thought in the sense that we have seen, but in modern mechanized work that thought does not belong to the worker but to the executive who directs the work. The consequence of the division of labor, as exemplified by Smith's example of the pin factory, is that maximum efficiency is derived precisely from eliminating the occasion of thought from the labor process. In Weil's summation, in a situation like this there is method in the activity of the worker but none in her mind. Yet work requires thought, and thought requires a mind; it's just that the mind in question is that of the manager or the director, not the worker herself. Indeed, injecting thought into the labor process would not only be impossible but, quite literally, counterproductive.[30] Again, this is alienation as Weil sees it: "Man is a slave in so far as, between action and its effect, between effort and the finished product, there is the interference of alien wills."[31] The worker acts without needing to think, and the boss thinks (or commands) without needing to act. The two poles of Weil's labor dialectic are thus in this way thoroughly dirempted from one another by modern working processes.[32]

Years after she undertook her factory labor, Weil reflected further on her experience in an essay simply entitled "Factory Work," the contents of which attest to the fact that she had forgotten nothing of her earlier travail and was now able to approach it with a more refined spiritual sensibility.[33] In a choice of words that will prove important later, Weil opens her meditation with the claim that "it has become more obvious than ever that factory workers are, in a sense, truly uprooted beings, exiles in their own land," but she maintains that the reasons for this condition are not well known because superficial exposure to the outward circumstances of working people's lives is insufficient (Weil is presumably thinking by contrast of her own more immersive experience of factory labor).[34] Furthermore, working people themselves find it difficult to "write, speak, or even reflect on such a subject, for the first effect of suffering is the attempt of thought to *escape*."[35]

Weil concedes that a factory could be the site of "a powerful awareness of collective—one might well say, unanimous—life"[36] with its rhythmic noises and buzzing activity under shining electric light "where nothing recalls nature, where nothing is gratuitous, where everything is sheer impact,"[37] but alas, it is not so, because the people who work in a factory are not free. Among their afflictions are the tyranny of the time clock, which demands punctual arrival at an arbitrary time;[38] mounting resentment at slights ("One comes to acquiesce down deep that he counts for nothing"); submission to the need to take orders without question;[39] expectation that one will rapidly adapt without warning to new unexplained demands, resulting in the feeling that the worker is "incessantly at someone else's beck and call."[40] Weil does not hesitate to attribute "monotony" to a working day in a factory, but even this monotony "is mingled with a thousand little incidents that stud each working-day," including injuries, accidents, and items gone missing. "Nothing is worse," she puts forward, "than a mixture of monotony and accident."[41] Some light on this can be shed by Weil's brief essay "The Mysticism of Work." There she speaks of two kinds of monotony, which can be "the most beautiful or the most atrocious thing. The most beautiful if it is a reflection of eternity. The most atrocious if it is the sign of an unvarying perpetuity. It is time surpassed or time sterilized. The circle is the symbol of monotony which is beautiful, the swinging of the pendulum, monotony which is atrocious."[42]

It is probably no accident that the pendulum is the mechanism by which a clock tells time. The tyranny of time in the factory is governed by the monotonous ticktock of the pendulum, its deathly alternation interrupted only by the occasional and unforeseeable jolt that disrupts but by no means detains the succession of one leaden moment after another. We will see more on the other form of monotony soon, but here it is worth noting that eternity, life itself, has a kind of vital monotony, a rhythm or circuit of healthy routine that might characterize work of a different kind. As a hint of what that difference might mean, Weil only mentions here in "Factory Work" the all-too-rare moments of comradeship and the delights of victory over obstacles won by your own hands. "The more the work throws up such difficulties, the more the heart is lifted. But this joy remains incomplete for want of men, whether companions or superiors, to judge and appreciate what has been successfully overcome."[43] In the factory the work itself is isolating, and each worker is absorbed in her own task, and so "the joys of work are relegated to the plane of unformulated feelings, impressions, that vanish as swiftly as they come to birth."[44]

Cutting to the heart of the matter, and sounding rather like Ruskin, Weil baldly asserts, "Things play the role of men, men the role of things. There lies the root of the evil."[45] Distinctive to Weil is that for her the worker plays the role of a thing, the worker is reduced to an object, but horrifyingly, the worker cannot actually *be* a thing, so she endures a dehumanizing shift at work while never actually ceasing to be a thinking person. The workers are, as Weil puts it, "not licensed to put their consciousness into abeyance," and yet they must work on, more thing than person.[46] On the next page she says that it is like being plunged into a kind of sleep without actually falling asleep.[47] According to another metaphor, Weil says that the pattern of a factory worker's labor is conducted according to "cadence" and not by "rhythm." Weil's example is of a world-record-setting runner, who glides to a smooth, effortless finish while his nearest rivals with awkward haste sprawl across the line behind him. The most accomplished performance looks as if it requires no exertion at all, while the imperfect looks ungainly and forced.

By contrast,

> the spectacle presented by men over machines is nearly always one of wretched haste destitute of all grace and dignity. It comes natural to a man, and it befits him, to pause on having finished something, if only for an instant, in order to contemplate his handiwork, as God did in Genesis. Those lightning moments of

thought, of immobility and equilibrium, one has to learn to eliminate utterly in a working-day at the factory.[48]

Factory work prohibits the graceful accomplishment of work and instead forces a kind of artless clumsiness upon the worker. This impact is felt on thought, inasmuch as any momentary pause from work to contemplate the work produced is forbidden. Significantly likening this natural rhythm to the pattern of creation, according to which God created for six days and then "rested" on the seventh day, Weil asserts that this rest is not available to the factory worker. The impact of factory work also turns up in the body, cramping movement and forcing an inept haste. Recalling the deathly monotony of the pendulum, Weil writes,

> Manual operations upon machines can attain the required cadence only if those second-long movements follow one another uninterruptedly in something like the tick-tock succession of a timepiece, with nothing to mark the end of something concluded and something about to begin. This tick-tock, the barren monotony of which is scarcely bearable to human ears over any length of time, workingmen are obliged to reproduce with their bodies.[49]

The result is that time itself becomes emptied of significance and weighs upon the worker like a suffocating burden. Recalling one of Marx's formulas from the *Manuscripts*, Weil declares that for the factory worker, "Time drags for him and he lives in a perpetual exile. He spends his day in a place where he cannot feel at home."[50] Weil's twist on this classic Marxist thesis is that while the worker is not at home at work, the machine is. It is the machine that is the object of solicitude in the factory, not the person. Riffing once more on another valence of Marx's account of estranged labor, Weil says, "The working man is made to feel that he is an alien. Nothing could be more impelling in a man than the need to appropriate, not materially or juridically, but in thought, the places and objects amidst which he passes his life. A cook says, 'My kitchen,' a gardener, 'My lawn,' and this is as it should be."[51] The worker is entirely entitled to claim a right to their own working domain and its yield, but this is impossible in a factory, because the machines in no way belong to the worker; in fact, the worker is made to serve the machine, and the machine in fact does not serve her.

Yet again providing her own take on a Marxist theme, Weil points out (and we have seen something of this already) that the factory worker does not know anything about the process of which she is a part and is only one step in a multistage process, on no part of which has she left any personal mark of her own.[52] The ideal social arrangement would allow all workers to have some sense of personal ownership of, and involvement in, her own labors. Hinting at a more positive theory of what working life should look like, Weil writes, "*The perfect social organization would be one which, by that and other means, would give a proprietary feeling to all men.*"[53] The reality of the time of course did not approach this ideal and arguably still does not. Wrapping up her indictment of factory labor, Weil concludes that uprootedness at work is tantamount to uprootedness at large, homelessness at work is also homelessness in the culture as a whole: "As long as workingmen are homeless in their own places of work, they will never truly feel at home in their country, never be responsible members of society."[54]

Turning to constructive suggestions, Weil says the factory should be a place where working people "can taste joy and nourish themselves on it," while admitting (as she always did) that "physical and spiritual travail" cannot thereby be eliminated (and indeed never can be). Customary measures undertaken in service of such an aim, Weil contends, try to do either too much or too little. Ludicrous reductions in the length of the working day, for example, wouldn't banish slavery but supplement a briefer period thereof with a period of total idleness. She recommends that incentives be changed, the sources of disgust with work be abolished, and the relation of the worker to the factory, its machines, and the passage of time at work be transformed. Most especially, "In all work one of the most powerful incentives is the feeling of an end to be accomplished and a job to be done."[55] This motive is almost always absent from a factory, and instead the worker feels as if she is being kept occupied with a meaningless task so as not to get into trouble, like a small child in dread of punishment if she doesn't stay out from underfoot of her authorities.[56]

Beginning a refreshingly practical set of modest but helpful work-related suggestions, Weil argues that if a worker is to have a job that makes a small contribution to a larger process, she should know something about the whole of that process, what it produces when it is concluded, and what part the whole factory operation plays in the society in which it is embedded. The worker's family should be permitted to visit the workplace, and the worker should have sufficient pride therein that he should be happy to show it off to his loved ones.[57] Quite beyond the benefit of receiving pay for their work, Weil says that the workers should understand in their very bones that "through all their travail they are creating objects called up by the needs of society, and that they have a real if finite right to be proud of them."[58]

Most important to the whole problem of work are "time and rhythm." The work itself, Weil says, is not at issue. "It is at once inevitable and fitting that work should involve monotony and tedium ... we are truly flesh and blood; we have been thrown out of eternity; and we are indeed obliged to journey painfully through time, minute in and minute out. This travail is our lot."[59] Recalling though her intimations about a positive sort of monotony, Weil says that everything that is in some way beautiful and good reproduces a mixture of uniformity and variety, and everything that is bad and degrading does not. Referring to the toil of a farming peasant, she observes that his work is obedient to the rhythm of the world, the diurnal course of the sun, the rolling of the seasons. This rhythm is absent from the factory, which obeys the clock, not constellations.[60] The blinders of the working man must be removed so that his power of foresight is unleashed. The worker must be allowed to know how his work is oriented toward the future, the accomplishment of the end goal and beyond that even the goal that the factory production process itself attains on the part of the society and its needs.[61] In all these recommendations, Weil is distinctly modest in her aims. It must be recalled that she is not a revolutionary but an incrementalist. These are not sweeping reforms she is putting forward, and she cautions against the twin dangers of timidity in the face of reform and illusory revolutionary promises. Her conclusion is just as modest.

Our factories have become festering-grounds of evil, and the evil of the factories must be corrected. It is difficult, but perhaps not impossible. It is high time that specialists, engineers, and others concerned, should be exercised not only to make objects, but also not to destroy men. Not to render them docile, nor even to make them happy, but quite simply not to force them to abase themselves.[62]

Before her stint in the factory, Weil had already written her "Theoretical Picture of a Free Society," in which she clearly speaks about the true nature of liberty and the sort of aspiration that a society ought reasonably to have with regard to the question of work. There she opined, "Perfect liberty is what we must try to represent clearly to ourselves, not in the hope of attaining it, but in the hope of attaining a less imperfect liberty than is our present condition; for the better can be conceived only by reference to the perfect. One can only steer towards an ideal."[63] The reason Weil is content with an approach to an ideal rather than its revolutionary imposition is because she is convinced that necessity, with which work brings us into contact, can never be eliminated, and she regards as perniciously idealistic any worldview that dangles this illusion before the eyes of the poor. "Perfect liberty cannot be conceived," she maintains, "as consisting merely in the disappearance of that necessity whose pressure weighs continually upon us; as long as man goes on existing, that is to say as long as he continues to constitute an infinitesimal fraction of this pitiless universe, the pressure exerted by necessity will never be relaxed for one single moment."[64]

Because necessity is always with us, we needn't lament the loss of a notion of liberty that was chimerical to begin with. Freedom is not acting without constraint; on the contrary, constraint is required for productivity. "There is no self-mastery without discipline, and there is no other source of discipline for man than the effort demanded in overcoming external obstacles. ... It is the obstacles we encounter and that have to be overcome which give us the opportunity for self-conquest."[65] For the full realization of human potential, even the sort of activities that seem to be "freest" in the depleted sense of being unchecked by necessity have to "imitate the accuracy, rigour, scrupulousness which characterize the performance of work, and even exaggerate them."[66] So not only should work be work but according to Weil art and sport should bear the marks of work as well. Absent such spurs to activity, human beings would realize none of their potential. "We have only to bear in mind the weakness of human nature to understand that an existence from which the very notion of work had pretty well disappeared would be delivered over to the play of the passions and perhaps to madness."[67]

Turning to a more positive theory of work, and now overbidding perhaps a little, Weil argues that "the key to all the practical problems of human existence" is twofold: "A workman's happiness consists above all in a certain attitude of mind towards his work" and "this attitude of mind can be brought about only if certain objective conditions—impossible to know without making a serious study of the subject—have been fulfilled."[68]

Weil does not specify what the objective conditions of work that will be satisfying to the worker are here. She has just said that study of these conditions has to take place as a preferable alternative to the usually cramped manner in which managers imagine they can make workers happy, that is, by raising their wage, so clearly here she has in mind improvement in the objective conditions of work that extend beyond the mere inflation of salary. If we turn to other sources though, we can learn more about what Weil thinks good, wholesome work consists in. For instance, her essay "The First Condition for the Work of a Free Person," penned in 1942 but not published until 1947, outlines some ways of enhancing work. She opens this essay with a reaffirmation of a point we have seen already: "There is in the work of human hands and, in general, in the skilled performance of a task, which is work properly understood, an irreducible element of servitude that even a perfectly just society cannot remove. This is because it is governed by necessity, not by finality."[69]

By necessity here Weil is clear that she has in mind the mere securing of what is required for the perpetuation of life. If we think of work at its most primitive, it secures nothing added to the basic demands of our existence but merely the extension of our existence, and this alone is as she puts it "not an end for a human being."[70] This is why she says work of this sort is not governed by finality, because it does not aim at any good above and beyond that of perpetuation of human existence. Goods, Weil insists in the sense she means here, are "added to existence," and without them existence is rendered naked and proffers nothing desirable save its own exposure. This is the condition of the slave, whether lifelong or momentary, and the situation of a worker resembles that of a slave exactly when and where the worker finds it impossible to desire anything other than what one has, the minimum necessary to go on living.[71] In this vicious cycle, one literally works in order to eat and eats in order to work.[72] That such a state of affairs is utterly demoralizing is not surprising, so Weil turns instead to what it was in times past that prevented such lassitude and disgust. Certainly not palliatives like ambition, "easy and violent pleasure," debauchery, and least of all the vain hope of revolution: "Insofar as it is a revolt against social injustice, the revolutionary idea is good and healthy. Insofar as it is a revolt against the essential evil of the workers' condition, it is a lie, because no revolution will wipe out this evil."[73]

Similarly, fobbing the workers off with more money is just another piece of naivety. Sounding just like Ruskin, Weil argues that a worker inasmuch as she becomes wealthy thereby precisely ceases to be a worker. The attainment of great wealth means exit from the condition of having to strive to supply yourself with what is necessary. No one, Weil alleges, who has not shared in this condition can judge the actions of those who are consigned to it for their whole lives. It is not a fatal state of affairs, but Weil likens it to a kind of hunger, a hunger "for which bread is less necessary than the remedy for this pain." Yet there is only one remedy, and that is beauty, the "light from eternity" that alone makes this monotony bearable.[74] The reason that beauty can be a consolation within the pain of the worker's condition is that beauty alone conducts desire not away from yourself toward some good that is absent or to look upon what is present with a jaundiced eye, such that you wish it were different, but leads you to affirm the desirability of what is present in its fullness. "Everything that is beautiful is an object of desire, but one does not desire that it be different, one does not desire to change anything, one desires the very thing that exists." Like gazing upon a starry sky, one desires just what one sees and nothing else.[75]

Moving to the next stage of her argument, Weil points out that "some people are forced to place all their desire on what they already possess." Presumably these people are in the main working persons, and because they are driven primarily by their needs rather than their aims, they *must* find beauty in what they possess. Indeed, the condition of the working class is reciprocally bound to beauty: "Beauty is made for them and they are made for beauty." Striking a rather poetic note herself, Weil says that while poetry is a luxury for most, "the common people need poetry like they need bread." She does not have in mind literal poetry of the written word but demands that "the daily substance of their lives be poetry itself."[76] The exclusive source of such poetry is, in turn, God.

Religion is the only means of poetizing reality, because "by no trick, by no process, no reform, no upheaval can finality enter into the universe where workers are placed by their very condition. But this universe can be completely linked to the only end that is true. It can be hooked onto God."[77] Nothing within, one might say, the worker's condition, affords this life-enriching poetry; so its source can only be from outside the boundaries of her condition, and that source is nothing less than divine. Here is the secret blessing within the worker's condition: All people desire finality, all people pursue ends, but the worker's desire is only satisfiable by the one true end that is outside the scope of finite projects and mundane possibilities. Any such particular end can always supplant for the one true end, the only and absolute aim of human desire, God. For the worker there is no such interposing distraction, or "screen," as Weil puts it here. "When it is a question of the salvation of one soul or many, there is no particular end that cannot make a screen and hide God. By detachment it is necessary to pierce through the screen. For the workers there is no screen. Nothing separates them from God. They only have to lift their heads."[78] Simple as that sounds, Weil admits that it is not easy for the workers to lift their heads because they are immersed in the realm of their own needs. They only have what is essential, and they possess nothing that they can be rid of only with effort. They therefore have no "intermediaries," as Weil dubs them.

In a church, for instance, she points out that people's prayers are facilitated by intermediaries: the imagery, the architecture, the words of the liturgy, the ritual gestures, and so on direct one's attention *through* them *to* God. In a workplace though there are no intermediaries. One goes there only to work, and "there everything binds one's thought to earth."[79] In a workplace though you can't place religious images or pause to look at them, and "neither can one propose that they recite prayers while working."[80] What is needed is that the "matter, the instruments, and the gestures" of the work itself, the implements and material features of work themselves be intermediaries of the divine, that they be polished like "mirrors" to reflect the celestial light. "There is no necessity more pressing than this transformation." So how to effectuate it?

There is no need, Weil argues, to fabricate arbitrary symbols. Rather what is needed is to clean the mirror that is the material basis of working activity, to restore to its luster the matter that is constitutive of work and thus to behold in this matter the riches of eternity. The first source of some such symbolic associations of profundity and poetry Weil culls from the Gospels. The truth of Jesus's proclamation that unless a grain of wheat falls to the ground and dies it remains alone but that if it dies it bears much fruit[81] is one that is best known by the farmer. Furthermore, the farmer knows this precisely *not* by contemplation or study but by and in the act of sowing grain;

plainly in fact the farmer knows this *better* than the academician, for her attention is by no means impeded by this "intermediary"; quite the opposite: It is brought to the highest possible degree of intensity by her bodily movements and gestures. Borrowing another example from John's Gospel, Weil references Jesus's proclamation of himself as the vine and the disciples as his branches, indicating their total dependence upon him for the bearing of spiritual fruit.[82] Weil observes that the process of cutting vines "takes days and days on large estates. But also there is a truth there that can be examined for days and days without being exhausted."[83] Using examples like these, Weil suggests that deep symbolism is available not just for drawing closer to the profound meaning of work in general but even for any number of specific unique tasks. It would be shocking indeed, she quips, if a church built by human beings should be loaded with manifold symbolic depth while the universe should be bereft of any symbolic meaning. The trick is to attend to such meanings with sympathy and without interruption.[84]

Deepening this way of looking at the universe, Weil reveals that "the greatest thing in the world" is solar energy, of which "the sun and the sap in the plants speak continually in the fields." This is obviously not a scientific claim, or rather, it is not only a scientific claim. For the energy of the sun comes unbidden to all things and sustains the life of all things down to the very molecular level.

> We eat it, and it keeps us on our feet, it makes our muscles move, it operates bodily in all our acts. It is, perhaps under diverse forms, the only thing in the universe that constitutes a force opposed to gravity ... It comes from an inaccessible source that we cannot approach even by one step. It comes down on us continually. But although it bathes us perpetually, we cannot capture it.

In its remoteness and yet omnipresence, in its gratuitousness and supremacy, the power of life that radiates from the sun is, dazzlingly, "a perfect image of Christ." Only the peasant, in his work, cares for and caters to this biological power that drives all the world and its activities, and thus (it would seem) only the work of the peasant furnishes us with a "perfect image" of service to Christ.[85] The imagery of the sun of course cannot help but also bring Plato to mind.

It remains the case that

> a certain subordination and a certain uniformity are forms of suffering included in the very essence of work and inseparable from the supernatural vocation that corresponds to it. They do not degrade a person. Everything that is added to them is unjust and does degrade. Everything that prevents poetry from crystallizing around these sufferings is a crime. For it is not enough to rediscover the lost source of such poetry; it is also necessary that the very circumstances of work permit it to exist.[86]

Work itself is not an evil, but the accretions that attach to work and prevent it from being poetic are. Recall that Weil claimed that the worker's attitude toward her work depended on the realization of certain objective conditions. At the very least, work must be free of circumstances that impair the poetization of labor. The supernatural vocation she speaks of here has to be unobstructed. How to achieve this vital state of affairs? Weil proves herself a perfect Augustinian in her diagnosis of what ails humanity and her prescription for the cure. "Everything that belongs to creatures is limited," she contends, "except the desire in us that is the mark of our origin; and our covetousness that makes us seek the unlimited down here is the unique source of error and crime."[87] Weil has a number of practical ideas in mind.

First, she condemns in the strongest terms "all advertising, all propaganda … that arouses the desire for the superfluous in the countryside and among the workers." She despises advertising for stimulating needless desires, provoking a restless hankering for change or a resentful fear of it. The point though as we have seen is to find contentment in the reality in which one finds oneself. There is a respect in which the worker's life "simply needs to be accepted." Diversion from the potential for such satisfaction Weil regards as a "crime."[88] Instead, change should be confined to the promotion of one's own well-being as measured by the general achievement thereof. The working person should neither have occasion to fear falling below the level of the general welfare and the security that comes with it nor the baseless aspiration to exceed it. The worker should even be shielded as far as possible from the fluctuations of supply and demand.[89]

Second, because arbitrariness compels one toward both fear and hope by turns, its influence over the life of the worker should be limited as much as possible. Weil seems to have foremost in mind the sort of arbitrariness almost inevitably imposed by bosses. Accordingly, she advises that authority figures should hover only when their presence is absolutely required, and that in general small-scale property is better than large. By this logic, producing machine-finished pieces in a small workshop is preferable to doing so on a factory line under the orders of a foreman. Referring to the book of Job, Weil says that the commanding voice of the taskmaster should be replaced by silence whenever possible.[90]

Third, "the worst outrage," the one she says is like the biblical sin against the Holy Spirit, which cannot be forgiven,[91] is "the crime against the attention of the workers. It kills the faculty in the soul that is the very root of every supernatural vocation."[92] Recall that above Weil said that nothing about work can obstruct the supernatural vocation of the worker; here is her most important statement on that matter. The worker's attention must be required for work to be salutary and open to its potential for supernatural plenitude. Referring to the organizational theory of Frederick Taylor, Weil heaps scorn on work that requires no active mental awareness on the part of the worker and sacrifices all thought and care to the idol of speed. This kind of work alone she says cannot be transformed or improved but must simply be suppressed.[93]

Finally, Weil recommends that the poetry of which she has spoken, which ought to permeate all aspects of working life, should also be periodically concentrated in "outstanding festivals," which serve to mark the progress of work. Though she does not say so here, we can surmise as well that a festival is uniquely suited to punctuate the seasons and rhythms of life, which Weil was at pains to stress the importance of earlier in the same essay.[94] All in all, the problems of technology and economy she concludes should be resolved to the benefit of the working person: "The entire society should be constituted in such a way that work does not drag down those who perform it."[95] Again notice that Weil's goal is not overambitious.[96] The aim is conservative: not to glorify work or overhype its importance but simply to avoid adding greater burdens to those that already shoulder the burden of work, which is and will forever have its own inherent difficulties. The working person, though, as Weil reminds her reader in the final words of this essay, is ideally positioned to realize the joy to which all human beings are summoned, a joy that is only discoverable within the ineradicable difficulty of labor. "If the vocation of the human being is to achieve pure joy through suffering, they are better placed than others to accomplish this in the most real way."[97]

Speaking specifically of rural life and work in another essay, "Le Christianisme et la vie des champs," Weil laments that calling a village "Christian" nowadays entails little more than that the residents go to mass on Sunday and teach their kids not to say swear words.[98] This superficial religiosity coexists with a stifling ennui, relieved only by alcohol and debauchery. Yet people say that to work is to pray. Weil sniffs that it is easy enough to say this, "but in fact it is only true under certain rarely realized conditions."[99] The countryside though should be a natural place for such conditions to obtain. Jesus used largely agricultural imagery, but the parables that draw on the symbolism of life lived close to nature "do not appear in the Sunday liturgy. This liturgy has no connections with the succession of the seasons of the year. The cosmic element is so absent from Christianity as it is currently practiced that one could forget that the universe was created by God."[100] Weil proposes two reforms that she thinks should be easy to implement. First, she suggests that clergy should comment in their sermons on some part of the Gospel that pertains to whatever seasonal work is then being done and bid the peasantry to think on the relevant Scripture while they do that work, and she offers some of the examples we have already seen in other writings among others. In every case, "It is a question of transforming, as far as possible, daily life itself into a metaphor with divine meaning, into a parable."[101]

The second reform is putting the Eucharist at the center of daily life. The priest, she points out, has the privilege of consecrating the elements at the altar, but the peasant she claims enjoys no less sublime a privilege, because through work he sacrifices his flesh to produce the wheat and the grapes. "Manual labor is either a degrading servitude for the soul or a sacrifice. In the case of work in the fields, the link to the Eucharist, if it is only felt, is enough to make it a sacrifice."[102] Simple gestures like announcing who donated the bread and wine for consecration, blessing the tools of the workers perhaps annually, and holding a liturgy to inaugurate a young person's entry into independent work, Weil feels, will contribute to a spiritual transformation of rural life and work.[103]

Overall, Weil contends that "Christianity will permeate society only if each social category has its specific, unique, inimitable link with Christ."[104] The peasant is connected to Christ through the work of producing bread and wine, the shepherd to the Good Shepherd, mothers through the "intermediary" Virgin Mary, judges through the Great Judge, students to the one who called himself the truth, beggars to the triumphant Christ of Matthew 24 who says he was hungry and fed by the faithful under the auspices of "the least of these," servants to him who in the words of Paul "took the form of a servant."[105] In this way just as the religious life is sorted into different orders with distinct charisms, so social life too could be organized, with Christ at the center and each profession representing a worldly but spiritualized "order" of labor.[106]

Weil's most complete statement on work can be found in her last writing, her only book-length undertaking. The occasion for this work was a planned policy prospectus for implementation after the liberation of France.[107] Remember above that Weil described the condition of the factory worker as being "uprooted." The title of this final work of hers, *L'Enracinement*, simply means "rootedness," and the book includes a diagnosis of the problem of uprootedness as it manifests itself in various sectors of French life and culture. It is in one such chapter, on uprootedness in the countryside, that Weil speaks at greater length on work and in particular peasant work. Paradoxically in Weil's estimation, the land is now worked by persons who are uprooted. This state of affairs is the very opposite of the ideal for human beings: "To be rooted," as Weil argues in the opening words of these chapters, "is perhaps the most important and least recognized need of the human soul."[108] Rootedness is a "real, active, and natural participation in the life of a community, which preserves in living shape certain particular treasures of the past and certain particular expectations for the future."[109] By the same token, "uprootedness is by far the most dangerous malady to which human societies are exposed."[110]

In the present case, rootedness has been destroyed by military conquest, which is nearly always an evil, while in other instances colonization or just economic domination is the cause.[111] Quite apart from the reality of the conquest and occupation of France, Weil names two other toxins that contribute to prevailing uprootedness: money and education, only the first of which will concern us briefly here. Here she recapitulates some of her thoughts on the cramped situation of workers who are motivated only by pay. "Money destroys human roots wherever it is able to penetrate, by turning desire for gain into the sole motive." This destruction is most thoroughgoing in the case of piece work, which "obliges each workman to have his attention continually taken up with the subject of his pay."[112] Thus once more she declares that the modern working person is in a condition of uprootedness; though he never leaves his familiar haunts, he is at home in none of them, and should he find himself completely unemployed, this "is, of course, an uprootedness raised to the second power."[113]

Rootedness in one's work can only be achieved by restoring it to its "rightful place in a man's thoughts. Instead of being a kind of prison, it becomes a point of contact between this world and the world beyond."[114] Here again the capacity for work must be understood as a contact point with transcendence. Revisiting her earlier examples about pastoral imagery drawn from the Gospels, Weil reaffirms the importance of poetizing labor and imbuing it with symbolic spiritual depth. "Thus only would the dignity of work be fully established. For, if we go to the heart of things, there is no true dignity without a spiritual root and consequently one of a supernatural order."[115] The objective of societal institutions ought to be then to infuse work with thought rather than divide the working person into "compartments, which sometimes works and sometimes thinks." This contention is perfectly consistent with what we saw from Weil's earlier writings, where action and thought are not to be divorced but dialectically play off one another. Weil asserts that of course a peasant at work in the fields has to think about what he is doing, not think about the Bible's use of agricultural metaphors, but she cautions that the focus of our attention is not the whole of it. This point is now memorably illustrated with a striking example:

A happy young woman, expecting her first child, and busy sewing a layette, thinks about sewing properly. But she never forgets for an instant the child she is carrying inside her. At precisely the same moment, somewhere in a prison workshop, a female convict is also sewing, thinking, too, about sewing properly, for she is afraid of being punished. One might imagine both women to be doing the same work at the same time, and having their attention absorbed by the same technical difficulties. And yet a whole gulf of difference lies between one occupation and the other.[116]

The difference is surely self-evident, but we should take care to ensure we are clear about its basis. The first woman is joyfully sewing a layette for the child she is carrying in her womb—this is work of an uplifting and ennobling character. The second is also sewing but doing so in misery, under confinement, and in fear of punishment. Superficially, they are doing what would appear to be the exact same work at the exact same time, but clearly these are two wildly different circumstances. Inese Radzins offers a careful and detailed reading of this divergence. She observes that there is a deep significance to the detail of the first woman's pregnancy, which may have more than one valence of meaning here.[117] For one thing, there is a certain gratuitousness common to parenting and the best kind of work: Both are inexplicable in terms of stock, generic causal explanations. We do them because they are worth doing. Furthermore, the impetus for the task at hand is actually derived from an unseen reality. Like thought or attention, the child about to be born, for whom the mother sews the layette, is an invisible reality and thus "offers a link to spirit."[118] Like the pondering of Scripture while working the fields, the unseen child is the inspiration for and companion to the mother's work. At the same time, as Radzins is correct to emphasize, the work requires and elevates the mundane material involved (needle, thread, fabric); the key is that work brings together the unseen reality and the material circumstances in their very exclusion of one another.[119]

Put simply, the goal of any society should be to shift the character of its work from the condition of the woman in prison to the condition of the pregnant mother. "The whole social problem consists in making the workers pass from one to the other of these two occupational extremes. What is required is that this world and the world beyond, in their double beauty, should be present and associated in the act of work, like the child about to be born in the making of the layette."[120] Work is or at least can be this point of contact, where two beauties meet, the intricate intersection of matter and spirit, necessity and liberty. In the case of the laboring prisoner, this connection has been severed. Her work affords no opening onto the world of the spirit.[121] The prisoner's work is nothing but drudgery, and thus emptied of spirit, her only consolation can be found in activities *other* than work.

For Weil, all human activities should be in touch with spirit, and work seems the most apt activity for this potential connection. As Radzins puts it, for Weil, "persons should be just as much 'at home' when at work as when in their home."[122] Or in other words, they should be rooted in work as much as in any other human setting and activity. How to forge this connection? According to Weil, such an association can be achieved by a mode of presenting thoughts which relates them directly to the movements and operations peculiar to each sort of work, by a process of assimilation sufficiently complete to enable them to penetrate into the very substance of the individual being, and by a habit impressed upon the mind and connecting these thoughts with the work movements.[123]

Presumably discipline and formation will play a role here, as will education conceived on more radical (in the root meaning of that word) terms as a kind of spiritual apprenticeship,[124] and as we have just seen the practices of infusing work with spiritual and symbolic significance would be needed as well.[125] Weil expresses skepticism about present prospects for such a revival of the spirituality of work, but she firmly announces that this is the task of the moment. "Our age has its own particular mission, or vocation—the creation of a civilization founded upon the spiritual nature of work."[126] This is the one task that belongs to the contemporary era and is the unique contribution that the present time has to make to the philosophical tradition. Anticipations of a fully developed spirituality of work she says can be gleaned from Rousseau, George Sand, Tolstoy, Proudhon, Marx, and the papal encyclicals, and these stand as "the only original thoughts of our time, the only ones we haven't borrowed from the Greeks."[127] If this project can be completed, then Weil is ultimately hopeful that

a civilization based upon the spirituality of work would give to Man the very strongest possible roots in the wide universe, and would consequently be the opposite of that state in which we find ourselves now, characterized by an almost total uprootedness. Such a civilization is, therefore, by its very nature, the object to which we should aspire as the antidote to our sufferings.[128]

As a potential sign of hope, Weil is of the belief that such a civilization may have existed before. At the very close of *The Need for Roots*, Weil returns to her theory of labor and proclaims the following:

Physical labor willingly consented to is, after death willingly consented to, the most perfect form of obedience. The penal character of labor, suggested by the account in Genesis, has been misunderstood for want of a just notion regarding punishment. It is a mistake to read into this text the slightest hint of a disdain for labor. It is more likely that it was handed down by some very ancient civilization in which physical labor was honored above every other activity.[129]

So to work at a physically demanding task is a kind of submission to necessity, a form of obedience, like acceptance of death. This strikes a somewhat different tone from previous, more academic discourses on the relationship of liberty and necessity. Now Weil speaks not just of a dialectical tension but the need for obedience and acceptance. In keeping with a large swath of traditional readings of Genesis, Weil too rejects the interpretation that would imply that work is a curse. Characteristically for her though, she declines to credit the Hebrew Bible with this discovery, citing instead what sounds at first like a hypothetical, not to say fantastical, historical source.[130]

Yet Weil is apparently in earnest: "There are numerous signs indicating that such a civilization did exist, that long ago physical labor was pre-eminently a religious activity and consequently something sacred."[131] For evidence of this contention Weil refers to a wide swath of mythical sources. She names the mystery religions and claims they "were founded upon symbolical expressions concerning the salvation of the soul, drawn from agriculture," the same symbolism found in the New Testament. She also names Hephaestus and Prometheus ("the nontemporal projection of Christ, a crucified and redemptive God who came down to cast fire upon the earth") as divine figures who are connected with fire and labor, as is the Holy Ghost. Hypothesizing a common truth translated into different symbol sets that were adapted to different types of physical labor for the purpose of drawing out that labor's sacred character, Weil concludes,

> All the religious traditions of antiquity, including the Old Testament, make the various trades originate in the receipt of direct instructions from God. ... Whatever the truth may be, which is hidden in these extremely mysterious accounts, the belief in direct instruction in the various trades by God implies the memory of a time when the exercise of these trades was above all a sacred activity.[132]

She hypothesizes a long and speculative history, in which this place of social centrality is lost in high ancient Greek culture, totally crushed by the Roman Empire, and briefly restored to honor by the Albigenses, Machiavelli's Florence, and the Romanesque era.[133] Following the decadence of the thirteenth and fourteenth centuries, a hopeful "first Renaissance," and the disappointing reactionary "second Renaissance," the modern world came into its own. "We are very proud of it," Weil says, "but we also know that it is sick. And everybody is agreed about the diagnosis of the sickness. It is sick because it doesn't know exactly what place to give to physical labor and to those engaged in physical labor."[134] We can question perhaps Weil's confidence about the extent of the consensus supporting her diagnosis of the ills of the modern world, but we know already that this disease has a cure or, as she said above, an antidote.

Here in the final pages of *The Need for Roots*, Weil returns to Genesis, exhorting us to situate it in its proper atmosphere. Surprisingly, she now speaks the language of punishment and curse, having just refused this association with the text of Genesis only a couple of pages prior.

> When a human being has, by committing a crime, placed himself outside the current of the Good, his true punishment consists in his reintegration into the plenitude of that current by means of suffering. There is nothing so marvelous as a punishment. Man placed himself outside the current of Obedience. God chose as his punishments labor and death. Consequently, labor and death, if Man undergoes them in a spirit of willingness, constitute a transference back into the current of supreme Good, which is obedience to God.[135]

So labor and death now appear to be punishment for sin after all. The trick of human life is to accept this punishment in an act of obedience. This is clear, Weil argues, if we look at the issue in the manner of the ancients, who interpreted "the passivity of inert matter as the perfection of obedience to God."¹³⁶

Death of course is a kind of final giving of one's self over to inert matter, at least from an earthly perspective (and Weil here leaves open the question of whether death might appear differently from a heavenly perspective). Death though is a largely impotent and abstract thought to us as long as death itself is not an immediate prospect. Work, however, physical labor, "is a daily death," and as such it is a more powerful witness to and more insistent invitation to obedience. "To labor is to place one's own being, body and soul, in the circuit of inert matter, turn it into an intermediary between one state and another of a fragment of matter, make of it an instrument." Thus labor is a form of obedience and thus also a restoration to the current of supreme Good, as she said above. To labor willingly is to obey necessity, to accept punishment for sin and be returned to goodness.

> Death and labor are things of necessity and not of choice. The world only gives itself to Man in the form of food and warmth if Man gives himself to the world in the form of labor. But death and labor can be submitted to either in an attitude of revolt or in one of consent. They can be submitted to either in their naked truth or else wrapped around with lies. Labor does violence to human nature.¹³⁷

This hard truth cannot be avoided. It can only be accepted without sugarcoating or prevarication. Consent to death is of course the final loss of everything "one calls 'I,'" and while consent to labor is less violent, "it is renewed each morning throughout the entire length of a human existence, day after day, and each day it lasts until the evening, and it starts again on the following day, and this goes on often until death."¹³⁸ It goes on every day all day regardless of the worker's mood or level of enthusiasm or energy. Thus it is the only activity that approaches the dignity and demand of death, and so "it follows that all other human activities, command over men, technical planning, art, science, philosophy, and so on, are all inferior to physical labor in spiritual significance."¹³⁹ On this final formulation from Weil's pen, it is the depth of submission to necessity, to punishment, that stands out. For her, labor is still the center of human life, but it is now charged with substantially more moralistic severity. This is the solution to the central problem of human affairs. Her last words on work were also the last words of this final book intended for publication. There is no better way to end our treatment than to end with the last words of *The Need for Roots*: "It is not difficult to define the place that physical labor should occupy in a well-ordered social life. It should be its spiritual core."¹⁴⁰

Conclusion

It is one thing of course to say that work should be the spiritual core of a renewed society; it is another thing to do it. Add to that perennial reality the fact that much has changed since Weil outlined her original proposals for postwar France, none of which she lived long enough to even try to see implemented and few of which ever were. On the one hand, working conditions have changed dramatically for the better thanks to widespread social reforms, certainly for the workers in developed nations by comparison to the days of Ruskin. These advances are obviously welcome, and they could be seen as vindication of many calls for moral reform. Other aspects of the Ruskinian and Weilian vision though are nowhere in evidence, and hard work remains with us, at least in some sectors.

Ruskin, for example, thought it wise to recruit workers for difficult jobs, which he believed would always be with us such that someone will always have to do hard work:

> Men are enlisted for the labour that kills—the labour of war: they are counted, trained, fed, dressed, and praised for that. Let them be enlisted also for the labour that feeds: let them be counted, trained, fed, dressed, praised for that. Teach the plough exercise as carefully as you do the sword exercise, and let the officers of troops of life be held as much gentlemen as the officers of troops of death; and all is done.[1]

Often this sort of suggestion, that hard work be rendered more enticing to those inclined to it by putting some patina of glamor on the practice—a smart uniform perhaps, the giving of honors to the most accomplished, the attaching of esteem to the people who do hard work—strikes readers as quixotic I suspect; it smacks of a discredited Soviet-style propagandism.

Yet on the other hand it also seems simple, cheap, and perhaps not entirely impractical. We frequently hear, as we did in 2015 from Senator Rubio, that difficult work *should* be held in more esteem, but we still just *don't* hold it in more esteem. Is it possible that the relatively easy proposals, which would cost our society next to nothing, *would* begin building a sense of esteem for workers who do tough jobs? Furthermore, while there is a certain kind of elitism that can lead to being dangerously out of touch with respect to work, one to which philosophers are particularly vulnerable, doesn't that same elitism endanger our appreciation for the esteem in which tough work is held precisely by the people who do it? I happened to hear then-President Trump praise the ongoing work of truckers, who had kept at their essential tasks during the Covid-19 crisis, which has overtaken only the writing of the very end of this book.[2] A cynical viewer would say that handing symbolic keys to four truckers invited to take part in a White House ceremony in their honor is a hollow gesture. Maybe it is, but I was struck more by what one of the truck drivers, Charlton Paul, had to say than by anything that the president said. Mr. Paul drives for UPS, and in the course of his remarks he said, "growing up, the only thing I wanted to do was sit behind the wheel of one of these massive trucks."[3] I take him at his word. Philosophers, and people who write books about philosophers, don't generally grow up wanting to sit behind the wheel of a massive truck. But Mr. Paul did. And he is not alone.

Would it be so foolish or quixotic to make a determined societal effort to recruit people like Mr. Paul for work they want to do, remunerate them handsomely for it, and reward them with plenty of time off for improving leisure? Not only that, would it not be entirely consistent with the Platonic tradition for the Mr. Pauls of the world to have likewise been educated well enough to appreciate that time of leisure with whatever pursuits he sees fit?[4] These are not incompatible aims according to the Platonic tradition. I myself have met a lineman who knew Plato's *Republic* better than I.

Furthermore, we might also duly note that we already glamorize certain kinds of work, just not very hard work, and that elite form of employment is actually costing us leisure, not gaining it. Derek Thompson of *The Atlantic* wrote an important piece recently called "The Religion of Workism Is Making Americans Miserable."[5] In it he documents how the wealthy are working more than ever and taking less rather than more time for leisure. He postulates that this drive toward more work is no longer primarily economically motivated but spiritually so: Workism is a new ersatz religion. For the workist youth, work is a promised source of meaning and community and transcendence, not just a paycheck. Work in fact outranks many other priorities according to a Pew Research report on youth anxiety cited by Thompson:

> 95 percent of teens said "having a job or career they enjoy" would be "extremely or very important" to them as an adult. This ranked higher than any other priority, including "helping other people who are in need" (81 percent) or getting married (47 percent). Finding meaning at work beats family and kindness as the top ambition of today's young people.[6]

While Thompson grants of course that there is nothing wrong with good old-fashioned work and that indeed there is some evidence that long-term unemployment is unhealthy, he does seem convinced nevertheless that "our desks were never meant to be our altars."[7] As a result of this perverse sleight of hand, "the only real reward from work is the ineffable glow of purpose. It is a diabolical game that creates a prize so tantalizing yet rare that almost nobody wins, but everybody feels obligated to play forever."[8] Thompson's conclusion is that it might help to make work less central in our lives rather than more so.

The Platonic tradition can perhaps steer a middle way here. We have seen that there is a danger in underappreciation for work, especially the tough kind. We really should have more welders, and welders should be better paid. It is easy for an elitist perspective to misunderstand the attractions of work that would not seem "meaningful" in their own eyes or to view with a jaundiced eye efforts to draw greater admiration toward the people who do hard work. There is a real danger here, because there is some evidence that even jobs that objectively appear meaningless are not experienced as such by the people who do them.[9] Similarly, those who are motivated by the internal goods of their jobs (which as we have seen the Platonic tradition certainly highlights) tend to be immune from the presence of external motivators and free from a number of damaging attitudes and behaviors.[10] The more you love your job for its own sake, the less your pay matters, and more pay does not help much if you hate your job to begin with.

At the same time, we cannot assign to work more weight than it can bear. At the end of Thompson's piece he admits he is a thoroughgoing workist himself, and he wonders whether it might be better to subordinate work to some other more traditional goods like relationships. The Platonic tradition never made this mistake: There is always something more important than work, call it the Good, call it God, call it nature or necessity. For the Platonic tradition work plays out in a horizon of reality that encircles it and within which work operates. This means that work can never really be itself an ersatz religion but can only be in service of some higher aim. Since for the Platonic tradition work can never be ultimate, there is always an interplay between it and leisure. The Platonic philosopher is a contemplator as well as a doer; the monastic heritage intersperses labor with rest, from Benedict to Petrarch; Ruskin demands that hard work be relieved by rest from labor.

In our current situation, however, Michael Hanby may be right to say,

> There is little work, little in the *nature* of work as conceived and practiced in our technological society, that is inherently ordered, by its own internal logic, to the sacramental order of creation and that permits the one who undertakes it to understand and reflect upon that order or to live a maximally coherent life in view of that reality.[11]

This is just to say in capsule form that it's hard to be a Platonist about work, especially when you live in a workist society.

Yet as I have said I think with the help especially of the more recent figures studied in this text we can at least think about changes of attitudes if not changes in society (though again, why these should not come as well I think is often a question that is not so much answered as not really asked seriously).

For starters, we can ask about whether our job is responsive to a genuine need or secures a real good. This simple question ought to cast into doubt entire industries that cater to luxury and foment needless desires, as we have seen from Plato down to Weil. It could be argued that what makes the "bullshit jobs" famously identified by David Graeber the bullshit they are is that they just don't in fact serve any genuine human need.[12] If the job is not bullshit though, then we might be able to see how its internal good motivates us to do it in conjunction with whatever external goods might also attach to it. Recall that from the start we affirmed that for Plato the best kind of goods will be both good in themselves and for what they get us, they will come with both internal and external goods, so there is every right to expect that both kinds of good will be present in our jobs, but we of course have been concentrating on the internal, which are much harder to appreciate in our current cultural setting.

If the job does have an internal good, then it must also be responsive to some aspect of reality. From work with that aspect of the real we learn to submit to limits, to be content with what we can bring about through disciplined effort and without aid or inducement, to refine one area of needfulness and be satisfied with whatever improvement can be realized through concentrated but humble exertion. This is true from the very beginning of our study: Xenophon cautioned that the wise farmer will know what the land can and cannot sustain. For an alternate, modern tradition, work is just the opposite. Beginning with Locke, who made labor the basis of all property, and Marx, who made it the origin of all human culture, we now tend to think of work as the unstoppable engine of all production that takes nature and perhaps in the end humanity itself to be infinitely malleable and manipulable. The corollary is that we think of our realm of activity as one of our own sovereign dominion, linking for the first time in Western history "propriety" with "property." The consequences to the environment are obvious, to humanity not at all heartening.[13]

Perhaps nothing can avert them. The philosopher has often been lampooned as useless, but for Plato, even the philosopher is productive, if of nothing else than his own life, set in order, which is at once work and artistry. If we are to make a more just society, it will have to be in this sense beautiful as well, and such a project can only begin by grasping what is. No one of us can grasp the whole of what is, but all of us can in some way through what we choose to work on, knowing that at the same time we are working necessarily on ourselves. Labor is not ultimate, but it is a way we can love and live in the reality that is.

I will close with a personal anecdote. When I was in college my father and I decided to build a new fence behind our suburban home. I worked on it every day during the sweltering Texas summer until he came home from work early to help. We planned on tearing down the old fence and building the new one with vertical posts at eight-foot intervals. The boards came down easily enough; the posts did not. We broke the cement with pickaxes and rocked the posts out of their holes, which then had to be refilled with dirt. After weeks of that toil I measured the eight-foot intervals for the new posts, only to discover that before the fence that I had just torn down was built there was an older fence. The posts had been cut flush with the ground and left in cement pilings. They all had to be busted out with the pickaxe. With no post to gain leverage, I dug holes adjacent to the cement to rock out the bigger pieces. Using a post-hole digger, the next thing to do was to dig two-foot-deep holes all around the perimeter of the yard. The vertical poles were not wood but ten-foot-high galvanized steel, and each one had to be sunk upright into concrete, which we stirred by hand and dumped from a wheelbarrow. We carved our initials and the date into the last framed pole base. Then the slats had to be sealed with a weatherproofing solution and nailed up to three cross-pieces that were anchored to each pole. We did every bit of the work by hand: every piece of cement busted, every drop of concrete poured, every nail driven. Years later I took my best friend, to whom I dedicated this book, to see my old childhood home, which my family had long since vacated. It was a dilapidated mess, a heartbreaking memorial to over a decade of neglect. We drove around back. The fence still stood.

Notes

Introduction

1. https://theweek.com/speedreads/588149/marco-rubio-wants-more-welders-less-philosophers. Accessed October 14, 2021.
2. https://www.forbes.com/sites/katiesola/2015/11/11/rubio-welders-philosophers/#513b874741b8. Accessed October 14, 2021.
3. https://www.washingtonexaminer.com/red-alert-politics/marco-rubio-upsets-philosophers-higher-education-reform-speeches. Accessed October 14, 2021.
4. Plato, *Republic*, trans. G. M. A. Grube and C. D. C. Reeve (Indianapolis, IN: Hackett, 1992), 357b–357d.
5. Interestingly Senator Rubio expressed a change of heart in 2018 on his Twitter account. Then he wrote, "I made fun of philosophy 3 years ago but then I was challenged to study it, so I started reading the stoics. I've changed my view on philosophy. But not on welders. We need both! Vocational training for workers & philosophers to make sense of the world." Retrieved from https://www.insidehighered.com/quicktakes/2018/03/29/rubio-changes-tune-philosophers. Accessed October 14, 2021.
6. Michael Hanby, "*Homo Faber* and/or *Homo Adorans*: On the Place of Human Making in a Sacramental Cosmos," *Communio* 38.2 (2011): 198–236, p. 230.
7. Howard M. Weiss, "Working as Human Nature," in *The Nature of Work: Advances in Psychological Theory, Methods, and Practice*, ed. J. Kevin Ford, John R. Hollenbeck, and Ann Marie Ryan (Washington, DC: American Psychological Association, 2014), 35–47, p. 39.
8. Rémi Brague, *The Kingdom of Man: Genesis and Failure of the Modern Project*, trans. Paul Seaton (Notre Dame, IN: University of Notre Dame Press, 2018), 44.
9. Oren Cass's recent book *The Once and Future Worker: A Vision for the Renewal of Work in America* (New York: Encounter Books, 2018) is interesting because it lays out public policy proposals specifically designed to stimulate work of all kinds. I would like to think of this book as providing philosophical reasons for judging that Cass's proposals would be worth considering and implementing.
10. See the introduction by Ron Beadle and Geoff Moore, "MacIntyre on Virtue and Organization," *Organization Studies* 27.3 (2006): 321–40, p. 330.
11. This language became more prevalent as of the publication of *Whose Justice? Which Rationality?* (Notre Dame, IN: University of Notre Dame Press, 1998).
12. According to one analysis, MacIntyre—despite his skepticism about business ethics—(see Alasdair MacIntyre, "The Irrelevance of Ethics," in *Virtue and Economy: Essays on Morality and Markets*, ed. Andrius Bielskis and Kelvin Knight (Abingdon, UK: Routledge, 2016), 7–22) is cited more often than any other virtue ethicist in business ethics literature, aside from Aristotle himself. See Ignacio Ferrero and Alejo José G. Sison, "A Quantitative Analysis of Authors, Schools, and Themes in Virtue Ethics Articles in Business Ethics and Management Journals (1980–2011)," *Business Ethics: A European Review* 23.4 (2014): 375–400.

13. Alasdair MacIntyre, *After Virtue: A Study in Moral Theory*, 2nd ed. (Notre Dame, IN: University of Notre Dame Press, 1984), 188.
14. Kelvin Knight, "Goods," *Philosophy of Management* 7.1 (2008): 107–22, p. 114.
15. Ibid.
16. MacIntyre, *Whose Justice? Which Rationality?*, 35.
17. Alasdair MacIntyre, "How to Seem Virtuous without Actually Being So," in *Education in Morality*, ed. J. Mark Halstead and Terence H. McLaughlin (London: Routledge, 1999): 118–31, pp. 127–8.
18. Alasdair MacIntyre, *Ethics in the Conflicts of Modernity: An Essay on Desire, Practical Reasoning, and Narrative* (Cambridge: Cambridge University Press, 2016), 237.
19. Ibid., 171.
20. Ibid., 130–1.
21. Ibid., 172.
22. Ibid., 178–82.
23. Ibid., 131.
24. Ibid., 131–2. Similar sentiments can be found elsewhere in MacIntyre's writings. See for instance *Dependent Rational Animals: Why Human Beings Need the Virtues* (Chicago: Open Court Press, 1999), where he writes: "Market relationships can only be sustained by being embedded in certain types of local nonmarket relationship, relationships of uncalculated giving and receiving, if they are to contribute to overall flourishing, rather than, as they so often in fact do, undermine and corrupt communal ties" (117). Further explorations of the suitability (or adaptability) of MacIntyre's conceptuality to issues in respect of labor are supplied by Matthew Sinnicks, "Moral Education at Work: On the Scope of MacIntyre's Concept of a Practice," *Journal of Business Ethics* 159.1 (2019): 105–18; Russell Keat, "Ethics, Markets, and MacIntyre," in *Revolutionary Aristotelianism: Ethics, Resistance, and Utopia*, ed. Kelvin Knight and Paul Blackledge (Stuttgart: Lucius and Lucius, 2008), 243–57; and David Miller, "Virtue, Practices, and Justice," in *After MacIntyre: Critical Perspectives on the Work of Alasdair MacIntyre*, ed. John Horton and Susan Mendus (Notre Dame, IN: University of Notre Dame Press, 1994), 245–64.
25. This point may occasion a final potential objection to the use of MacIntyre's thought. MacIntyre himself is of course principally inspired by Aristotle, so our exploration of the Platonic tradition will complement, rather than rival, I trust, MacIntyre's thinking on this subject. That such complementarity is possible is signaled by Knight, who observes that MacIntyre departs from Aristotle in one crucial respect: he does not make a firm distinction between productive practices and nonproductive practices. See Knight, "Goods," 121. To my mind Aristotle's fanatical insistence on driving a wedge between theory and practice is a significant hindrance to his usefulness as a thinker on labor. MacIntyre himself (rightly) recognizes that on this point Aristotle is more ideological than philosophical. See Knight, "Goods," 120.

Part One Ancient Greece

1. Readers might consult Gustave Glotz, *Ancient Greece at Work: An Economic History of Greece from the Homeric Period to the Roman Conquest*, trans. M. R. Dobie (London: Kegan Paul, Trench, Trubner; New York: Alfred A. Knopf, 1926) and Alison

Burford, *Craftsmen in Greek and Roman Society* (London: Thames and Hudson, 1972). For an explicit attempt to use the categories of Karl Marx in application to ancient Greek society, see G. E. M. de Ste. Croix, *The Class Struggle in the Ancient Greek World from the Archaic Age to the Arab Conquests* (Ithaca, NY: Cornell University Press, 1981). A differing perspective trained on a much narrower slice of history comes from M. I. Finley, *The World of Odysseus*, 2nd ed. (London: Penguin Books, 1979).

1 Work among the Ancient Greeks

1. Jean-Pierre Vernant, *Myth and Thought among the Greeks* (London: Routledge & Kegan Paul, 1983), 248.
2. Ibid.
3. Ibid.
4. Ibid., 249.
5. Finley, *The World of Odysseus*, 55.
6. Ibid., 56.
7. Ibid., 58. See also the useful introduction by David W. Tandy and Walter C. Neale to their edition of Hesiod's *Works and Days: A Translation and Commentary for the Social Sciences* (Berkeley: University of California Press, 1996), 25. This recent, readable edition contains an abundance of helpful notes designed to be of value to persons interested in social science and may prove especially useful to readers of this book as well for that reason.
8. Ibid., 56.
9. Both Finley and Tandy and Neale note the poignancy of Achilles's preference for the life of a *thes* among the living over that of rule in the underworld. See Finley, *The World of Odysseus*, 57, and Tandy and Neale (trans.), *Works and Days*, 114 n150.
10. Vernant, *Myth and Thought among the Greeks*, 249.
11. Adriano Tilgher, *Work: What It Has Meant to Men through the Ages (Homo Faber)*, Arno Press 1977 repr. ed., trans. Dorothy Canfield Fisher (New York: Harcourt, Brace, 1930), 3. It should be noted further that Tilgher's work is not without impact on subsequent reflections on work, some of which take this summary judgment at face value. Yves Simon quotes his interpretation of Kant at some length from a French translation of the original Italian text in "Work and Workman," *Review of Politics* 2.1 (January 1940): 63–86, p. 73. Lee Hardy quotes this same sentence, without caveat, contradiction, or criticism, in *The Fabric of This World: Inquiries into Calling, Career Choice, and the Design of Human Work* (Grand Rapids, MI: Eerdmans, 1990), 7.
12. Ibid., 249–50.
13. Ibid., 250.
14. Ibid.
15. Ibid., 251.
16. Vernant may be overestimating this; the ancient mind generally did not compartmentalize the "religious" in the fashion expected after modernity, and farming may not have been especially charged with religious significance compared to other sorts of work. Reading Hesiod's *Works and Days* does not leave one with the impression that farming is any more ritualistically significant than other forms of work, an impression that may be partly attributable to the fact that the text's focus is reasonably narrow—Hesiod for example knows only a little about seafaring, but what

he knows he offers up (618–94); but on the sea too the gods are to be placated, and diligent attentiveness to what must be done and when it must be done is rewarded.
17. Finley, *The World of Odysseus*, 56.
18. Ibid.
19. Hesiod, *Works and Days*, 33, 35. See also Finley, *The World of Odysseus*, 61, and Vernant, *Myth and Thought among the Greeks*, 254.
20. Xenophon, *Oeconomicus: A Social and Historical Commentary with a New English Translation*, trans. Sarah B. Pomeroy (Oxford: Clarendon Press, 1994), 131.
21. Hesiod, *Works and Days*, 398–404.
22. Ibid., 39–42.
23. See also Vernant, *Myth and Thought among the Greeks*, 251–2:

> Land, with all its religious connotations and the special links binding it to its owner, was quite a different type of possession from money. It was only with the greatest difficulty that it eventually became integrated into the economic system based on currency. It is therefore not so very surprising that for a long time psychological attitudes toward agricultural work continued to remain very similar to Hesiod's.

24. Hesiod, *Works and Days*, 37.
25. Ibid., 420–4.
26. Ibid., 398, 634.
27. Ibid., 461–2.
28. Vernant, *Myth and Thought among the Greeks*, 253.
29. Xenophon, *Oeconomicus*, 203. Quoted in part at Vernant, *Myth and Thought among the Greeks*, 253.
30. Xenophon, *Oeconomicus*, 181.
31. Ibid., 183.
32. Ibid., 183, 185.
33. Ibid., 193.
34. Ibid., 199.
35. Ibid.
36. Ibid. Note the invocation of debt, which so troubled Hesiod.
37. Ibid.
38. Ibid., 203.
39. Ibid., 205.
40. Ibid.
41. Ibid.
42. Hesiod, *Works and Days*, 32; Finley, *The World of Odysseus*, 61.
43. Vernant, *Myth and Thought among the Greeks*, 252.
44. Ibid.
45. Ibid., 255.
46. We will see in our examination of Plato that this is an aspect of his narrative about the origin of political community.
47. Interestingly Vernant uses the same Greek word that Tandy and Neale discuss as a central component of Hesiod's advice on economy. Citing Louis Gernet, they point out that the range of possible meanings for the term *chreos* is very wide, including at least four interrelated significations: "the idea of a constraint that weighs on the debtor; the idea of an obligation that is punishable in case of default; the idea of the very thing that, once received, 'obligates'; the ideas, in addition, of propriety, duty, and even religious observation" (39–40).

48. Vernant, *Myth and Thought among the Greeks*, 258. See also John Peter Oleson, ed., *The Oxford Handbook of Engineering and Technology in the Classical World* (Oxford: Oxford University Press, 2008), 4.
49. Ibid., 258–60. This is why Vernant cautions against applying the term "division of labor" to ancient Greek society in any but the most attenuated sense. The Greeks never thought of the aim of techne as maximizing efficiency or even of production in an abstract sense as the goal of techne, much less that production or technological development could be in principle unlimited. Rather the point was to meet needs in a way that made the products of techne as good as they could be.
50. Vernant, *Myth and Thought among the Greeks*, 260–1.
51. Oleson, *The Oxford Handbook of Engineering and Technology in the Classical World*, 4.
52. Aristotle, *Politics*, 1253a.
53. Vernant, *Myth and Thought among the Greeks*, 261.
54. Plato, *Republic*, 369c.
55. Ibid., 369d.
56. Ibid., 370c–d.
57. Ibid., 372a–b.
58. Ibid., 372d.
59. Ibid., 373e.
60. Ibid., 372d–373a.
61. On this point Patrick Coby makes an interesting but incomplete observation. He contrasts Plato's front-and-center placement of the technai in a supposedly primitive civic arrangement with Aristotle's argument that the family is the first social association and that it is the family's purpose to satisfy daily needs. Coby thinks Plato does this in order to "plausibly aver the primacy of knowledge in all human activity. Man does not begin as child, father, mother, but as a technically wise artisan who plies his trade for his own welfare and the welfare of his fellow artisans." See his "On Warriors and Artisans: The Case for Moral Virtue in Plato's *Republic*," *Polity* 15.4 (1983): 515–35, p. 518. This is a point worth taking on board for any broader discussion about politics and the origins of human communities, but it is not quite the case that Plato's primitive city says nothing interesting at all about the place of family in social life, though for our focus on the philosophy of work it is not as relevant.
62. Plato, *Republic*, 373d–e.
63. Ibid., 371e–372a.
64. Xenophon, *Oeconomicus*, 121, 123.
65. Oleson, *The Oxford Handbook of Engineering and Technology in the Classical World*, 5. Sometimes "banausic" is associated with the later term "mechanical." See "mechanical, adj. and n.", *The Compact Edition of the Oxford English Dictionary*, I:A–O (Oxford: Oxford University Press, 1971), 1725. The term "mechanical" though is bound to seem anachronistic as a translation of "banausic."
66. Plato, *Republic*, 495d.
67. Oleson, *The Oxford Handbook of Engineering and Technology in the Classical World*, 5.
68. Ibid., 6.
69. Hesiod, *Works and Days*, 105.
70. Vernant, *Myth and Thought among the Greeks*, 251.
71. Hesiod, *Works and Days*, 104. *Odyssey*, XVIII, 327–9.
72. Cicero, trans. Walter Miller, *Loeb Classical Library*, vol. XXI (Cambridge, MA: Harvard University Press, 1913), 153, 155.
73. Finley, *The World of Odysseus*, 72.

74. The scene from the *Odyssey* is recounted by David Roochnik in his *Of Art and Wisdom: Plato's Understanding of Techne* (University Park: Pennsylvania State University Press, 1996), 22. Roochnik goes on to point out that in the Homeric corpus techne generally is connected with wiles and trickery, since skill can overcome even superior strength. The etymological association between skill and wiliness survives most completely in modern English in the word "craft."

2 Plato on Work

1. This number is attributed to the Ibycus computer system at Princeton University by David Roochnik in his "Socrates's Use of the Techne-Analogy," *Journal of the History of Philosophy* 24.3 (July 1986): 295–310, p. 308. Another "very rough count" is provided by Robert S. Brumbaugh in his *Platonic Studies of Greek Philosophy: Form, Arts, Gadgets, and Hemlock* (Albany, NY: State University of New York Press, 1989), 198. Brumbaugh tallies "two hundred and six references to arts and crafts in the *Republic*" (198) and provides the following statistics as well: "The brief *Laches* has twenty-one references to the arts, the briefer *Ion* ten, the transitional *Euthydemus* twenty-four, and the *Charmides* a surprising thirty-four references … The *Timaeus* has thirty-five, which, considering its subject-matter is not surprising, indeed a bit unexpectedly low; the *Statesman*, however, comes up with twenty-six, and the notorious *Sophist* scores sixty-two!" (199).
2. Brumbaugh, *Platonic Studies of Greek Philosophy*, 198.
3. Ibid., 199. The Spanish philosopher José Ortega y Gasset is convinced that Plato was a hunter. See his *Meditations on Hunting*, trans. Howard B. Wescott (New York: Charles Scribner's Sons, 1972), 151–2.
4. These examples are suggested as of prime importance by Roochnik (2) as well as C. D. C. Reeve in his "The Role of *Techne* in Plato's Construction of Philosophy," *Proceedings of the Boston Area Colloquium in Ancient Philosophy*, vol. 16 (Leiden: Brill, 2000), 207–22, pp. 213, 207.
5. Plato, "Laches," *Complete Works*, ed. John M. Cooper, trans. Rosamond Kent Sprague (Indianapolis, IN: Hackett, 1997), 184d. The term "expert" translates the Greek "technikos."
6. Ibid., 185a.
7. Ibid., 20a–b.
8. Roochnik, *Of Art and Wisdom*, 2.
9. Ibid., 4.
10. Ibid., 4–6.
11. Ibid., 6, emphasis in the original.
12. Plato, "Apology," *Complete Works*, ed. John M. Cooper, trans. G. M. A. Grube (Indianapolis, IN: Hackett, 1997), 21a–b.
13. Ibid., 22a.
14. Ibid., 22b–c.
15. Ibid., 22d.
16. Ibid., 22d–e.
17. Joel A. Martinez provides a list in the course of his exposition of the implications of this principle for the argumentation of the *Republic*. See his "Rethinking Plato's Conception of Knowledge: The Non-philosopher and the Forms," *Apeiron* 44 (2011): 326 n1.

18. Plato, *Republic* 601d–602a.
19. Ibid., 340d–e.
20. Ibid., 338c–339b.
21. Ibid., 339b–e.
22. Ibid., 340b–c.
23. Ibid., 341c–d.
24. Ibid., 341d–e.
25. Ibid., 342b.
26. Ibid.
27. Ibid., 342c.
28. Ibid., 342d.
29. Ibid., 343e.
30. It is worth noting that Plato uses related terms to refer to both the specific activity of political rulers and the sense in which all technai "rule over and are stronger than the things of which they are the crafts" (342c). A term in English that might capture this parallelism more successfully would be "govern," in that we might say both that rulers govern their subjects and that medicine governs sick bodies.
31. Plato, *Republic*, 343b.
32. Ibid., 346a.
33. Ibid., 346b–c.
34. Ibid., 346e.
35. Ibid.
36. Kenneth Knies, "Taking the Strict Account of Techne Seriously: An Interpretive Direction in Plato's *Republic*," *Schole* 8.1 (2014): 111–125, p. 112.
37. Despite the fact that this clarification is brought forward in the context of a polemic with Thrasymachus, it is important to second Knies's observation that "At no point will Socrates challenge Thrasymachus' decision to view work as under the perfect guidance of knowledge" (113).
38. Knies, "Taking the Strict Account of Techne Seriously," 115. A more complete analysis of this dynamic is provided in the last paragraph of the same page of Knies's article.
39. Knies, "Taking the Strict Account of Techne Seriously," 116. This point about the "wearer of the garment" is relevant to the discussion in Book X of the "user" of different works of artifice. The relevance to the debate with Thrasymachus about justice should also be apparent: The shepherd does not put himself in the master's place, considering the fitness of the sheep for consumption as food but *qua* shepherd only looks to the needs of the sheep and makes use of his techne to repair those needs.
40. Plato, *Republic*, 420e–421a.
41. Ibid., 421a–c.
42. Knies, "Taking the Strict Account of Techne Seriously," 122.
43. Plato, *Republic*, 422a.
44. Ibid., 422e–423a.
45. Ibid., 370b.
46. Ibid., 423d. I owe these citations to Knies, who writes the following on this point:

> Already in the construction of the first city, Socrates shows that the political division of labor responds to concerns other than the efficient production of high-quality products. It is right for each citizen-worker to perform one task, not only because it will yield a greater quantity of better goods, but because it gives expression to the diversity of human nature and because each worker is

one person, not many. Later, Socrates will assert that the worker *becomes one* by doing the one task for which she is suited. (122–3)

47. Knies, "Taking the Strict Account of Techne Seriously," 123.
48. Coby, "On Warriors and Artisans," 524.
49. Ibid.
50. Ibid., 531.
51. Ibid., 534.
52. Plato, *Republic*, 428b.
53. Ibid., 428c–d.
54. Many others of a like character could be enumerated. Tom Angier, in his lucid overview of techne in Plato's writings (which introduces his book-length study of the same theme in Aristotle's ethical philosophy), catalogues many such relevant passages. See *Techne in Aristotle's Ethics* (London: Continuum, 2010), 20–2.
55. See Reeve's "The Role of *Techne* in Plato's Construction of Philosophy" and Roochnik's *Of Art and Wisdom* (Roochnik denies that for Plato philosophical expertise is a form of techne, but he concedes that on the face of it many passages seem to imply as much (1–6)).
56. In an earlier publication, Roochnik nominates Terrence Irwin's *Plato's Moral Theory* (Oxford: Clarendon Press, 1977) as a representative of the classic view and a foil to his own. He quotes Irwin as holding that for Socrates "virtue is simply craft-knowledge" (7). Quoted in Roochnik, "Socrates's Use of the Techne-Analogy," 296. On the same page he mentions Gregory Vlastos's disagreement with Irwin and endorsement of only a partial analogy in his "The Virtuous and the Happy," *Times Literary Supplement* (February 24, 1978): 230–1: "For though Socrates certainly wants moral knowledge to be in some respects like that of carpenters ... he knows that it is radically different in others." As an ally on this point at least Roochnik claims George Klosko, "The Technical Conception of Virtue," *Journal of the History of Philosophy* 18 (1981): 98–106.
57. Reeve, "The Role of *Techne* in Plato's Construction of Philosophy," 207.
58. Ibid., 221.
59. Ibid.
60. Ibid., 215–20.
61. Ibid., 222.
62. Roochnik, *Of Art and Wisdom*, 176.
63. Ibid., 177.
64. Ibid., 89.
65. Ibid., 170–3.
66. Ibid., 174–5.
67. Ibid., 150.
68. Roochnik settles for this rather thin conclusion more than once. See also 94: "We learn precious little about what he [Socrates] thinks moral knowledge actually is. It is clear only that he thinks it is desirable and should be sought." See also 233, a concluding passage that repeats rather than expands upon the basic point: "What does Socrates know? That moral knowledge is good and should be sought and that, as a result, philosophy is superior to the power politicking of a Callicles."
69. Roochnik, *Of Art and Wisdom*, 15. See also 244.
70. Ibid., 245.
71. Ibid., 246.

72. Ibid., 146.
73. See page xii of his introduction:

> In writing this book I take up themes that have long preoccupied me. For better or worse, and whatever my intentions, all my writings have, from a variety of angles, approached, elaborated, and tried to hammer out a single thought. As a result the present book covers some of the same ground as my first, *The Tragedy of Reason*. In both I try to articulate Plato's conception of reason or moral knowledge. In the first book, I do so via the lens of tragedy; in this the second, of techne. The connection is straightforward enough: for Plato reason is tragic because it cannot achieve a moral techne, a stable body of reliable knowledge able to tell us, in fixed terms readily teachable to others, how we ought to live.

74. See his review of Schindler's book in *Ancient Philosophy* 30.1 (2010): 180–2.
75. D. C. Schindler, *Plato's Critique of Impure Reason: On Goodness and Truth in the Republic* (Washington, DC: Catholic University of America Press, 2008), 267 n135.
76. Plato, "Greater Hippias," *Complete Works*, ed. John M. Cooper, trans. Paul Woodruff (Indianapolis, IN: Hackett, 1997), 281d.
77. Schindler, *Plato's Critique of Impure Reason*, 268–9.
78. Ibid., 269.
79. Ibid., 114.
80. Ibid., 267.
81. Roochnik, *Of Art and Wisdom*, 170; see also his use of Aristotle to articulate a view of the humanities as indirectly useful through uselessness in "The Useful Uselessness of the Humanities," *Expositions* 2.1 (2008): 19–26; Schindler, *Plato's Critique of Impure Reason*, 265–9.
82. Schindler, *Plato's Critique of Impure Reason*, 267. See also Roochnik, *Of Art and Wisdom*, 173: "Techne (or episteme) is linear; it is *tinos*, of something specific other than itself."
83. Roochnik, *Of Art and Wisdom*, 105.
84. Ibid., 106.
85. Ibid., 107.
86. Schindler, *Plato's Critique of Impure Reason*, 325.
87. Ibid., 170.
88. Ibid., 168. In connection with this "matching up" Schindler refers (as Roochnik did above) to Laches's appreciation for a man whose words and deeds harmonize in the Doric fashion.
89. Roochnik, *Of Art and Wisdom*, 172–3.
90. Schindler, *Plato's Critique of Impure Reason*, 269.
91. Ibid.
92. Plato, "Greater Hippias," 281b.
93. Ibid., 283b.
94. Schindler, *Plato's Critique of Impure Reason*, 189–96. The parallels to MacIntyre's thought should be obvious.
95. Ibid., 269.
96. Ibid., 275.
97. Ibid., 271.
98. Ibid.
99. Ibid., 272, emphasis in the original.
100. Ibid., 273.

101. Ibid.
102. Ibid., 274. Schindler does concede that both Roochnik and Griswold (among a host of others) are attentive to the dialogue form as well and argue that it is crucially tied to the content of Plato's thinking (30 n45).
103. Ibid., 275.
104. Plato, *Republic*, 516e–517a.
105. As we have seen, Schindler and Roochnik agree on much structurally, but Schindler you might say refuses to draw the tragic conclusion from the structural difficulties in Plato's thinking.
106. The truth too is that we are simply not capable of taking in the wide range of possible answers to this question. One approach not fully considered here is the potential for a "kingly techne" model of philosophy. We have seen the reservations that Roochnik and Schindler express around this idea, but a powerful advocacy of it can be found in the writings of Mark Moes, chief among them his "Dialectical Rhetoric and Socrates' Treatment of Mimetic Poetry in Book 10 of the *Republic*," *Philosophy Study* 1.1 (2011): 1–21.
107. Plato, *Republic*, 371e–372a.
108. Ibid., 443c.
109. Ibid., 443c–d.
110. For further development in this idea in a different direction see Coby, "On Warriors and Artisans," 515.
111. Schindler, *Plato's Critique of Impure Reason*, 275 n166.
112. Desmond Lee, *The Republic*, reissued ed. (London: Penguin Books, 2003), 335.
113. I prefer this term to Reeve and Grube's "imitative" because it recalls the Greek term, which is well known in philosophical, literary, and aesthetic circles and properly understood encompasses a rich array of significations that go well beyond mere imitation. This latter term in academic conversations around the topic of mimesis is often understood to be restrictive, meaning only the most slavish or depleted sort of aping. While Plato I think recognizes that mimesis can be understood restrictively, and his cautions against it suggest this concern is foremost on his mind, the term "mimesis" is less prejudicial in this direction and acknowledges that Plato himself is a great, perhaps the greatest, philosophical practitioner of mimesis himself.
114. Plato, *Republic*, 595b.
115. Ibid., 595c.
116. Ibid., 596a.
117. Ibid., 596b.
118. Ibid.
119. Ibid., 596c.
120. Ibid.
121. Ibid., 596d.
122. Ibid., 596e.
123. Ibid.
124. Ibid., 596e–597a.
125. Ibid., 597b.
126. Interestingly the term "demiourgos" is associated only with the carpenter, not the god, who is called a *pepoieken*. In the *Timaeus* Plato will call the divine craftsman responsible for the shaping of the cosmos a demiourgos.
127. Plato, *Republic*, 597e.
128. Ibid., 598a.

129. Ibid., 598b.
130. Ibid.
131. Ibid., 598b–598c.
132. Ibid., 598c–598d.
133. Ibid., 598d–598e.
134. Ibid., 599a.
135. Ibid., 599a–599b.
136. Ibid., 599b.
137. Ibid., 600b.
138. Ibid., 600d.
139. Ibid., 601a.
140. Ibid., 601b.
141. Ibid., 601c.
142. Ibid.
143. Ibid.
144. Ibid., 601d.
145. Ibid.
146. Ibid., 602a.
147. Ibid., 602d.
148. Ibid., 602b.
149. Schindler learns this lesson from Francisco J. Gonzalez, whom he claims

> shows that Plato offers *two* hierarchies in book X: he initially presents the nature-craftwork-artistic image, and *then* he rates the user's knowledge above the maker's or the artist's. To explain the discrepancy here, Gonzalez argues that the *use* of a thing does not mean the instrumentalization of it, but the appreciation of its goodness. This is exactly right: a grasp of the good of a thing is not a merely intellectual act but involves a more comprehensive relationship that can be called a "use" of it. *This* is what it means to understand something in the light of the good. (*Plato's Critique of Impure Reason*, 316–17 n100)

> See also Francisco J. Gonzalez, *Dialectic and Dialogue: Plato's Practice of Philosophical Inquiry* (Evanston, IL: Northwestern University Press, 1998), 129–49.

150. Plato, "Meno," in *Complete Works*, ed. John M. Cooper, trans. G. M. A. Grube (Indianapolis, IN: Hackett, 1997), 99c–d.
151. Ibid., 98a–b.
152. Plato, "Apology," 22c.
153. Ibid., 22d–22e.
154. This conclusion is supported interestingly by the *Protagoras*, where Socrates has the following exchange with Hippocrates:

> "Then tell me what you think a sophist is." "I think," he said, "that, as the name suggests, he is someone who has an understanding of wise things." "Well, you could say the same thing about painters and carpenters, that they understand wise things." But if someone asked us "wise in what respect?" we would probably answer, for painters, "wise as far as making images is concerned," and so on for the other cases. (Plato, "Protagoras," in *Complete Works*, ed. John M. Cooper, trans. Stanley Lombardo and Karen Bell (Indianapolis: Hackett Publishing Company, 1997), 312c–312d)

155. Plato, *Republic*, 602c.

214 Notes

156. Ibid., 602d–602e.
157. Ibid., 603b.
158. Ibid., 603d–603e.
159. Ibid., 603e.
160. Ibid.
161. Ibid., 604a–604b.
162. Ibid., 604b–604c.
163. Ibid., 604d.
164. Ibid., 604e.
165. Ibid., 605a.
166. Ibid., 605b–605c.
167. Ibid., 605d.
168. Ibid.
169. Ibid., 606b. I read Book III of Augustine's *Confessions* as making a very similar point about the morally questionable aspects of tragedy. As I read Augustine, a major part of his concern is that tragedy is a spectacle, that is, a scene staged for the benefit of being looked at, not for being engaged with directly. Acclimating oneself to scenes of counterfeit suffering in his argument blunts our capacity to respond concretely to actual suffering that we confront in our own reality.

> Surely this is the most wretched lunacy? For the more a man feels such sufferings in himself, the more he is moved by the sight of them on the stage. Now when a man suffers himself, it is called misery; when he suffers in the suffering of another, it is called pity. But how can the unreal sufferings of the stage possibly move pity? The spectator is not moved to aid the sufferer but merely to be sorry for him; and the more the author of these fictions makes the audience grieve, the better they like him. If the tragic sorrows of the characters—whether historical or entirely fictitious—be so poorly represented that the spectator is not moved to tears, he leaves the theatre unsatisfied and full of complaints; if he is moved to tears, he stays to the end, fascinated and revelling in it. … But today I have more pity for the sinner getting enjoyment from his sin than when he suffers torment from the loss of pleasure which is ultimately destructive, and the loss of happiness which is only misery. This clearly is the truer compassion, but the sorrow I feel for him gives me no pleasure. (Augustine, *Confessions*, 2nd ed., trans. F. J. Sheed (Indianapolis: Hackett Publishing Company, 2006), 38)

170. Plato, *Republic*, 606d.
171. Ibid., 607a.
172. Ibid.
173. Ibid., 607c.
174. Ibid., 607d.
175. Ibid.
176. Ibid., 607e.
177. See the Coda to *Plato's Critique of Impure Reason*.
178. Plato, *Republic*, 612b.
179. Ibid., 612d.
180. Schindler, *Plato's Critique of Impure Reason*, 288.
181. Ibid.

182. Plato, "Timaeus," in *Complete Works*, ed. John M. Cooper, trans. Donald J. Zeyl (Indianapolis, IN: Hackett, 2004), 29e.
183. Schindler, *Plato's Critique of Impure Reason*, 302–3. Attend to his comments on the *Symposium* about the "fruitfulness" of beauty in footnote 60 as well.
184. The converse of course does not follow: An artist *qua* artist cannot be a philosopher. Significantly for this argument, at one key point in the argument of the *Republic*, Socrates explicitly likens the philosopher to a painter:

    Do you think, then, that there's any difference between the blind and those who are really deprived of the knowledge of each thing that is? The latter have no clear model in their souls, and so they cannot—in the manner of painters—look to what is most true, make constant reference to it, and study it as exactly as possible. (484c)

    The word translated as "model" is *paradeigma*, which occurs also at a key moment in the *Euthyphro*, where Socrates urges the priest to define piety in such a way that it can be used as a "model" to judge any action as pious (and thus in conformity with the paradigm) or not (and thus unlike the paradigm). Clearly the suggestion is that the form of piety itself will work as a model in much the same way that a painter consults a model for study and reproduction in action. See "Euthyphro," *Plato: Complete Works*, ed. John M. Cooper, trans. G. M. A. Grube (Indianapolis, IN: Hackett, 2997), 6e.

185. Plato, *Republic*, 519c.
186. Ibid., 519d.
187. See Andrea Wilson Nightingale, *Spectacles of Truth in Classical Greek Philosophy: Theoria in Its Cultural Context* (Cambridge: Cambridge University Press, 2004), 130:

    The philosopher who has contemplated reality will understand the nature of Form and particular and the ontological relation of the one to the other: he knows that the entities in the cave are in fact *eidola* and also understands what they are "images" of. This leads to a surprising conclusion: that the philosopher's vision and understanding are broader when he dwells in the world than when he engages in theoretical contemplation (at which point he sees only the Forms).

188. Nightingale appreciates the importance of the "return" to the cave as well. See her *Spectacles of Truth in Classical Greek Philosophy*, especially the section on "Return and Reentry" in chapter 3, 131–8.
189. Ibid., 520c.
190. These arguments are given fuller and convincing explanation by Schindler in the remainder of his book's final chapter. See pages 307–18. My hope is that some of the original insights I offered earlier in this part of my chapter will complement Schindler's persuasive account. I cannot reproduce all of that here, since Schindler is concerned with the *Republic* as a whole, but I situate my study of Plato's attitude toward a certain kind of work within his frame and make my own contribution to enriching his interpretation.
191. Andrea Wilson Nightingale, *Spectacles of Truth* (Cambridge: Cambridge University Press, 2004), 29.
192. Ibid.
193. Ibid., 199.
194. Ibid., 198.

195. Ibid., 40.
196. Ibid., 41.
197. Ibid., 43–4.
198. Ibid., 48.
199. Ibid., 69.
200. Ibid., 70.
201. Schindler, *Plato's Critique of Impure Reason*, 160–1.
202. Plato, *Republic*, 327a.
203. Ibid., 2 n1. See also Nightingale, *Spectacles of Truth*, 75.
204. Nightingale, *Spectacles of Truth*, 75.
205. Plato, *Republic*, 328a.
206. Nightingale, *Spectacles of Truth*, 75 n13.
207. Ibid., 77.
208. Ibid., 109.
209. Ibid., 117.
210. Ibid.
211. Ibid., 118. This is Nightingale's own translation, which preserves (as I too am doing) the term "banausic" without translation. Quoted from *Symposium* 203a.
212. Ibid., 119. Again this is Nightingale's translation of a passage occurring at *Theaetetus* 176c–d.
213. Plato, *Republic*, 493a–c.
214. Ibid., 495e.
215. Ibid., 495d.
216. Nightingale, following Kenneth Dover's observations, suggests the sophists and rhetoricians are included here. See *Spectacles of Truth*, 119 n40.
217. Nightingale, *Spectacles of Truth*, 120.
218. Plato, *Republic*, 590c.
219. Ibid., 588c–589a.
220. Oleson, *The Oxford Handbook of Engineering and Technology in the Classical World*, 6. The first two chapters of this volume document much more fully the written (chapter 1) and visual (chapter 2) sources for ordinary persons' view of manual labor produced by the ancient world.
221. Nightingale, *Spectacles of Truth*, 120. Nightingale quotes from David Whitehead, *The Ideology of the Athenian Metic*, supplementary volume no. 4 (Cambridge: Cambridge Philological Society, 1977), 119. See also the whole of chapter 4, section C on "Banausia."
222. Nightingale, *Spectacles of Truth*, 120–1.
223. Ibid., 117.
224. For additional important insights into Socrates's poverty as an index of his commitment to the truth, see Schindler, *Plato's Critique of Impure Reason*, 188–91.
225. Nightingale, *Spectacles of Truth*, 177.
226. Plato, *Republic*, 487a–503e.
227. Plato, *Timaeus*, 46e. Nightingale's translation.
228. Nightingale, *Spectacles of Truth*, 177.
229. Ibid.
230. Plato, "Apology," in *Complete Works*, ed. Cooper, 29d–e, 31c.
231. That a kind of mutual reinforcement could arise between the sustenance of practices and the cultivation of virtue is a possibility glimpsed by Knight in MacIntyre's latest writings. See Knight, "Goods," 121.

232. As the example of Thrasymachus's predatory shepherd implies, a rival candidate for the force that could coordinate working activity might be money. As we have seen, money is arguably for Plato a sort of ersatz substitute for philosophy: It is abstract, infinitely convertible with other values, and unreal, and because of this it can influence a great many human actions and choices.
233. Plato, *Republic*, 421c.

Part Two The Middle Ages

1. See his *La force motrice animale à travers les âges* (Nancy: Berger-Levrault, 1924) and *L'attelage: Le cheval de selle à travers les âges: Contribution a l'histoire de l'esclavage* (Paris: Picard, 1931). As the titles of these works suggest, Lefebvre des Noëttes was primarily interested in the differences between ancient and medieval implementation of equine technologies like collars, hitches, and traction systems. His study of alleged medieval advancements in horse-based cultivation and carriage techniques has since been called into question.
2. See his *Feudal Society* vols. 1 and 2, trans. L. A. Manyon (London: Routledge and Kegan Paul, 1961); and "The Advent and Triumph of the Watermill," in *Land and Work in Medieval Europe: Selected Papers by Marc Bloch*, trans. J. E. Anderson (Berkeley: University of California Press, 1967). An important critical response to Bloch's work on the use of watermill technology in the medieval period is supplied by Örjan Wikander in his *Exploitation of Water-Power or Technological Stagnation? A Reappraisal of the Productive Forces in the Roman Empire* (Lund: Gleerup, 1984).
3. Many books could be listed here, but see especially Jacques LeGoff, *Time, Work, and Culture in the Middle Ages*, trans. Arthur Goldhammer (Chicago: University of Chicago Press, 1980); Jacques LeGoff, *Pour un autre Moyen Âge* (Paris: Gallimard, 1991); Jacques LeGoff, *The Medieval Imagination*, trans. Arthur Goldhammer (Chicago: University of Chicago Press, 1992); and Jacques LeGoff, *Medieval Civilization*, trans. Julia Barrow (Oxford: Blackwell, 1990).
4. See his *The Medieval Machine: The Industrial Revolution of the Middle Ages* (London: Penguin, 1981). A critical review (that nonetheless notes the relative youth of the field of medieval history of technology) is supplied by Bert S. Hall in *Speculum* 53.2 (1978): 366–8.
5. See his *The Axe and the Oath: Ordinary Life in the Middle Ages*, trans. Lydia G. Cochrane (Princeton, NJ: Princeton University Press, 2010).
6. Kevin Greene supplies a fine summary of some of these revised contemporary appraisals in his "Technology and Innovation in Context: The Roman Background to Medieval and Later Developments," *Journal of Roman Archaeology* 7 (1994): 22–33. An outstanding resource on the progress made during the twelfth century particularly is available in *Renaissance and Renewal in the Twelfth Century*, Medieval Academy Reprints for Teaching 26, ed. Robert L. Benson and Giles Constable with Carol D. Lanham (Toronto: Toronto University Press, 1991).
7. George Ovitt, Jr., *The Restoration of Perfection: Labor and Technology in Medieval Culture* (New Brunswick, NJ: Rutgers University Press, 1987), 72. Other works of importance cited frequently in these chapters are Elspeth Whitney's "Paradise Restored: The Mechanical Arts from Antiquity through the Thirteenth Century," *Transactions of the American Philosophical Society* 80.1 (1990): 1–169 and Birgit van den Hoven's *Work in Ancient and Medieval Thought: Ancient Philosophers,*

Medieval Monks and Theologians, and Their Concept of Work, Occupations, and Technology (Amsterdam: J. C. Gieben, 1996). Van den Hoven's overall judgment is somewhat unusual compared to the majority of scholars who emphasize a strong contrast in attitudes about work between the ancient and medieval worlds, in that she argues ultimately that there is more continuity than distinction between the two eras. However, she achieves this position (despite the title of her book) by comparing not the ancient world as a whole but the Stoic Imperial era (which featured some of the most favorable attitudes toward work in antiquity) with the medieval period (which, as we will see, ranges in favorability toward work). By selectively using only Stoic perspectives and highlighting some of the more negative attitudes in the Middle Ages, she concludes that antiquity and the medieval era were closer together with respect to work than most historians appreciate. Arthur T. Geoghegan's dissertation, *The Attitude towards Labor in Early Christianity and Ancient Culture*, The Catholic University of America Studies in Christian Antiquity 6 (Washington, DC: Catholic University of America Press, 1945), is rather more comprehensive and furnishes a dazzling number of citations from primary texts; merely reproducing Geoghegan's many references would make for a tedious and repetitive laundry list, but anyone interested in delving more deeply into the particular writings of any of the figures surveyed in these chapters and a great many not included here could profitably consult his publication.

3 The Early Medieval Period

1. Coby, "On Warriors and Artisans," 535.
2. See his "'Mary Needs Martha': The Purposes of Manual Labor in Early Egyptian Monasticism," *St. Vladimir's Theological Quarterly* 43.2 (1999): 163–207. Another even more extensive taxonomy is provided in two companion publications of extraordinary scholarly value by Pierre Bonnerue, "Concordance sur les activités manuelles dans les règles monastiques anciennes," *Studia Monastica* 35.1 (1993): 69–96; and Pierre Bonnerue, "*Opus* et *labor* dans les règles monastiques anciennes," *Studia Monastica* 35.2 (1993): 265–92. The former is an index of over two dozen monastic rules that organizes numerous references to manual labor under an admirably detailed list of subtopics, ranged in turn under the broad headings of "la raison et la destination du travail, l'attitude au travail, place et quantité, les cas particuliers, l'artisanat, les activités agricoles, les services, le matériel" (69–70). The latter is a concordance of the same rules, tabulating over seven hundred occurrences of the terms "opus" and "labor" (282). As Bonnerue himself admits, "The ancient monastic rules form a relatively homogeneous set of texts" (286, translation my own), so there is much repetition here, too much to even try to distill into this chapter, but scholars interested in delving more deeply into the particulars can do no better than avail themselves of Bonnerue's thorough and detailed resources.
3. Geoghegan, *The Attitude towards Labor in Early Christianity and Ancient Culture*, 169.
4. Geoghegan, *The Attitude towards Labor in Early Christianity and Ancient Culture*, 167. Geoghegan concludes from testimonies like this that "a Tabennesiot monastery was a veritable beehive of industry, with each monk busily engaged in his own craft and all contributing to the common good through a well-ordered division of labor" (ibid., 167).

5. Ibid.
6. Metteer, "'Mary Needs Martha,'" 164 n3. See also Ovitt, *The Restoration of Perfection*, 95: "The commitment to manual labor in both the eremitic and cenobitic communities was, therefore, substantial."
7. Ovitt, *The Restoration of Perfection*, 90.
8. Hoven, *Work in Ancient and Medieval Thought*, 119–20.
9. 2 Thessalonians 3, a passage that as we will see comes up constantly in these discussions and in numerous rules of monastic life.
10. For Aristotle the philosophical contemplator becomes godlike, but he does so at the price it would seem of something of his humanity. See Aristotle, *Nicomachean Ethics*, trans. Hippocrates G. Apostle (Des Moines: Peripatetic Press, 1984), 1177b-c. The early monks acknowledged that their enterprise, while aimed at God, remained human.
11. Cited in Hoven, *Work in Ancient and Medieval Thought*, 121–2; see also Metteer, "'Mary Needs Martha,'" 172.
12. Hoven, *Work in Ancient and Medieval Thought*, 118. She also abbreviates the anecdote provided in full above about Silvanus at this stage, again conveniently omitting the point of the story. Her account ends with Silvanus being chided by a brother in the words of Luke 10:42 and fails to mention Silvanus's dramatic response until she moved on to a different point, at which later stage she completes the story (ibid., 121–2). The connection between the two parts of the story is thereby attenuated misleadingly.
13. Metteer, "'Mary Needs Martha,'" 172.
14. Hoven, *Work in Ancient and Medieval Thought*, 118.
15. Ibid.
16. The character of this work was however up for debate. Those who argued that manual labor was not to be part of a monk's life did not excuse themselves on the grounds that work was not required but that they were called to a specific and thoroughgoing devotion to spiritual works like prayer and hymnody. Van den Hoven cites examples of spokespersons for this view, but as we will see, it was rejected decisively by the most influential authorities, among them no lesser figures than Basil and Augustine.
17. Genesis 3:17–19. Eve receives a complementary judgment against her, where God declares "I will greatly multiply thy sorrow and thy conception; in sorrow thou shalt bring forth children," such that the feminine companion to the characteristically masculine curse placed upon work is that childbearing will be painful. It is remarkable that even in contemporary English we call the travail of a woman in childbirth "labor."
18. Adriano Tilgher once again goes seriously astray when he claims that "Like the Greeks, the Hebrews thought of work as painful drudgery, but ... The Hebrew felt that he knew why our race is obliged to work. It was because it is its duty to expiate the original sin committed by its forefathers in the earthly Paradise" (11).
19. Examples could be multiplied, but Metteer notes its occurrence in Jerome's account of Hilarion's life and practice as well as Cassian's general report on Egyptian monasticism. See Metteer, "'Mary Needs Martha,'" 173.
20. Verses 8–10.
21. Verse 11.
22. Verse 12.
23. Matthew 6:34.

24. Athanasius, *The Life of Saint Antony*, trans. Robert T. Meyer (Westminster, MD: Newman Press, 1950), 19.
25. Ibid., 20–1.
26. Ibid., 21, emphasis in the original.
27. Ibid., 25.
28. Metteer, "'Mary Needs Martha,'" 165–8.
29. Ibid., 169–70. See also Ovitt, *The Restoration of Perfection*, 93–4.
30. Ovitt, *The Restoration of Perfection*, 91–2.
31. Metteer, "'Mary Needs Martha,'" 171.
32. Ibid.
33. Ovitt, *The Restoration of Perfection*, 92–3.
34. Metteer, "'Mary Needs Martha,'" 171 n19.
35. Quoted at Geoghegan, *The Attitude towards Labor in Early Christianity and Ancient Culture*, 170. Geoghegan also points out that Pachomius demanded that an aspiring monk serve a three-year period of probation, during which they had to bear up under some of the harsher tasks (170).
36. Ibid.
37. Ibid.
38. Metteer, "'Mary Needs Martha,'" 175.
39. Ibid., 178.
40. Hoven, *Work in Ancient and Medieval Thought*, 122. We have seen enough already to judge her contention that a monk "should" engage in "overproduction" to be a bit exaggerated. The truth of the matter was that overproduction would have been a needless source of temptation, whereas the ability to do work expressly for charitable purposes with whatever there might be in slight excess over the strictly necessary was praised. See Metteer, "'Mary Needs Martha,'" 200.
41. Metteer, "'Mary Needs Martha,'" 188–9.
42. Ibid., 189.
43. Ibid.
44. W. H. Mackean, *Christian Monasticism in Egypt to the Close of the Fourth Century* (London: Society for Promoting Christian Knowledge, 1920), 135. See also Geoghegan, *The Attitude towards Labor in Early Christianity and Ancient Culture*, 165.
45. Metteer, "'Mary Needs Martha,'" 190. As Metteer points out, the tension between charity and withdrawal is isomorphic with the ongoing debate between the anchoritic and cenobitic paths, but in many cases the strengths of both were combined, as we will see.
46. Graham Gould, *The Desert Fathers on Monastic Community* (Oxford: Clarendon Press, 1993), 172.
47. Ibid., 172–3.
48. See also Metteer, "'Mary Needs Martha,'" 190.
49. Gould, *The Desert Fathers on Monastic Community*, 173.
50. Ibid., 174.
51. Ovitt, *The Restoration of Perfection*, 93. Also commented upon by Metteer at "'Mary Needs Martha,'" 191.
52. Ovitt, *The Restoration of Perfection*, 93–4. He also cautions against taking Pambo's judgment to be universally held (94). There were debates between these two paths, though the most conciliatory approaches affirmed them both.
53. Metteer, "'Mary Needs Martha,'" 192.

54. Gould, *The Desert Fathers on Monastic Community*, 173. Gould cautions that we should not engage in "an undue attempt at harmonization; we should not deny in principle that the fervor of their desire for prayer and salvation led some to hold back from the corporate reality of monastic life. This too was a valid *ergasia* [way of life]" (177). Note that ergasia is etymologically derived from ergon, such that "way of life" here could also mean working, business, or practice.
55. Metteer, "'Mary Needs Martha,'" 192.
56. Ovitt, *The Restoration of Perfection*, 95. As we have seen, the productivity of monastic labor, should it generate a surplus beyond the immediate needs of those who generated it by their own effort, could always and was often passed on to those in need, whether fellow monastics or laypersons.
57. Geoghegan, *The Attitude towards Labor in Early Christianity and Ancient Culture*, 174. Metteer uses the exact same comparison at "'Mary Needs Martha,'" 194.
58. Metteer, "'Mary Needs Martha,'" 192.
59. Ovitt, *The Restoration of Perfection*, 95.
60. Ibid., 193.
61. Geoghegan, *The Attitude towards Labor in Early Christianity and Ancient Culture*, 165–6. See also Metteer, "'Mary Needs Martha,'" 193.
62. 1 Corinthians 3:8.
63. Metteer, "'Mary Needs Martha,'" 194.
64. Ibid.
65. Ibid., 203.
66. Ibid. This monk also ran afoul not only of the call to humility but also obedience. Cassian records the words of one abba he met in the desert: "It is one and the same kind of disobedience to go against an elder's command either because of zealous activity or because of laziness" (ibid., 198), thus proving that obedience was to be observed strictly, avoiding both excess and defect. See also Jonathan Malesic, "'Nothing Is to Be Preferred to the Work of God': Cultivating Monastic Detachment for a Postindustrial Work Ethic," *Journal of the Society of Christian Ethics* 35.1 (2015): 45–61, p. 56: "Ultimately, the abbot, who must always be obeyed, sets the limits on monastic work."
67. Metteer, "'Mary Needs Martha,'" 203.
68. On this important point, see Malesic, "'Nothing Is to Be Preferred to the Work of God,'" 52–3.
69. Hoven, *Work in Ancient and Medieval Thought*, 125.
70. Ovitt, *The Restoration of Perfection*, 97.
71. Malesic, "'Nothing Is to Be Preferred to the Work of God,'" 53.
72. Ibid. Quote from Benedict of Nursia, *RB 1980: The Rule of St. Benedict*, ed. Timothy Fry (Collegeville, MN: Liturgical Press, 1981), 265.
73. Malesic, "'Nothing Is to Be Preferred to the Work of God,'" 54. See also Hoven, *Work in Ancient and Medieval Thought*, 127: "Connected with this was the active avoidance of specialisation in work, through the weekly rotation of tasks within the cloister. A monk should not become too fond of a particular skill or activity, but must be ready to obey every order. A monk should not undertake his work with pride, but in humility."
74. See Ovitt, *The Restoration of Perfection*, 97: "Even in the best-organized monastic communities labor had primarily a spiritual purpose."
75. Geoghegan, *The Attitude towards Labor in Early Christianity and Ancient Culture*, 165.
76. Ibid., 173.

77. Hoven, *Work in Ancient and Medieval Thought*, 121.
78. Ibid., 127.
79. Ovitt, *The Restoration of Perfection*, 97.
80. Ibid.
81. Metteer, "'Mary Needs Martha,'" 197. The case of John the Dwarf's superior is impressive on this score. To test whether John's obedience was genuine or merely affected, his superior ordered him to water a dry stick stuck in the desert ground every day until it blossomed. After three years the superior was satisfied, and in some accounts, the stick actually did blossom (ibid., 197–8 n119).
82. Metteer, "'Mary Needs Martha,'" 200-1.
83. Metteer tells of one account in which "an elderly monk was divinely led to an industrious and humble farmer who greatly pleased the Lord. After meeting the 'brother,' the monk admitted that his *askesis* and virtues fell short of the man's character and simple lifestyle" (ibid., 204). That the comparison is to a lowly agricultural laborer is not insignificant.
84. Ovitt, *The Restoration of Perfection*, 91. See also Hoven, *Work in Ancient and Medieval Thought*, 127: "Humility is an essential concept in the link between work and asceticism."
85. Hoven, *Work in Ancient and Medieval Thought*, 127. Ovitt too concludes that "the legacy, then, of the first ascetics and the first monastic theorists favored manual labor, but always as a means to a spiritual end" (Ovitt, *The Restoration of Perfection*, 106). That is fair enough, but one should not downplay the significance of the very idea that manual labor could even be a means to a spiritual end.
86. LeGoff, *Time, Work, and Culture in the Middle Ages*, 110.
87. Ibid., 110–11.
88. Ibid., 80. The language of penitence of course to modern ears sounds like devotion to self-flagellation, but the work of penance was indeed essential to monastic life and was not necessarily self-lacerating but a joyful renunciation of the comforts and consolations of worldly goods. This is perhaps why many commentators prefer to speak of ascesis as opposed to the unduly harsh term "penitence."
89. Ibid., 80-1.
90. With the arguable exception of Musonius Rufus, the Stoic teacher of Epictetus, who not only argued that the philosopher could farm but indeed argued that he should do so. See "What Means of Livelihood Are Appropriate for a Philosopher?" in *Musonius Rufus: The Roman Socrates*, trans. Cora Lutz, Yale Classical Studies X, ed. A. R. Bellinger (New Haven, CT: Yale University Press, 1947).
91. Metteer, "'Mary Needs Martha,'" 196-7.
92. Ovitt, *The Restoration of Perfection*, 94.
93. Ibid., 106.
94. Susanna Barsella, "*Ars* and Theology: Work, Salvation, and Social Doctrine in the Early Church Fathers," *Annali d'Italianistica* 32 (2014): 53–72, p. 53.
95. Ibid.
96. Barsella credits Chrysostom for making this chain of imitation explicit:

> Chrysostom expands the idea of *imitatio Dei* to encompass three moments: imitation of God in the act of creation; imitation of Christ's redemptive work; imitation of Saint Paul, who for the Christian orator represented an archetypical figure as perfect example of Christ. His idea of imitation, besides its doctrinal importance, contributed to the recognition of

authority to apostolic teaching and thus to the strengthening of the spiritual and political role of the Church. Following Paul's admonition in 2 *Thess.* 3:10 according to which "if any man will not work, neither let him eat," Chrysostom identifies in the exercise of charity in the material form of almsgiving the privileged way to attain similitude to God. (ibid., 61)

97. Barsella, "*Ars* and Theology," 55.
98. Recall from the prior chapter Knies's argument that in Plato's *Republic* while need may be the origin of the political community it cannot be its ultimate rationalization; the Platonic community on his reading of it would be more than a need-coordinating mechanism of the sort that we get in modern political economy but more like a civic horizon for the achievement of individuals in their respective callings. If Knies and Barsella are right, then the monastery may be the first historically realized instantiation of that Platonic ideal.
99. Barsella, "*Ars* and Theology," 56.
100. Ibid., 59.
101. Ibid. Basil uses a telling analogy in *The Long Rules*:

    As the secular arts are directed toward certain specific aims and adapt their particular activities to these aims, so also, inasmuch as our actions have as their rule and guide the keeping of the commandments in a manner pleasing to God, it is impossible to do this with exactitude unless it be done as He wills who gave [the commandments]. And by our painstaking zeal to do the will of God in our work, we shall be united to God through our memory. As the smith, when he is forging an axe, for example, thinks of the person who commissioned the task, and with him in mind calculates its shape and size, suiting this work to the wish of him who ordered it done (for if he is unmindful of this, he will fashion something quite different from what he was ordered to make), so the Christian directs every action, small and great, according to the will of God, performing the action at the same time with care and exactitude, and keeping his thoughts fixed upon the One who gave him the work to do. (Basil of Caesarea, *Saint Basil: Ascetical Works*, The Fathers of the Church: A New Translation 9, trans. M. Monica Wagner, ed. Roy Joseph Deferrari (New York Fathers of the Church, 1950), 243–4)

102. Barsella, "*Ars* and Theology," 60.
103. Ibid.
104. Ibid., 62.
105. Ibid.
106. Ibid.
107. Ibid., 63. The term "instrumental" here may not be the best choice, but if one reads it as meaning "essential to" rather than "merely useful for," then that might be the more charitable interpretation.
108. Malesic, "'Nothing Is to Be Preferred to the Work of God,'" 46.
109. Ibid.
110. Ibid., 51.
111. Ibid.
112. Ibid., 52.
113. Ibid. Here again a MacIntyrean distinction between internal and external goods might be applicable.

114. Ibid., 54. The same priority is obvious in the rule of Basil, which, significantly, enumerates the hours of prayer in the same question that deals with work. Question 37 of *The Long Rules* is: "Whether prayer and psalmody ought to afford a pretext for neglecting our work, what hours are suitable for prayer, and, above all, whether labor is necessary." Basil's answer, in brief, is that work is necessary and cannot be neglected, but that he combines this answer with a detailed account of when the monks should pray and the rationalization for each hour's office is no accident. See Basil of Caesarea, *Ascetical Works*, 306–11.
115. Malesic, "'Nothing Is to Be Preferred to the Work of God,'" 50–1.
116. Quoted to good effect in Ovitt, *The Restoration of Perfection*, 106.
117. Rudolph Arbesmann, "The Attitude of Saint Augustine toward Labor," in *The Heritage of the Early Church: Essays in Honor of the Very Reverend Georges Vasilievich Florovsky*, ed. David Neiman and Margaret Schatkin (Rome: Pontificum Institutum Studiorum Orientalium, 1973), 245–59, p. 245. Similarly Barsella hails *The Work of Monks* as "the first organic text in western thought dedicated to the theme of work" (66).
118. Augustine, "The Work of Monks," in *Saint Augustine: Treatises on Various Subjects*, The Fathers of the Church: A New Translation 16, ed. Roy J. Deferrari, trans. Mary Sarah Muldowney (New York: Fathers of the Church, 1952), 323–94, p. 323. See also Arbesmann, "The Attitude of Saint Augustine toward Labor," 247.
119. It is possible that these dissenting monks were influenced by or even identified with the sectarian and frequently censured Messalians, though this is debated. The thesis was raised first by Georges Folliet in his "Des moines euchites à Carthage en 400–401," *Studia Patristica* 2, Texte und Untersuchungen 64 (Berlin: Akademie Verlag, 1957), 386–99. The Messalians (whose name derives from the Syriac for "one who prays," were known in Greek as Euchites. See also Barsella, "*Ars* and Theology," 66; Hoven, *Work in Ancient and Medieval Thought*, 199–20; Arbesmann, "The Attitude of Saint Augustine toward Labor," 246–7. See also Kenneth B. Steinhauser, "The Cynic Monks of Carthage: Some Observations on *De opera monachorum*," in *Augustine: Presbyter Factus Sum*, ed. Joseph T. Lienhard, Earl C. Muller, and Roland J. Teske (New York: Peter Lang, 1993), 455–62. Steinhauser raises the possibility that the recalcitrant monks were more influenced by Cynic philosophy than Messalian sectarianism but cautions that in neither case can a firm historical connection be made (459). Finally, see Maria E. Doerfler, "'Hair!': Remnants of Ascetic Exegesis in Augustine of Hippo's *De opere monachorum*," *Journal of Early Christian Studies* 22.1 (2014): 79–111. She maintains that "a spate of recent scholars has argued convincingly, however, that we might speak rather of a strand of asceticism running through many of the more highly Christianized areas of the fourth and fifth centuries" (82 n7). See also 86–7, where she concludes that speculation about influence, whether Cynic or Messalian, is "of limited value" (87).
120. Steinhauser, "The Cynic Monks of Carthage," 455. A more fulsome account of Augustine's wider perspective on work follows our discussion of *The Work of Monks*.
121. Furthermore, some of the most influential accounts of Egyptian monasticism had yet to be written, John Cassian's *Institutes*, The Works of the Fathers in Translation 58, trans. Boniface Ramsey (New York: Newman Press, 2000), perhaps chief among them.
122. Augustine, *Confessions*, 14–15.
123. For a summary of the various positions, see Pierre Courcelle, *Late Latin Writers and Their Greek Sources*, trans. Harry E. Wedeck (Cambridge, MA: Harvard University

Press, 1969), 149–50. See also Berthold Altaner, "Augustinus und die Griechische Patristik: Eine Einführung und Nachlese zu den Quellenkritischen Untersuchungen," *Revue Bénédictine* 62.3 (1952): 201–215, wherein the author concludes that "we may assert that Augustine, in his theological thought, and especially in his exegetical expositions, could only be influenced by the intellectual achievements of the Greek East to the extent that they were available to him in Latin translations, or by detour through other Latin authors" (207, translation my own).

124. Courcelle, *Late Latin Writers and Their Greek Sources*, 151–55.
125. Altaner, "Augustinus und die Griechische Patristik," 213.
126. Courcelle, *Late Latin Writers and Their Greek Sources*, 201. *The Life of Saint Antony* in fact had a major impact on Augustine's decision to commit fully to Christianity. See chapters VI–VIII in Book Eight of the *Confessions*, where the not-yet-converted Augustine meets Ponticianus, a devout Christian who tells Augustine of how a companion of his had been inflamed with zeal for the religious life upon reading *The Life of Saint Antony* and immediately renounced the world, his courtly ambition, and his impending marriage. Augustine and his friend Alypius had never heard of Antony before (150), but Ponticianus's story arouses in Augustine the same passion Antony's life aroused in Ponticianus's friend, whereupon Augustine upbraids Alypius,

> wild in look and troubled in mind, crying out: "What is wrong with us? What is this that you heard? The unlearned arise and take heaven by force, and here are we with all our learning stuck fast in flesh and blood! Is there any shame in following because they have gone before us, would it not be a worse shame not to follow at once?" These words and more of the same sort I uttered, then the violence of my feeling tore me from him while he stood staring at me thunderstruck. For I did not sound like myself. (153)

127. Altaner, "Augustinus und die Griechische Patristik," 213. A thorough accounting of Augustine's acquaintance with the Greek Fathers is provided by Courcelle in *Late Latin Writers and Their Greek Sources*, 196–208.
128. Doerfler, "'Hair!': Remnants of Ascetic Exegesis in Augustine of Hippo's *De opere monachorum*," 106.
129. Geoghegan, *The Attitude towards Labor in Early Christianity and Ancient Culture*, 207. An excerpt from it was compiled by Thomas Aquinas in his *Catena Aurea* as well.
130. One exceptional passage should be cited, which will strike readers of this chapter as reminiscent of monastic themes:

> Let us suppose a person is converted to this [monastic] life from a life of luxury, and that he is afflicted with no physical infirmity. Are we so incapable of understanding the sweetness of Christ that we do not know how great a swelling of deeply rooted pride is healed when, after the removal of the superfluities with which his spirit was fatally possessed, the humility of the worker does not refuse to perform lowly labors to obtain the few supplies which remain necessary for this natural life? If, however, a person is converted to this life from poverty, let him not consider that he is doing merely what he used to do, if, turning from the love of increasing his own private fortune, however little, and no longer seeking what things are his own but rather those of Jesus Christ, he has devoted himself to the charity of common life, intending to live in companionship with

those who have one heart and one soul in God, so that no one calls anything his own but all things are held in common. (Augustine, *The Work of Monks*, 377)

One significant reference to the value of labor in producing alms occurs near the passage just cited. The most interesting thing about it perhaps is Augustine's appeal to the "one commonwealth of all Christians," which deploys a Ciceronian use of the term *res publica* to describe the universal fellowship of all Christian believers. The context of this invocation, which aligns the Christian church with the Stoic aspiration to a universal cosmopolitan fraternity, is Augustine's argument that no attention should be paid to which monasteries receive the largest bequests from wealthy novices. Almsgiving is important because "whoever has requested necessary help for Christians in any region whatsoever receives it from the goods of Christ, no matter where he himself receives his own necessities" (Augustine, *The Work of Monks*, 378–9). See also Geoghegan, *The Attitude towards Labor in Early Christianity and Ancient Culture*, 304.

131. Barsella, "*Ars* and Theology," 67 n45.
132. Augustine, *The Work of Monks*, 331–2. It should be borne in mind throughout that just about everything we know about the monks that Augustine is criticizing comes to us from his pen, which he of course wields against them. His own attribution of views to his opponents is not necessarily altogether suspect, but it is surely not dispassionately objective.
133. Ibid., 333.
134. Ibid., 334.
135. Ibid., 335.
136. Ibid., 336.
137. Ibid., 335.
138. Ibid., 340.
139. Ibid., 342.
140. Ibid., 348.
141. Ibid., 350.
142. Ibid., 353.
143. Ibid., 354.
144. These were not innocuous occupations according to Augustine. He frequently condemned the bloodlust of gladiatorial games and the distracting spectacle of the theater, which was often lewd and low-minded as well, and he lamented the extent to which these popular diversions enticed the faithful away from church. Furthermore, the Council of Arles had already in 314 AD threatened with excommunication any Christian working as a gladiator or comic actor. See Geoghegan, *The Attitude towards Labor in Early Christianity and Ancient Culture*, 219–20.
145. Augustine, *The Work of Monks*, 354.
146. Ibid.
147. Ibid.
148. The suggestion is raised, but not explored, by Geoghegan, who is following Joseph Mausbach. See Geoghegan, *The Attitude towards Labor in Early Christianity and Ancient Culture*, 211 n98.
149. See Ronald F. Hock, "Simon the Shoemaker as an Ideal Cynic," *Greek, Roman and Byzantine Studies* 17.1 (1976): 41–53; see also John Sellars, "Simon the Shoemaker and the Problem of Socrates," *Classical Philology* 98.3 (2003): 207–16.
150. Sellars, "Simon the Shoemaker and the Problem of Socrates," 208.
151. Ibid., 212.

152. Ibid., 214.
153. If this reading is correct, Steinhauser's verdict that while early Christian monasticism "could easily assimilate Stoic indifference (*apatheia*), there appears to have been no place for Cynic individualism (autarkeia)" cannot be accepted as it stands (Steinhauser, "The Cynic Monks of Carthage," 460). Augustine's Paul, if he is at all like Simon the Shoemaker, in fact embodies autarkeia, as did all the monks who devoted themselves to self-sustenance.
154. It is possible that Augustine is not thinking of Simon in particular but that he has in mind a general Cynical association between philosophers and shoemakers, which Hock proves became something of a recurrent trope. See Hock, "Simon the Shoemaker as an Ideal Cynic," 46–7. Sellars surmises that the Cynics may have associated with shoemakers because like Socrates they went barefoot, such that conversation between a Cynic and a shoemaker could not be motivated by anything but free mutual interest; "such a relationship would have been one free from any ulterior motive, existing purely for the mutual benefit of philosophical discussion. Socrates, well known for his barefoot lifestyle, would have at last found someone to talk with in [*sic*] the environs of the Agora who was not intent upon selling him anything" (213).
155. Augustine, *The Work of Monks*, 354.
156. Barsella, "*Ars* and Theology," 69.
157. Augustine, *The Work of Monks*, 356–7.
158. See Barsella, "*Ars* and Theology," 68: "Augustine shared the common judgment of the Fathers on the various categories of professions but his major goal was to dignify manual work."
159. Augustine, *The Work of Monks*, 362–3.
160. Ibid., 372.
161. Ibid., 372–4.
162. Ibid., 374–5.
163. Ibid., 375. Augustine was not alone in this exegetical task. Slightly different tacks were taken by Basil of Caesarea and John Chrysostom. Basil argued that work was evidently commanded of all and that idleness was obviously a great evil. Furthermore, it was valuable for the disciplining of the body and for the supplying of alms for the needy. See Question 37 from *The Long Rules* in *Saint Basil: Ascetical Works*, 306–11. The primary purpose of work is not to serve one's own needs but to fulfill Jesus's command to provide food for the hungry, since "to be solicitous for oneself is strictly forbidden by the Lord … Everyone, therefore, in doing his work, should place before himself the aim of service to the needy and not his own satisfaction" (317). As if anticipating the objection, Basil continues: 'Nor should anyone think that the Apostle is at variance with our words when he says: 'that working they would eat their own bread'; this is addressed to the unruly and indolent, and means that it is better for each person to minister to himself at least and not be a burden to others than to live in idleness" (ibid.). For more on Basil's discussion of work, see Terrence G. Kardong, *Pillars of Community: Four Rules of Pre-Benedictine Monastic Life* (Collegeville, MN: Liturgical Press, 2010), 57–9. John Chrysostom, in his sermon for the fourteenth Sunday after Pentecost (the Gospel reading for which was the birds of the air and lilies of the field passage from the Sermon on the Mount), recites the Pauline instructions about work only to catch himself up short:

> But all these sayings seem to be in strong conflict with what was said in the beginning (*Labour not for the food that perisheth*, etc.). So we must find an

explanation. What therefore shall we say in reply? That we are *to take no thought* does not mean we are *not to work*. It means that we are not to be bound fast to the things of this life; that is, that we are not to be solicitous for the morrow's rest: to look upon that as something of secondary importance. For a man may work, yet lay up nothing for the morrow. A man may work, yet have no care for the morrow. For work and solicitude are not the same thing. Let a man work, not as trusting to himself in his work, but so that he may have something to give to another in need. (*The Sunday Sermons of the Great Fathers: Volume Four*, trans. and ed. M. F. Toal (San Francisco, CA: Ignatius Press, 2000), 108–9)

164. Augustine, *The Work of Monks*, 379. Quoted from Matthew 6:24.
165. Ibid.
166. This point actually anticipates a crucial element of Augustine's overall philosophy, according to which the objective good of a thing can be corrupted by its misuse. In this case, even the excellence of the Gospel message is not immune from the misconduct of the Gospel preacher. As we will see, Augustine places significant ethical weight on the subjective side of moral evaluation, attributing a situation's goodness or badness not so much to the objective thing used in action but much more to the manner in which the agent acts.
167. Augustine, *The Work of Monks*, 380, translation modified.
168. Ibid., 383. See also Geoghegan, *The Attitude towards Labor in Early Christianity and Ancient Culture*, 202–3.
169. Ibid., 380.
170. Michael Fiedrowicz, "General Introduction," in *On Genesis*, The Works of Saint Augustine: A Translation for the 21st Century 13, ed. John E. Rotelle, trans. Matthew O'Connell (Hyde Park, NY: New City Press, 2002), 13–22, pp. 13–14. Hexameral literature, which examined the six days of divine creation, was a flourishing genre before Augustine's time. For a brief introduction to Augustine's influences see also pp. 17–19 in Fiedrowicz's "General Introduction." See also Ovitt, *The Restoration of Perfection*, chapter 2.
171. Ibid., 21.
172. See, for example, Vitruvius, *Ten Books on Architecture*, trans. Ingrid D. Rowland (Cambridge: Cambridge University Press, 1999), 34; and Letter 90 in Seneca, *Epistles, Volume II: Epistles 66–92*, trans. Richard M. Gummere, Loeb Classical Library 76 (Cambridge, MA: Harvard University Press, 1920).
173. Augustine, *On Genesis*, 356.
174. Ibid.
175. Ibid., 357.
176. Arbesmann cites some of Augustine's sermons to support his claim that

> the first place among all occupations is assigned by Augustine to agriculture. In this he follows some authors of the O. T. ["Old Testament"] and a long series of Roman writers who depict the human tasks which husbandry involves with the most enthusiastic appreciation, and find no lot throughout all the range of human employments more enviable than that of a man who has to till the soil or to rear flocks and herds. Besides, cultivation of the soil was Adam's occupation in Paradise. (252)

177. Augustine, *On Genesis*, 357, author's emphasis.
178. Ibid., 356.

179. Ibid., 357.
180. Ibid., 359.
181. Carol Harrison, "Augustine and the Art of Gardening," in *The Use and Abuse of Time in Christian History*, Studies in Church History 37, ed. R. N. Swanson (Suffolk, UK: Boydell Press, 2002), 13–33, p. 15. See also Steinhauser, "The Cynic Monks of Carthage," 455:

   > In *De Genesi ad literam* Augustine observes that work existed before the fall. Therefore, work in itself is not evil; nor may human work be considered the result of original sin. Before the fall, agricultural labor—the ideal work in antiquity—was a tremendous pleasure to the laborer. In the work of husbandry, the laborer could see the activity of God in his creation. Augustine does concede that work would not be such a burden today if the bliss which prevailed in the garden had endured. Only after the fall does work become difficult and painful.

182. Augustine, *On Genesis*, 357.
183. Ibid.
184. Harrison, "Augustine and the Art of Gardening," 16.
185. Ibid.
186. Ibid., 17.
187. Ibid., 20–1.
188. Augustine, *The City of God against the Pagans*, vol. 7, Loeb Classical Library 417, trans. William M. Green (Cambridge, MA: Harvard University Press, 2014), 327, 329, 331.
189. Whitney, "Paradise Restored," 52. See also 54:

   > Beginning with arts producing material objects (cloth-making, architecture) he follows with the arts he describes in the *De doctrina christiana* as "aiding God" (agriculture, navigation), the arts we would now call "fine arts" (sculpture, painting), a group of arts perhaps characterized by the importance of process rather than product (hunting, medicine, warfare and cookery) and ends with the liberal arts, and finally, philosophy.

190. Augustine, *The City of God against the Pagans*, 321.
191. Ibid., 305.
192. Ibid., 317.
193. Ibid., 323.
194. Ibid., 323–7.
195. Ibid., 335–7.
196. Ibid., 331–5.
197. Ibid., 339–85.
198. Whitney, "Paradise Restored," 52.
199. Ibid., 53.
200. Ibid.
201. Ibid.
202. Cicero, *De natura deorum*, Loeb Classical Library 268, trans. Harris Rackham (Cambridge, MA: Harvard University Press, 1933), 271.
203. It should also be said that Balbus's views are not necessarily those of Cicero himself, such that to conclude that this praise is representative of Cicero's own view of craftsmanship is a bit precarious; all the more precarious it is to assert that this passage from *De natura deorum* therefore constitutes "one of the most positive

statements on technology in classical literature" without the qualification that it may be attributed to a spokesperson by the author precisely to distance himself from it.
204. Augustine, *The City of God against the Pagans*, 321 n1.
205. Seneca also diverged from Cicero on this point; he argued that ingenuity [*sagacitas*] and wisdom [*sapientia*] were heterogeneous. The former was the source of inventions and technical practices, while the latter was the source of philosophical thinking and contented living. Speaking of crafts like weaving, farming, and milling, he writes, "Reason did indeed devise all these things, but it was not right reason. It was man, but not the wise man, that discovered them." See Seneca, *Epistles, Volume II: Epistles 66–92*, trans. Richard M. Gummere, Loeb Classical Library 76 (Cambridge, MA: Harvard University Press, 1920), 413.
206. Whitney, "Paradise Restored," 53–4. Emphasis in the original.
207. Augustine, *The City of God against the Pagans*, 327.
208. Whitney, "Paradise Restored," 54.
209. Van den Hoven falls into the same interpretive error, partly under Whitney's influence. See Hoven, *Work in Ancient and Medieval Thought*, 97: "Augustine regards—although not without irony—philosophy as the highest of the arts and places primary education, rhetoric, grammar, music, geometry, arithmetic and astronomy in the highest category but one of the liberal arts." Her reconstruction is dependent upon Henri-Irénée Marrou, who seems to be somewhat creative in his reading of this passage, and she again, following Whitney, accuses Augustine of being "ironic" (99 n108).
210. Augustine, *Confessions*, 119.
211. Ibid., 120.
212. Ibid., 121.
213. Ibid., 129.
214. Ibid., 130.
215. Ibid.
216. Ibid.
217. Augustine, *On the Free Choice of the Will*, trans. Thomas Williams (Indianapolis, IN: Hackett, 1993), 26.
218. Ibid., 97.
219. Augustine, *Confessions*, 29–30.
220. Ibid., 30.
221. Ibid., 32.
222. Harrison, "Augustine and the Art of Gardening," 21; Arbesmann, "The Attitude of Saint Augustine toward Labor," 251.
223. Augustine, "The Excellence of Widowhood," in *Saint Augustine: Treatises on Various Subjects*, The Fathers of the Church: A New Translation 16, trans. M. Clement Eagan, ed. Roy J. Deferrari (New York: Fathers of the Church, 1952), 315.
224. Harrison, "Augustine and the Art of Gardening," 21.

4 The Late Medieval Period

1. Ovitt, *The Restoration of Perfection*, 138.
2. For a more compact assessment of the period leading up to what he calls a "Carolingian Renaissance of Labor," see LeGoff's chapter "Labor, Techniques, and

Craftsmen in the Value Systems of the Early Middle Ages (Fifth to Tenth Centuries)," in his *Time, Work, and Culture in the Middle Ages*.
3. Ibid., 138–41.
4. Ibid., 142.
5. Ibid.
6. Brian Stock, "Activity, Contemplation, Work and Leisure between the Eleventh and the Thirteenth Centuries," in *Arbeit-Musse-Meditation: Betrachtungen zur Vita Activa und Vita Contemplativa*, ed. Brian Vickers (Zurich: Verlag der Fachvereine, 1985), 88.
7. Ovitt, *The Restoration of Perfection*, 143–4.
8. Ibid., 145.
9. A somewhat more critical view of the reality of Cistercian labor practices ought also to be considered, and this is provided by Isabel Alfonso in her "Cistercians and Feudalism," *Past and Present* 133.1 (1991): 3–30. Alfonso argues that Cistercians practiced rather more traditional custodial ownership of land than previously (and optimistically) surmised, such that their prosperity was not entirely unpredictable. Rather than develop a truly innovative scheme of land and labor management, the monasteries often exercised seigneurial rights that extended even to simply recruiting as lay brothers those tenant laborers who were effectively displaced by their occupancy of and administration over newly acquired land holdings. Ovitt (*The Restoration of Perfection*, 144) and Christopher J. Holdsworth both speculate about the attractions that lay brotherhood might have held for peasant farmers, but if Alfonso is right, then the lay brothers may have had less choice in the matter than they realize. See Christopher J. Holdsworth, "The Blessings of Work: The Cistercian View," in *Sanctity and Secularity: The Church and the World*, ed. Derek Baker (Oxford: Basil Blackwell, 1973), 59–76, pp. 67–8.
10. Holdsworth, "The Blessings of Work: The Cistercian View," 60.
11. Ibid., 60–1.
12. Ibid., 64.
13. "Blessed is the exchange [*vicissitudo*], when from the heart of the bride some streams of honey flow into the Beloved and from him return in waves to the bride. Indeed to the source whence these rivers of honey emerge they are restored that they may continue to flow." Gilbert of Hoyland, *Sermons on the Song of Songs* III, Cistercian Fathers Series 26, trans. Lawrence C. Braceland (Kalamazoo, MI: Cistercian, 1979), 416. For the Latin see Sancti Bernardi Abbatis Claræ-Vallensis, *Opera Omnia*, vol. 2, Pars Prior, ed. Jean Mabillon (Paris: Gaume Fratres, 1839), 238 (Sermo XXXIV).
14. Brian Stock, "Experience, Praxis, Work, and Planning in Bernard of Clairvaux: Observations on the *Sermones in Cantica*," in *The Cultural Context of Medieval Learning*, ed. J. E. Murdoch and E. D. Sylla (Dordrecht: Springer, 1975), 219–68, p. 229. See also Emero Stiegman's introduction to Volume III of Bernard's sermons on the Song of Songs: "Action and Contemplation in Saint Bernard's Sermons on the Song of Songs," in *On the Song of Songs III*, Cistercian Fathers Series 21, trans. Kilian Walsh (Kalamazoo, MI: Cistercian Publications, 1979), vii–xix. Stiegman contends that action and contemplation share a "coordinate nature" (x) in Bernard's sermons, such that their "integration" (xiii) is realized when we rightly see that "the ascetic and the apostle share in a common labor, and in its fruit" (ibid.). Their work is common because "the *affective* charity of prayer and the *actual* charity of fraternal care are motions of the same Spirit" (xvii).
15. A similar dynamic is detectable in the Cistercian tradition's handling of the classic trope of Mary and Martha as symbolic figures for the contemplative and active lives,

respectively, again paired as they often are with Rachel and Leah. See Holdsworth, "The Blessings of Work," 64–6.
16. Quoted at Holdsworth, "The Blessings of Work," 66. Bernard-Joseph-Maurice Vignes makes a similar point, choosing the word "alternance" to describe how Bernard advocates a life devoted to three different sorts of work: physical, intellectual, and moral-religious. The third of three principles on work he isolates in Bernard's writings is that "everyone's labors should be alternated," such that no one is confined to "one unique task." See his "Les doctrines économiques et morales de Saint Bernard sur la richesse et le travail," *Revue d'histoire économique et sociale* 16.3 (1928): 547–85, p. 575 (all translations my own). Speaking specifically of manual labor, Vignes argues that in Bernard's hands "it thus loses the degrading and damaging character that was assigned to it by classical antiquity; it stops being a cause of humiliation and is definitively rehabilitated" (581). It does so on his reading because it is as obligatory as intellectual and moral or spiritual cultivation and should be accommodated into everyone's daily routine along with these other two (admittedly higher) pursuits. Stressing that for Bernard the monastery is the model of a rationally ordered spiritual existence that is proposed as a model for the whole of Christian society (575), Vignes further argues that alternation in tasks provides the benefit of securing the development of the full personality across its physical, intellectual, and moral nature; makes each kind of work easier in a "reciprocal" relationality between them; and valorizes the harmonious development of all the human faculties (583–4).
17. Stock, "Experience, Praxis, Work, and Planning in Bernard of Clairvaux," 226. This logic is also present in a sentence from Bernard's sermon III on the vigil of the Nativity, which Stock quotes but without explicitly connecting it to the dialectical movement he identifies elsewhere in Bernard's preaching: "Purity of intention takes as its purpose that the simple eye should make the whole body radiant: that, whatever you may do, you may do it according to God, so that grace may flow back to the place from which it pours forth" (239). This language is quite strikingly similar to what we saw above when Gilbert of Hoyland exclaimed, "blessed is the exchange [*vicissitudo*], when from the heart of the bride some streams of honey flow into the Beloved and from him return in waves to the bride. Indeed to the source whence these rivers of honey emerge they are restored that they may continue to flow."
18. Ibid., 228.
19. Ibid., 230.
20. Ibid. Ovitt gets this right too. See Ovitt, *The Restoration of Perfection*, 146.
21. Ibid., 233.
22. Ibid.
23. Ibid., 231.
24. Ibid., 227.
25. John 2.
26. Bernard of Clairvaux, *Monastic Sermons*, Cistercian Fathers Series 68, trans. Daniel Griggs (Collegeville, MN: Liturgical Press, 2016), 260 (Sermo 55).
27. Ibid., 261.
28. Ibid., 261–2.
29. Ibid., 262.
30. Bernard of Clairvaux, *On the Song of Songs* II, Cistercian Fathers Series 7, The Works of Bernard of Clairvaux 3, trans. Kilian Walsh (Kalamazoo, MI: Cistercian, 1983), 243–4.

31. Ibid., 244. See also Stiegman, "Action and Contemplation in Saint Bernard's Sermons on the Song of Songs," xiii.
32. Stock is right that "statements therefore about human work and labor in Bernard should not be artificially separated from their contexts" (247) and here is conscious that Bernard's Sermon 46 on the Song of Songs is speaking not so much about literal work but spiritual. Nevertheless, I think it established that Bernard speaks of both, depending on context.
33. Quoted at Stock, "Experience, Praxis, Work, and Planning in Bernard of Clairvaux," 249.
34. Stock's concluding question is a good one to consider: "Had the topos of *docta ignorantia* ever reached so low in the social order in the previous history of the classical tradition?" (Stock, "Experience, Praxis, Work, and Planning in Bernard of Clairvaux," 249).
35. Included with "An Argument on Four Questions," in *Cistercians and Cluniacs: The Case for Cîteaux*, Cistercian Fathers Series 33, trans. Jeremiah F. O'Sullivan (Kalamazoo, MI: Cistercian, 1977). The translator is to be congratulated for his admirable preservation of many of Idung's amusing and incisive Latin word plays.
36. *Cistericans and Cluniacs*, 6. See also his own defense in the mouth of the Cistercian at 48.
37. Ibid., 25–6.
38. Ibid., 22.
39. Holdsworth has this to say on the subject:

    Broadly speaking after the time of Benedict of Aniane it was very rare for monks to work in the fields, less rarely they were occupied for some period in domestic work, or at producing say metal work or some other craft work. Increasingly, however, from the foundation of Cluny onwards, the only work shared in by monks was the *opus Dei*, which came to fill more and more of the hours of darkness as well as those of light. Anything else became exceptional and distinctly secondary in importance, so that it does not surprise one to find not a single reference to field or garden work being a "common exercise" among English black monks in the twelfth century. The literary tradition provided ample reinforcement for the disappearance of manual work from the monk's life since it conveyed the idea that it was not fit for free men because contact with matter was soiling. (Holdsworth, "The Blessings of Work,' 68)

40. *Cistercians and Cluniacs*, 27–8.
41. Ibid., 28.
42. Ibid., 28, 37.
43. Ibid., 42.
44. Ibid., 44.
45. Ibid.
46. Ibid., 47.
47. Ibid.
48. Ibid., 63.
49. Ibid., 64.
50. Ibid., 64–5.
51. Ibid., 65.
52. Ibid.
53. Ibid., 66.

54. Ibid., 92.
55. Ibid.
56. Ibid., 93.
57. Ibid.
58. Ibid.
59. Ibid., 94.
60. Ibid.
61. Ibid.
62. Ibid., 138. Passing references to manual labor can still be found on pages 104, 108, and 128.
63. Ibid., 112.
64. Ovitt, *The Restoration of Perfection*, 151.
65. Ibid., 155.
66. *Libellus de diversis ordinibus et professionibus qui sunt in aecclesia*, ed. and trans. G. Constable and B. Smith (Oxford: Clarendon Press, 1972), xxiii.
67. Ibid., xxv–xxvii. Tellingly, the introduction makes this point:

   > In spite of his tolerant and impartial tone and his determination to find what good he could in each religious order, the author of the *Libellus* was far from approving everything, and he was as ready to condemn those who clung blindly to the "the chalice of ingrained custom" and refused to change their old ways as he was to condemn those members of the new orders who criticized without charity and created scandal by their innovations. Nor was he simply an apologist for the *status quo*. His high praise for the monks and canons who lived far from other men, and the Biblical prototypes he chose for them, can leave no doubt of his admiration and sympathy for the reformers, even though he doubted whether their standards and ideals should be applied to all other orders and callings of the Church. (xxvii)

   For the author of the *Libellus* too, there could be no universal return to the "good old days."
68. *Libellus de diversis ordinibus*, 95.
69. Ibid.
70. Ibid., 97.
71. Ovitt, *The Restoration of Perfection*, 158.
72. Ibid.
73. Quoted at Kellie Robertson and Michael Uebel (eds.), *The Middle Ages at Work: Practicing Labor in Late Medieval England* (New York: Palgrave Macmillan, 2004), 7.
74. See the "Introduction" to Theophilus, *The Various Arts*, ed. and trans. C. R. Dodwell (Oxford: Clarendon Press, 1986), x: "It is this rational organization, the detailed presentation of each method and the integration of the methods into a complete craft that so much distinguishes the *De Diuersis Artibus* from other comparable medieval works, which normally resolve themselves into a miscellaneous series of hints and recipes." See also xiii–xiv:

   > The difference between Theophilus and other comparable medieval works is this: the latter are normally compilations—whether gathered together at one time or assembled over a period—whereas the *De Diuersis Artibus* represents the deliberate attempt by one person to give shape to his own personal

knowledge and experience and present it in a rational and ordered way. If it is true to say that the Middle Ages has left us a number of miscellanies of art techniques, it is also true to say that it has left us only one treatise.

See also John van Engen, "Theophilus Presbyter and Rupert of Deutz: The Manual Arts and Benedictine Theology in the Early Twelfth Century," *Viator* 11 (1980): 147–64, p. 147.

75. See the "Introduction" to *The Various Arts*: "The hints he suggests, the details he goes into, the reservations he makes, the warnings he gives, all indicate a person with practical experience of the methods he is discussing" (xxxvii–xxxviii).
76. Theophilus, *The Various Arts*, x.
77. Ibid., 1.
78. Ibid.
79. Ibid.
80. Engen, "Theophilus Presbyter and Rupert of Deutz," 150–1. As van Engen says, this is a totally unprecedented move but finds an echo in Rupert's writings on the Trinity.
81. Ibid., 1–2.
82. Ibid., 2.
83. Ibid.
84. Ibid., 3. Could there be an echo and conflation here of two of Jesus's brief parables in Matthew 13?

> Again, the kingdom of heaven is like unto treasure hid in a field; the which when a man hath found, he hideth, and for joy thereof goeth and selleth all that he hath, and buyeth that field. Again, the kingdom of heaven is like unto a merchant man, seeking goodly pearls: Who, when he had found one pearl of great price, went and sold all that he had, and bought it.

85. Theophilus, *The Various Arts*, 3–4.
86. See Engen, "Theophilus Presbyter and Rupert of Deutz," 148. This free bestowal of technical knowledge revises the classical Greek conception of techne, according to which the practitioner guards his secrets and conveys his specialized knowledge only to his few chosen apprentices. Theophilus is adherent to a more profligate Christian charity.
87. Theophilus, *The Various Arts*, 4
88. Ibid., 36.
89. Ibid.
90. Ibid.
91. Ibid., 37. It is possible that this unusual phrase, *atrium agiae Sophiae*, which features a borrowing from Greek, was retrieved by Theophilus from Alcuin's sacramentary, which uses it in a post-communion prayer for a ferial mass devoted to Holy Wisdom. The attribution was made by Bernhard Bischoff in his *Mittelalterliche Studien: Ausgewählte Aufsätze zur Schriftkunde und Literaturgeschichte* 2 (Stuttgart: Anton Hiersemann, 1967), 182.
92. As van Engen contends, Theophilus uses the familiar themes of Benedict's Rule on labor—the avoidance of idleness and the means of supplying the needs of the community and of the impoverished—but puts them together in a unique manner. See Engen, "Theophilus Presbyter and Rupert of Deutz," 151.
93. Theophilus, *The Various Arts*, 61.
94. Ibid.

95. Van Engen demonstrates that the use of this verse, and the interpretation that Theophilus gave it, is very probably a foursquare opposition to the spiritualizing interpretation of the exact same verse put forward by Bernard of Clairvaux in his *Apologia*. See Engen, "Theophilus Presbyter and Rupert of Deutz," 159–60.
96. Theophilus, *The Various Arts*, 62.
97. Exodus 31:3–5.
98. Exodus 31:2.
99. Heidi C. Gearhart, *Theophilus and the Theory and Practice of Medieval Art* (University Park, PA: Pennsylvania State University Press, 2017), 83–6.
100. Are even these works, which seem to belong to craftsmanship, to be attributed to the gift of the Holy Spirit? Or is this stated symbolically, so that the things that are signified by these objects pertain to the divine spirit of wisdom and understanding and knowledge? But still, even here, although he is said to be filled with the divine spirit of wisdom and understanding and knowledge, it is not yet called the Holy Spirit.

    See Augustine, *Writings on the Old Testament*, The Works of Saint Augustine: A Translation for the 21st Century 14, trans. Joseph T. Lienhard (Hyde Park, NY: New City Press, 2016), 156. Van Engen also observes that Theophilus departs from the Augustinian precedent here and once more shows that only Rupert of Deutz shared in Theophilus's opinion. See Engen, "Theophilus Presbyter and Rupert of Deutz," 153–4.
101. Theophilus, *The Various Arts*, 62.
102. Ibid.
103. Augustine, *Commentary on the Lord's Sermon on the Mount with Seventeen Related Sermons*, The Fathers of the Church: A New Translation 11, trans. Denis J. Kavanagh (New York: Fathers of the Church, 1951), 27. The sevenfold gifts of the Holy Spirit were prominent in Hugh of St. Victor, who wrote a short treatise on them, and were the organizing principle of part of Rupert's work on the Trinity and his commentary on Revelation. See Engen, "Theophilus Presbyter and Rupert of Deutz," 154 n40, n41. Van Engen speculates that Theophilus is once again following Rupert here, who also reversed the order of the seven gifts. This was so unusual that Gerhoch of Reichersberg stirred controversy among the cardinals of the Roman curia when he preached a sermon on the seven gifts and followed Rupert's sequence. Gerhoch wrote a long treatise explaining his view on the matter. See Engen, "Theophilus Presbyter and Rupert of Deutz," 155.
104. Gearhart, *Theophilus and the Theory and Practice of Medieval Art*, 85.
105. "Diligence" is extolled no fewer than thirty-five times in *The Various Arts*, and the word "diligently" is Theophilus's most frequently used adverb. See Gearhart, *Theophilus and the Theory and Practice of Medieval Art*, 76.
106. Gearhart, *Theophilus and the Theory and Practice of Medieval Art*, 87–8. See also Engen, "Theophilus Presbyter and Rupert of Deutz," 151: "Theophilus made the craftsman's labor both a religious duty and a religious exercise."
107. Engen, "Theophilus Presbyter and Rupert of Deutz," 162.

5 Petrarch

1. Brief discussions of Pico della Mirandola, Giannozzo Manetti, and Marsilio Ficino do occur in Burckhardt's seminal text, but even then the contents of their writings do not occupy the author. See Jacob Burckhardt, *The Civilization of the Renaissance in Italy*, trans. S. G. C. Middlemore (Vienna: Phaidon Press, 1937). Overall, the verdict of Ernst Cassirer stands: "Jacob Burckhardt, for one, in his great portrayal of Renaissance civilization, granted no place to philosophy. He does not even consider it as a constitutive moment of the entire intellectual movement." See Ernst Cassirer, *The Individual and the Cosmos in Renaissance Philosophy*, trans. Mario Domandi (Oxford: Blackwell, 1963), 3.
2. Cassirer, *The Individual and the Cosmos in Renaissance Philosophy*, 3–4.
3. Paul Oskar Kristeller, *Renaissance Philosophy and the Mediaeval Tradition*, Wimmer Lecture XV (Latrobe, PA: Archabbey Press, 1966), 13. Kristeller has written more on the relationship between the medieval period and the Renaissance than anyone. See his *Medieval Aspects of Renaissance Learning: Three Essays by Paul Oskar Kristeller*, Duke Monographs in Medieval and Renaissance Studies 1, ed. and trans. Edward P. Mahoney (Durham, NC: Duke University Press, 1974); Paul Oskar Kristeller, *Renaissance Thought and Its Sources*, ed. Michael Mooney (New York: Columbia University Press, 1979); and Paul Oskar Kristeller, *Renaissance Thought: The Classic, Scholastic, and Humanist Strains* (New York: Harper & Row, 1961).
4. See his *The Scope of Renaissance Humanism* (Ann Arbor: University of Michigan Press, 1983), x.
5. Charles Trinkaus, *In Our Image and Likeness: Humanity and Divinity in Italian Humanist Thought in 2 Volumes*, 1 (London: Constable, 1970), 248.
6. See, for example, the massive *Renaissance and Renewal in the Twelfth Century*, which exhaustively documents the many cultural developments afoot in the twelfth century that initiated the reforms and innovations previously attributed exclusively to the Italian Renaissance. Note also Bernard Murchland's caution against falling into clichéd contrasts between the eras, with Innocent III as the token for the Middle Ages and Giannozzo Manetti as the Renaissance spokesman: "The Middle Ages were by no means as dark as Innocent's vision would indicate; nor was the Renaissance as healthily optimistic as it has often been interpreted to be." See the introduction to his *Two Views of Man: Pope Innocent III On the Misery of Man/Giannozzo Manetti On the Dignity of Man* (New York: Frederick Ungar, 1966), vi.
7. Trinkaus, *In Our Image and Likeness*, xiii–xiv.
8. Consider the verdict of Marjorie O'Rourke Boyle, whose particular point about Petrarch is also corroborative of what was said above about the relationship of the Renaissance as a whole to the medieval period: "Petrarch the poet as irreligious, even idolatrous, is the legacy of an obsolete historiography that demarcated the Middle Ages and the Renaissance as sacred and secular cultures." See her *Petrarch's Genius: Pentimento and Prophecy* (Berkeley: University of California Press, 1991), 1–2.
9. Trinkaus, *The Scope of Renaissance Humanism*, 349–51.
10. Ibid., 352.
11. Ibid., 352–3.
12. See Robert E. Proctor, *Defining the Humanities: How Rediscovering a Tradition Can Improve Our Schools*, 2nd ed. (Bloomington: Indiana University Press, 1998), 26; Trinkaus, *The Scope of Renaissance Humanism*, 353–4.

13. Proctor, *Defining the Humanities*, 38–9; Charles Trinkaus, *The Poet as Philosopher: Petrarch and the Formation of Renaissance Consciousness* (New Haven, CT: Yale University Press, 1979), 116.
14. The influence of Augustine on Petrarch has been thoroughly discussed by Alexander Lee in his *Petrarch and St. Augustine: Classical Scholarship, Christian Theology and the Origins of the Renaissance in Italy* (Leiden: Brill, 2012).
15. Trinkaus, *The Poet as Philosopher*, 120. See also F. Edward Cranz, "Some Petrarchan Paradoxes," in *Reorientations of Western Thought from Antiquity to the Renaissance*, ed. Nancy Struever (Aldershot, UK: Ashgate, 2006), 13. Cranz calls the popularity of this work, extending well into the eighteenth century with over two dozen Latin editions and fifty translations into nine different languages, "off the scale" compared to the success of other Italian humanists.
16. Petrarch, *Remedies for Fortune Fair and Foul*, trans. Conrad H. Rawski, Volume 2, Book I Commentary (Bloomington: Indiana University Press, 1991), 69–70 n19. As we will see, the same logic appears in *On Religious Leisure*, where Petrarch distinguishes between the complete truth of Christianity and the imperfect truth of the pagans, who held virtue to be paramount in life. Echoing *The City of God*, Book XIX, chapter 4, Petrarch is contending that all pagan ethics (and he names Aristotle, Plato, Cicero, Seneca, the Cynics, and the Epicureans) fails by resting content with a humanly achievable virtue as necessary and sufficient for the securing of the good life. "Therefore, although the illustrious philosophers of all nations relate everything to virtue, the philosopher of Christ relates virtue itself to God, the Creator of virtue. Using virtues, he enjoys God and never lets his mind stop short of that goal" (130).
17. Petrarch, *Remedies for Fortune Fair and Foul*, Volume 1, Book I, 62–3. The many passages in Petrarch's work that draw such a distinction, which should be kept in mind during the discussion of *On Religious Leisure* below, are traced out in admirable detail by Lee in his *Petrarch and St. Augustine*, 117–24.
18. Petrarch, *Remedies for Fortune Fair and Foul*, Volume 1, Book I, 63.
19. Ibid.
20. Petrarch, *Remedies for Fortune Fair and Foul*, Volume 3, Book II, 24.
21. Ibid., 36.
22. Ibid., 37.
23. Ibid. In Cicero's *De re publica* Scipio misattributes this anecdote to Plato "or perhaps someone else." See Cicero, *On the Republic/On the Laws*, Loeb Classical Library 213, trans. Clinton W. Keyes (Cambridge, MA: Harvard University Press, 1928), 51, 53. Petrarch seems to have copied it from Vitruvius, since like him, he follows this anecdote with a saying from Theophrastus. See Vitruvius, *Ten Books on Architecture*, 75.
24. Petrarch, *Remedies for Fortune Fair and Foul*, Volume 3, Book II, 39.
25. Ibid., 131.
26. Ibid., 132.
27. Ibid., 132–3.
28. Ibid., 292.
29. Ibid., 132, 292. At his most pedestrian, Petrarch suggests that work, in combination with other treatments, can be useful as a remedy for obesity (244), slow-wittedness (246), and scabies (201), with which he was personally afflicted on more than one occasion (Petrarch, *Remedies for Fortune Fair and Foul*, Volume 4, Book II, 315–17).
30. See Ronald G. Witt, "Introduction," in *On Religious Leisure*, ed. and trans. Susan S. Schearer (New York: Italica Press, 2002), ix.

31. Petrarch, *On Religious Leisure*, 4.
32. Ibid., 5.
33. Ivan Illich, *In the Vineyard of the Text: A Commentary to Hugh's* Didascalicon (Chicago: University of Chicago Press, 1993), 61.
34. Ibid., 62.
35. Aristotle, *Nicomachean Ethics*, 1177b6.
36. Petrarch, *On Religious Leisure*, 6.
37. Ibid., 7.
38. Ibid.
39. Ibid.
40. Ibid.
41. Ibid., 7–8.
42. Verses 6–9:

    I have planted, Apollos watered; but God gave the increase. So then neither is he that planteth any thing, neither he that watereth; but God that giveth the increase. Now he that planteth and he that watereth are one: and every man shall receive his own reward according to his own labour. For we are labourers together with God: ye are God's husbandry, ye are God's building.

    The verse has come up before in Augustine's *On Genesis*.
43. Petrarch, *On Religious Leisure*, 130.
44. Ibid., 8.
45. Ibid.
46. Ibid., 12.
47. Ibid., 9.
48. Ibid., 10.
49. Ibid., 14.
50. Quoted at Demetrio S. Yocum, *Petrarch's Humanist Writing and Carthusian Monasticism: The Secret Language of the Self* (Turnhout, Belgium: Brepols, 2013), 251.
51. See his excellent discussion of the background for this idea, including Petrarch's borrowings from Augustine on how to translate Psalm 46:10 at *Petrarch's Humanist Writing and Carthusian Monasticism*, 91–7.
52. Ibid., 249–54.
53. Ibid., 134.
54. Ibid., 134–8.
55. Ibid., 138–9.
56. Ibid., xvii.
57. Ibid., 64
58. Ibid., 22–3.
59. Lee, *Petrarch and St. Augustine*, 119, 144.
60. For further thoughts on *On Religious Leisure* see Susanna Barsella, "A Humanistic Approach to Religious Solitude," in *Petrarch: A Critical Guide to the Complete Works*, ed. Victoria Kirkham and Armando Maggi (Chicago: University of Chicago Press, 2009), 197–208. One of her more important conclusions:

    Petrarch's redefinition of Christian "vacatio" in terms of *otium* indicates that a rethinking of the social function of the *literatus* [man of letters] was already in progress in the second half of the fourteenth century. In his humanistic view of society, as monastic and secular *otia* were similar and complementary, so were the functions of the monk and the man of letters, for both were committed to the moral perfection of earthly experience. While monks testified to a perfect spiritual life through their sanctity, philosophers, poets, and princes were the moral and political guides to the edification of Christian society. Although ethical goals were common to secular and religious solitudes, a crucial difference existed in Petrarch's new intellectual perspective. While the monks sought virtue as a way of anticipating celestial beatitude on earth, the literate sought in virtue the blossoming of human nature. While monks aimed at becoming examples of sanctity that may guide others, poets preserved, transmitted, and created works to inspire virtue in their readers. Their goals were different but connected; in both the action of the will to direct the soul toward virtue was crucial. (206–7)

6 Martin Luther

1. Martin Luther, *On the Freedom of a Christian with Related Texts*, ed. and trans. Tryntje Helfferich (Indianapolis: Hackett, 2013), 1.
2. Ibid.
3. Ibid., 18–19.
4. Ibid., 19.
5. Ibid., 19–20.
6. Ibid., 20.
7. Ibid.
8. Ibid., 22. See also the interesting choice of metaphor at 27, where Luther likens faith to a kind of workman who does righteous works: "Works, however, are dead things, which can neither honor nor praise God, no matter how they are done or even if they are intended to honor and praise God. But here we do not seek which works are to be done, but rather the builder and master workman who honors God and does the works." See also the same image in his "Treatise on Good Works": "Now faith is the master workman and the motivating force behind the good works of generosity, just as it is in all the other commandments" (Martin Luther, *Luther's Works*, Volume 44, ed. James Atkinson, gen. ed. Helmut T. Lehmann, "Treatise on Good Works," trans. W. A. Lambert, rev. James Atkinson (Philadelphia, PA: Fortress Press, 1966), 109).
9. As the editor and translator notes, the term "estates" [*Ständen*] is a quasi-technical one for Luther, and it is worth noting here because it will be relevant to Luther's theory of work. According to Helfferich's explanatory footnote,

> "Estates" is a term meaning social position or rank. Elsewhere in his writings Luther adopted the common medieval idea that all people (even unbelievers) naturally and by God's will belong within one (or more) of the three major walks of life or estates, including the church, the household or economic life, and civil government or political life. He then distinguishes this from vocations or callings, to which believing Christians are drawn by the Holy Spirit. (*On the Freedom of a Christian*, 23 n27)

Luther uses the German term *Beruf* to refer to a vocation or calling, and he will, in revolutionary fashion, argue that a Christian can be *called* to dutiful service in any estate, not just to clerical or monastic life. To the medieval mind, a person cannot be

called to or have a vocation for any job, only to a priestly or monastic life, but Luther will argue that a person can indeed be called to parenthood or farming or military, civic, or domestic service or any number of "secular" occupations. This book cannot address the complexity of the topic of vocation in Luther's writing, which is admittedly related to the topic of work but outside the scope of this treatment. An excellent summary of Luther on estates and callings is provided by F. Edward Cranz in his *An Essay on the Development of Luther's Thought on Justice, Law, and Society*, Harvard Theological Studies XIX (Cambridge, MA: Harvard University Press, 1959), 153–9.
10. Luther, *On the Freedom of a Christian*, 23.
11. Ibid., 23–4.
12. Ibid., 25.
13. Ibid., 31.
14. Ibid. Ian Hart points out that Luther somewhat infrequently highlights the ascetic value of labor, but he seems mystified as to the source of this inspiration, calling it "a strange idea" and speculating that it might have been a commonplace in the medieval era since it comes up in John Chrysostom. Our study so far has surely removed any mystery about where Luther might have picked up this theme. See Ian Hart, "The Teaching of Luther and Calvin about Ordinary Work: 1. Martin Luther (1483–1546)," *Evangelical Quarterly* 67.1 (1995): 35–52, pp. 42–3.
15. Luther, *On the Freedom of a Christian*, 31.
16. Ibid., 32.
17. Ibid.
18. Ibid.
19. See Luther's personal remarks on this subject, which reiterate the classic view that work is good for bodily self-discipline but caution against overexertion:

   > The body does indeed have the purpose, not of loafing around, but of working; however, a person should work in such a way that he stays healthy and does not destroy his body in the process. God doesn't want us to abuse and harm our bodies, which is what many people did under the papacy in the monasteries. They spent so much time in prayer, fasting, singing, self-torture, reading, sleeping on stone floors, that as a result they died prematurely; and I, too, did that and so tortured myself, that I still haven't recovered and won't recover from it as long as I live. God doesn't want us to do such things, because that is deliberately shortening your life. Christ is also concerned with our stomachs, which are mortal. Therefore, we should take good care of our bodies, use them to perform useful work, but in such a way that they remain healthy. (Martin Luther, *Sermons of Martin Luther: The House Postils*, Volume 2, ed. Eugene F. A. Klug, trans. Eugene F. A. Klug, Erwin W. Koehlinger, James Lanning, Everette W. Meier, Dorothy Schoknecht, and Allen Schuldheiss (Grand Rapids, MI: Baker Books, 1996), 332)

20. Luther, *On the Freedom of a Christian*, 33.
21. That such a convergence is possible, maybe even necessary, is noted by a Roman Catholic commentator.

   > All that a genuinely Catholic theology has to say about things that *cannot* be merited in any way by the *actus humanus*, taken together with all that such a theology says about the ways in which other human actions by God's grace can co-merit that eternal salvation, where grace crowns the gifts of an earlier grace,

all this holds true for the relatively perfective dynamic of labor. What is usually discussed under the title of "work" and what is usually discussed under the title of "good works" must at some point converge; for both, their lasting and perfective merits are real but relative.

See Richard Schenk, "Work: The Corruption or Perfection of the Human Being?" *Nova et Vetera* 2.1 (2004): 129–46, pp. 139–40.
22. Ibid.
23. Ibid.
24. Ibid., 34.
25. 1103b1–3.
26. Martin Luther, *Martin Luther's Basic Theological Writings*, 3rd ed., ed. Timothy F. Lull and William R. Russell (Minneapolis, MN: Fortress Press, 2012), 3. Aristotle of course also argues that the will is disposed neither to good nor to evil but is equipoised between them (*Nicomachean Ethics*, 1103a24–26).
27. 1103a33–1103b1.
28. Luther, *On the Freedom of a Christian*, 34.
29. Ibid., 37.
30. Ibid., 37–8.
31. Ibid., 39.
32. Ibid., 40.
33. Ibid., 41.
34. Luther, *Luther's Works*, Volume 44: The Christian in Society I, 108. See also his remark in a sermon for the Fifteenth Sunday after Trinity on the Sermon on the Mount: "For God has mandated that we are to work, as it is written in Genesis 3:19: 'In the sweat of thy face shalt thou eat bread'; again, 2 Thessalonians 3:10: 'If any would not work, neither should he eat'" (Luther, *Sermons of Martin Luther: The House Postils*, Volume 3, 18).
35. Martin Luther, *Luther's Works*, Volume 1: Lectures on Genesis Chapters 1–5, ed. Jaroslav Pelikan, trans. George V. Schick (St. Louis: Concordia Publishing House, 1958), 210.
36. Ibid., 211.
37. Ibid., 210–11.
38. Ibid., 211.
39. Ibid. Luther targeted the mendicant orders for criticism on this score, sounding an Augustinian note in his condemnation of monastic abstention from work:

> But the religious orders are not supported by their labor. They are like a lazy rogue who does not exert himself bodily but lets others work for him, filling his belly through the sweat and blood of others. Nor does he anticipate the slightest danger or damage to his possessions, so that, in short, there is in that situation very little "sweat of the face." His way of life follows the pattern of Psalm 73:5–6: "They are not in trouble as other men are; they are not stricken like other men. Therefore pride is their necklace, etc." And although they pray and sing and pursue their spiritual occupations, this in no way contributes to the exercise of the body. (Martin Luther, *Luther's Works*, Volume 28: Commentaries on 1 Corinthians 7/1 Corinthians 15/Lectures on 1 Timothy, ed. Hilton C. Oswald, trans. Edward Sittler (St. Louis: Concordia Publishing House, 1973), 20–1)

40. Luther, *Luther's Works*, Volume 1, 211. By "when the Gospel was first proclaimed" it is possible that Luther does not mean for the first time, that is, first-century Palestine, but in his own day and age, that is, when he himself restored the true meaning to the Gospel, so long suppressed and mutilated by the medieval church.
41. Ibid.
42. Ibid., 212.
43. Ibid., 214.
44. Luther, *Luther's Works*, Volume 28, 349.
45. Luther, *Luther's Works*, Volume 1, 212.
46. See Georges Duby, *The Three Orders: Feudal Society Imagined*, trans. Arthur Goldhammer, repr. ed. (Chicago: University of Chicago Press, 1982).
47. Luther, *Luther's Works*, Volume 1, 212.
48. Ibid.
49. Ibid.
50. Ibid., 213.
51. Ibid.
52. Ibid.
53. Ibid.
54. Ibid., 213–14.
55. Martin Luther, *Luther's Works*, Volume 24: Sermons on the Gospel of St. John Chapters 14–16, ed. Jaroslav Pelikan, asst. ed. Daniel E. Poellot, trans. Martin H. Bertram (St. Louis: Concordia Publishing House, 1961), 161.
56. Ibid, 162.
57. Ibid.
58. Martin Luther, *Sermons of Martin Luther: The House Postils*, Volume 3, 47.
59. Ibid., 47–8.
60. Ibid., 48.
61. Ibid.
62. Ibid., 47. See also Luther, *Luther's Works*, Volume 21: The Sermon on the Mount (Sermons) and the Magnificat, ed. Jaroslav Pelikan, trans. Jaroslav Pelikan (St. Louis: Concordia Publishing House, 1956), 265:

    > Nothing but good fruit can come from the station that God has created and ordained, and from the man who works and lives in this station on the basis of the Word of God. With this you can now comfort your heart against thoughts like these: "Oh, it was this person or that who got me into this station. It causes me nothing but disgust and trouble." I have often been tempted this way in connection with my own office, and still am. If it had not been for the Word of God, I would have stopped preaching a long time ago and would have said farewell to the world, the way the monks used to do. It is the devil himself doing this and making everyone's station hard for him.

63. Luther, *Luther's Works*, Volume 24: Sermons on the Gospel of St. John Chapters 14–16, 162.
64. Martin Luther, *Luther's Works*, Volume 45: The Christian in Society II, ed. Walther I. Brandt, gen. ed. Helmut T. Lehmann, "Exposition of Psalm 127, for the Christians at Riga in Livonia," trans. Walther I. Brandt (Philadelphia, PA: Muhlenberg Press, 1962), 323.
65. Ibid.
66. Ibid.

67. Ibid., 324–5.
68. Ibid., 326.
69. Martin Luther, *Luther's Works*, Volume 9: Lectures on Deuteronomy, ed. Jaroslav Pelikan, asst. ed. Daniel Poellot, trans. Richard R. Caemmerer (St. Louis: Concordia Publishing House, 1960), 96.
70. Ibid.
71. Martin Luther, *Luther's Works*, Volume 15: Notes on Ecclesiastes/Lectures on the Song of Solomon/Treatise on the Last Words of David, ed. Jaroslav Pelikan, assoc. ed. Hilton C. Oswald, trans. Jaroslav Pelikan (St. Louis: Concordia Publishing House, 1972), 151.
72. Ibid., 152.
73. Luther, *Luther's Works*, Volume 45: The Christian in Society II, 325.
74. Ibid.
75. See Martin Luther, *Luther's Works*, Volume 3: Lectures on Genesis Chapters 15–20, ed. Jaroslav Pelikan, trans. George V. Schick (St. Louis: Concordia Publishing House, 1961), 290: "But the diligent and godly the Lord will make rich, for 'He fulfills the desire of all who fear Him' [Psalm 145:19]." See also *Luther's Works*, Volume 9, 75: "For while it is true that the busy hand produces riches, nevertheless what Solomon also said is true, that only the blessing of the Lord makes wealthy men, namely, through the busy hand (Prov. 10:22). For if the busy hand were to be hindered by force, the blessing of the Lord would still enrich." Finally, see Luther, *Luther's Works*, Volume 17: Lectures on Isaiah Chapters 40–66, ed. Hilton C. Oswald, trans. Herbert J. A. Bouman (St. Louis: Concordia Publishing House, 1972), 248.

> This is the way it goes in the physical realm: the one does the work, the other reaps. But a Christian who has the Spirit will have both the work and the fruit, and no one else shall have it. Therefore it is a great comfort to know that God approves of his work and toil, and it is certain that we may look for the reward.

76. Martin Luther, *Luther's Works*, Volume 45: The Christian in Society II, 325. Johann Heinz, in his "Luther's Doctrine of Work and Reward," *Andrews University Seminary Studies* 22.1 (Spring 1984): 45–69, does not deal with these exact passages of Scripture but with a host of others, and he effectively shows how Luther accounted for biblical passages that implied a direct reward for effort.
77. Ibid., 326.
78. Ibid. See also the second sermon for the Fifteenth Sunday after Trinity, on the Sermon on the Mount in *The Sermons of Martin Luther: The House Postils*, Volume 3, 18:

> By this, however, Christ does not command that people should not work. For even birds, though they neither sow nor reap, nor gather into granaries, nor do the kind of work that man does, nevertheless, have their work cut out for them; they have to spread their wings and fly about to get their food. Similarly we, too, must work ... Worry is forbidden, that people think God has deserted them and believe they must occupy their minds with anxiety. Even though they have enough of everything, some still do not want to trust in God. This is forbidden; for when we fret, we are fools. If grain is to thrive in the ground, God alone must grant it; our worrying will not accomplish it. For what can we do about it if this year everything in the field wilts and dies off? Clearly, right before our eyes, everything is in God's hands; he is the one who must bring it to pass. However, we are doubting people; we have not learned to believe, but instead we worry.

79. Ibid., 327. Hannah Arendt makes an interesting observation on Luther's theology of labor. She interprets him as scrupulously purging his remarks on labor of any suggestion that it involves making or producing. "Human labor," she writes of Luther, "according to him is only 'finding' the treasures God has put into the earth. Following the Old Testament, he stresses the utter dependence of man upon the earth, not his mastery." See Hannah Arendt, *The Human Condition* (Chicago: University of Chicago Press, 1958), 139–40 n3.
80. Ibid.
81. Ibid. See also Luther, *Luther's Works*, Volume 3, Lectures on Genesis Chapters 15–20, 290:

> To be sure, God does everything; but we, too, must do what belongs to our calling. He gives bread to nourish and preserve the body; but He gives it to him who labors, sows, reaps, etc. And when you sow the land, you must not think that nothing will result from your labor. For it is God's command that you should do your duty, and He wants to work through you. Therefore you must devote yourself to your work and duty with all your strength and attention, and leave the rest to God.

82. Luther, *Luther's Works*, Volume 9, Lectures on Deuteronomy, 96.
83. Incidentally, Luther cited Bernard more than any other non-biblical source, over five hundred times. See Theo. M. M. A. C. Bell, "Luther's Reception of Bernard of Clairvaux," *Concordia Theological Quarterly* 59.4 (October 1995): 245–77, p. 248; and Franz Posset, "Bernard of Clairvaux as Luther's Source," *Concordia Theological Quarterly* 54.4 (October 1990): 281–304, p. 299.
84. Luther, *Luther's Works*, Volume 15: Notes on Ecclesiastes/Lectures on the Song of Solomon/Treatise on the Last Words of David, 8.
85. Ibid., 9.
86. Luther, *Luther's Works*, Volume 9: Lectures on Deuteronomy, 41.
87. Ibid.
88. Ibid., 75.
89. Luther, *Sermons of Martin Luther: The House Postils*, Volume 2, 288.
90. Ibid., 288–9.
91. Ibid., 41.
92. Martin Luther, *Luther's Works*, Volume 14: Selected Psalms III, ed. Jaroslav Pelikan, asst. ed. Daniel E. Poellot, trans. Edward Sittler (St. Louis: Concordia Publishing House, 1958), 114.
93. Ibid.
94. Martin Luther, *Luther's Works*, Volume 30: The Catholic Epistles, ed. Jaroslav Pelikan, assoc. ed. Walter A. Hansen, trans. Martin H. Bertram (St. Louis: Concordia Publishing House, 1967), 94.
95. Ibid., 95.
96. Luther, *Luther's Works*, Volume 15, 98.
97. Ibid.
98. Ibid., 99.
99. Luther, *Sermons of Martin Luther: The House Postils*, Volume 3, 49.
100. Luther, *Luther's Works*, Volume 21, 193.
101. Ibid., 194.
102. Luther, *Sermons of Martin Luther: The House Postils*, Volume 3, 11.
103. Luther, *Luther's Works*, Volume 21, 265.

104. Ibid., 266.
105. See Luther, *Sermons of Martin Luther: The House Postils*, Volume 3, 10: "In the world's eyes it's a big deal when a monk denies himself everything, enters a cloister, leads a disciplined, austere life, fasts, prays, and so on. No lack of activity exists there, except only that God's command is lacking to do these things. Therefore, this cannot be extolled as serving God."
106. Ibid.
107. Luther, *Luther's Works*, Volume 24: Sermons on the Gospel of St. John Chapters 14–16, 231.
108. Ibid.
109. Ibid.
110. Ibid., 232.
111. Ibid.
112. Luther, *Luther's Works*, Volume 30: The Catholic Epistles, 96.
113. Ibid., 95.
114. Hart rightly suggests that Luther may have been influenced in this direction by Johannes Tauler and exponents of the devotio moderna movement. See Hart, "The Teaching of Luther and Calvin about Ordinary Work: 1. Martin Luther (1483–1546)," 40–1.
115. Luther, *Sermons of Martin Luther: The House Postils*, Volume 3, 10.

7 John Ruskin

1. P. D. Anthony, *John Ruskin's Labour: A Study of Ruskin's Social Theory* (Cambridge: Cambridge University Press, 1983), 173. See also John Ruskin, *Unto This Last*, in *The Works of John Ruskin*, Library Edition XVII, ed. E. T. Cook and Alexander Wedderburn (London: George Allen, 1905), 73–4.
2. John Ruskin, *Præterita: Outlines of Scenes and Thoughts Perhaps Worthy of Memory in My Past Life* (Orpington: George Allen, 1886), in *The Works of John Ruskin*, Library Edition XXXV (London: George Allen, 1908), 13.
3. Anthony, *John Ruskin's Labour*, 10–11; 30–1.
4. Ibid., 15–19.
5. John D. Rosenberg notes that this was his lifelong habit: "Almost from infancy Ruskin was forced to find in his powers of eye and mind the chief pleasures of his being." See his *The Darkening Glass: A Portrait of Ruskin's Genius* (New York: Columbia University Press, 1986), 1.
6. John Ruskin, "A Joy for Ever," in *The Works of John Ruskin*, Library Edition XVI, ed. E. T. Cook and Alexander Wedderburn (London: George Allen, 1906), 10. Ruskin was not an admirer of Smith, to say the least. He proclaimed him an evangelist of the "gospel of Covetousness" (Ruskin, *Fors Clavigera Volume VI*, 511), the gist of which Ruskin summarized as follows:

> Indeed, when Adam Smith formally, in the name of the philosophers of Scotland and England, set up this opposite God, on the hill of cursing against blessing, Ebal against Gerizim; and declared that all men "naturally" desire their neighbours' goods; and that in the name of Covetousness, all the nations of the earth should be blessed,—it is true, that the half-bred and half-witted Scotchman had not gift enough in him to carve so much as his own

calf's head on a whin-stone with his own hand; much less to produce a well molten and forged piece of gold, for old Scottish faith to break its tables of ten commandments at sight of. But, in leaving to every artless and ignorant boor among us the power of breeding, in imagination, each his own particular calf, and placidly worshipping that privately fatted animal; or, perhaps,—made out of the purest fat of it in molten Tallow instead of molten Gold,—images, which may be in any inventive moment, misshapen anew to his mind, Economical Theology has granted its disciples more perfect and fitting privilege. (ibid., 516)

More than once Ruskin attributes to Smith the promulgation of a commandment to hate God and our neighbors. See *Fors Clavigera Volume VI*, 764 and *Volume VII*, 134.

7. John Ruskin, *The Two Paths: Being Lectures on Art and Its Application to Decoration and Manufacture, Delivered in 1858-9* (London: Smith, Elder, 1859), in *The Works of John Ruskin*, Library Edition XVI, ed. E. T. Cook and Alexander Wedderburn (London: George Allen, 1906), 406n.
8. Frederick William Roe, *The Social Philosophy of Carlyle and Ruskin*, repr. ed. (originally published 1921) (Fort Washington, NY: Kennikat Press, 1969), 187.
9. Quoted in Roe, *The Social Philosophy of Carlyle and Ruskin*, 179–80.
10. The chapter was powerfully influential on William Morris, whose Kelmscott Press reprinted it in a standalone volume, and Ruskin himself acknowledged it as "precisely and accurately the most important chapter in the whole book," containing "all that I have to bring forward respecting architecture." See Roe, *The Social Philosophy of Carlyle and Ruskin*, 180.
11. Roe, *The Social Philosophy of Carlyle and Ruskin*, 181.
12. John Ruskin, *The Stones of Venice Volume II*, Library Edition X, ed. E. T. Cook and Alexander Wedderburn (London: George Allen, 1904), 189–90.
13. Ibid., 190.
14. Ibid., 191.
15. Roe, *The Social Philosophy of Carlyle and Ruskin*, 182.
16. Ruskin, *The Stones of Venice*, 197.
17. Ibid., 192.
18. Ibid., 193–4.
19. Ibid., 194.
20. Ibid., 196.
21. Ibid. In fairness to Smith, against both Ruskin and Marx, it should be noted that in *The Wealth of Nations* Smith himself acknowledged this very drawback with respect to division of labor in no uncertain terms. He writes,

In the progress of the division of labor, the employment of the far greater part of those who live by labor, that is, of the great body of people, comes to be confined to a few very simple operations; frequently to one or two. But the understandings of the greater part of men are necessarily formed by their ordinary employments. The man whose whole life is spent in performing a few simple operations, of which the effects too are, perhaps, always the same, or very nearly the same, has no occasion to exert his understanding, or to exercise his invention in finding out expedients for removing difficulties which never occur. He naturally loses, therefore, the habit of such exertion, and generally becomes as stupid and ignorant as it is possible for a human creature to become. ... But in every improved and civilized society this is the state into which the laboring poor, that is, the great

body of the people, must necessarily fall, unless government takes some pains to prevent it. (Vol. 3 (New York: P. F. Collier, 1909), 162, 163)
22. Ruskin, *The Stones of Venice*, 196.
23. Ibid., 196–7.
24. Ibid., 197.
25. John Ruskin, *Lectures on Architecture and Painting, Delivered at Edinburgh in November, 1853* (London: Smith, Elder, 1854), in *Works of John Ruskin*, Library Edition XII, ed. E. T. Cook and Alexander Wedderburn (London: George Allen, 1904), 68.
26. Ruskin, *The Stones of Venice*, 200.
27. Ibid.
28. Ibid.
29. Ibid., 201.
30. Ruskin, *Unto This Last*, 74.
31. The provision of such an education is what Ruskin calls the second duty of government, behind the provision of "food, fuel, and clothes" necessary for life. See John Ruskin, *Fors Clavigera: Letters to the Workmen and Labourers of Great Britain Volume VI* (Orpington: George Allen, 1876), in *The Works of John Ruskin*, Library Edition XXVIII, ed. E. T. Cook and Alexander Wedderburn (London: George Allen, 1907), 651. He despairs that such education has not been extended to the working class, showing not that the working classes are unsusceptible to being so educated but only that the effort has not been tried. As Cook and Wedderburn note, "that education should be mainly an ethical process, and not a machinery for the acquisition of knowledge, was a constant theme with Ruskin." See their additional references at 429 n2.
32. John Ruskin, *Fors Clavigera: Letters to the Workmen and Labourers of Great Britain Volume I* (Orpington: George Allen, 1871), in *The Works of John Ruskin*, Library Edition XXVII, ed. E. T. Cook and Alexander Wedderburn (London: George Allen, 1907), 39. See also John Ruskin, *Sesame and Lilies: Two Lectures Delivered at Manchester in 1864* (London: Smith, Elder, 1865), in *The Works of John Ruskin*, Library Edition XVIII (London: George Allen, 1905), 184: "You will find nearly every educational problem solved, as soon as you truly want to do something; everybody will become of use in their own fittest way, and will learn what is best for them to know in that use."
33. Ruskin, *The Stones of Venice*, 201.
34. Ibid., 201.
35. Ibid.
36. Ibid., 202. Again note that for Ruskin it is fair and right that differences in the quality and outlay of work should attract different levels of reward and esteem.
37. John Ruskin, *Lectures on Art Delivered before the University of Oxford in Hilary Term, 1870* (Oxford: Clarendon Press, 1870), in *The Works of Ruskin*, Library Edition XX, ed. E. T. Cook and Alexander Wedderburn (London: George Allen, 1905), 113. Ruskin perhaps for the first time in Western thought weds a classical objection to banausia to an incipient modern proto-environmentalism.
38. Ibid., 114.
39. Ibid. See also additional references in Roe, *The Social Philosophy of Carlyle and Ruskin*, 214 n2, where the author documents extensive support for his claim that "Ruskin recognized certain kinds of work as debasing and 'mechanical':—'*simply* or *totally*

manual work; that, alone, *is degrading.*'" Ruskin means here of course manual work that involves no contribution from the intellect, not manual work per se but work that is only manual and not at all creative or "inventive" as he often says.

40. Ruskin, *Fors Clavigera Volume I*, 180.
41. Ruskin, *The Two Paths*, 396.
42. John Ruskin *The Crown of Wild Olive: Three Lectures on Work, Traffic, and War* (London: Smith, Elder, 1866), in *The Works of John Ruskin*, Library Edition XVIII, ed. E. T. Cook and Alexander Wedderburn (London: George Allen, 1905), 418.
43. John Ruskin, *Munera Pulveris: Six Essays on the Elements of Political Economy* (London: Smith, Elder, 1872), in *The Works of John Ruskin*, Library Edition XVII, ed. E. T. Cook and Alexander Wedderburn (London: George Allen, 1905), 182–3. This is actually a more expansive version of a briefer definition provided in *Unto This Last*, from the same volume, 94–5:

> Labour is the contest of the life of man with an opposite;—the term "life" including his intellect, soul, and physical power, contending with question, difficulty, trial, or material force. Labour is of a higher or lower order, as it includes more or fewer of the elements of life: and labour of good quality, in any kind, includes always as much intellect and feeling as will fully and harmoniously regulate the physical force.

44. Ruskin waxes eloquent on effort and its rewards at the close of chapter V of *The Seven Lamps of Architecture*, in *The Works of John Ruskin*, Library Edition VIII, ed. E. T. Cook and Alexander Wedderburn (London: George Allen, 1903), 219: "We have certain work to do for our bread, and that is to be done strenuously; other work to do for our delight, and that is to be done heartily: neither is to be done by halves and shifts, but with a will; and what is not worth this effort is not to be done at all."
45. Supritha Rajan, *A Tale of Two Capitalisms: Sacred Economics in Nineteenth-Century Britain* (Ann Arbor: University of Michigan Press, 2015), 70.
46. Ibid., 69.
47. Ruskin, *Unto This Last*, 75, quoting himself from *Modern Painters*, Library Edition III–V, in *The Complete Works of John Ruskin*, ed. E. T. Cook and Alexander Wedderburn (London: George Allen, 1903).
48. Ruskin, *Modern Painters*, 205.
49. Ibid., 206, 207.
50. Rajan, *A Tale of Two Capitalisms*, 70.
51. Ruskin, *Unto This Last*, 105. Relying again on classical etymology, Ruskin links "value" to the Latin "valere," meaning to be well or strong, such that "To be 'valuable,' therefore, is to 'avail towards life.'" See Ruskin, *Unto This Last*, 84.
52. Ruskin, *Unto This Last*, 105.
53. Ibid.
54. John Ruskin *Fors Clavigera Volume V* (Orpington: George Allen, 1875), in *The Works of John Ruskin*, Library Edition XXVIII, ed. E. T. Cook and Alexander Wedderburn (London: George Allen, 1907), 332.
55. Ruskin, *Sesame and Lilies*, 182.
56. Ibid. Ruskin claims that this is not only an individual obligation but also the first duty of any decent government. See Ruskin, *Fors Clavigera Volume VI*, 651.
57. Ruskin, *Sesame and Lilies*, 182.
58. Ibid.

59. Ruskin is outraged by the condescending and self-righteous attitude of the wealthy to the poor. To the (Lutheran?) suggestion that "everybody ought to remain content in the position in which Providence has placed them," Ruskin responds,

> Ah, my friends, that's the gist of the whole question. *Did* Providence put them in that position, or did *you*? You knock a man into a ditch, and then you tell him to remain content in the "position in which Providence has placed him." That's modern Christianity. You say—"*We* did not knock him into the ditch." We shall never know what you have done, or left undone, until the question with us, every morning, is not how to do the gainful thing, but how to do the just thing, during the day; nor until we are at least so far on the way to being Christian, as to acknowledge that maxim of the poor half-way Mahometan, "One hour in the execution of justice is worth seventy years of prayer." (Ruskin, *The Crown of Wild Olive*, 422)

60. Ibid., 182–3.
61. See Ruskin, "*Unto This Last*," 75. Ruskin's denunciations pull no punches:

> The writings which we (verbally) esteem as divine, not only denounce the love of money as the source of all evil, and as an idolatry abhorred of the Deity, but declare mammon service to be the accurate and irreconcilable opposite of God's service: and, whenever they speak of riches absolute, and poverty absolute, declare woe to the rich, and blessing to the poor. Whereupon we forthwith investigate a science of becoming rich, as the shortest road to national prosperity. (ibid., 75–6)

62. John Ruskin, *On the Old Road*, Library Edition XXXIV, ed. E. T. Cook and Alexander Wedderburn (London: George Allen, 1908), 206.
63. It's unfortunate that this thought is not followed up by Ruskin: The theological implications seem potentially weighty. We will soon see that Simone Weil pursued the suggestion with more interest.
64. Ruskin, *Munera Pulveris*, 192.
65. Ruskin, *On the Old Road*, 206–7. Ruskin also associates 2 Thessalonians 3:10 with his discussion of property, which he divides into no fewer than five categories. Briefly, the first is the common property of humanity, necessary to life and which cannot be obtained by work and to which all persons are entitled a share (air to breathe and water to drink); second is property necessary to life but brought about only by work and to which again all persons are entitled a share, provided that they work for it indeed and such that it would be immoral to hoard more of it than required (food, clothing, shelter, tools needed for labor); third is property that provides pleasure but is unnecessary for life (luxuries like delicate foodstuffs, racing horses, gold and jewels) and of questionable moral value; fourth is property affording intellectual gratification (which Ruskin admits is difficult to distinguish finally from the third sort, the value here being context-sensitive); and fifth is property of only documentary value (money). Ruskin invokes 2 Thessalonians 3:10 in his discussion of the second type of property, to which interested readers should refer for illuminating details and provocative arguments. See the whole of his discussion at 130–9 of "*A Joy for Ever," (and Its Price in the Market): Being Substance (with Additions) of Two Lectures on the Political Economy of Art* (Orpington: George Allen, 1880), in *The Works of John Ruskin*, Library Edition XVI, ed. E. T. Cook and Alexander Wedderburn (London: George Allen, 1905).

66. Ruskin, *Munera Pulveris*, 264.
67. John Ruskin, *Time and Tide, by Weare and Tyne: Twenty-Five Letters to a Working Man of Sunderland on the Laws of Work* (London: Smith, Elder and Co., 1867), in *The Works of John Ruskin*, Library Edition XVII, ed. E. T. Cook and Alexander Wedderburn (London: George Allen, 1905), 388.
68. Ibid., 389.
69. Ibid. See also *The Two Paths*, where Ruskin again asserts,

> Generally modern speculation involves much risk to others, with chance of profit only to ourselves; even in its best conditions it is merely one of the forms of gambling or treasure-hunting: it is either leaving the steady plough and the steady pilgrimage of life, to look for silver mines beside the way; or else it is the full stop beside the dice-tables in Vanity Fair—investing all the thoughts and passions of the soul in the fall of the cards, and choosing rather the wild accidents of idle fortune than the calm and accumulative rewards of toil. And this is destructive enough, at least to our peace and virtue. But it is usually destructive of far more than *our* peace, or *our* virtue. (403)

Ruskin's example of this wide-ranging impact of such bogus speculation is one that is eerily relevant to our own setting: "the suffering, the guilt, and the mortality caused necessarily by the failure of any large-dealing merchant, or largely-branched bank" (ibid.).

70. Ruskin, *The Two Paths*, 396.
71. Ibid., 401–2.
72. Ibid., 402. Once again Ruskin unleashes an avalanche of Scriptural citations to support his point that the Bible plainly forbids all manner of taking advantage of the poor, and yet not only is buying goods that cannot possibly have properly recompensed the work undertaken to produce them not censured but congratulated. See Ruskin, *The Two Paths*, 397–401.
73. Ruskin, *The Two Paths*, 405–6.
74. Ibid., 406. See also Ruskin, *Time and Tide*, 391–2, where Ruskin again solicits Scripture's horror at the sin of theft, which he thinks is practiced at the very fundament of modern economy.
75. Ruskin, *Unto This Last*, 90–1.
76. Ibid., 91.
77. Ruskin, *Unto This Last*, 92. Ruskin also came to the view at some stage in his thinking that the charging of interest is another widespread but immoral form of taking advantage over others in need. See Ruskin, *Munera Pulveris*, 220 n and 271 n. See also Ruskin, *Modern Painters*, 3–4: "And knavery is not the less knavery because it involves large interests, nor theft the less theft because it is countenanced by usage, or accompanied by failure in undertaken duty."
78. Ruskin, "A Joy for Ever," 139.
79. Ibid.
80. Ibid. Ruskin was clear on this point in *Modern Painters Volume V* and equally frustrated that so little mind was paid to it:

> I cannot repeat too often (for it seems almost impossible to arouse the public mind in the least to a sense of the fact) that the root of all benevolent and helpful action toward the lower classes consists in the wise direction of

purchase; that is to say, in spending money, as far as possible, only for products of healthful and natural labour. (427 n)

81. Ruskin, *Time and Tide*, 336.
82. Ruskin, *The Crown of Wild Olive*, 424.
83. Ibid., 425.
84. Ibid., 425–6.
85. Ruskin says this frequently. Earlier in the same lecture he said "rough work is at all events real, honest, and, generally, though not always, useful; while the fine work is, a great deal of it, foolish and false, as well as fine, and therefore dishonourable" (Ruskin, *The Crown of Wild Olive*, 418). See also Ruskin, *The Stones of Venice*, 453–4: "The evidence of labour becomes painful only when it is a *sign of Evil greater, as Evil, than the labour is great, as Good*." Ruskin goes on here to decry not work's difficulty but its foolishness when directed at aims not worth achieving or its fruitlessness when it fails to come to good issue. For Ruskin's further contention that hard work would improve the quality of the upper classes see Ruskin, *Modern Painters*, 344:

> Gentlemen have to learn that it is no part of their duty or privilege to live on other people's toil. They have to learn that there is no degradation in the hardest manual, or the humblest servile, labour, when it is honest. But that there *is* degradation, and that deep, in extravagance, in bribery, in indolence, in pride, in taking places they are not fit for, or in coining places for which there is no need. It does not disgrace a gentleman to become an errand boy, or a day labourer; but it disgraces him much to become a knave, or a thief.

See also *Modern Painters*, 427–9:

> And let all physical exertion, so far as possible, be utilised, and it will be found no man need ever work more than is good for him. I believe an immense gain in the bodily health and happiness of the upper classes would follow on their steadily endeavouring, however clumsily, to make the physical exertion they now necessarily take in amusements, definitely serviceable. It would be far better, for instance, that a gentleman should mow his own fields, than ride over other people's.

86. Ruskin, *The Crown of Wild Olive*, 426. Ruskin was blunter and more succinct in *Fors Clavigera Volume I*, 39: "The labour producing no useful result was demoralizing. All such labour is. The labour producing useful result was educational in its influence on the temper. All such labour is."
87. See Karl Marx, "Economic and Philosophical Manuscripts," in *Karl Marx: Early Writings*, ed. Quintin Hoare, trans. Gregor Benton (New York: Vintage Books, 1975).
88. Ruskin, *The Crown of Wild Olive*, 427.
89. Ibid.
90. Ibid., 427–8.
91. Ibid., 429.
92. Ibid., 430–1.
93. Ibid., 424 n3.
94. Ruskin, *Fors Clavigera Volume IV*, 174.
95. Ibid.
96. Ibid., 175.

97. Ibid.
98. Ibid., 176. Ruskin criticizes hothouses as an ersatz and overly delicate substitute for the work of real gardening. In the same letter he replies to a young lady's question for why he advises that they abstain from working in hothouses. He submits four reasons:

> First, then—The primal object of your gardening, for yourself, is to keep you at work in the open air, whenever it is possible. The greenhouse will always be a refuge to you from the wind; which, on the contrary, you ought to be able to bear; and will tempt you into clippings and pottings and pettings, and mere standing dilettantism in a damp and over-scented room, instead of true labour in fresh air.
> Secondly.—It will not only itself involve unnecessary expense—(for the greenhouse is sure to turn into a hot-house in the end; and even if not, is always having its panes broken, or its blinds going wrong, or its stands getting rickety); but it will tempt you into buying nursery plants, and waste your time in anxiety about them.
> Thirdly.—The use of your garden to the household ought to be mainly in the vegetables you can raise in it. And, for these, your proper observance of season, and of the authority of the stars, is a vital duty. Every climate gives its vegetable food to its living creatures at the right time; your business is to know that time, and be prepared for it, and to take the healthy luxury which nature appoints you, in the rare annual taste of the thing given in those its due days. The vile and gluttonous modern habit of forcing never allows people properly to taste anything.
> Lastly, and chiefly.—Your garden is to enable you to obtain such knowledge of plants as you may best use in the country in which you live by communicating it to others; and teaching them to take pleasure in the green herb, given for meat, and the coloured flower, given for joy. And your business is not to make the greenhouse or hothouse rejoice and blossom like the rose, but the wilderness and solitary place. (Ruskin, *Fors Clavigera Volume IV*, 182)

99. John Ruskin, *Valle Crucis: Studies in Monastic History and Architecture*, in *The Works of John Ruskin*, Library Edition XXXIII, ed. E. T. Cook and Alexander Wedderburn (London: George Allen, 1908), 236.
100. Ibid., 237.
101. Ibid. Put in fewer words, "In the proclamation, then, of useful labour as man's duty upon earth, and of the Sun of Righteousness as his Lord in Heaven, you have the Benedictine gospel" (Ruskin, *Valle Crucis*, 239). See also Ruskin's treatment of Francis, with whom he associates a form of "Universal Monasticism," in *The Aesthetics and Mathematic Schools of Art in Florence* (London and Orpington: George Allen, 1906) in *The Works of John Ruskin*, Library Edition XXIII, ed. E. T. Cook and Alexander Wedderburn (London: George Allen, 1906), 256.
102. Ibid., 425 n3.
103. For Ruskin's own awareness of this charge, see Ruskin, *Munera Pulveris*, 270, as well as the introduction to the same volume (Library Edition XVII), cxi.
104. Earlier in the same lecture, Ruskin inveighs against this very same hypocrisy of outwardly professing belief while failing to actually serve God in the way that Scripture commands, which is through concrete, tangible acts of justice. See Ruskin, *The Crown of Wild Olive*, 420: "That is the one thing constantly reiterated by our

Master—the order of all others that is given oftenest—'Do justice and judgment.' That's your Bible order; that's the 'Service of God'—not praying nor psalm-singing."
105. Matthew 7:23.
106. Ibid.

8 Simone Weil

1. Robert Chenavier, "Simone Weil: Completing Platonism through a Consistent Materialism," in *The Christian Platonism of Simone Weil*, ed. E. Jane Doering and Eric O. Springsted (Notre Dame, IN: University of Notre Dame Press, 2004), 61–93, p. 65.
2. Simone Weil, *Œuvres Complètes I: Premieres écrits philosophiques*, ed. Gilbert Kahn and Rolf Kühn (Paris: Gallimard, 1988), 246. Translations from *Œuvres Complètes I* my own.
3. Ibid., 249.
4. Ibid., 246.
5. Ibid.
6. Ibid.
7. Ibid., 246–7.
8. Ibid., 247. In yet another example, one that only Weil could devise, she says when you read in the newspaper about the cruelties of a tyrant and find your fist clenched in anger, this is a spontaneous movement of the living body that only becomes work when transformed or perhaps better yet, I would say disciplined, such that you learn how to shoot accurately in order to kill the tyrant. As Weil wryly notes, the aim of this project would actually be thwarted by anger (ibid.). Weil reuses the example of picking a fruit in "De la perception ou l'aventure de Protée," concluding there as well that "To act indirectly is to work" (Weil, *Œuvres Complètes I*, 125).
9. For this reason Weil also associates work with "distance" and its overcoming (Weil, *Œuvres Complètes I*, 247).
10. "Work is done, not in consequence of a need, but in view of an end" (Weil, *Œuvres Complètes I*, 247).
11. Weil, *Œuvres Complètes I*, 246.
12. Ibid., 248.
13. Ibid., 378.
14. Simone Weil, "The Pythagorean Doctrine," in *Intimations of Christianity among the Ancient Greeks*, ed. and trans. Elizabeth Chase Geissbuhler (London: Routledge and Kegan Paul, 1957), 178.
15. Ibid. James Gordon Calder puts this well in his dissertation, "Labour and Thought in the Philosophy of Simone Weil (1909–1943): Preface to a Philosophy of Education." PhD dissertation, (Dalhousie University, 1985): "For Weil there is, in actuality, only one kind of thought, free thought, and liberty has certain objective conditions. It cannot be conceived of as the simple disappearance of necessity. On the contrary, it lies in the very attempt to conceive the necessary" (52).
16. Simone Weil, *Oppression and Liberty*, trans. Arthur Wills and John Petrie (Amherst: University of Massachusetts Press, 1973), 85.
17. Calder, "Labour and Thought in the Philosophy of Simone Weil," 51.
18. This doctrine is of a piece with her reconstructed Platonism, which she argued in order to complete itself as a rigorous philosophical outlook had to embrace a kind

of materialism. The complexities of her remarkable ontology cannot be limned here, but interested readers should consult Robert Chenavier, "Simone Weil: Completing Platonism through a Consistent Materialism" and Patrick Patterson and Lawrence E. Schmidt, "The Christian Materialism of Simone Weil," in *The Christian Platonism of Simone Weil*.

19. Weil, *Œuvres Complètes I*, 379.
20. Ibid.
21. Ibid., 248.
22. Part of the reason for this self-separation, and unfortunately this theme takes us too far afield in a study of this length, is because work exposes us to time. Elsewhere Weil writes,

> The perpetual dialectic of time by which, either in memory or in the project, I find myself always far from myself, is the law of work. There was no time in the earthly Paradise, and it is in this that the earthly Paradise consisted; at the same time that man was condemned to work, he was condemned to grow old. Growing old is going from project to work. Not that time follows the rhythm of our work; it expresses the very condition of work, a condition that never, and not even when we are sleeping, ceases to be our condition. In this respect time is outside of time; time is eternal; time is in some way always present, because the world cannot be absent. (ibid., 245)

The final phrase recalls a twist on Arthur Rimbaud's "true life is elsewhere. We are not in the world," an aphorism also twisted as the opening line of Emmanuel Levinas's *Totality and Infinity*: "The true life is absent. But we are in the world." For our purposes, Weil seems here to imply that work is a condemnation imposed upon humanity as a result of expulsion from the earthly Paradise, a minority, not to say heterodox, position, as we have seen. Weil does seem to endorse this position though, as can be seen from an aside in her essay "Classical Science and After." There she writes, "The totality of geometrical and mechanical necessities to which the action is always subject constitutes the primal curse which fell upon Adam, which makes the difference between the world and an earthly paradise, the curse of labor." The essay is available in Simone Weil, *On Science, Necessity, and the Love of God*, ed. Richard Rees (Oxford: Oxford University Press, 1968), 3–43, p. 6.

23. Quoted at Chenavier, "Simone Weil: Completing Platonism through a Consistent Materialism," 74.
24. Simone Weil, "Introduction" to Factory Journal, in *Formative Writings: 1929–1941*, ed. and trans. Dorothy Tuck McFarland and Wilhelmina van Ness (Amherst: University of Massachusetts Press, 1987), 151.
25. Weil, Factory Journal, in *Formative Writings: 1929–1941*, 155–235. See also Françoise Meltzer, "The Hands of Simone Weil," *Critical Inquiry* 27.4 (2001): 611–28, p. 614.
26. "Reflections Concerning the Causes of Liberty and Social Oppression," in *Oppression and Liberty*, 37–124, p. 110.
27. It should be noted that for Weil this dynamic is partly attributable to the character of the machine itself. Calder puts this best:

> A machine is composed of bits of matter arranged in relation to one another according to the pattern of linguistic relations present to the mind of its inventor. In this sense it is a piece of language. Matter is thus capable of embodying, independently of mind, linguistic relations. The sounds of the

> human voice, like the marks of a hand writing on a sheet of paper, are things and they can be artificially arranged in relation to one another according to the rules of custom and convention. From this perspective a machine is a piece of language that functions to produce a certain effect without the need [or even the opportunity] of its thought being present to the mind of the individual using it. Customary forms of behaviour, formulaic expressions of all kinds, skills, habits, techniques, and the very social organization of labour, are all collective ways in which human activity is governed and directed by the material establishment of linguistic relations outside the sphere of individual consciousness.

See Calder, "Labour and Thought in the Philosophy of Simone Weil," 207–8. See also Meltzer, "The Hands of Simone Weil," 617: "The machine, she writes, liberates thought, unless the work is assembly line, which abases the worker. But that, she adds, is not the machine's fault."

28. "Reflections Concerning the Causes of Liberty and Social Oppression," 110. See also Calder, "Labour and Thought in the Philosophy of Simone Weil," 240: "For Weil the increasing chaos in all spheres of our society, and in the economic sphere in particular, is directly due to the thoughtless and therefore irresponsible subordination of the labouring masses to leaders who are, themselves, irresponsibly thoughtless and, in any case, overwhelmed by an unthinkable mass of detail."
29. Calder, "Labour and Thought in the Philosophy of Simone Weil," 30.
30. Ibid., 33–4.
31. Simone Weil, *Gravity and Grace*, trans. Arthur Wills (New York: Putnam's, 1952), 212.
32. Note here that unlike in Marx's later thought, the issue is not that the boss controls the means of production and the worker does not. For Weil the opposition of worker to boss is not a function of class (she critiqued Marx for his understanding of class) but of the separation of the working and thinking activities of the human being. On Weil's early, preconversion difference from Marx on this point, see Johanna Selles-Roney, "'Is This Not the Kind of Fasting I Have Chosen?' Simone Weil's Life and Labor," in *Political Theory and Christian Vision: Essays in Memory of Bernard Zylstra*, ed. Jonathan Chaplin and Paul Marshall (Lanham, MD: University Press of America, 1994), 269:

> Marx had recognized the power of bureaucracy to oppress, particularly in the form of the bureaucratic and military machine of the state. Marx had, however, located the problem of the separation of spiritual forces of labor from manual labor in the operation of capitalist economy. By contrast, she [Weil] believed that in any economic system the existence of a managerial class or a bureaucratic caste guaranteed the existence of an oppressive system.

On Weil's critique of Marx (and in fact for a rather sensitive and careful study of Weil's relationship to Marx in general), see Robert Sparling, "Theory and Praxis: Simone Weil and Marx on the Dignity of Labor," *Review of Politics* 74 (2012): 87–107, pp. 95–6, 100–5. See also Lawrence A. Blum and Victor J. Seidler, *A Truer Liberty: Simone Weil and Marxism* (New York: Routledge, 1989). Some of Weil's own concentrated critiques of Marx, which she claims she intimated in her youth and found unanswered by Marxists, are available in "On the Contradictions of Marxism," in *Oppression and Liberty*.
33. Selles-Roney, "'Is This Not the Kind of Fasting I Have Chosen?'," 273.
34. Simone Weil, "Factory Work," in *The Simone Weil Reader*, ed. George A. Panichas (New York: David McKay Company, 1977), 53–72, p. 54.

35. Ibid. Indeed, one of the impressions Weil took away from her experience was how reluctant the factory worker is to protest; factory work itself takes away all such initiative and defeats any attempt to challenge it. See Selles-Roney, "'Is This Not the Kind of Fasting I Have Chosen?,'" 273. This realization of hers is part of the reason why Weil was skeptical of revolution as either possible or desirable (269–72). See also Sparling, "Theory and Praxis: Simone Weil and Marx on the Dignity of Labor."
36. Weil, "Factory Work," 54.
37. Ibid., 55.
38. Ibid.
39. Ibid., 56.
40. Ibid., 57.
41. Ibid., 58.
42. Weil, "The Mysticism of Work," in *Gravity and Grace*, 232–236, p. 233.
43. Weil, "Factory Work," 59.
44. Ibid.
45. Ibid., 60.
46. Ibid.
47. Ibid., 61.
48. Ibid.
49. Ibid.
50. Ibid., 62.
51. Ibid.
52. Ibid., 63.
53. Ibid. Emphasis in the original.
54. Ibid., 64.
55. Ibid., 66.
56. Ibid., 66–7.
57. Ibid., 67.
58. Ibid., 68.
59. Ibid., 69.
60. Ibid.
61. We will see shortly that in later writings Weil makes additional suggestions for how to infuse work with the requisite sense of rhythm.
62. Weil, "Factory Work," 72.
63. Weil, *Oppression and Liberty*, 84.
64. Ibid.
65. Ibid.
66. Ibid., 85.
67. Ibid., 84.
68. Ibid., 179.
69. Simone Weil, "The First Condition for the Work of a Free Person," in *Simone Weil: Late Philosophical Writings*, ed. Eric O. Springsted and Lawrence E. Schmidt (Notre Dame, IN: University of Notre Dame Press, 2015), 131–43, p. 131.
70. Ibid., 132.
71. Ibid.
72. Ibid., 132–3.
73. Ibid., 133.
74. Ibid., 135. Needless to say, the conception of beauty here is not a dilettante's. Elsewhere Weil writes of beauty that it is something that the aesthete has turned into a

sacrilege by treating it as if it were to be handled and inspected. "Beauty is something to be eaten; it is a food. If we are going to offer the people Christian beauty purely on account of its beauty, it will have to be as a form of beauty which gives nourishment." See Simone Weil, *The Need for Roots: Prelude to a Declaration of Duties to Mankind*, trans. Arthur Wills (Boston, MA: Beacon Press, 1952), 93.

75. Ibid.
76. Ibid. The conjunction of the appeal to "bread" and the phrase "daily substance" so closely together implies a covert reference to the "daily bread" of the Lord's Prayer. This conceit is at the heart of Desmond Avery's *Beyond Power: Simone Weil and the Notion of Authority* (Lanham, MD: Lexington Books, 2008). Avery's commentary on "The First Condition for the Work of a Free Person" (131–42) is associated with the petition to "give us this day our daily bread." The parallel is sound, since Weil said the Our Father every day and wrote an essay on it. See *Waiting for God*, 71–2, and "Concerning the Our Father" in *Waiting for God*.
77. Weil, "The First Condition for the Work of a Free Person," 135.
78. Ibid., 136.
79. Ibid.
80. Of course this is exactly what the early monks did. Perhaps the very idea of it seems unthinkable in twentieth-century Europe. I suppose though that no one could *prevent* someone from praying while working.
81. John 12:24. Weil does not actually quote or cite the text directly here.
82. John 15:5. Again Weil does not directly refer to John's text.
83. Weil, "The First Condition for the Work of a Free Person," 137.
84. Ibid. See also Weil, *The Need for Roots*, 90:

> Just as the young *Jocistes* [members of the young Christian workers' movement] feel exalted at the thought of Christ as a workingman, so the peasants should take a similar pride in the part devoted in the New Testament parables to the life of the fields and in the sacred function ascribed to bread and wine, and derive therefrom the feeling that Christianity is something which belongs to them.

85. Ibid., 138. A similar passage occurs in *The Need for Roots*, without mention of Christ.

> Everything should be centered around the wonderful cycle whereby solar energy, poured down into plants, is retained in them by the action of chlorophyll, becomes concentrated in seeds and fruits, enters into Man in the form of food or drink, passes into his muscles and spends itself on preparing the soil. … Were the thought of this cycle to sink deep into the minds of peasants, it would permeate their labor with poetry. (87)

86. Ibid., 141. See also Springsted and Schmidt (eds.), *Late Philosophical Writings*, 112: "Physical labor, though it may be painful, is not in itself degrading. It is not art and it is not science; but it is something else which has a value that is absolutely equal to art and science."
87. Weil, "The First Condition for the Work of a Free Person," 138.
88. Ibid., 141.
89. Ibid., 142.
90. She seems to have in mind Job 3:18. See also Weil, *The Need for Roots*, 59–60:

> If the majority of workmen were highly qualified professionals, fairly frequently called upon to show inventiveness and initiative, each responsible for his

production and machine, the present discipline in regard to work would no longer serve any useful purpose. Some men could work at home; others in small workshops, which could very often be organized on a co-operative basis. At present, the rule of authority is exercised in an even more intolerable fashion in small factories than in large ones; but that is because they try to imitate the large ones. Such workshops would not be small factories, they would be industrial organisms of a new kind, in which a new spirit could blow; though small, they would be bound together by organic ties strong enough to enable them to form as a whole a large concern. There is about large concerns, in spite of all their defects, a special sort of poetry, and one for which workmen have nowadays acquired a taste.

91. Mark 3:28–30.
92. Weil, "The First Condition for the Work of a Free Person," 142. Unfortunately we cannot delve as deeply into the topic of attention as it deserves. It is a central theme of Weil's thought, and here we will simply remark that in this essay she says at its highest pitch attention is for her equivalent to prayer (139).
93. Weil, "The First Condition for the Work of a Free Person," 142.
94. For a classic discussion of how the festival relieved even the working person's burdens in the ancient world, affording the worker occasional opportunities for leisure, which was normally reserved for the nonworking, see Josef Pieper, *Leisure: The Basis of Culture*, trans. Alexander Dru (New York: Pantheon Books, 1952).
95. Ibid.
96. Given free rein to imagine an ideal situation to be implemented in postliberation France, Weil's extensive suggestions for how to organize working people's lives are rather more aspirational, not to say utopian. See Weil, *The Need for Roots*, 73–8.
97. Ibid., 143. There is likely an autobiographical element to Weil's thinking on the poetry of workers in and amidst the difficulty of their work. She attested to a series of experiences that progressively led her into a lifelong attraction to Christianity, the first of which was a visit with her parents after her stressful stint in the factories to a small fishing village in Portugal. There she witnessed a procession of fishermen's wives, who she recalled sang "hymns of heart-rending sadness." It was there she remembered that "the conviction was suddenly borne in upon me that Christianity is pre-eminently the religion of slaves, that slaves cannot help belonging to it, and I among others." See Simone Weil, *Waiting for God*, trans. Emma Craufurd (New York: Harper and Row, 1973), 67.
98. Simone Weil, "Le Christianisme et la vie des champs," in *Pensees sans ordre concernant l'amour de Dieu* (Paris: Gallimard, 1962), 21–33, p. 21.
99. Ibid. All translations of this essay are my own.
100. Ibid., 22.
101. Ibid., 24.
102. Ibid., 25.
103. Ibid., 26–9.
104. Ibid., 31.
105. Ibid., 31–2.
106. Ibid., 33. Such proposals have met with some skepticism. Thomas R. Nevin for one (who does comment directly on this rather obscure essay) writes,

> Weil believes that work, if regarded as a sacrifice, can be rescued from degradation; it can transform the worker's daily life. That this transformation presupposes a rather sophisticated, *normalien* consciousness and attention does not deter her. She feels that thinking about God should be like the leavening in bread, infinitely small. Besides, the priest would keep the faithful going with ceremonies and readings. But it is exactly these reflective exertions that betray the scheme: the farmer reckoning his labor a sacrifice, the priest delivering homilies on labor's religious symbolism—Weil forgets that symbols and rituals work best, if at all, on a nonreflected level, where considerations and reminders have no part. To rationalize a mystery is to destroy it. In her uncompromising way of uniting thought and action, Weil does not appreciate the irrational dynamic at the root of religious culture. ... The urge to uplift the farmer's mental life, to make a program of rituals, is an intellectual's mistake. (Thomas R. Nevin, *Simone Weil: Portrait of a Self-Exiled Jew* (Chapel Hill: University of North Carolina Press, 1991), 370)

107. See the "Preface" by T. S. Eliot to *The Need for Roots*, x–xi.
108. Ibid., 43.
109. Ibid.
110. Ibid., 47.
111. Ibid., 43–4.
112. Ibid., 44.
113. Ibid., 45.
114. Ibid., 94.
115. Ibid.
116. Ibid., 95.
117. Inese Radzins, "Simone Weil on Labor and Spirit," *Journal of Religious Ethics*, 45.2 (2017): 291–308. Her discussion of this vignette is on pages 297–301.
118. Ibid., 298.
119. Radzins does not quite say this, but I would add that implicit in the choice of a pregnant mother is a parallel between labor in the sense of bearing a child and labor in the sense of working at a task. Interestingly, the gendered nature of the example would have found the approval of John Ruskin, who frequently nominated sewing as the characteristically feminine labor and paired it with the characteristically masculine work of agriculture. The needle, he said more than once, is the woman's plow.

> I say, first, on our understanding the right use of the plough, with which, in justice to the fairest of our labourers, we must always associate that feminine plough—the needle. The first requirement for the happiness of a nation is that it should understand the function in this world of these two great instruments: a happy nation may be defined as one in which the husband's hand is on the plough, and the housewife's on the needle; so in due time reaping its golden harvest, and shining in golden vesture: and an unhappy nation is one which, acknowledging no use of plough nor needle, will assuredly at last find its storehouse empty in the famine, and its breast naked to the cold. (Ruskin, *The Two Paths*, 395–6)

> See also John Ruskin, *The Shepherd's Tower* in *The Works of John Ruskin*, Library Edition Volume XXIII, ed. E. T. Cook and Alexander Wedderburn (London: George

Allen, 1906), 417. Speaking of Adam and Eve, he writes, "The meaning of which entire myth is, as I read it, that men and women must both eat their bread with toil. That the first duty of man is to feed his family, and the first duty of the woman to clothe it."

120. Weil, *The Need for Roots*, 92.
121. It should be noted with Radzins that for Weil the realm of spirit is not just transcendent to the material world, which it is, but is also immanent to it at the same time. Work is at the pivot point between this world and the world beyond, so much so that the latter is realizable only in the former, as if on the flip side of it. Again the image of pregnancy might be a helpful clue. The unseen reality is incipient within the material world, not hovering above it like a ghost but unseen, alive, and incarnate. Radzins also accurately I think observes that pregnancy implies an irreplaceable individuality to work; no two children are exactly alike, and in the same way no meaningful task is accomplished in the exact same way as another. See Radzins, "Simone Weil on Labor and Spirit," 298–301.
122. Radzins, "Simone Weil on Labor and Spirit," 302.
123. Weil, *The Need for Roots*, 95.
124. More than once in this book Weil mentions the abandoned practice of sending apprentices on a "tour de France," not the bicycle race but a circuit that took student workers around a fixed itinerary of visits to the major production sites in the nation. This practice she regards as salutary, building camaraderie among the journeymen and perhaps (though she does not say this directly) imparting to work something of the meaning and moment of a pilgrimage. See Weil, *The Need for Roots*, 52, 76, and 84.
125. Radzins also advances some proposals that are in keeping with her interpretation of Weil, including the imperative to "prioritize the spiritual concerns of workers" (304) and to assign religion to a different place in society (305).
126. Weil, *The Need for Roots*, 96.
127. Ibid.
128. Ibid., 98–9.
129. Ibid., 295.
130. The tortured conflicts around Weil and Judaism are too thorny for us to disentangle here. Though born into a secular, agnostic Jewish family, Weil declined to take up that identity herself, famously penning a letter to the Vichy regime in which she rejected the government's attempt to classify her as a Jew. In *The Need for Roots* she expressly disqualifies Judaism alone from being taught in public schools (93). For expert treatments of this subject, see Palle Yougrau, *Simone Weil* (London: Reaktion Books, 2011), especially the chapter entitled "The Jewish Question." See also his "Was Simone Weil a Jew?," *Partisan Review* 68.4 (2001): 629–41. See also Thomas R. Nevin, *Simone Weil: Portrait of a Self-Exiled Jew* and most recently Christy Wampole, *Rootedness: The Ramifications of a Metaphor* (Chicago: University of Chicago Press, 2016). Wampole correctly shows that the accusation that the Jewish people are "rootless" is a long-standing anti-Semitic trope, so omnipresent that Weil could not have failed to know about it (124). Emmanuel Levinas knew Weil personally and confronted her views in his essay "Simone Weil against the Bible," in *Difficult Freedom: Essays on Judaism*, trans. Seán Hand (Baltimore, MD: Johns Hopkins University Press, 1997), 133–41.
131. Weil, *The Need for Roots*, 295–6.
132. Ibid., 296.

133. Ibid., 297–8.
134. Ibid., 299.
135. Ibid., 300.
136. Ibid. Hence the epistle to the Hebrews (which Weil attributes to Paul, though the scholarly consensus today is that it was not likely written by Paul at all) says that even Christ himself learned obedience through his sufferings.
137. Weil, *The Need for Roots*, 301.
138. Ibid.
139. Ibid., 302.
140. Ibid.

Conclusion

1. Ruskin, *The Crown of Wild Olive*, 419.
2. I hope in view of these disturbing recent events that we can revisit the use of the term "essential" vs. "nonessential" with respect to people's work. I imagine everyone's work is essential if you are the one doing it and moreover that a crisis has a way of drawing out with greater clarity what sort of work really is and isn't essential.
3. See https://trumpwhitehouse.archives.gov/briefings-statements/remarks-president-trump-celebrating-americas-truckers/. Accessed October 22, 2021.
4. Ruskin, *The Crown of Wild Olive*, 422–4.
5. https://www.theatlantic.com/ideas/archive/2019/02/religion-workism-making-americans-miserable/583441/. Accessed October 22, 2021.
6. Ibid.
7. Ibid.
8. Ibid.
9. See the references at Ron Beadle and Kelvin Knight, "Virtue and Meaningful Work," *Business Ethics Quarterly* 22.2 (April 2012): 433–50, p. 441.
10. Ibid., 442.
11. Hanby, "*Homo Faber* and/or *Homo Adorans*," 223.
12. See David Graeber, *Bullshit Jobs* (New York: Simon & Schuster, 2018).
13. Hanby, "*Homo Faber* and/or *Homo Adorans*," 220.

Bibliography

Alfonso, Isabel. "Cistercians and Feudalism." *Past and Present* 133.1 (1991): 3–30.
Altaner, Berthold. "Augustinus und die Griechische Patristik: Eine Einführung und Nachlese zu den Quellenkritischen Untersuchungen." *Revue Bénédictine* 62.3 (1952): 201–15.
Angier, Tom. *Techne in Aristotle's Ethics*. London: Continuum, 2010.
Anthony, P. D. *John Ruskin's Labour: A Study of Ruskin's Social Theory*. Cambridge: Cambridge University Press, 1983.
Arbesmann, Rudolph. "The Attitude of Saint Augustine toward Labor." In *The Heritage of the Early Church: Essays in Honor of the Very Reverend Georges Vasilievich Florovsky*. Ed. David Neiman and Margaret Schatkin, 245–59. Rome: Pontificum Institutum Studiorum Orientalium, 1973.
Arendt, Hannah. *The Human Condition*. Chicago: University of Chicago Press, 1958.
Aristotle. *Nicomachean Ethics*. Trans. Hippocrates G. Apostle. Des Moines: Peripatetic Press, 1984.
Athanasius. *The Life of Saint Antony*. Trans. Robert T. Meyer. Westminster, MD: Newman Press, 1950.
Augustine. *Commentary on the Lord's Sermon on the Mount with Seventeen Related Sermons*. The Fathers of the Church A New Translation 11. Trans. Denis J. Kavanagh. New York: Fathers of the Church, 1951.
Augustine. *Confessions*, 2nd ed. Trans. F. J. Sheed. Indianapolis: Hackett, 2006.
Augustine. "The Excellence of Widowhood." In *Saint Augustine: Treatises on Various Subjects*. The Fathers of the Church: A New Translation 16. Trans. M. Clement Eagan. Ed. Roy J. Deferrari, 279–319. New York: Fathers of the Church, 1952.
Augustine. *On Genesis*. The Works of Saint Augustine: A Translation for the 21st Century 13. Ed. John E. Rotelle. Trans. Matthew O'Connell, 13–22. Hyde Park, NY: New City Press, 2002.
Augustine. *On the Free Choice of the Will*. Trans. Thomas Williams. Indianapolis: Hackett, 1993.
Augustine. *The City of God against the Pagans* vol. 7. Loeb Classical Library 417. Trans. William M. Green. Cambridge, MA: Harvard University Press, 2014.
Augustine. "The Work of Monks." In *Saint Augustine: Treatises on Various Subjects*. The Fathers of the Church: A New Translation 16. Ed. Roy J. Deferrari. Trans. Mary Sarah Muldowney, 323–94. New York: Fathers of the Church, 1952.
Augustine. *Writings on the Old Testament*. The Works of Saint Augustine: A Translation for the 21st Century 14. Trans. Joseph T. Lienhard. Hyde Park, NY: New City Press, 2016.
Avery, Desmond. *Beyond Power: Simone Weil and the Notion of Authority*. Lanham, MD: Lexington Books, 2008.
Barsella, Susanna. "*Ars* and Theology: Work, Salvation, and Social Doctrine in the Early Church Fathers." *Annali d'Italianistica* 32 (2014): 53–72.

Barsella, Susanna. "A Humanistic Approach to Religious Solitude." In *Petrarch: A Critical Guide to the Complete Works*. Ed. Victoria Kirkham and Armando Maggi, 197–208. Chicago: University of Chicago Press, 2009.

Basil of Caesarea. *Saint Basil: Ascetical Works*. The Fathers of the Church: A New Translation 9. Trans. M. Monica Wagner, ed. Roy Joseph Deferrari. New York: Fathers of the Church, 1950.

Beadle, Ron, and Knight, Kelvin. "Virtue and Meaningful Work." *Business Ethics Quarterly* 22.2 (April 2012): 433–50.

Beadle, Ron, and Moore, Geoff. "MacIntyre on Virtue and Organization." *Organization Studies* 27.3 (2006): 321–40.

Bell, Theo M. M. A. C. "Luther's Reception of Bernard of Clairvaux." *Concordia Theological Quarterly* 59.4 (October 1995): 245–77.

Benedict of Nursia. *RB 1980: The Rule of St. Benedict*. Ed. Timothy Fry. Collegeville, MN: Liturgical Press, 1981.

Benson, Robert L., and Constable, Giles, with Lanham, Carol D. Eds. *Renaissance and Renewal in the Twelfth Century*. Medieval Academy Reprints for Teaching 26. Toronto: Toronto University Press, 1991.

Bernard of Clairvaux. *Monastic Sermons*. Cistercian Fathers Series 68. Trans. Daniel Griggs. Collegeville, MN: Liturgical Press, 2016.

Bernard of Clairvaux. *On the Song of Songs* II. Cistercian Fathers Series 7. The Works of Bernard of Clairvaux 3. Trans. Kilian Walsh. Kalamazoo, MI: Cistercian, 1983.

Bischoff, Bernhard. *Mittelalterliche Studien: Ausgewählte Aufsätze zur Schriftkunde und Literaturgeschichte* 2. Stuttgart: Anton Hiersemann, 1967.

Bloch, Marc. "The Advent and Triumph of the Watermill." In *Land and Work in Medieval Europe: Selected Papers by Marc Bloch*. Trans. J. E. Anderson, 136–66. Berkeley: University of California Press, 1967.

Bloch, Marc. *Feudal Society*, vols. 1 and 2. Trans. L. A. Manyon. London: Routledge and Kegan Paul, 1961.

Blum, Lawrence A., and Seidler, Victor J. *A Truer Liberty: Simone Weil and Marxism*. New York: Routledge, 1989.

Bonnerue, Pierre. "Concordance sur les activités manuelles dans les règles monastiques anciennes." *Studia Monastica* 35.1 (1993): 69–96.

Bonnerue, Pierre. "*Opus* et *labor* dans les règles monastiques anciennes." *Studia Monastica* 35.2 (1993): 265–92.

Boyle, Marjorie O'Rourke. *Petrarch's Genius: Pentimento and Prophecy*. Berkeley: University of California Press, 1991.

Brague, Rémi. *The Kingdom of Man: Genesis and Failure of the Modern Project*. Trans. Paul Seaton. Notre Dame, IN: University of Notre Dame Press, 2018.

Brumbaugh, Robert S. *Platonic Studies of Greek Philosophy: Form, Arts, Gadgets, and Hemlock*. Albany: State University of New York Press, 1989.

Burckhardt, Jacob. *The Civilization of the Renaissance in Italy*. Trans. S. G. C. Middlemore. Vienna: Phaidon Press, 1937.

Burford, Alison. *Craftsmen in Greek and Roman Society*. London: Thames and Hudson, 1972.

Calder, James Gordon. "Labour and Thought in the Philosophy of Simone Weil (1909–1943): Preface to a Philosophy of Education," PhD diss. Dalhousie University, 1985.

Cass, Oren. *The Once and Future Worker: A Vision for the Renewal of Work in America*. New York: Encounter Books, 2018.

Cassian, John. *Institutes*. The Works of the Fathers in Translation 58. Trans. Boniface Ramsey. New York: Newman Press, 2000.
Cassirer, Ernst. *The Individual and the Cosmos in Renaissance Philosophy*. Trans. Mario Domandi. Oxford: Blackwell, 1963.
Chenavier, Robert. "Simone Weil: Completing Platonism through a Consistent Materialism." In *The Christian Platonism of Simone Weil*. Ed. E. Jane Doering and Eric O. Springsted, 61–76. Notre Dame, IN: University of Notre Dame Press, 2004.
Cicero. *De natura deorum*. Loeb Classical Library 268. Trans. Harris Rackham. Cambridge, MA: Harvard University Press, 1933.
Cicero. *De officiis*. Trans. Walter Miller. Loeb Classical Library, vol. XXI. Cambridge, MA: Harvard University Press, 1913.
Cicero. *On the Republic/On the Laws*. Loeb Classical Library 213. Trans. Clinton W. Keyes. Cambridge, MA: Harvard University Press, 1928.
Claræ-Vallensis, Sancti Bernardi Abbatis. *Opera Omnia*. Vol. 2, Pars Prior. Ed. Jean Mabillon. Paris: Gaume Fratres, 1839.
Coby, Patrick. "On Warriors and Artisans: The Case for Moral Virtue in Plato's *Republic*." *Polity* 15.4 (1983): 515–35.
The Compact Edition of the Oxford English Dictionary. I:A-O. Oxford: Oxford University Press, 1971.
Courcelle, Pierre. *Late Latin Writers and Their Greek Sources*. Trans. Harry E. Wedeck. Cambridge, MA: Harvard University Pres, 1969.
Cranz, F. Edward. *An Essay on the Development of Luther's Thought on Justice, Law, and Society*. Harvard Theological Studies XIX. Cambridge, MA: Harvard University Press, 1959.
Cranz, F. Edward. "Some Petrarchan Paradoxes." In *Reorientations of Western Thought from Antiquity to the Renaissance*. Ed. Nancy Struever, 1–21. Aldershot, UK: Ashgate, 2006.
Crawford, Matthew B. *Shop Class as Soulcraft: An Inquiry into the Value of Work*. New York: Penguin Press, 2009.
Doerfler, Maria E. "'Hair!': Remnants of Ascetic Exegesis in Augustine of Hippo's *De opere monachorum*." *Journal of Early Christian Studies* 22.1 (2014): 79–111.
Duby, Georges. *The Three Orders: Feudal Society Imagined*. Trans. Arthur Goldhammer. Repr. ed. Chicago: University of Chicago Press, 1982.
Ferrero, Ignacio, and Sison, Alejo José G. "A Quantitative Analysis of Authors, Schools, and Themes in Virtue Ethics Articles in Business Ethics and Management Journals (1980-2011)." *Business Ethics: A European Review* 23.4 (2014): 375–400.
Fiedrowicz, Michael. "General Introduction." In *On Genesis. The Works of Saint Augustine: A Translation for the 21st Century* 13. Ed. John E. Rotelle. Trans. Matthew O'Connell, 13–22. Hyde Park, NY: New City Press, 2002.
Finley, M. I. *The World of Odysseus*, 2nd ed. London: Penguin Books, 1979.
Folliet, Georges. "Des moines euchites à Carthage en 400-401." *Studia Patristica* 2. Texte und Untersuchungen 64 (Berlin: Akademie Verlag, 1957): 386–99.
Fossier, Robert. *The Axe and the Oath: Ordinary Life in the Middle Ages*. Trans. Lydia G. Cochrane. Princeton, NJ: Princeton University Press, 2010.
Gearhart, Heidi C. *Theophilus and the Theory and Practice of Medieval Art*. University Park, PA: Pennsylvania State University Press, 2017.
Geoghegan, Arthur T. *The Attitude towards Labor in Early Christianity and Ancient Culture*. The Catholic University of America Studies in Christian Antiquity 6. Washington, DC: Catholic University of America Press, 1945.

Gilbert of Hoyland. *Sermons on the Song of Songs* III. Cistercian Fathers Series 26. Trans. Lawrence C. Braceland. Kalamazoo, MI: Cistercian, 1979.

Gimpel, Jean. *The Medieval Machine: The Industrial Revolution of the Middle Ages.* London: Penguin, 1981.

Glotz, Gustave. *Ancient Greece at Work: An Economic History of Greece from the Homeric Period to the Roman Conquest.* Trans. M. R. Dobie. London: Kegan Paul, Trench, Trubner; New York: Alfred A. Knopf, 1926.

Gould, Graham. *The Desert Fathers on Monastic Community.* Oxford: Clarendon Press, 1993.

Graeber, David. *Bullshit Jobs.* New York: Simon & Schuster, 2018.

Greene, Kevin. "Technology and Innovation in Context: The Roman Background to Medieval and Later Developments." *Journal of Roman Archaeology* 7 (1994): 22–33.

Hall, Bert S. "Review of *The Medieval Machine: The Industrial Revolution of the Middle Ages.*" *Speculum* 53.2 (1978): 366–8.

Hanby, Michael. "*Homo Faber* and/or *Homo Adorans*: On the Place of Human Making in a Sacramental Cosmos." *Communio* 38.2 (2011): 198–236.

Hardy, Lee. *The Fabric of This World: Inquiries into Calling, Career Choice, and the Design of Human Work.* Grand Rapids, MI: Eerdmans, 1990.

Harrison, Carol. "Augustine and the Art of Gardening." In *The Use and Abuse of Time in Christian History, Studies in Church History* 37. Ed. R. N. Swanson, 13–33. Suffolk, UK: Boydell Press, 2002.

Hart, Ian. "The Teaching of Luther and Calvin about Ordinary Work: 1. Martin Luther (1483–1546)." *Evangelical Quarterly* 67.1 (1995): 35–52.

Heinz, Johann. "Luther's Doctrine of Work and Reward." *Andrews University Seminary Studies* 22.1 (Spring 1984): 45–69.

Hesiod. *Works and Days: A Translation and Commentary for the Social Sciences.* Trans. David W. Tandy and Walter C. Neale. Berkeley: University of California Press, 1996.

Hock, Ronald F. "Simon the Shoemaker as an Ideal Cynic." *Greek, Roman and Byzantine Studies* 17.1 (1976): 41–53.

Holdsworth, Christopher J. "The Blessings of Work: The Cistercian View." In *Sanctity and Secularity: The Church and the World.* Ed. Derek Baker, 59–76. Oxford: Basil Blackwell, 1973.

Idung of Prufening. *Cistercians and Cluniacs: The Case for Cîteaux.* Cistercian Fathers Series 33. Trans. Jeremiah F. O'Sullivan. Kalamazoo, MI: Cistercian, 1977.

Illich, Ivan. *In the Vineyard of the Text: A Commentary to Hugh's Didascalicon.* Chicago: University of Chicago Press, 1993.

Irwin, Terrence. *Plato's Moral Theory.* Oxford: Clarendon Press, 1977.

Kardong, Terrence G. *Pillars of Community: Four Rules of Pre-Benedictine Monastic Life.* Collegeville, MN: Liturgical Press, 2010.

Keat, Russell. "Ethics, Markets, and MacIntyre." In *Revolutionary Aristotelianism: Ethics, Resistance, and Utopia.* Ed. Kelvin Knight and Paul Blackledge, 243–57. Stuttgart: Lucius and Lucius, 2008.

Klosko, George. "The Technical Conception of Virtue." *Journal of the History of Philosophy* 18 (1981): 98–106.

Knies, Kenneth. "Taking the Strict Account of Techne Seriously: An Interpretive Direction in Plato's *Republic.*" *Schole* 8.1 (2014): 111–26.

Knight, Kelvin. "Goods." *Philosophy of Management* 7.1 (2008): 107–22.

Kristeller, Paul Oskar. *Medieval Aspects of Renaissance Learning: Three Essays by Paul Oskar Kristeller.* Duke Monographs in Medieval and Renaissance Studies 1. Ed. and trans. Edward P. Mahoney. Durham, NC: Duke University Press, 1974.

Kristeller, Paul Oskar. *Renaissance Philosophy and the Mediaeval Tradition*. Wimmer Lecture XV. Latrobe, PA: Archabbey Press, 1966.

Kristeller, Paul Oskar. *Renaissance Thought and Its Sources*. Ed. Michael Mooney. New York: Columbia University Press, 1979.

Kristeller, Paul Oskar. *Renaissance Thought: The Classic, Scholastic, and Humanist Strains*. New York: Harper & Row, 1961.

Lee, Alexander. *Petrarch and St. Augustine: Classical Scholarship, Christian Theology and the Origins of the Renaissance in Italy*. Leiden: Brill, 2012.

Lefebvre des Noëttes, Richard. *L'attelage: Le cheval de selle à travers les âges: Contribution a l'histoire de l'esclavage*. Paris: Picard, 1931.

Lefebvre des Noëttes, Richard. *La force motrice animale à travers les âges*. Nancy: Berger-Levrault, 1924.

LeGoff, Jacques. *Medieval Civilization*. Trans. Julia Barrow. Oxford: Blackwell, 1990.

LeGoff, Jacques. *Pour un autre Moyen Âge*. Paris: Gallimard, 1991.

LeGoff, Jacques. *The Medieval Imagination*. Trans. Arthur Goldhammer. Chicago: University of Chicago Press, 1992.

LeGoff, Jacques. *Time, Work, and Culture in the Middle Ages*. Trans. Arthur Goldhammer. Chicago: University of Chicago Press, 1980.

Levinas, Emmanuel. "Simone Weil against the Bible." In *Difficult Freedom: Essays on Judaism*. Trans. Seán Hand, 133–41. Baltimore, MD: Johns Hopkins University Press, 1997.

Libellus de diversis ordinibus et professionibus qui sunt in aecclesia. Ed. and Trans. G. Constable and B. Smith. Oxford: Clarendon Press, 1972.

Luther, Martin. *Luther's Works*. Volume 1: Lectures on Genesis Chapters 1–5. Ed. Jaroslav Pelikan. Trans. George V. Schick. St. Louis: Concordia Publishing House, 1958.

Luther, Martin. *Luther's Works*, Volume 9: Lectures on Deuteronomy. Ed. Jaroslav Pelikan, Asst. ed. Daniel Poellot, Trans. Richard R. Caemmerer. St. Louis: Concordia Publishing House, 1960.

Luther, Martin. *Luther's Works*. Volume 14: Selected Psalms III. Ed. Jaroslav Pelikan. Asst. Ed. Daniel E. Poellot. Trans. Edward Sittler. St. Louis: Concordia Publishing House, 1958.

Luther, Martin. *Luther's Works*. Volume 15: Notes on Ecclesiastes/Lectures on the Song of Solomon/Treatise on the Last Words of David. Ed. Jaroslav Pelikan. Assoc. Ed. Hilton C. Oswald. Trans. Jaroslav Pelikan. St. Louis: Concordia Publishing House, 1972.

Luther, Martin. *Luther's Works*. Volume 17: Lectures on Isaiah Chapters 40–66. Ed. Hilton C. Oswald. Trans. Herbert J. A. Bouman. St. Louis: Concordia Publishing House, 1972.

Luther, Martin. *Luther's Works*. Volume 21: The Sermon on the Mount (Sermons) and the Magnificat. Ed. Jaroslav Pelikan. Trans. Jaroslav Pelikan. St. Louis: Concordia Publishing House, 1956.

Luther, Martin. *Luther's Works*. Volume 24: Sermons on the Gospel of St. John Chapters 14–16. Ed. Jaroslav Pelikan. Asst. Ed. Daniel E. Poellot. Trans. Martin H. Bertram. St. Louis: Concordia Publishing House, 1961.

Luther, Martin. *Luther's Works*. Volume 28: Commentaries on 1 Corinthians 7/1 Corinthians 15/Lectures on 1 Timothy. Ed. Hilton C. Oswald. Trans. Edward Sittler. St. Louis: Concordia Publishing House, 1973.

Luther, Martin. *Luther's Works*. Volume 30: The Catholic Epistles. Ed. Jaroslav Pelikan. Assoc. Ed. Walter A. Hansen. Trans. Martin H. Bertram. St. Louis: Concordia Publishing House, 1967.

Luther, Martin. *Luther's Works*. Volume 44: The Christian in Society I. Ed. James Atkinson. Gen. Ed. Helmut T. Lehmann. "Treatise on Good Works." Trans. W. A. Lambert. Rev. James Atkinson. Philadelphia, PA: Fortress Press, 1966.

Luther, Martin. *Luther's Works*. Volume 45: The Christian in Society II. Ed. Walther I. Brandt. Gen. Ed. Helmut T. Lehmann. "Exposition of Psalm 127, for the Christians at Riga in Livonia." Trans. Walther I. Brandt. Philadelphia, PA: Muhlenberg Press, 1962.

Luther, Martin. *Martin Luther's Basic Theological Writings*, 3rd ed. Ed. Timothy F. Lull, William R. Russell. Minneapolis, MN: Fortress Press, 2012.

Luther, Martin. *On the Freedom of a Christian with Related Texts*. Ed. and trans. Tryntje Helfferich. Indianapolis: Hackett, 2013.

Luther, Martin. *Sermons of Martin Luther: The House Postils*. Ed. Eugene F. A. Klug. Trans. Eugene F. A. Klug, Erwin W. Koehlinger, James Lanning, Everette W. Meier, Dorothy Schoknecht, and Allen Schuldheiss. Grand Rapids, MI: Baker Books, 1996.

MacIntyre, Alasdair. *After Virtue: A Study in Moral Theory*. 2nd ed. Notre Dame, IN: University of Notre Dame Press, 1984.

MacIntyre, Alasdair. *Dependent Rational Animals: Why Human Beings Need the Virtues*. Chicago: Open Court Press, 1999.

MacIntyre, Alasdair. *Ethics in the Conflicts of Modernity: An Essay on Desire, Practical Reasoning, and Narrative*. Cambridge: Cambridge University Press, 2016.

MacIntyre, Alasdair. "How to Seem Virtuous without Actually Being So." In *Education in Morality*. Ed. J. Mark Halstead and Terence H. McLaughlin, 118–31. London: Routledge, 1999.

MacIntyre, Alasdair. "The Irrelevance of Ethics." In *Virtue and Economy: Essays on Morality and Markets*. Ed. Andrius Bielskis and Kelvin Knight, 7–22. Abingdon, UK: Routledge, 2016.

MacIntyre, Alasdair. *Whose Justice? Which Rationality?* Notre Dame, IN: University of Notre Dame Press, 1998.

Mackean, W. H. *Christian Monasticism in Egypt to the Close of the Fourth Century*. London: Society for Promoting Christian Knowledge, 1920.

Malesic, Jonathan. "'Nothing Is to be Preferred to the Work of God': Cultivating Monastic Detachment for a Postindustrial Work Ethic." *Journal of the Society of Christian Ethics* 35.1 (2015): 45–61.

Martinez, Joel A. "Rethinking Plato's Conception of Knowledge: The Non-philosopher and the Forms." *Apeiron* 44 (2011): 326–34.

Marx, Karl. "Economic and Philosophical Manuscripts." In *Karl Marx: Early Writings*. Ed. Quintin Hoare. Trans. Gregor Benton, 279–400. New York: Vintage Books, 1975.

Meltzer, Françoise. "The Hands of Simone Weil." *Critical Inquiry* 27.4 (2001): 611–28.

Metteer, Charles. "'Mary Needs Martha': The Purposes of Manual Labor in Early Egyptian Monasticism." *St. Vladimir's Theological Quarterly* 43.2 (1999): 163–207.

Miller, David. "Virtue, Practices, and Justice." In *After MacIntyre: Critical Perspectives on the Work of Alasdair MacIntyre*. Ed. John Horton and Susan Mendus, 245–64. Notre Dame, IN: University of Notre Dame Press, 1994.

Moes, Mark. "Dialectical Rhetoric and Socrates' Treatment of Mimetic Poetry in Book 10 of the *Republic*." *Philosophy Study* 1.1 (2011): 1–21.

Murchland, Bernard. "Introduction." In *Two Views of Man: Pope Innocent III On the Misery of Man/Giannozzo Manetti On the Dignity of Man*, iii–xix. New York: Frederick Ungar, 1966.

Nevin, Thomas R. *Simone Weil: Portrait of a Self-Exiled Jew*. Chapel Hill: University of North Carolina Press, 1991.

Nightingale, Andrea Wilson. *Spectacles of Truth in Classical Greek Philosophy: Theoria in Its Cultural Context*. Cambridge: Cambridge University Press, 2004.

Oleson, John Peter, Ed. *The Oxford Handbook of Engineering and Technology in the Classical World*. Oxford: Oxford University Press, 2008.

Ortega y Gasset, José. *Meditations on Hunting*. Trans. Howard B. Wescott. New York: Charles Scribner's Sons, 1972.

Ovitt, George Jr. *The Restoration of Perfection: Labor and Technology in Medieval Culture*. New Brunswick, NJ: Rutgers University Press, 1987.

Patterson, Patrick, and Schmidt, Lawrence E. "The Christian Materialism of Simone Weil." In *The Christian Platonism of Simone Weil*. Ed. E. Jane Doering and Eric O. Springsted, 77–94. Notre Dame, IN: University of Notre Dame Press, 2004.

Petrarch. *On Religious Leisure*. Ed. and trans. Susan S. Schearer. New York: Italica Press, 2002.

Petrarch. *Remedies for Fortune Fair and Foul*. Trans. Conrad H. Rawski. Bloomington: Indiana University Press, 1991.

Pieper, Josef. *Leisure: The Basis of Culture*. Trans. Alexander Dru. New York: Pantheon Books, 1952.

Pirsig, Robert M. *Zen and the Art of Motorcycle Maintenance*. New York: Harper Collins, 1999, 1974.

Plato. "Apology." In *Complete Works*. Ed. John M. Cooper. Trans. G. M. A. Grube. Indianapolis: Hackett, 1997.

Plato. "Greater Hippias." In *Complete Works*. Ed. John M. Cooper. Trans. Paul Woodruff. Indianapolis: Hackett, 1997.

Plato. "Laches." In *Complete Works*. Ed. John M. Cooper. Trans. Rosamond Kent Sprague. Indianapolis: Hackett, 1997.

Plato, "Meno." In *Complete Works*. Ed. John M. Cooper. Trans. G. M. A. Grube. Indianapolis: Hackett, 1997.

Plato. *Republic*. Trans. G. M. A. Grube and C. D. C. Reeve. Indianapolis: Hackett, 1992.

Plato. "Timaeus." In *Complete Works*. Ed. John M. Cooper. Trans. Donald J. Zeyl. Indianapolis: Hackett, 1997.

Posset, Franz. "Bernard of Clairvaux as Luther's Source." *Concordia Theological Quarterly* 54.4 (October 1990): 281–304.

Proctor, Robert E. *Defining the Humanities: How Rediscovering a Tradition Can Improve Our Schools*. 2nd ed. Bloomington: Indiana University Press, 1998.

Radzins, Inese. "Simone Weil on Labor and Spirit." *Journal of Religious Ethics* 45.2 (2017): 291–308.

Rajan, Supritha. *A Tale of Two Capitalisms: Sacred Economics in Nineteenth-Century Britain*. Ann Arbor: University of Michigan Press, 2015.

Reeve, C. D. C. "The Role of *Techne* in Plato's Construction of Philosophy." *Proceedings of the Boston Area Colloquium in Ancient Philosophy* 16 (2000): 207–22.

Robertson, Kellie, and Uebel, Michael, Eds. *The Middle Ages at Work: Practicing Labor in Late Medieval England*. New York: Palgrave Macmillan, 2004.

Roe, Frederick William. *The Social Philosophy of Carlyle and Ruskin*. Repr. ed. Port Washington, NY: Kennikat Press, 1969.

Roochnik, David. *Of Art and Wisdom: Plato's Understanding of Techne*. University Park, PA: Pennsylvania State University Press, 1996.

Roochnik, David. "Review of *Plato's Critique of Impure Reason: On Goodness and Truth in the Republic*" *Ancient Philosophy* 30.1 (2010): 180–2.

Roochnik, David. "Socrates's Use of the Techne-Analogy." *Journal of the History of Philosophy* 24.3 (1986): 295–310.

Roochnik, David. "The Useful Uselessness of the Humanities." *Expositions* 2.1 (2008): 19-26.

Rosenberg, John D. *The Darkening Glass: A Portrait of Ruskin's Genius*. New York: Columbia University Press, 1986.

Rufus, Musonius. "What Means of Livelihood Are Appropriate for a Philosopher?" In *Musonius Rufus: The Roman Socrates*. Trans. Cora Lutz. Yale Classical Studies X. Ed. A. R. Bellinger. New Haven, CT: Yale University Press, 1947.

Ruskin, John. *The Aesthetics and Mathematic Schools of Art in Florence*. London: George Allen, 1906. In *The Works of John Ruskin*. Library Edition XXIII. Ed. E. T. Cook and Alexander Wedderburn. London: George Allen, 1906.

Ruskin, John. *The Crown of Wild Olive: Three Lectures on Work, Traffic, and War*. London: Smith, Elder, 1866. In *The Works of John Ruskin*, Library Edition XVIII. Ed. E. T. Cook and Alexander Wedderburn. London: George Allen, 1905.

Ruskin, John. *Fors Clavigera: Letters to the Workmen and Labourers of Great Britain Volumes I-VIII*. Orpington: George Allen, 1871. *The Works of John Ruskin*, Library Edition XXVII. Ed. E. T. Cook and Alexander Wedderburn. London: George Allen, 1907.

Ruskin, John. *"A Joy for Ever," (and Its Price in the Market): Being Substance (with Additions) of Two Lectures on the Political Economy of Art*. Orpington: George Allen, 1880. In *The Works of John Ruskin*. Library Edition XVI, ed. E. T. Cook and Alexander Wedderburn. London: George Allen, 1905.

Ruskin, John. *Lectures on Architecture and Painting, Delivered at Edinburgh in November, 1853*. London: Smith, Elder, 1854. In *The Works of John Ruskin*. Library Edition XII. Ed. E. T. Cook and Alexander Wedderburn. London: George Allen, 1904.

Ruskin, John. *Lectures on Art Delivered before the University of Oxford in Hilary Term, 1870*. Oxford: Clarendon Press, 1870. In *The Works of Ruskin*. Library Edition XX. Ed. E. T. Cook and Alexander Wedderburn. London: George Allen, 1905.

Ruskin, John. *Modern Painters*. In *The Works of John Ruskin*. Library Edition III-V. Ed. E. T. Cook and Alexander Wedderburn. London: George Allen, 1903.

Ruskin, John. *Munera Pulveris: Six Essays on the Elements of Political Economy*. London: Smith, Elder, 1872. In *The Works of John Ruskin*. Library Edition XVII. Ed. E. T. Cook and Alexander Wedderburn. London: George Allen, 1905.

Ruskin, John. *On the Old Road*. In *The Works of John Ruskin*. Library Edition XXXIV. Ed. E. T. Cook and Alexander Wedderburn. London: George Allen, 1908.

Ruskin, John. *Præterita: Outlines of Scenes and Thoughts Perhaps Worthy of Memory in My Past Life*. Orpington: George Allen, 1886. In *The Works of John Ruskin*. Library Edition XXXV. London: George Allen, 1908.

Ruskin, John. *Sesame and Lilies: Two Lectures Delivered at Manchester in 1864*. London: Smith, Elder, 1865. *The Works of John Ruskin*, Library Edition XVIII. Ed. E. T. Cook and Alexander Wedderburn. London: George Allen, 1905.

Ruskin, John. *The Seven Lamps of Architecture*. In *The Works of John Ruskin*. Library Edition VIII. Ed. E. T. Cook and Alexander Wedderburn. London: George Allen, 1903.

Ruskin, John. *The Shepherd's Tower*. In *The Works of John Ruskin*. Library Edition Volume XXIII. Ed. E. T. Cook and Alexander Wedderburn. London: George Allen, 1906.

Ruskin, John. *The Stones of Venice Volume II*. In *The Works of John Ruskin*. Library Edition X. Ed. E. T. Cook and Alexander Wedderburn. London: George Allen, 1904.

Ruskin, John. *Time and Tide, by Weare and Tyne: Twenty-Five Letters to a Working Man of Sunderland on the Laws of Work*. London: Smith, Elder, 1867. In *The Works of John Ruskin*, Library Edition XVII. Ed. E. T. Cook and Alexander Wedderburn. London: George Allen, 1905.

Ruskin, John. *The Two Paths: Being Lectures on Art and Its Application to Decoration and Manufacture, Delivered in 1858-9*. London: Smith, Elder, 1859. In *The Works of John Ruskin*, Library Edition XVI, ed. E. T. Cook and Alexander Wedderburn. London: George Allen, 1906.

Ruskin, John. *Unto This Last*. *The Works of John Ruskin*. Library Edition XVII. Ed. E. T. Cook and Alexander Wedderburn. London: George Allen, 1905.

Ruskin, John. *Valle Crucis: Studies in Monastic History and Architecture*. In *The Works of John Ruskin*. Library Edition XXXIII. Ed. E. T. Cook and Alexander Wedderburn. London: George Allen, 1908.

Schenk, Richard. "Work: The Corruption or Perfection of the Human Being?" *Nova et Vetera* 2.1 (2004): 129–46.

Schindler, D. C. *Plato's Critique of Impure Reason: On Goodness and Truth in the Republic*. Washington, DC: Catholic University of America Press, 2008.

Sellars, John. "Simon the Shoemaker and the Problem of Socrates." *Classical Philology* 98.3 (2003): 207–16.

Selles-Roney, Johanna, "'Is This Not the Kind of Fasting I Have Chosen?' Simone Weil's Life and Labor." In *Political Theory and Christian Vision: Essays in Memory of Bernard Zylstra*. Ed. Jonathan Chaplin and Paul Marshall, 267–79. Lanham, MD: University Press of America, 1994.

Seneca. *Epistles, Volume II: Epistles 66–92*. Trans. Richard M. Gummere. Loeb Classical Library 76. Cambridge, MA: Harvard University Press, 1920.

Simon, Yves. "Work and Workman." *Review of Politics* 2.1 (January 1940): 63–86.

Sinnicks, Matthew. "Moral Education at Work: On the Scope of MacIntyre's Concept of a Practice." *Journal of Business Ethics* 159.1 (2019): 105–18.

Sparling, Robert. "Theory and Praxis: Simone Weil and Marx on the Dignity of Labor." *Review of Politics* 74 (2012): 87–107.

Ste. Croix, G. E. M. de. *The Class Struggle in the Ancient Greek World from the Archaic Age to the Arab Conquests*. Ithaca, NY: Cornell University Press, 1981.

Steinhauser, Kenneth B. "The Cynic Monks of Carthage: Some Observations on *De opera monachorum*." In *Augustine: Presbyter Factus Sum*. Ed. Joseph T. Lienhard, Earl C. Muller, and Roland J. Teske, 455–62. New York: Peter Lang, 1993.

Stiegman, Emero. "Action and Contemplation in Saint Bernard's Sermons on the Song of Songs." In *On the Song of Songs III*. Cistercian Fathers Series 21. Trans. Kilian Walsh, vii–xix Kalamazoo, MI: Cistercian, 1979.

Stock, Brian. "Activity, Contemplation, Work and Leisure between the Eleventh and the Thirteenth Centuries." In *Arbeit–Musse–Meditation: Betrachtungen zur Vita Activa und Vita Contemplativa*. Ed. Brian Vickers, 87–108. Zurich: Verlag der Fachvereine, 1985.

Stock, Brian. "Experience, Praxis, Work, and Planning in Bernard of Clairvaux: Observations on the *Sermones in Cantica*." In *The Cultural Context of Medieval Learning*. Ed. J. E. Murdoch and E. D. Sylla, 219–68. Dordrecht: Springer, 1975.

Theophilus. *The Various Arts*. Ed. and trans. C. R. Dodwell. Oxford: Clarendon Press, 1986.

Tilgher, Adriano. *Work: What It Has Meant to Men through the Ages (Homo Faber)*. Arno Press 1977 repr. ed. Trans. Dorothy Canfield Fisher. New York: Harcourt, Brace, 1930.

Toal, M. F., Trans. and Ed. *The Sunday Sermons of the Great Fathers*. San Francisco, CA: Ignatius Press, 2000.

Trinkaus, Charles. *In Our Image and Likeness: Humanity and Divinity in Italian Humanist Thought in 2 Volumes*, 1. London: Constable, 1970.

Trinkaus, Charles. *The Poet as Philosopher: Petrarch and the Formation of Renaissance Consciousness*. New Haven, CT: Yale University Press, 1979.

Trinkaus, Charles. *The Scope of Renaissance Humanism*. Ann Arbor: University of Michigan Press, 1983.

Van den Hoven, Birgit. *Work in Ancient and Medieval Thought: Ancient Philosophers, Medieval Monks and Theologians, and Their Concept of Work, Occupations, and Technology*. Amsterdam: J. C. Gieben, 1996.

Van Engen, John. "Theophilus Presbyter and Rupert of Deutz: The Manual Arts and Benedictine Theology in the Early Twelfth Century." *Viator* 11 (1980): 147–64.

Vernant, Jean-Pierre. *Myth and Thought among the Greeks*. London: Routledge & Kegan Paul, 1983.

Vignes, Bernard-Joseph-Maurice. "Les doctrines économiques et morales de Saint Bernard sur la richesse et le travail." *Revue d'histoire économique et sociale* 16.3 (1928): 547–85.

Vitruvius. *Ten Books on Architecture*. Trans. Ingrid D. Rowland. Cambridge: Cambridge University Press, 1999.

Vlastos, Gregory. "The Virtuous and the Happy." *Times Literary Supplement* (February 24, 1978): 232–3.

Wampole, Christy. *Rootedness: The Ramifications of a Metaphor*. Chicago: University of Chicago Press, 2016.

Weil, Simone. "Le Christianisme et la vie des champs." In *Pensees sans ordre concernant l'amour de Dieu*. Paris: Gallimard, 1962.

Weil, Simone. "Factory Work." In *The Simone Weil Reader*. Ed. George A. Panichas, 53–72. New York: David McKay, 1977.

Weil, Simone. *Factory Journal*. In *Formative Writings: 1929–1941*. Ed. and trans. Dorothy Tuck McFarland and Wilhelmina van Ness. Amherst: University of Massachusetts Press, 1987.

Weil, Simone. "The First Condition for the Work of a Free Person." In *Simone Weil: Late Philosophical Writings*. Ed. Eric O. Springsted and Lawrence E. Schmidt, 131–43. Notre Dame, IN: University of Notre Dame Press, 2015.

Weil, Simone. *Gravity and Grace*. Trans. Arthur Wills. New York: Putnam's, 1952.

Weil, Simone. *The Need for Roots: Prelude to a Declaration of Duties to Mankind*. Trans. Arthur Wills. Boston, MA: Beacon Press, 1952.

Weil, Simone. *Œuvres Complètes I: Premieres écrits philosophiques*. Ed. Gilbert Kahn and Rolf Kühn. Paris: Gallimard, 1988.

Weil, Simone. *On Science, Necessity, and the Love of God*. Ed. Richard Rees. Oxford: Oxford University Press, 1968.

Weil, Simone. *Oppression and Liberty*. Trans. Arthur Wills and John Petrie. Amherst: University of Massachusetts Press, 1973.

Weil, Simone. "The Pythagorean Doctrine." In *Intimations of Christianity among the Ancient Greeks*. Ed. and Trans. Elizabeth Chase Geissbuhler, 151–202. London: Routledge and Kegan Paul, 1957.

Weil, Simone. *Waiting for God*. Trans. Emma Craufurd. New York: Harper and Row, 1973.

Weiss, Howard M. "Working as Human Nature." In *The Nature of Work: Advances in Psychological Theory, Methods, and Practice*. Ed. J. Kevin Ford, John R. Hollenbeck, and Ann Marie Ryan. Washington, DC: American Psychological Association, 2014.

Whitehead, David. *The Ideology of the Athenian Metic*. Supplementary volume no. 4. Cambridge: Cambridge Philological Society, 1977.

Whitney, Elspeth. "Paradise Restored: The Mechanical Arts from Antiquity through the Thirteenth Century." *Transactions of the American Philosophical Society* 80.1 (1990): 1–169.

Wikander, Örjan. *Exploitation of Water-Power or Technological Stagnation? A Reappraisal of the Productive Forces in the Roman Empire.* Lund: Gleerup, 1984.

Witt, Ronald G. "Introduction." In *On Religious Leisure*. Ed. and trans. Susan S. Schearer, ix–xxii. New York: Italica Press, 2002.

Xenophon. *Oeconomicus: A Social and Historical Commentary with a New English Translation.* Trans. Sarah B. Pomeroy. Oxford: Clarendon Press, 1994.

Yocum, Demetrio S. *Petrarch's Humanist Writing and Carthusian Monasticism: The Secret Language of the Self.* Turnhout, Belgium: Brepols, 2013.

Yougrau, Palle. *Simone Weil*. London: Reaktion Books, 2011.

Yougrau, Palle. "Was Simone Weil a Jew?" *Partisan Review* 68.4 (2001): 629–41.

Index of Biblical Citations

Genesis	142, 150, 182, 193, 194	Luke 10:5-7	141
Genesis 2	70, 92, 137	Luke 10:42	69, 219 n.12
Genesis 2:15	70	Luke 12	73
Genesis 3:16	219 n.17	John 2	108
Genesis 3:17-19	70–1	John 6	134
Genesis 3:19	71, 140, 143, 147, 165, 166, 242 nn.34, 39	John 6:27	227 n.163
		John 12:24	187
Exodus 31:2	119	John 14	144
Exodus 31:3-5	119	John 15:5	188
Deuteronomy	149	Romans 7	136
Deuteronomy 8:17	147	Romans 13	134
Deuteronomy 25:4	141	Galatians	135
Job	127, 189	Philippians	139
Job 3:18	258 n.90	1 Corinthians	93
Job 5:7	140	1 Corinthians 3	129
Psalm 26	118	1 Corinthians 3:6-7	147
Psalm 46:10	127, 128, 239 n.51	1 Corinthians 3:6-9	239 n.42
Psalm 73:5-6	242 n.39	1 Corinthians 3:8	77
Psalm 127:1	146, 148, 149	1 Corinthians 7:20	141
Psalm 145:19	244 n.75	1 Corinthians 7:29-31	107
Proverbs 10:4	149	1 Corinthians 9	134, 141
Proverbs 10:22	149, 244 n.75	1 Corinthians 9:14	141
Ecclesiastes	118, 128, 140, 148, 150, 152	1 Thessalonians 5:17	69
		2 Thessalonians	69, 71, 81, 108–9, 111
Ecclesiastes 12:12	v		
Song of Songs	107, 109, 231 n.14, 233 n.32	2 Thessalonians 3:10	71, 79, 87, 113, 114, 140, 141, 143, 165, 167, 168, 219 n.9, 223 n.96, 242 n.34, 250 n.65
Matthew 6	149		
Matthew 6:24	91		
Matthew 6:34	71, 228 n.163		
Matthew 7	138, 175		
Matthew 7:23	175		
Matthew 13	235	1 Timothy 3:21	145
Matthew 17	139	Hebrews	261 n.136
Matthew 19	71	1 Peter 3	151
Matthew 24	190	1 John	144
Mark 3:28-30	189	Revelation	236 n.103
Luke 2	139		

General Index

Abraham 75
Achilles 16, 205 n.9
Adam 70, 93–4, 137–8, 140, 143, 147, 228 n.176, 255 n.22, 260 n.119
Address to the Christian Nobility of the German Nation 133
Adeimantus 19, 29, 32, 37, 53, 58, 62
agriculture, *see* farming
Aholiab 119
Albigenses 194
alienation 172, 180–1
alms, *see also* charity 73, 76, 83–6, 102, 107, 174, 220 n.45, 223 n.96, 225–6 n.130, 227 n.163
Altaner, Berthold 87, 225 n.123
Ambrose, St. 83, 110
anchorite 68–75, 78, 219 n.6, 220 n.45
angel 70, 75–7, 99, 118, 166
Antony, St. 68, 71–2, 87, 225 n.126
Aphrodite 20
Apollo, Abba 74
Apollos 42
Apology 21–3, 30, 45, 59
Aquinas, Thomas 225 n.129
Arbesmann, Rudolph 86, 102, 223 n.176
Archebius, Abba 73
architecture, *see also* building 82, 187, 229 n.189, 238 n.23, 247 n.10
  in Ruskin 157–64, 174
Ares 20
arete, *see also* virtue 11
Aristippus 126–7
Aristotle 52, 55, 128, 219 n.10, 238 n.16
  medieval responses to 82–4, 106
  Luther's criticisms of 138–9, 242 n.26
  and MacIntyre 203 n.12, 204 n.25
  and Plato 207 n.61, 210 n.54, 211 n.81
Arsenius, Abba 74
art, fine 39, 43, 49, 82, 114–16, 119–20, 157–67, 174, 185, 195, 234–5 n.74, 258 n.86

asceticism 67–78, 81, 85, 124, 222 nn.83, 84, 85, 88, 224 n.119, 231 n.14, 241 n.14
Athanasius, St. 71
Athens 9, 38–9, 51, 53, 58–9, 63
Augustine, St. 3, 65, 83, 86–103, 105–6, 108, 111–12, 119, 172–3, 189, 214 n.169, 219 n.16, 225 nn.123, 126, 225–6 n.130, 226 nn.132, 144, 227 nn.153, 154, 158, 163, 228 nn.166, 170, 176, 229 nn.181, 189, 230 n.209, 236 n.100, 238 n.14, 239 n.51, 242 n.39
  influence on Petrarch 125, 129–31
  influence on Luther 133, 140–3, 149–50, 154
Aurelius 86
autarkeia, *see* self-sufficiency

Balbus 97
banausia 9, 19–20, 51–7, 164, 207 n.65, 216 nn.211, 221, 248 n.37
Barnabas, St. 88
Barsella, Susanna 81–4, 90, 222–3 n.96, 223 n.98, 224 n.117, 227 n.158, 239–40 n.60
Basil, St. 82–4, 219 n.16, 223 n.101, 224 n.114, 227 n.163
beatific vision 97, 129
Benedict of Aniane, St. 233 n.39
Benedict of Nursia, St. 77, 79, 83–5, 106, 110, 112, 114, 174, 199
Bernard of Clairvaux, St. 105–9, 113–14, 150, 231 n.14, 232 nn.16, 17, 233 n.32, 236 n.95, 245 n.83
Berry, Wendell 6
Bezaleel 119
birds of the air, *see also* lilies of the field, Sermon on the Mount 69, 85, 90–2, 149, 227–8 n.163, 244–5 n.78
Black Death 127
Bloch, Marc 65, 217 n.2

body 20, 99, 107, 111–12, 115, 118, 143, 152, 173, 227 n.163, 232 n.17, 241 n.19, 242 n.39, 245 n.81, 254 n.8
  discipline of in Luther 134–9
  in Plato 25–6, 55
  in the Middle Ages 72, 80, 83, 87, 92–4, 97
  in Weil 177–8, 183, 195
Boethius 126
Brague, Rémi 3
building, *see also* architecture 17, 21, 60, 81–3, 118–19, 138–9, 146, 160, 239 n.42, 240 n.8
bullshit jobs 199
Burckhardt, Jacob 123, 237 n.1
Burns, Tom 6

Cain 140
Calder, James Gordon 179, 181, 254 n.15, 255–6 n.27
calling, *see also* vocation 20, 54, 94, 112, 119, 140–1, 145, 151–5, 223 n.98, 234 n.67, 240–1 n.9, 245 n.81
capitalism 5–6, 166, 170, 256 n.32
Carlstadt, Andreas 140–2
carpentry 3, 17, 21, 30, 37, 39–41, 68, 82, 89, 108–9, 139, 210 n.56, 212 n.126, 213 n.154
Carthusians 105, 127–31
Cassian, John 74, 110–11, 219 n.19, 221 n.66, 224 n.121
Cassirer, Ernst 123, 237 n.1
cenobite 68, 73–5, 219 n.6, 220 n.45
character 4–5, 15, 46–7, 59, 109, 124, 138, 157, 163, 173, 222 n.83
charity, *see also* alms 73–4, 78–83, 108, 220 nn.40, 45, 222–3 n.96, 225–6 n.130, 231 n.14, 235 n.86
chess 4–5
Chitty, Derwas 70
chrea 13, 16
"Christianisme et la vie des champs, Le" 190
Chrysostom, St. John 83–5, 222–3 n.96, 227–8 n.163, 241 n.14
Cicero 20, 97–8, 226 n.130, 229–30 n.203, 230 n.205, 238 nn.16, 23
Cistercians 105–14, 231–2 n.15
City of God, The 95–8, 101, 238 n.16

Civilization of the Renaissance in Italy, The 123, 237 n.1
Cleitophon 25
Cluny 106, 109–13, 233 n.39
cobblery 17–18, 21, 27, 37, 41–4, 60, 68, 83, 89–90, 109, 227 n.154
Coby, Patrick 29–30, 67, 207 n.61
"Concerning Six Spiritual Water Pots" 108–9
Confessions 86, 92, 99, 101, 214 n.169, 225 n.126
contemplation, *see also* theory 3, 9, 199, 215 n.187, 219 n.10, 231–2 n.15
  in Petrarch 123–4, 130
  in the Middle Ages 67–9, 75, 78, 82–3, 95, 105–11, 115
  in Plato 29, 49–54, 57–9
  in Weil 182–3, 187
Courcelle, Pierre 86, 224 n.123
craft 3, 9, 15–21, 208 nn.74, 1, 209 nn.30, 39, 210 n.55, 212 n.106, 213 n.149, 218 n.4, 229–30 n.203, 233 n.39, 234 n.74, 236 nn.100, 106
  in Luther 138–9
  in Plato 23–31, 37–45, 48–52, 55–63
  in the Middle Ages 67–69, 77–8, 82, 85, 89, 92, 97–101, 109, 114–16, 120
  in Ruskin 163–4
Crawford, Matthew 1
creation 199, 222–3 n.96, 228 n.170, 229 n.181, 238 n.16, 243 n.62
  in Luther 137, 149–50
  in the Middle Ages 70, 81–2, 89, 92–4, 97–103, 111, 115–16
  in Plato 57
  in Ruskin 166, 173–4
  in Weil 183, 190
Critobulus 13, 19
Crown of Wild Olive, The 165, 172, 173, 249–50 n.59, 252 n.85, 253 n.104
Cyclopes 16–17
Cynicism 89, 224 n.119, 227 nn.153, 154, 238 n.16

David, King 118–19
De diversis artibus, see Various Arts, The
De doctrina christiana 229 n.189
De Genesi ad literam, see Literal Commentary on Genesis

De natura deorum 97–8, 229–30 n.203
De officiis 20
De opificio hominis 124
De opera monachorum, see *Work of Monks, The*
De ortu scientiarum 114
De otio religioso, see *On Religious Leisure*
De re publica 238 n.23
death 241 n.19, 244 n.78
  in Luther 133, 145–6, 149
  in the Middle Ages 73, 75, 80, 85, 87
  in Petrarch 126–7
  in Ruskin 164–6, 170, 175
  in Weil 187, 193–7
debt 13, 15, 73, 206 nn.36, 47
Demeter 12
Deming, W. Edwards 6
demiurge 2, 11–13, 40–4, 48–50, 56–7, 212 n.126
demos 11
Desert Fathers, *see also* individual Abbas 75, 106
Devil 97, 116, 145–6, 175, 243 n.62
dialogue, genre 21–2, 31–7, 49, 89, 125–7, 212 n.102
"Dialogue between a Cluniac and a Cistercian, A" 109–13
Didascalicon 128
dignity, human 82, 124, 137, 143, 151, 157–8, 182, 191, 195
Diogenes Laertius 89
Dionysius the Pseudo-Areopagite 124
Diotima of Mantinea 54
Disputation against Scholastic Theology 138
division of labor 77, 160, 181, 207 n.49, 209 n.46, 218 n.4, 247 n.21
Dodwell, C. R. 115, 234–5 n.74
Doerfler, Maria 87

Eden, Garden of 70, 92–4, 137–8, 219 n.18, 228 n.176, 255 n.22
eidolon, *see also* image 42, 51
eidos, *see also* form 17
Elias 75
Epicurean 93, 98, 238 n.16
epimeleia 15
erga 41
ergasia 221 n.54
ergon 11–12, 33, 221 n.54

Eriugena, John Scotus 124
eros 32, 54
eschatology 81–4
estate 135, 139, 143–4, 152, 240–1 n.9
Eucharist, *see also* liturgy 74, 139–40, 155, 190, 235 n.91
Euclid 158
Eumaeus 11
Euthydemus 31, 34, 208 n.1
Euthymius, St. 78
Evagrius of Antioch 87
Eve 137, 219 n.17, 260 n.119
"Excellence of Widowhood, The" 102

Factory Journal 180
"Factory Work" 182
faith 173, 190, 226 n.144, 240 n.8, 246–7 n.6, 259–60 n.106
  in Luther 133–40, 145–55
  in the Middle Ages 69, 72, 82, 88, 96–8, 119
  in Petrarch 124–5
Fall, the 70, 80, 93–7, 103, 115, 137, 229 n.181
farming, *see also* gardening 128, 170, 200, 205–6 n.16, 222 nn.83, 90, 228 n.176, 229 n.181, 230 n.205, 231 n.9, 240–1 n.9, 259–60 n.106, 260 n.119
  in the ancient Greeks 11–17, 20, 22, 28, 30, 60
  in Luther 140–3, 154–5
  in the Middle Ages 78, 81, 87–9, 93, 103, 111
  in Weil 184, 187–91, 194
Faust 181
Ferrer, Amy 1–2
Fiedrowicz, Michael 92
Finley, Moses 11–13, 16, 19–20
"First Condition for the Work of a Free Person, The" 186
form, Platonic 17, 32–3, 36, 40–4, 47–9, 215 nn.184, 187
Fors Clavigera 174, 246–7 n.6, 249 n.56, 252–3 n.98
fortune 125–7, 238 n.15, 251 n.69
Fossier, Robert 65
Francis, St. 180, 253 n.101
freedom 54–6, 69, 74, 88, 128, 130, 160, 179, 185, 192–3, 254 n.15

Christian, Luther's theory of 134–6, 147–9

Garden of Eden, *see* Eden
gardening, *see also* farming 68, 111, 131, 140–1, 151, 233 n.39, 252–3 n.98
Gearhart, Heidi 119
Geoghegan, Arthur 67–8, 72, 76, 218 n.4, 220 n.35, 226 n.148
Georgics 142
Gilbert of Hoyland 107, 231 n.13, 232 n.17
Gimpel, Jean 65
Glaucon 18, 30, 37, 40–4, 47, 50, 53, 55, 58
God 9, 17, 20, 199, 212 n.126, 219 nn.10, 17, 222 n.83, 222–3 n.96, 223 n.101, 225–6 n.130, 229 nn.181, 189, 232 n.17, 238 n.16, 239 n.42, 240 n.8, 241 n.19, 241–2 n.21, 242 n.34, 243 n.62, 244 nn.75, 78, 245 nn.79, 81, 246 n.105, 246–7 n.6, 259–60 n.106
  divine Demiurge, Plato's theory of 37, 41, 54, 57
  in Luther 133–55
  in the Middle Ages 67–75, 81–5, 88–9, 92–103, 107, 110–19
  in Petrarch 123–30
  in Ruskin 164–5, 173–5
  in Weil 182–3, 187, 190, 194–5
Goethe 181
Good, the 32–6, 47–51, 57–60, 99–103, 149–50, 194–5, 199
Gospel 69, 87–91, 108, 134, 139–44, 187–91, 227–8 n.163, 228 n.166, 243 n.40, 246–7 n.6, 253 n.101
Gothic 158–60
Gould, Graham 74–6, 221 n.54
Graeber, David 199
Greater Hippias 32
Greeks, ancient 4, 9–63, 84–9, 125, 193–4, 205 n.1, 205–6 n.16, 206 nn.23, 47, 207 n.49, 208 n.74, 212 n.113, 219 n.18, 224–5 n.123, 225 n.127, 235 n.86
Gregory of Nyssa 124
Griswold, Charles 35–6, 53, 212 n.102

Hanby, Michael 3, 199
Harrison, Carol 94–5, 102–3
Hephaestus 9, 20, 194
Hercules 11, 127, 174

Hesiod 9, 12–15, 20, 48–9, 205–6 n.16
hesychia 74–6
hexameral literature 82–3, 124, 228 n.170
Hexameron, of Ambrose 83
Hexameron, of Basil 82
Hippias 35
Historia monachorum in Aegypto 87
Holdsworth, Christopher 106–7, 231 n.9, 233 n.39
Holy Spirit 119, 189, 194, 236 nn.100, 103, 240 n.9
Homer 9, 11, 17, 20, 39, 42, 46–9, 208 n.74
Hugh of St. Victor 128, 236 n.103

idleness 14, 20, 28, 62, 111–18, 221 n.66, 227 n.163, 235 n.92, 242 n.39, 251 n.69
  Luther's critique of 135–40, 144–5, 149
  monastic condemnation of 69–71, 81, 85–7
  in Petrarch 126, 130
  in Ruskin 163, 167–8
  in Weil 184
Idung of Prüfening 109–13, 233 n.35
Iliad 16
Illich, Ivan 128
image 37, 42–4, 49–51, 60, 213 n.154, 215 n.187, 246–7 n.6
  of God 115–16, 174
imitation, *see mimesis*
Incarnation 81
Institutes, The 110, 224 n.121
Irwin, Terrence 37, 210 n.56
Isaac, Abba 74
Isaias, Abba 74–5
Ischomachus 14–16

Jerome, St. 68, 72, 77–8, 87, 110, 219 n.19
Jesus 222–3 n.96, 225–6 n.130, 227 n.163, 235 n.84, 238 n.16, 241 n.19, 244 nn.75, 78, 253 n.101, 258 nn.84, 85, 261 n.136
  according to Luther 134–6, 138–9, 141, 149–50, 153–5
  according to the Middle Ages 69, 71, 76, 81, 87–9, 91–2, 95, 97, 107–8, 110
  according to Petrarch 129–30
  according to Ruskin 173, 175
  according to Weil 187–8, 190, 194

Job 127, 140, 189
John of Lycopolis 87
John the Dwarf, Abba 70, 76, 78, 222 n.81
John the Persian, Abba 78
"Joy for Ever, A" 157, 250 n.65
Judgment Day 136
Julius Caesar 127
justice 2–5, 13, 17–19, 200, 209 n.39, 249–50 n.59, 253 n.104, 260 n.119
  in Luther 138, 152
  in the Middle Ages 67, 81, 89, 94
  in Plato 24–30, 37–8, 48–51, 54–5, 58–63
  in Ruskin 157, 164, 169–71, 175
  in Weil 186–8, 193
justification 133–7

Kilwardby, Robert 114
kleros 13
Knies, Kenneth 27–9, 62, 209–10 n.46, 223 n.98
Knight, Kelvin 5, 204 n.25, 216 n.231
knowledge 13–16, 19–25, 29–34, 37–55, 58, 67, 96, 114–19, 129, 164, 207 n.61, 209 n.37, 210 nn.56, 68, 211 n.73, 213 n.149, 215 nn.184, 187, 235 n.86, 236 n.100, 248 nn.31, 32, 253 n.98
Kristeller, Paul Oskar 123, 237 n.3
Kunigunde of Niedermunster 110

Laches 21, 30, 33, 34, 208 n.1, 211 n.88
Lausiac History 75
Lazarus of Bethany 69
Leah, wife of Jacob 109, 231–2 n.15
Lectures on Art 164
Lefebvre des Noëttes, Richard 65, 217 n.1
LeGoff, Jacques 65, 79–80, 83, 230–1 n.2
leisure 56, 95, 105, 110, 125–31, 142–3, 174, 183, 198–9, 259 n.94
lerche 20
Libellus de diversis ordinibus 113, 234 n.67
liberal arts 20, 108, 163, 229 n.189, 230 n.209
liberalism 179
liberty, *see* freedom
Life of Saint Antony, The 71, 87, 225 n.126
Life of Solitude, The 130
lilies of the field, *see also* birds of the air, Sermon on the Mount 69, 91–2, 227 n.163

Literal Commentary on Genesis 92, 229 n.181
liturgy, *see also* Eucharist 77, 187, 190
Locke, John 167, 200
Lombard, Peter 124
Lord's Prayer 173, 258 n.76
love 16, 29, 54, 74, 100–3, 107, 110–12, 133–9, 145–5, 151, 154, 162, 173, 199–200, 225–6 n.130
Lucretius 93
Luther, Martin 131, 133–55, 240 n.8, 240–1 n.9, 241 nn.14, 19, 242 nn.34, 39, 243 nn.40, 62, 244 nn.75, 76, 78, 245 nn.79, 81, 83, 246 nn.105, 114, 249 n.59

Macarius, Abba 74
Machiavelli, Niccolo 194
MacIntyre, Alasdair 4–6, 203 n.12, 204 nn.24, 25, 211 n.94, 216 n.231, 223 n.113
Mackean, William Herbert 73, 75
Malesic, Jonathan 77–8, 84–5, 221 n.66
management 6, 12, 90, 94, 146, 153, 181, 185, 231 n.9, 256 n.32
Manicheanism 99
manual labor 20, 54–5, 65, 200–1, 216 n.220, 218 n.2, 219 n.6, 222 n.85, 227 n.158, 232 n.16, 233 n.39, 234 n.62, 244 n.75, 248 n.39, 252 n.85, 256 n.32
  in Luther 140–3, 149
  in the Middle Ages 67–73, 76–91, 95, 106–15, 118
  in Petrarch 126, 131
  in Ruskin 158–65, 168–70
  in Weil 180–3, 190, 194
manufacturing 6, 44, 159–61, 164
marketplace 16, 63, 73, 162, 204 n.24
Martha of Bethany 69–70, 110–11, 231 n.15
Martinez, Joel 24, 208 n.17
Marx, Karl 157, 159–60, 172, 177, 183, 193, 200, 205 n.1, 247 n.21, 256 n.32
Mary, Blessed Virgin 89, 139, 190
Mary of Bethany 69–70, 110–11, 231 n.15
mass, *see* Eucharist
materialism 179, 254 n.18
Matthew the Precentor of Rievaulx 107
Maximilian, Emperor 142

mechanical arts 19, 55, 78, 85, 108, 161–4, 180, 207 n.65, 248 n.39
Megethius, Abba 78
Meletus 23
Meno 45
Metteer, Charles 67–8, 70, 73, 75–8, 80, 219 n.6, 220 n.45, 221 n.57, 222 n.83
mimesis 38–41, 46–51, 212 n.113
Modern Painters 157, 165, 251 nn.77, 80, 252 n.85
monasticism 67–92, 103–20, 127–33, 138–41, 154–5, 163, 173–4, 180, 199, 218 n.2, 219 n.10, 220 n.45, 221 nn.54, 56, 74, 222 n.85, 225–6 n.130, 239–40 n.60, 242 n.39, 246 n.105
money 1–4, 15, 206 n.23, 216 n.224, 226 n.130, 244 n.75, 249 n.51, 250 nn.61, 65, 251 n.80
  in Luther 139–40, 143, 146–7, 153
  in the Middle Ages 72–5, 91, 102, 105–6
  in Plato 25–9, 35–6, 48, 55–6, 59–63
  in Ruskin 160, 164–71
  in Weil 186, 191, 198
moral knowledge 22–3, 30–1, 34, 37, 210 n.56, 211 n.73
Moses 119, 147
Moses, Abba 74–5
Munera Pulveris 165, 168
"Mysticism of Work, The" 182

Nature 3, 13–16, 28, 41–2, 63–5, 82, 93–4, 97, 162–5, 181, 190, 199–200, 213 n.149, 253 n.98
Neale, Walter 13, 16, 20, 205 nn.7, 9, 206 n.47
necessity 62, 94–5, 142, 168–9, 179, 185–7, 192–5, 199, 254 n.15
Need for Roots, The 191, 193–5, 257 n.74, 258 nn.84, 85, 258–9 n.90, 259 n.96, 261 n.124
Nesteros, Abba 75
Nicomachean Ethics 138, 219 n.10, 242 n.26
Nightingale, Andrea Wilson 51–4, 56–7, 59, 215 nn.187, 188, 216 nn.211, 212
nomos 17

Odyssey 20, 208 n.74
Oeconomicus 16, 164

Of True Religion 129
oichos 11–16, 22, 43
Oleson, John Peter 16, 19, 56, 216 n.220
Olympus 9, 20
On Religious Leisure 127–8, 131, 238 n.16, 239–40 n.60
On the Babylonian Captivity of the Church 133
"On the Care of the Dead" 87
On the Freedom of a Christian 133, 136, 140, 153, 240 n.9
Oracle of Delphi 23
otium, see also leisure 95, 118, 126–31, 239–40 n.60
Ovitt, George Jr. 65, 68, 72, 75–9, 81, 105–6, 112–14, 219 n.6, 220 n.52, 221 n.74, 222 n.85, 231 n.9, 232 n.20

Pachomius, St. 68, 73, 76–8, 220 n.35
Paesius, Abba 74–5
painting 15, 18, 38–46, 51, 96, 110, 114, 118, 164–6, 213 n.154, 215 n.184, 229 n.189
Palaemon, Abba 73
Palladius 68, 72, 75
Pambo, Abba 75, 220 n.52
parable 73, 88, 190, 235 n.84, 258 n.84
parrhesia 89
Patroclus 16
Paul, Abba 111
Paul, Apostle 3, 222–3 n.96, 227–8 n.163, 261 n.136
  according to Luther 133–6, 139–43, 145
  according to the Middle Ages 69, 71–3, 76–7, 79, 81, 85, 87–91, 107–9, 111–14, 118
  according to Petrarch 129
  according to Ruskin 167–8
  according to Weil 190
Paul, Charlton 198
Pelagius 86
Penelope 20
Pericles 89
Perses 12–13, 15, 20
Peter, Apostle 139, 150–1
Petrarch 123–31, 155, 163, 199, 237 n.8, 238 nn.14, 15, 16, 17, 23, 29, 240 n.51, 240–1 n.60
Pharisees 135

physis 17, 40
Pirsig, Robert 1
Pistamon, Abba 76
Plato 2–3, 5–7, 9, 15, 17, 19, 21–65, 200,
    204 n.25, 206 n.46, 207 n.61,
    208 n.3, 209 n.30, 210 n.54, 211
    n.73, 212 nn.102, 105, 113, 126,
    213 n.149, 215 n.190, 217 n.232,
    223 n.98, 238 nn.16, 23, 254 n.18
  in Luther 153
  in the Middle Ages 67, 80–1, 84, 92,
    102, 115
  in Petrarch 124
  in Ruskin 157, 165, 173–4
  in Weil 177–8, 188, 198
pleonexia 5
Poemen, Abba 73, 75, 78
poetry 9, 23, 38–51, 96, 110, 124–7,
    187–91, 237 n.8, 239–40 n.60, 258
    n.85, 258–9 n.90, 259 n.97
poiesis 82–3
polis 3, 17, 24, 27–30, 47, 52–4, 58, 61–3,
    81–3, 87
political economy 157–8, 161, 164–70,
    223 n.98
politicians 23, 55–6
Pompey 127
ponos 11
praxis 54, 83
prayer 53, 219 n.16, 221 n.54, 224 nn.114,
    119, 231 n.14, 235 n.91, 241 n.19,
    242 n.39, 246 n.105, 249–50 n.59,
    253 n.104, 258 nn.76, 80, 258–
    9 n.92
  in Luther 134, 140–2, 154
  in the Middle Ages 69–75, 78, 85,
    88–90, 107, 110–13, 117–18
  in Petrarch 130–1
  in Ruskin 173–4
  in Weil 187, 190
price 20, 73, 117, 161–2, 169–70, 235 n.84
production 2–3, 6, 11–13, 23, 57, 63, 73,
    81–4, 95, 180, 184, 200, 207 n.49,
    209–10 n.46, 220 n.40, 255 n.32, 258
    n.90, 261 n.124
profit 13, 16, 20, 26–30, 63, 73, 78, 90, 116,
    169–71, 251 n.69
Prometheus 194
Proudhon, Pierre-Joseph 193

psalms 78, 88–90, 108, 111–12, 174, 224
    n.114, 253 n.104

Rachel, wife of Jacob 109, 231–2 n.15
Radzins, Inese 192, 260 n.119, 260–1
    n.121, 261 n 125
Rajan, Supritha 165–6
Reeve, C. D. C. 30–1, 37, 212 n.113
"Reflections Concerning the Causes of
    Liberty and Social Oppression" 180
Reformation 135, 142
"Religion of Workism Is Making
    Americans Miserable, The" 198
Remedies for Fortune Fair and Foul 125,
    238 n.29
Renaissance 123–4, 127, 194, 237 nn.1, 6, 8
*Renaissance Philosophy and the Mediaeval
    Tradition* 123
Republic 2–3, 17, 24, 29–30, 32–4, 38–9,
    48–9, 51, 53–5, 57–62, 67, 198, 208
    nn.1, 17, 215 nn.184, 188, 190, 223 n.98
Resurrection 97
revolution 28, 157, 161, 184–6, 256 n.35
Robert of Molesme 106
Roe, F. W. 158–159, 247 n.10, 248 n.39
Romans, ancient 19, 95, 125–7, 194,
    228 n.176
Roochnik, David 22, 30–7, 208 nn.74, 1,
    4, 210 nn.55, 56, 68, 211 nn.73, 74,
    81, 82, 212 nn.102, 105, 106
Rousseau, Jean-Jacques 193
Rubio, Marco 1–2, 197, 203 n.5
Rufinus of Aquileia 87
rule, monastic 72, 77–8, 86, 218 n.2,
    219 n.9, 223 n.101, 224 n.114,
    227 n.163
Rule, of Benedict 77–9, 83–5, 106, 109–12,
    114, 235 n.92
Ruskin, John 157–75, 180, 182, 186, 197,
    199, 246 n.5, 246–7 n.6, 248 nn.31, 32,
    36, 37, 39, 249 nn.43, 44, 51, 56, 249–
    50 n.59, 250 nn.61, 63, 65, 251 nn.69,
    72, 74, 77, 80, 252 nn.85, 86, 252–3
    n.98, 253 nn.101, 103, 104, 260 n.119
Rusticus 78

salary 1–2, 185–6, 198
salvation 72, 81–4, 96, 107–11, 115, 133–6,
    139, 150, 187, 194, 221 n.54, 241 n.21

Sand, George 193
Schenoudi, Abba 73
Schindler, D. C. 32–8, 48–9, 53, 211 n.88, 213 n.149, 215 n.190
scholasticism 123–5, 138
Scipios, the 127
self-sufficiency 13, 67–9, 72–6, 86, 89, 106, 149, 227 n.153
Sellars, John 89, 227 n.154
Sentences 124
Serapion, Abba 73
Sermon on the Mount, *see also* birds of the air and lilies of the field 69–71, 87, 91–2, 119, 129, 175, 227–8 n.163, 242 n.34, 244 n.78
servanthood 12, 56, 75–8, 88, 133–6, 139, 142–5, 151–5, 188–90, 227 n.163, 240 n.9, 250 n.61, 253 n.104
Sesame and Lilies 167, 248 n.32
Seven Lamps of Architecture, The 157–8, 249
Silvanus, Abba 69–70, 78, 219 n.12
Simon the Shoemaker 89–90, 227 n.44
sin 92–3, 97–8, 101–2, 118, 135–7, 140, 143, 155, 173–5, 189, 194–5, 214 n.169, 251 n.74
 original 79, 107, 219 n.18, 229 n.181
slavery 79, 82, 88, 158, 162, 181, 184–6, 259 n.97
Smith, Adam 157, 160, 165–6, 181, 246–7 n.6, 247 n.21
smithing 19–21, 55, 68, 223 n.101
socialism 157
Socrates 89, 209 n.37, 209–10 n.46, 210 nn.56, 68, 213 n.154, 215 n.184, 216 n.224, 227 n.154
 according to Plato 2, 17–19, 21–35, 37, 39–51, 53–63
 according to Xenophon 13–15, 19
Solomon, King 118, 146, 148–50, 152, 244 n.75
sophistry 17, 22–4, 33–6, 45, 55–6, 213 n.154, 216 n.216
soul 3, 17–20, 215 n.184, 225–6 n.130, 240 n.60, 249 n.43, 251 n.69
 in Plato 28–9, 37–9, 45–9, 55–61
 in Luther 134–6
 in the Middle Ages 67, 72, 76, 81, 90, 99–102, 107, 112, 118

 in Ruskin 158–60, 164, 168, 173
 in Weil 177–8, 187–91, 194–195
Sozomen, Abba 73
Steinhauser, Kenneth 86, 224 n.119, 227 n.153, 229 n.181
Stock, Brian 105, 107–8, 232 n.17, 233 nn.32, 34
Stoicism 97, 126, 203 n.5, 218 n.7, 222 n.90, 226 n.130, 227 n.153
Stones of Venice, The 157–8, 161–3, 252 n.85
sun 14, 50, 59–60, 173, 184, 188, 253 n.101, 258 n.85
Symposium 54–5, 215 n.183

Tandy, David 13, 16, 20, 205 nn.7, 9, 206 n.47
Taylor, Frederick 189
telos 11, 17, 20
Tertullian 79
Testard, Maurice 98
Theaetetus 54–6, 216 n.212
Theodore of Enaton 73
theology 12, 79–86, 92–3, 99–101, 105–8, 123–4, 138, 146, 155–7, 171–3, 225 n.123, 241 n.21, 245 n.79, 250 n.63
Theophilus Presbyter 105, 114–20, 234–5 n.74, 235 nn.86, 92, 236 n.95
"Theoretical Picture of a Free Society" 185
theoria, see also theory 52–7
theoros 52–6
theory 2, 52–8, 116, 204 n.25, 215 n.187
thes 12, 205 n.9
Thompson, Derek 198
Thrasymachus 24–7, 60, 209 nn.37, 39
Timaeus 49, 56–7, 208 n.1, 212 n.126
Time and Tide 169, 171, 251 n.74
Timothy, St. 141–2
Tolstoy, Leo 193
Trinkaus, Charles 123–4
Trump, Donald 198
Two Paths, The 164, 251 n.69, 260 n.119

Ulysses 127
Unto This Last 170, 249 nn.43, 51, 250 n.61

Valle Crucis 174, 253 n.101
Van den Hoven, Birgit 68–71, 73, 77–9, 85, 100, 218 n.7, 219 nn.12, 16, 220 n.40, 221 n.73, 222 n.84, 230 n.209

Van Engen, John 116, 120, 235 nn.80, 92, 236 nn.95, 100, 103
Various Arts, The 105, 114–15, 234–5 n.74, 235 n.75, 236 n.105
Vernant, Jean-Pierre 11–12, 14–17, 20, 205 n.16, 206 nn.23, 47, 207 n.49
Virgil 129, 142
virtue 4–5, 11, 203 n.12, 210 n.56, 216 n.231, 222 n.83, 238 n.16, 240 n.60, 251 n.69
  in Luther 136–8, 153
  in the Middle Ages 67–8, 76, 79–82, 85–6, 95–6, 109, 119
  in Petrarch 126–7, 129
  in Plato 29–31, 38, 42–5, 55, 58–62
vocation, *see also* calling 28–9, 80, 188–90, 193, 240–1 n.9

Waldensians 141–2
Wealth of Nations, The 160, 247 n.21
weaving 17, 21, 27, 68, 78, 82–3, 109–11, 192, 230 n.205, 260 n.119

Weil, Simone 2–3, 6, 177–95, 197, 199, 250 n.63, 254 nn.8, 15, 18, 255 n.22, 255–6 n.27, 256 nn.28, 32, 35, 257 nn.61, 74, 258 nn.76, 81, 82, 84, 85, 86, 90, 259 nn.92, 96, 97, 259–60 n.106, 260–1 n.121, 261 nn.124, 130, 136
Whitehead, David 56
Whitney, Elspeth 97–8, 100, 229 n.189, 230 n.209
Work of Monks, The 86–7, 89, 91–2, 110–11, 224 nn.117, 120, 225–6 n.130, 226 n.132
workism 198
Works and Days 12–13, 16, 205 nn.7, 16

Xenophon 13–14, 16, 19, 55, 200

Yocum, Demetrio 130–1

Zacharias 69

www.ingramcontent.com/pod-product-compliance
Lightning Source LLC
Chambersburg PA
CBHW052215300426
44115CB00011B/1694